Rod Moss grew up in Melbourne, completing his schooling in Boronia and gaining qualifications to teach art at secondary level. Moss was invited to teach in the avant garde, experimental Brinsley Road School founded in Melbourne during the early 1970s. After a year's interlude in West Virginia, learning the practical disciplines of Armenian philosopher, George Gurdjieff, Moss relocated to central Australia, where he has lived since 1984. Moss lectured, in Art at the southern campus of Charles Darwin University in Alice Springs until his retirement in 2008.

Moss is an award-winning artist and writer. His first memoir, *The Hard Light of Day,* received the Prime Minister's Literary Award for Non-Fiction and the Northern Territory Book of the Year. His second, *A Thousand Cuts,* won the 2014 Chief Minister's Northern Territory Book of the Year Award. Moss exhibits in Alice Springs, Brisbane, Melbourne and the USA.

PRAISE FOR *CROSSING THE GREAT DIVIDE*

Crossing the Great Divide is a monumental achievement. Epic in scope, it encompasses a life journey recorded in luminous detail, driven by an unwavering intellectual curiosity, and graced by unsparing self-reflection and humanity. It is both a portrait of a young man as aspiring artist, working his way towards his calling, and the reflections of the mature artist, who has truly crossed the divide between Indigenous and non-Indigenous peoples, and found a way to express his findings, and his vision, as a painter, craftsman, lateral thinker and writer.

— Arnold Zable, author

When I read Rod Moss's masterpiece *The Hard Light of Day*, I marvelled at the wonderful goodness and profound humanism of the man who wrote it. Ditto when I read *One Thousand Cuts*. Where could such a man come from, I wondered. Many readers who felt as I did will look eagerly for answers in *Crossing the Great Divide*. They won't be surprised that Moss' rich life confirms the ancient insight that wisdom comes only to people who were neither wise nor prudent when they were young. In his early and middle years, Moss's ferocious hunger for experience—physical, intellectual, artistic and spiritual, in their many forms—was tempered by a sense of humanity as it existed in himself and others that went deep even then. The idiosyncratic, gritty but sensuous, realism of Moss's paintings shows also in his prose, enlivening while disciplining its attention to the details of events, persons and places he describes. I know of no one like him.

— Raimond Gaita, philosopher, author

The writing of Rod Moss has already opened a unique gate into Central Australia: his *The Hard Light of Day* and *One Thousand Cuts* were revelatory of the landscape and those dwelling in its tissues of tragedy and love. What made this writing possible? How did Moss's goodness of heart and his intelligent eye so come together as to produce these unique contributions to Australian art-making? This gritty memoir, both prosaic and textured, is a good place to tackle the mystery. It is vivid with detail, open-hearted, redolent with drollery and authenticity as the author draws himself back into his originations.

— Barry Hill, author

Rod Moss's memoir takes us all over the thriving world, and his eye sees everything. But his story is not a travelogue, far more the quest of a great writer and artist to deepen his experience of life. This is what it means to retain a curiosity about the world, and the skill to thrill the reader.

— Robert Hillman, award-winning author.

CROSSING THE GREAT DIVIDE

MEMOIR OF AN ARTIST

ROD MOSS

Published by Wild Dingo Press
Melbourne, Australia
books@wilddingopress.com.au
www.wilddingopress.com.au

First published by Wild Dingo Press 2019

Cover image: Rod Moss, *The Gift Of Butterflies*, 2016
Designer: Debra Billson
Editor: Catherine Lewis
Printed in Australia

Moss, Rod, 1948-
Crossing the Great Divide / Rod Moss

A catalogue record for this
book is available from the
National Library of Australia

ISBN: 9780648349860 (paperback)
ISBN: 9780648349884 (ebook: pdf)
ISBN: 9781925893007 (eBook: ePub)

Acknowledgements

My thanks to the editors of Arena magazine for publishing 'Revelations: From Alice Springs to Sicily', an early version of the present text's chapter, 'Where gods once walked'.

Friends and siblings responded to various moments of the narrative. Some gulped the lot, none more than Tony Lintermans whose critical suggestions helped shape it.

Whatever their input I'm grateful for the attention given by the following: Ahmed Adam, John and Leonie Anderson, Frank Baada, Jan Blair, Philip Batty, Michael Bowden, Peggy Cole, Sharon Connolly, Bill and Annie Davis, Josh Davies, James Dean, Barry Hill, Graeme Drendel, Michael Eather, David Flannery, Rai Gaita, Howard Goldenberg, Royden Irvine, Vicki and Jock Jacobi, Martin King, Adam Knight, Rod McMillan, Jan Mittleman, Dave Morgan, Jack O'Dowd, Margaret O'Sullivan, Kristin Otto, Des O'Shannesy, Nic Ouchtomsky, Noel Price, Dianne Renkin, Craig San Roque, Astarte and Chris Rowe, Paul Satchel, Rosalin Sadler, Glendel Schrader, John Scott, Deon Sortino, Nick Tapper, Mandy Webb, Erica Seccombe and Nat Williams, Cate Young, Arnold Zable and Jenny Zimmer.

A big thank-you to Pat and Jeremy at Colemans Printers, Alice Springs, for unflagging co-operation with the numerous drafts leading to publication.

My siblings, Colin, Marilyn and Ian sharpened recall of Boronia in the 1950s, as did my parents. I've been blessed in having the support of my gifted children, Raffi, Ronja and Anjou Moss who graciously endured readings of drafts.

Wild Dingo publisher, Catherine Lewis's enthusiasm and care were crucial to the book's existence as was her skilled team.

Basking in my partner Gloria Morales's generosity I found the freedom to expose my many follies. For that I am grateful.

The world desires illusion, either the illusion antecedent to reason, which is poetry, or the illusion subsequent to reason, which is religion.

The world must be as Don Quixote wishes it to be, and inns must be castles, and he will fight with it and will, to all appearances, be vanquished, but he will triumph by making himself ridiculous. And he will triumph by laughing at himself and making himself the object of his own laughter.

Miguel de Unamuno, The Tragic Sense of Life

For Gloria, Raffi, Ronja and Anjou

Table of Contents

1

From fern tree gullies, I came

Animal in Botanics, Rod Moss, 1982.

Without multistoried buildings and air pollutants the skies of Alice Springs give freely of their monumental displays. Out west this afternoon, a cape of checked cloud was being towed to the horizon, broad above and tapering to its apex on the rim. As the sun slipped from sight it singed the checks copper and purple. Fifteen minutes of luminosity, beauty by its other name, reminded me of Swiss miniaturist, Paul Klee, who floated his shimmering patches in the decades separating the twentieth century's great wars. I cite Klee as he played another small role. His wish, 'to be as though new born, knowing nothing' was my mantra as Central Australia laid claims on me.

My previous memoirs were about being in Alice Springs, raising a family, teaching and making art. Rear vision reveals a road signposted with people, events, literature and cinema leading to the centre of Australia. I am no more an autonomous individual than anyone else, being constituted by parents, authority figures, peers, and rivals whom I've internalised as models and become the unconscious basis of my desires.

As children, my siblings and I played, unfettered, in the bush next to our home. We lived in the foothills of the Dandenong Ranges. Whichever way you looked from our place, trees dominated the skyline. Indeed, much of our time was spent climbing them. I've been hooked on bush ever since. Though Central Australia's climate and biota were foreign, that childhood immersion was essential preparation for embracing its incomparable and boundless beauty.

Whatever conscience and aesthetics generated from those bushy beginnings, these were enlarged and deepened through relationships, work and travel. How I developed an interest in the First People of Australia is, necessarily, party to my story. Its momentum was slow, and nuanced. While the decision to relocate in the Territory was clear, I knew not where it would lead, other than it would present relationships with Aboriginals. I hadn't the faintest intent of making art about those relationships.

Revising the determinants binding me to Alice Springs through writing, gives the illusion of a steady, linear track. The conundrum of which was nature and which nurture, even from this vantage, I can't distinguish. Painting and writing are valiant attempts at clearing the ground for myself. In Central Australia my abiding interests in art and in our First People coincided. I taught art, confided in it, and enduring friendships were nurtured through it.

2
Set adrift

Journal, Rod Moss, 1985.

Boronia, in foothills east of Melbourne, was where I took my first footsteps, and from where I came and went for twenty years. It's no longer a village. Nor is its community comprised of orchardists and horticulturists. That sense of community no longer attends. Our home and mum's mothers are the lone pre-1950s survivors of the street: hers, a weatherboard built by husband, Oswald, in 1922 with help from men from the newly established nearby Church of Christ. He was a joiner and had a furniture factory in Glenferrie until he fell and injured his spine in the backyard. It got infected and he died when mum was five.

While dad was building our weatherboard next door, I lived with older brother, Ian, and my parents at grandma's. Dad had bought the uncleared block from Oswald's sister for 50 pounds. I adored grandma and her kitchen with its animated wood-fired stove, the cords of yellow- box stacked in her shed where the axe and saws hung above the cutting jig, and orange lichen swarmed across its exterior walls.

Behind home Chandler's daffodil farm stretched to the base of the One Tree Hill, looming large in hazy blue. Nearby lay the more imposing *Corhanwarrabul*, we called Mt Dandenong, crowned with TV towers since the mid-1950s. Our village name proclaimed the flowers those daffodils supplanted. Over the ranges the sun emerged, stirring birdsong, tickling leaves and grasses. Our sloping backyard was groomed with native trees while freshly planted exotics—elms, maples and liquid ambers—slowly matured. These were fertile grounds for the deafening summer chorus of cicadas whose stridulations passed to crickets at sunset.

On the other side of our house were woodlands: striated stringybarks weathered grey in winter, salmon pink in spring; yellowbox and peppermint gum; the corded, peach-grey messmates; the festooning, amber sap of black wattles, wadded for masticating; the fluffy dogwood flowers mum said caused rashes; the sweet, dry fruit of cherry fir and nut grasses. We formed whistles from the rampant sword grass, snapping and laying a blade between clamped thumbs, and gently blowing. Filled with Blyton's fictions, I chose a twisted white box with footholds as my *Faraway Tree* and spent hours in its upper forks, fantasising the cloud lands that might attach to its canopy. Had possum hunters, long ago, notched these steps in the tree's fleshy underparts?

The rear boundary of our backyard was hedged with pittosporums whose sticky fruits exuded a pungent perfume. Autumn rain promoted Slippery Jacks and Saffron Cap mushrooms beneath this hedge. We picked and peeled the white tops whose pink or chocolate flesh had an earthy tang for mum to fry in butter and parsley. 'Don't you boys eat red stuff from the bush,' mum warned. Red meant danger, especially red-back spiders. Not so for rosellas who'd settle on the self-sown cotoneaster in the front yard, squabbling and scoffing berry clusters.

There were flowers mum planted which we were to avoid—the trumpet shaped datura lily and foxgloves. Blackberries were edible, and the lower side of our street was infested with them. Scratches and the occasional tiger or black snake were worth the bounty, and Ian and I filled billycans mum turned into jam. Grandma lent her woven wire snake rod, but we'd drop it as soon as we were out of sight. Unless it rained, we were in the bush from breakfast to dusk.

Dad fixed a swing to the low bough of an apple box for us. The same branch served as perch for a kookaburra couple that seem to command the rising sun. Nearby was the poultry yard. Though I never befriended chooks or ducks, I liked herding them around and nestling in the hay of their laying box, munching handfuls of wheat and pollard. Ant industry fascinated me. I'd pester orange sugar ants into frenzied defence of their minced mounds when I ruined them. They'd rally as one to re-build after initial confusion fashioning breathing holes in the earth. They foraged alone, but formed communal chains to ferry goods back home, or paired up to lug iridescent beetles and wasps. Unlike black jumping ants and plum-coloured bull ants, their bites were inoffensive. I couldn't locate the nests of bull-ants or jumping ants that dawdled through solitary days. I'd prod bull ants until they reared into action; and stirred jumping ants to compete in hopping challenges. Hordes of small black ants, with acidic stench, trod daily to and from the garden. In warm weather they formed long lines to the kitchen sink.

The whereabouts of a tea-tree glade, with water seeping through a sponge of mossy turf, I kept secret. In spring the canopy was alive with small white flowers and crowded with bees. Pollen in blossom and piled on their hind legs intoxicated. Were they destined to honeyfie dad's hive, tucked beneath our fledgling almond tree? My admiring fingers stroked the velvet that when punctured revealed peat-dark aggregate. Cress flourished. I peopled the place with imaginary friends and the benign powers of plants, egg-and-bacon creepers, sarsaparilla, and green-hooded orchids. At dusk boisterous possums shook the branches. Ever rarer was the gentle rustle of bandicoots. And once I came upon a bettong fretting midst this moss-lime baize.

I saw too a blue-tongued lizard, old and still as a rock, encased in shiny plated skin grinning thoughtlessly, unnerved by my presence. It looked to have been there forever and would be there when I'd gone. Immaculately groomed, eyes unblinking and obdurate, its slow pulse visible beneath the skin at the base of its skull. Small black ants swarmed across its face. It waited for them to venture lip-wards whereupon its dart-like tongue made of them an instant meal. Dad told me not to prod blue-tongue lizards as they deterred snakes. But I had not been alone in my observations. The skink was no more immortal than the ants. As I turned my back to walk and report my findings, a kookaburra made a clean sweep and had it back on his branch, dashing it this way and that, pulping it to digestibility.

****

I was little more than a toddler when the splendid green and gold Jubilee Train, celebrating fifty years of nationhood, rolled into town. We wandered with dad through the carriages, admiring exhibits. Dad poured over the Snowy Mountain Hydro-Electric Scheme exhibit, the post-war engineering triumph that attracted male migrants from southern Europe, some of who'd subsequently found employment at his workplace. We regrouped at the rail crossing to witness it lumber towards the Upper Ferntree Gully terminal, me astride dad's shoulders, waving at this glistening beast's trail of billowing plumes, thrilled at its hissing underparts. Dad said that before the war he'd served his boilermakers apprenticeship at the Newport Railway Workshops. Were trains like this what boilermakers made? This monstrous steaming steel thing, was it a boiler?

Lighter metals were aloft. Aircraft were a novelty in our skies. If engines whirled above, dad would call us from play. They flew low enough for him to identify the make from their shape and sound. He elaborated on these at the Essendon Aerodrome once, taking us by train to watch the arrival and departure of a dozen or so planes. His aeronautic fascination started at Flemington Racetrack during Melbourne's Centennial celebrations in 1934, where he witnessed participants of the London to Melbourne Air Race, touchdown. The crash of the *Kyeema* in 1938 on nearby Mt Dandenong was also writ large in his mind.

With Ian at school I'd track past grandma's woodshed and watch her scrub feet, clip nails, and tend the corns and bunions of old women taxied to her front gate. One woman forever walked. Goosey Kitty Chandler everywhere she wandered. Her friendship with grandma formed back in 1920s church days. Whatever the weather, she was garbed in coat and cloche hat, her chin set determinedly against its vagaries. The others I escorted up and back the winding concrete path, fringed with dancing fuchsias and smiling pansies. The ramp to her surgery was crowded with blue hydrangeas whose ferrous whiff was triggered by the women's heavy coats as they brushed by.

These dark woollen garments hung like separate selves on a hook behind the door. Walking sticks were stacked nearby. The room reeked of Wintergreen and Dettol. Those white legs shocked me when thick brown stockings were peeled and fell lifeless to the floor; ankles lost in fatty rolls, veins of various blues and purples mapping the pale flesh as they soaked their feet in her tawny china basin. I sat nearby in silence. Gentle patter was exchanged until five shillings was tendered and the garments re-fitted.

As far as I was concerned grandma was loving kindness incarnate except in springtime when, to control their population, she'd lean her stepladder against the spouting and grope in sparrow nests for eggs which she summarily crushed.

Grandma bought me a colouring book whose blank images I needed only hold to the outlines while brushing with water for them to spring to limpid life. She also made a gollywog, floppy and black with vermillion lips, white button eyes, and crinkly wool hair. His blue-and-white striped shorts were strapped over his shoulders. He was my bedmate but lacked mum's warmth. When worn beyond repair, mum bought a fleecy, gold teddy bear that I'd tuck underarm as I wandered to her bedside after a troubled sleep. Though I requested the kitchen door be left ajar for a comforting sliver of light to pierce the gloom, I was a frequent bed-wetter. Often, I dreamt I was outside the front of the house peeing on my parent's bedroom wall. I'd wake in a flood. As the warmth diminished I'd peel out of bed and dawdle the length of the house and tentatively whisper, 'Mum, here I am'. There'd be a groan and request to strip my pyjama pants before snuggling beside her. That was good. I was still her scrumptious, 'Scrumpy', whatever my impositions.

There were Victorian heirlooms in our house that felt like they belonged more at Grandma's: a black oval papier mâché tray, copal-varnished with mother-of-pearl inlay formed into cyclamen, butterflies and birds. I marvelled over the gilded rim's weave of leaves. They were accompanied by a set of four small plates. There was also a wind-up music box and C19th nautilus brought back from the Isle of Man by mum's paternal grandfather from a visit to his birthplace. The nacreous setting enhanced its delicate Chinese landscape, the figures ghosting in and out of vision with a twist of the wrist. A cruder carved tortoise shell kept it company on the mantelpiece. The rarity and skill of these artefacts was not shared by contemporary knick knacks displayed on kitchen and lounge-room shelves.

Grandma's goat, having butted her, earned the appellation, 'Hitler', for his aggressions. His excretions permeated the grass circles he chomped throughout her large backyard. Like his namesake, his life was terminated with poison. The circumference of his final tethering overlapped the rubbish dump. He fixed on some torch batteries, died painfully, and was composted on the site of his indiscretion. Was the goat stupid? Dad thought so. Whenever I broke something, or got instructions confused, he called me a stupid goat, and Hitler's bloated body flashed before me.

Grandma's outside toilet was emptied weekly by Mr Chipperfield in his green truck. 'Night soil' was what dad called the cans of shit Chipperfield shouldered to his truck. He sniggered at Chipperfield's euphemistic job title, 'sanitary engineer'. He wasn't needed at our place as dad had shovelled a deep pit and concreted the walls for a septic tank concealed on the bush side of the house.

Dad was an engineer for the State Electricity Commission and took the train every day to the Richmond substation in Church Street, next to the Yarra River. In the main it was used to supplement peak demand and avert power shortages. He did three shifts, day, afternoon and night so that two weeks out of three he was absent from supper. I sometimes wondered who the visitor at our meal table was, especially if he was angry. When he was home there was 'no monkey business' or turning up noses at unappealing foods.

Sunday mornings our parents strolled us through the bush to sit on a bench and gaze over daffodil expanses. Sometimes we took longer walks beyond Blind Creek to Ferntree Gully. Mum would have a leg of lamb in the oven and the spuds and pumpkin would be ready by the time we returned. There might be peas, or worse, bitter Brussels sprouts. For reasons mum kept to herself, she insisted our soup bowls had to be tilted away from our bodies and the spoon scooped accordingly. Never did I see anyone else doing likewise.

Dad relished carving with the bone-handled knife and fork with retractable safety lever. He sharpened the knife on a finely fluted steel rod. As each plate was passed around the table, dad reminded us that though his grandfather did the same, we would skip the sententious grace. The lamb was sliced and served cold on Mondays. Some Tuesdays there was enough to convert to patties. I hungered for the bone to suck, its remnant fat and marrow. The jelled blood captured below frozen lard was a treat on fresh bread. The shank's knucklebone was salvaged to play jacks though these became redundant with the advent of plastic replicas. Sausages, lambs fry, tripe and sheep brains rounded out our meaty diet.

My greatest challenges were the congealed blood sausage of black pudding and smoked cod. Objections to these were met with threats to pack us off to the nearby Salvation Army Boys' Home huddling in the lush valley of The Basin below Mt Dandenong. The Home, established in 1897 as a reformatory institution for wayward or orphaned youths, had been purchased from early settler, David Dobson. Threats of having food recycled the following meal, or being sent to the Boys' Home, had us grudgingly finish even the least appetising fare. When baulking certain offerings, we were enjoined to consider starving

Africans, though the brightly robed black people in our National Geographic magazines didn't validate mum's plea.

Desserts were a mixed blessing. Though invariably sweet, the texture of jelly, junkets and custards disgusted me. Ice sat in a semi-transparent glaze above the milk in most of mum's attempts at ice cream. Ground rice and sago were challenging. Two stood apart. Cake time I'd hover round the kitchen bench to lick the mixing bowl, no matter the make. Date loaf, baked in a cylindrical tin, was attractive. But heading the list were golden dumplings that floated in incomparably rich syrup.

Before supper, our washed hands and legs had to pass inspection. 'Rodney, you haven't washed behind your knees,' mum would say, to which I'd lamely protest, 'But no one sees back there,' before returning to the bathroom and removing offending dirt. Having finished eating, we placed our fork and knife in parallel in the middle of the plate, and were instructed to say we'd 'had an elegant sufficiency' and to ask, 'May I leave the table, please?' 'Please' and 'thank you' were essential manners and of paramount importance on the rare occasions we ate at the 'aunts'.

Mealtimes, dad used as occasions for correcting expression. 'You two, not youse. Ewes are sheep.' 'I, myself' need only be 'I'.' 'Those people' not, 'them people'. It grieved him to hear the superfluity of 'those ones', 'the honest truth', and 'in actual fact'. A thing couldn't be 'terribly good' but either 'terrible' or 'good'. When he sat at the table, all other voices were subjugated. No one countered his opinions, and at the slightest ruckus he threatened to 'spifflicate' us. Mum sometimes interjected. I'd gaze at the cloudy green laminated table as he belittled her, fingering the wisps of fleece that marbled the surface of a distant fertile planet. Her pain was my pain.

***

Marilyn was born in 1952. While I doted on her, Ian teased her unmercifully about her slightly knocked knees, or prominent incisors—a feature we shared with her. He felt she didn't share the pressure to finish meals and, exempt from punishment, was our parent's favourite. She amused us as we waited for supper, sitting in her high chair beating her spoon in sync to *She Wears Red Feathers* and *How Much is That Doggie in the Window*, playing on the kitchen radio. Ian delighted in the Animal Fair ditty, emphasising *the big baboon, by the light of the moon, was combing her auburn hair*, deriding her luxurious hair. Marilyn's shuffling around the house struck an odd note. Whereas we boys did the usual crawling thing prior to walking, she propelled herself by sitting cross-legged, tilting slightly forward, and with her weight centred at her axis, dragged her butt along the ground.

In dad's absence, Ian taunted us with inventive put-downs. He'd wrestle me to the floor, pin my arms and dribble on my chest. One of his favourite stunts was to slip out of our bedroom undetected and re-emerge at the window, face flattened against the glass, he would roll back his eyes and utter odd birdlike sounds. He was the bane of my existence, the cause of nightmares and likely, the bed-wetting. Despite mum's claim to the contrary, names hurt. He called me 'half-caste'. We didn't realise at the time that this referred to part-Aboriginality, but I knew it meant not being whole, that I didn't belong. I was Other. Repeated often enough, his fantasy gained credibility and he knew its venom grieved me.

Mum's attempts at discipline were futile. As her frustration rose she'd tell us she was 'floating' and reported our antics when dad made his 6 o'clock phone call. A leather strap was kept in the drawer below the cutlery. We knew its warmth too well. Ian was routinely woken and belted by dad on his 10 o'clock. return. I, too, was occasionally belted, but nothing like Ian, who was the inevitable perpetrator. If dad was on night shift, the strapping was after breakfast, on our hamstrings, as hands were needed for schoolwork. We'd loosen our school shorts to hide the welts from other kids. Thus shamed, I never asked classmates if they were punished. Perhaps it was normal? And though mum was clearly complicit in this and pleaded from the kitchen not to be too hard, she avoided our blame by cuddling us later in the day.

The routine didn't disrupt Ian's sleep, but I often lay awake anticipating his strapping. If I felt trapped, weather permitting, I'd slip out the back door and sit for 15 or so minutes amongst the trees in the backyard. There I was at home. The fresh air calmed and steadied me sufficiently to re-enter the house and crawl beneath welcoming blankets.

Some Saturdays we boarded the narrow-gauge Puffing Billy at Upper Ferntree Gully to visit aunts in Belgrave. The line had opened in 1900 primarily to serve Carl Nobelius's Emerald and Gembrook nurseries. We perched on the sills of the open-sided wooden carriages, braving the flecks of ash floating in coke-filled clouds and waving back to families gathered in backyards to greet us as we passed. We sat quietly inside those cramped gloomy lounge rooms, bored with adult talk. But several times we journeyed to the end of the line to stroll the nursery and test the waters of nearby Emerald Lake with kids from another branch of the Chandler family who farmed at Avonsleigh. Percy and Gwen Chandler had been school friends of mum's. These were big days out as we romped amongst hay bales in their shed, or squatted on the tractor pretending to drive, with energetic guttural grunts.

Another of mum's friends offered to drive us for a holiday at her beach house in the tiny fishing village of Rhyll on Phillip Island. Mum was pregnant with her fourth and desperate for a break. We squeezed into the Ford Prefect, my first substantial car trip. We crossed San Remo Bridge and passed strange wooden kilns which dad reckoned were where the chicory we drank was roasted. We could see French Island which served as a prison and where chicory also grew. Dad said it was named by French explorers. What were they doing in our country so long ago?

I nursed my Christmas present, a three-funnelled plastic model of the 1930s ocean liner, Queen Mary. At water's edge I carved passage through the jungle of putrid weed and set the boat on its maiden voyage. The first wave sucked it beyond reach and I watched in disappointment as it sailed further into Westernport Bay, perhaps returning to Mother England. The next day we set out to catch the morning ferry to the larger town of Cowes. I sprinted downhill after Ian when we heard the ferry's horn and tripped over a barbed wire fence ripping the underside of my arm. Mum staunched the bleeding with handkerchiefs and our Cowes focus shifted to the island's sole medical help.

The town's tawdry resort atmosphere was garnished with sea-front palms. The clinic was shut Sundays. We hurried uphill past the shops in search of the doctor's home. He answered dad's rapping on his flyscreen door, inviting us to sit in the lounge. As he pumped me with tetanus, he said I'd have to contend without anaesthetic as he has none at home. Taking a suturing needle from his drawer he made six, what he termed, double stitches, with sturdy twine. 'You've been a brave boy not crying,' he said reassuringly. Back home, the stitches itched as the wound healed. Mum re-dressed them daily and when the twine was removed I bore the scar's shiny statement as a record of bravery.

Dad brought a tin off-cut from work, undercoated it pale cream, then, following carefully pencilled letters, and painted 'Hastings Ave' in black gloss enamel, hammered it to the lamppost on the corner of Boronia Road. I thought he'd personally proclaimed Hastings Avenue. He said it acknowledged the Battle of Hastings in 1066, and the town was the birthplace of Boronia's first postmaster. The Norman's victory, he added, introduced French words to our Anglo-Saxon language. Mum's book of the 1930's movie, *The Adventures of Robin Hood*, with its stills of Errol Flynn and angelic Olivia de Havilland, that summed up my knowledge of those distant times. I had no idea of invasions, or people fighting to possess other people's land. And for that matter, that

Australia commenced as an English penal colony, and had been vigorously defended by its prior occupants.

Ours was the last house on the street. Where it finished, a root-rutted track wove 50 metres through bush and bracken and opened on an orchard of plums and apples. Adjoining its lower acres was a high, corrugated burgundy fence enclosing cottages of ancient nuns of the Good Shepherd's Order. Though built only a decade prior to my birth it seemed to have existed forever. On warm days small groups of this sisterhood sat inanimate beneath the shade of the trees. Ian and I assumed it was their fruit and crouched in the bush until they retired. Their severe black habits and ground-length white dresses rendered them exotics we daren't disturb. Three goats, tethered to stakes, grazed the surrounding grass. With the disappearance of the silent procession we'd warily skirt the goats, clamber the trees, wedge into a fork and feast.

From Ian's daily tormenting and competitive jousting, I found no escape. For better and worse we were thrown together. Yet complicity in these adventures was the upside of the relationship so that when he started school, I was often miserable and resorted to the kitchen, hanging out with mum as she endlessly cleaned, washed, cooked and shopped.

One day, with him at school and thinking 'plum', I dared enter the orchard alone. The big shaggy-bearded Billy forbade me entering the gate and told me to go straight home. 'You can't come in here little boy,' or so I explained to mum on my return, adding that he'd tossed me back over the gate on his large horns when I tried to pass. She advised against fibbing and that eating unripe plums was bound to cause a bellyache. For lying I would have to go the bedroom and miss lunch. Who was I attempting to deceive? Had I lied? I had no memory of eating plums, or the happy meeting of fruit and fingers. What lingered were images of the terrible troll and the urinous stench of the Billygoat Gruffs from bedtime readings.

***

How isolated were we in those car-less 1950s? There were three houses other than ours, all occupied by elderly, childless couples. Houses on the lower side fronted Turner Avenue so what we saw between scrub and trees was backyard fencing. We kids were our own company. Our dirt street lacked lighting save for a single-bulbed lamppost at its entrance peering down on dad's sign. Twice a year a slim man of solemn countenance pedalled to the corner of our property. There he'd dismount and raise a concrete lid exposing a steel pipe. Beneath his coat he wore a set of navy bib and braces and matching cotton drill cap. He'd unhitch a massive spanner from his crossbar and loosen the lid, releasing torrents of water. Dad said he was the 'mains man'. He'd stand studying the wild grass, bullied flat beneath the tide of water as it spent itself in the sword grass and onion weed, rewarding his endeavours with a rolled cigarette before disappearing back to town. Apart from geriatric Mrs Moorcroft, drizzle of grey hair on her upper lip hobbling with cane in one hand shopping jeep in the other to and fro the shops, no one tramped that track.

No men presented in the dim houses of the old we visited: neither the two maids tucked away behind our back hedge of pittosporums, nor those we had to call 'aunt'. I knew we had no actual aunts or uncles as both parents lacked siblings. Dad's mum died from septicaemia after his birth. His father abandoned him to his grandmother and his unmarried sister, our great 'aunt' Gwen. Those dark interiors were the abode of women in black. The houses exuded halitosis to which their shuffling occupants seemed oblivious. Shelves, dressers and sideboards were decked with photos of progeny and the missing men, glass, and china figurines. In the cabinets were bowls, dishes, and prized porcelain. On the walls were gold-framed reproductions of seascapes and flower arrangements.

A long driveway fed from Boronia Road's cliffs to the old maids' cottage. The mulchy underfoot suggested no vehicle had disturbed the lane in the half century since its construction. It had an aura of mystery. The cane-clutching ancients seemed housebound. Though intruders in the lane, it was our conduit to church and an orchard of prized blood plums, and we sensed surreptitious ownership of this dark corridor. Totally embowered with tall trees, it was something of a time tunnel; to go forward was to go back. Traversing its hundred metres in dappled light and encountering their dwelling clothed splendidly in hydrangea and rose arbours, was a window on another era. Surrounding their cottage, clumps of agapanthus proliferated, lilac-coloured blooms nodding on ungainly stems. The jasmine-latticed frame clinging to the brick chimney, the lichen-encrusted pavers, the rake and pruning shears left by the barrow in the garden crowded with quince, loquat, cumquat and crabapple, possessed a dense immobility absent from our block, and whose scents in fruiting season we carried into their home, sometimes returning with jars of their preserved sugary contents.

Miss Thomas and Miss Niven had an organ jammed behind their front door. Stretching on the wall above most of its length was the intimidating image of *The Charge of the Light Brigade*. Rows of white horses with flaring nostrils and terrified eyes, red-jacketed fusiliers with sabres drawn, thundered towards the crest of the organ. What this battle was about I hadn't a clue. Maybe the old women had fathers or uncles on those mounts? On the wall by their kitchen was a slender white-robed man rapping at a door just like theirs. He held a lamp by his thigh and a full moon surrounded his sad head. He sported a fulsome red beard and effeminate shoulder- length hair. Mum whispered that this was Jesus. So here was the guy I'd recently heard about at Sunday school, the gentle man, meek and mild, in whose name we dedicated coins when the wooden collection plate was passed along our pew.

Dad had no time for religion, regarding its devotees as wishful thinkers. He found more useful things to do on weekends. The hour's train ride to the city was a treat and, with Marilyn in her stroller, we took the 'red rattler', as dad dubbed the train, to Royal Park Zoo. It was stifling and our pants stuck to the green artificial leather benches with each vehicular jolt. At Box hill, halfway to the city was a huge hoarding representing handsome personnel of the Army, Navy and Air Force. Elsewhere were advertisements for *Griffiths Bros. Tea*, marking by the mile our advance upon the city. We never drank tea. Chicory was our hot beverage. Mostly we had water, sometimes flavoured with lemon or orange saline.

Once inside the zoo gates we bought peanuts for the voracious monkeys. 'You're looking at your ancestors there,' quipped dad. They even squabbled over the shells they impishly snatched from one another, and then readily dispatched. The bison's mournful eye suggested abandonment from its ancestors great, roaming herds. Fly hordes thrived around its long eyelashes, nostrils, and the few remaining islands of shaggy winter fur. Its solitary confinement haunted me. Zoos were prisons. The giraffe, whose height could be estimated by numerals painted on the wall next to his rubbly stable, looked lost and pitiful. Like the nearby zebra, its patterned coat painted with miraculous perfection, contrasted with its undignified enclosure. A cluster of kids clinging to parents tittered as a series of small dark pellets issued from its anus.

An elephant carted queues of children in a tidy, circular enclosure, its deeply creased hide seemingly the result of this tiresome duty. Another group of kids did a larger adjacent circuit in a miniature train. The dishevelled jungle king languished with his two queens looking profoundly disinterested, as well they might so far from the Serengeti. Other than the slightest flick of the tail at fly traffic, they were dormant.

A pair of Wildebeests and their calf grazed nonchalantly, indifferent to the sparrows sporting on their backs. The calf dropped on its front knees to access its mother's milk. The nippled world; I started looking for nipples on other beasts. Nearby a polar bear lay in the limited shade of its faux cave. Its painted white concrete rocks fooled no one. None of these exotics seemed to enjoy our inspection other than the otters and seals whose pools offered relief. The hippo's concrete tub was no substitute for wallowing in luxurious mud. There were so many species from so many countries housed in unrelated proximity to each other. The general desolation compromised the surprise of first sightings. The animals were both larger than life per depictions in our *National Geographics*, yet drastically diminished.

At the exit gate a grating, 'hello' startled us. We scanned the aviary where a sulphur-crested cockatoo fluttered to the front of the cage, gripping the bars and training its anthracitic eye on us. It had been an arduous day and we welcomed its interest. 'I've come a long way to see you,' jabbered Ian who, barely pausing, offered his name and address for future communications. It was a unique interactive pleasure given the universal muteness that repaid our day's voyeurism.

Just as rare an event as the zoo was the sight of a pregnant woman in the streets, at least one well advanced. As we passed a woman waddling from the grocery one morning, I asked mum what was wrong with her. She dismissed my query and whispered to look away. Though she, too, was showing the baby she'd begun to grow, in the midst of our post-war baby boom there endured some stigma about flaunting evidence of sexual activity. My errand-running no doubt helped maintain her 'confinement'. Just as unusual was an encounter with women smoking. When I saw a woman with short-cropped hair, pants, fag in mouth exit the bakery, I told mum I'd seen a man-lady. That aroused a fit of laughter.

I couldn't wait to terminate my lonely days and start school. There was no kindergarten before I commenced the same Boronia State mum had attended a few years after its construction in 1923. Its few acres of playground sloped gently to the single-platform station. Some kids wept as their mothers abandoned them at the school gate. Not me. I was impatient to be where Ian had boasted of grand events. Soon after enrolling, our family joined the queue of kids at the Progress Hall for inoculation jabs. The scourge of polio was near extinct, though one girl in class with callipers strapped to a mangled leg was a reminder of its crippling power. For all that, we were still visited by mumps, measles, chickenpox, and unsightly scabs of impetigo.

Each Monday morning assembly monitors hoisted Australia's flag. We repeated an oath to serve god, honour the queen and her country, and cheerfully obey our parents, teachers, and the law. I knew the queen existed as we'd attended her Coronation Parade in Swanston Street; she with stiff half-smile and white-gloved mitt raised as we waved national flags on sticks at her passing limousine. Country was the backyard and bush next door, extending up *One Tree Hill*. God remained a mystery.

No one wore hats. Now and then on hot days at assembly a kid fainted, and a teacher assisted him or her to the sick bay. Announcements were made by silver-haired, Miss Neil. At Rangeview Road School, where we graduated to third grade, Jenkins did the talking, occasionally relieved by balding headmaster, Maddocks, whose name honoured the new limestone school hall. Talk done, the blare of a recorded brass band made scratchy entry onto the address system to assist our marching to class.

We began days standing by our desks, singing the alphabet, followed by the times table up to twelve, without recourse to the printout on the back of our Vana exercise books. There were over 40 students in class, sitting at green wooden desks in pairs of girls and boys. Etched names from previous generations were discernible beneath the paint. Such was our unquestioning compliance, teachers had no difficulty maintaining order amongst what now would be regarded as impossible numbers. Chalked art was drawn on small blackboards, swiftly erased and stashed in desks at the conclusion of sessions.

Teacher's steady lettering covered the top of the blackboard with the alphabet in upper and lower case. Below were the date and the board sectioned in spelling, numbers, and Nature Study. We'd strike a margin on the left side of our exercise books with red pencil and copy the date and subject up top, following Miss Hutchison's script. On either side of the blackboard hung maps printed on canvas. The world was to the left declaring the pink estates of Empire. On the right was our colonised country, with its rigid state boundaries. We each had plastic templates of mainland Australia with which we'd replicate our coastline throughout the next decade, belatedly acknowledging Tasmania.

School was unproblematic for me. Reading, Numbers and Spelling came easily, though some things made little sense. Explanations of homographs like 'our' and 'hour', 'blew' and 'blue', 'ate' and 'eight', I took on trust from the teacher. Likewise, with homonyms like 'date', 'leaves', or 'bark', this last exemplified by a dog pursuing a cat and barking up the wrong tree. The biggest challenge came from Grade 2 teacher, Miss Allen, a Scottish woman bent on imparting her homeland's dances. She insisted that once a week we boys don kilts and jig about the quadrangle with the girls we otherwise kept at a distance. The half-hour walk to and from school in a tartan kilt with its great chrome safety pin shamed me, and I did my best to keep from sight, dodging behind trees and back lanes from imagined observers. If formal lessons concluded a few minutes before lunch we were treated with five minutes of game time, 'Simon Says', or Allen, tapping a student shoulder to leave the room while our eyes were shut, would ask us to open them and identify the absentee.

***

Dad re-lined our bedroom with pine panels and inserted a shelf to house a Astor Mickey radio. The world beyond Boronia flared to life. After school I snuggled beneath blankets to listen to serials: *The Sea Hound*, *Superman*, *Hop Harrigan*, and *Tarzan*. Keith Smith's *Pied Piper* had me struggling to remember jokes heard from Smith's *Pocket-money Riddle Round-up* to amuse school buddies. 'Did you hear about the man who had his left leg cut off? He's all right now.' 'What did the sea say to the boat? Nothing. It just waved.' Mum would sit on my bed after *Tarzan's* curtain call and read for a few minutes then whisper sweet nothings in my ear or play, *Can You Keep A Secret* or tap my toes while reciting, *This Little Piggy Went To Market*. Then she'd pump the green Mortein canister, bringing pesky mosquitoes to ground, before wish us 'little darlings', sweet dreams.

Redex Car Rallies around Australia fed images as I lay in bed co-driving with 'Gelignite' Jack Murray or Jack Davey. They battled outback dirt roads, and I'd slide beneath the blankets of my 'rally car' asking my imaginary co-driver if he needed relief at the wheel, food, or drink as we negotiated exotic Kalgoorlie, Camooweal, Meekatharra and Alice Springs. Broadcasts of boxing matches were also transfixing. And Sunday's police reports of overnight car crashes piqued my morbid curiosity.

Grieg's enchanting *Peer Gynt* suite transported me to lofty mountain realms; further than I'd ever travelled from home. There were stories such as *Bambi* and Danny Kaye's multi-voiced, *Tubby The Tuba* and the strange tale of *Gossamer Wump*. Gossamer sought mastery of the triangle. Together with his 27 peanut butter sandwiches and dog, George, in a suitcase, he packed off for a 10-year apprenticeship with Professor Cutty Nutty Dump. Several more attempts were made at the big-time before he resigned himself to the signifying notes of the local ice cream van. Whatever the moral about thwarted ambition, the sad fate of George's decade-long suitcase internment was baffling.

Wump's exploits emboldened me to ask mum to opt for the newly marketed crunchy peanut butter in my school lunches—I'd not wanted to offend her by voicing displeasure with the blackberry jam sandwiches that crystallised the bread by midday. We munched our sandwiches in gender-specific shelter sheds. Play was impermissible until the last crumb was swallowed. Then on wet days we'd stand on the benches to play 'pussy-in-the-corner' with the corners serving as safety zones from the tagger.

I was in Grade 2 when Colin was born, a brown-eyed handsome fellow, exciting us while wearing mum thin with his suckling. Misunderstanding the word 'caul' crowning Colin's scalp, I proudly informed my teacher of the good luck 'cow' on his head. 'He can't drown,' I repeated what mum had confided, imagining the mythic swimming prowess of cows. Little more than a vapour of fluff graced his scalp for close to two years during which dad called him the Bald Iggle, a character in Al Capp's *Lil' Abner* cartoon.

That year, Marie Street, which marked the perimeter of Chandler's property, was upgraded with bitumen. The daffodil fields were subdivided and an acre sold to form a Lawn Bowls Club. The launch of the clubhouse was celebrated with a screening of W C Field's *Hurry Hurry*. Mishearing often provided entertainment at my expense. Lumbering Harry Lovett presided over the evening. I thought he'd introduced himself as 'Hurry' the film's star, Fields, who'd graced us with a guest appearance and faked an Australian accent. After all Lovett, too, was a fat-jowled old grouch.

Such mishearing had no repercussions compared to classmate Jones's incident. For reasons escaping me, the freckle-faced boy was nicknamed 'Bluey'. He reminded me of comic-book character Ginger Megs, not only for his unruly spray of hair and piebald eyes. As if working from Meg's script, Jones's daily hi-jinx tested classroom protocols. Most memorably, when elected as milk-monitor, Jones absented himself and ran after the delivery van with his helper some paces behind. Some of us could see through the open door his failed leap at the rear of the moving vehicle. In one instant, his grip on the top crate of milk brought the stash, with him, to earth. The van came to a sudden halt. Jones was on his feet inspecting gravel-rashed palms and knees when the driver approached to assess damage. Milk and glass shards littered the track. And Jones's pluck took a severe hit, being relegated to standing in the corner of our classroom until lunchtime. The upside was that we missed the day's free milk. Whatever its alleged health benefits, it often soured sitting an hour outside the class door in the sun.

Our social life was augmented when mum's friend, Joyce Barker and husband Bill boarded with us for several months while their house was built. Together with their two children, they crammed into Marilyn's bedroom, while she shared with mum and dad. I thought Joyce rivalled mum's charm and beauty but disliked Bill who sometimes disciplined me in dad's absence. He sent me back to my room as I crept towards mum's bed after a nightmare. 'You're not my father,' I cried at this fellow, who looked like comic-strip hero, *Mandrake*, and possibly possessed kindred powers. Dapper Bill's Brylcreemed black hair was combed back in a single sweep to the right. He had cold, green goat's eyes and a pencil moustache that grimaced when grinning. He was a drummer but preserved the sense not to practice at our place.

When they moved, their eldest child, Doug, a little older than Ian, continued playing with us on weekends. Doug and Ian conspired to surprise his sister Carol on her birthday. We gathered caterpillars, leaf-rolling spiders, millipedes, and armadillo bugs, which we pummelled to gravy, and housed in a tobacco tin. Doug wrapped it up and called Carol from our kitchen. Her shriek before those carapaces floating midst their vile grey sea rewarded our labour as we ran beyond reach of our reproachful mothers.

We'd break into sides for games, each of us hoping for the advantage of Doug's partnership. Once a teenager who shacked up with his older brother on the far side of the bush, asked to join us. We'd no cause to ever speak before. He had a slug gun, so given his seniority and weapon, we all wanted to side with him; but he wished to go it alone. We ran and hid behind trees from this Andrew Harcourt. Then we heard gun reports. He disappeared as Doug yelped. A slug was wedged in the side of his nose and his eyes glistened. The game was over and Doug, though once or twice fishing and eeling the creeks with Ian, never again joined our bush amusements. Nor did Harcourt, who I hoped had secure residency at the Salvation Boys' Home.

Grandma visited the Royal Melbourne Show and returned with the showbag of liquorice I'd requested. Greed gripped me. To share my guilt the following afternoon, I invited Jeff Nicholls to duck school. Between rounds of Cowboys and Indians we worked through the bag in the neighbouring bush with delicious gluttony and dire gastronomic consequences. Mum knew what I'd been up to the instant I rushed to the toilet then fronted her with my partially cleansed chops. Tilting her head and fixing me with an enquiring gaze she said, nothing escaped her attention. This, I believed.

A few months later I heard grandma tapping on the kitchen window. I'd never seen her at our place before. She told mum she was about to go to hospital for a gall bladder operation. 'I'm going, now' she called. 'Is Geoff there?' Dad sloped off up the hallway as mum beckoned him to the kitchen, muttering that he hoped she'd die. His reaction confused me as I watched my precious grandma turn and disappear, weary and hurt. Something was wrong. I knew he'd once or twice locked mum out of the house at night, having threatened to do so if she went next door to wish her mother goodnight. We'd heard her weeping in our dog's kennel but had been too afraid to help her.

Arriving home from school the next week I found mum cradling Colin, rocking and weeping as she sat on the low brick holding wall bordering the path leading to her mother's. Between sobs she repeated, 'Mum's dead, darling. Mum's dead. I don't know what to do.' I couldn't believe this, and wrapped my arm over her shoulders telling her not to cry. 'You'll be okay,' I consoled. I didn't know this word 'aneurysm' that caused her passing. A chasm had opened for us. She must have felt terror with her loss. No parents or siblings, and a husband whose shift work made for irregular contact.

Grandma was buried next to her husband in a Box Hill grave, unmarked and unvisited. A recurring dream had me stretching the limits of the town's known geography on a bare hill to the west. Standing there, leafless, in a paddock was an old grey gumtree. Unrecognisable houses surrounded it. I wanted to go to the tree but couldn't reach it or even duck through the fence. I'd wake alone, weeping. Was it her?

3

A widening world

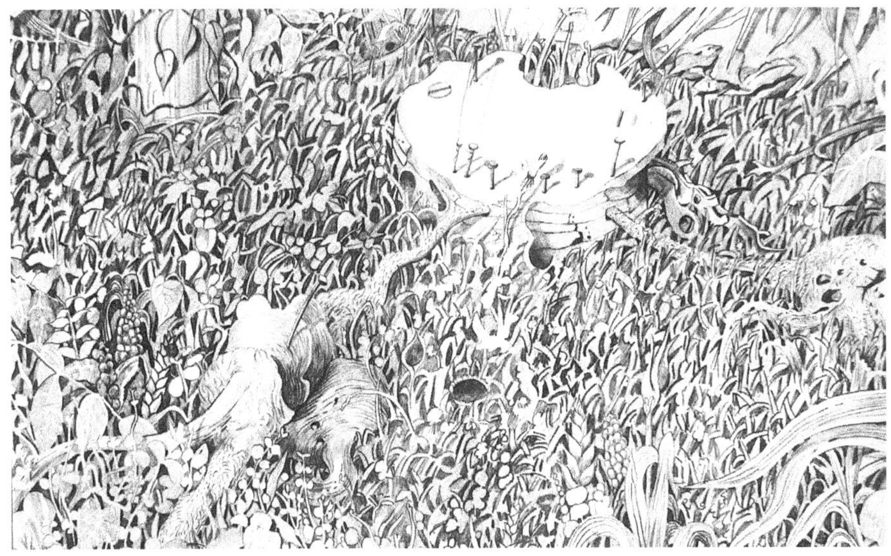

For a Southern Garden, Rod Moss, 1978.

There was a consoling certainty about Boronia's daily doings and fixture of friendly faces in the few dozen shops lining the two main streets that, unfortunately, intersected at the rail crossing. Doubtless, this design preceded the quantity of car traffic that even in the late 1950s rendered it hazardous and inconvenient for impatient commuters. Several horrific collisions with trains had earned the crossing its reputation as Australia's worse death trap. When I was four, a train had bisected a busload of Church of Christ worshippers, killing thirteen and injuring twenty. The horrific 1926 crash is memorialised with a monument to the boy scouts who assisted at the scene.

The first city-bound morning train honked its horn at 6 o'clock, heralding dairyman Colin Brown, whose Clydesdale clopped towards us from the dairy in Dorset road while I lay in bed. Unharnessed at the end of its duties, it jogged to the paddock at the end of our street behind the butchers. I clicked my tongue against the roof of my mouth to imitate its beating hooves, mouth music I varied when clattering my teeth to the rattling rails as trains approached from Ferntree Gully. Bigger milk herds grazed in the pastures that were losing ground to neighbouring Bayswater's expanding industrial zone. Dad had built a milk box, emulating our house, and it was up to me to fetch the four tinfoil-capped bottles. We used to save the caps and string them to decorate the Christmas tree.

Though only two streets and less than a hundred metres from the crossing, we lived almost exclusively east of the line. I was responsible for simpler shopping errands and needed no encouragement when it included the bakery. I'd buy an unsliced high-tin white loaf, a double if available. Sliced bread was yet to come. I'd often nibble its fleecy front on my amble home, denying my role in its refashioned concavity. If mum caught me sucking the penny or threepence change she'd warn me, 'take that money from your mouth. It might have been in the pocket of a dirty Chinaman'.

I knew only one Chinese man: pint-sized Artie Power. This elderly oriental rode a full-size bicycle whose pedals his toe-clipped feet barely reached. Chrome clips attended his cuffs, causing them to balloon over his calves. There was something unfathomable about his dark eyes, watchful without conceding thought. He was always immaculately attired in pressed grey strides and white shirt, tweed jacket and matching golf cap. I never saw him quit his saddle or converse. Did he know this tussle with elevation rendered him ridiculous? Mum told me that having once received compensation for the loss of a toe, Artie, strapped for cash, had lopped other toes for subsequent claims. I pondered the source of the coins tumbling in his pockets and the tiny stumps of feet powering those pedals.

On rare occasions we rejoiced with a Boston bun or lamington, sitting beside apple and custard tarts like crown jewels in the glass display case. I was bemused by the large script of the hoarding on the railway side of the bakery, one of the few advertisements in Boronia and the most resplendent. *Dr Morse's Indian Root Pills* in silver outlined in black, blazed over a cobalt field. Adverts generally shared the fatigued fawns, blues, and greens that also graced cars and clothes. Though mum occasionally resorted to Aspro or Bex pills, she knew nothing about Morse's product which remained a mystery.

Pinnock and Sims, both dapper in white, cotton drills and navy aprons, did the butchery next door; cheery guys nimbly footing through the saw-dusted floor. Sheep and pigs bobbed from the refrigerated truck as the deliveryman shouldered them through the door. The carcasses were soon unrecognisable save for the pigs' heads crowned with parsley in the window display, grinning stupidly on synthetic grass. The stench of the bloodied bench battled sawdust resins as the men broke from butchery to smile at mum. Beefy, pink-faced Sims honed his long knife with a steel stake, housed in a cylinder at his waist. The blade slid silently through the lamb's leg, making a comfy thud when returned to its sheath. Pinnock, small and swarthy, usually served. Sausage slugs, sheep's brains and chops were wrapped in white paper and laid on the counter. 'Anything else today, Mrs. Moss?' 'No thanks, that'll be all, Mr. Pinnock,' she'd smile, slipping the packages into her string bag.

Squeezed between the butchers and the bakery was a tiny tobacconist. Its tin billboards advertised Turf and Craven A cigarettes; the first sporting a black cat, the second, a winged horse. Did animals smoke? Less enigmatic was a kitted sailor nestled in a lifebuoy, proclaiming the benefits of Players Navy Cut smokes.

Across from the horse paddock was the Post Office where mum worked with Mrs Charters, towards the end of the Second World War, having left school at fourteen. Mum had also traced parts for Beaufort jets at Fisherman's Bend. It stood where Turner Avenue joined Boronia Road, honouring the name of the first postmaster who'd doubled duties as stationmaster. Except for Christmas cards, it wasn't postal business that brought us there, but transactions at the Commonwealth Bank from a partitioned booth. I liked Charter's beam behind steel-rimmed specs, and the thump and spirited scent of purple ink as she franked deposits and withdrawals. Her thinning faded ginger hair was worn close to her scalp in delicate ringlets, her talk filled with gentle concern.

Looking east up Boronia Road, 1950.

Over the road from the bakery was the grocer's corner. I'd cross the tree-lined creek running beside Boronia Road as it climbed to The Basin, occasionally encountering old Albert Zeising in his buggy, clopping along between the few cars. Zeising owned extensive property west of the station, and a modest court, formerly his driveway, was named after him. The two genial Falconer brothers, Colin and Hugh, in grey dustcoats, doled flour, sugar and rolled oats from hessian bags on the shop floor, and biscuits into paper bags from the brightly labelled cubed tins on the shelves behind the counter. The Falconer clan, with grocer credentials originating in Scotland, also had stores in neighbouring Bayswater and Ferntree Gully. Both pre-dated Boronia, and also housed populations of a few thousand.

Next door was Richardson's greengrocery—ruddy-faced father and son in their leather aprons. 'Grocer,' hollered Alan, the son, as he home-delivered mum's order of fruit and vegies in a wooden box later in the morning. Mrs Taylor and Mrs Adams served in the haberdashery further up Boronia Road hill. There, mum purchased cottons, buttons, and wools to knit and darn our pants and pullovers. At home she'd roll our socks over a wooden mushroom and, tin thimble on her pointer, renew balding toes and heels.

On Falconer's other flank, facing Dorset road was Laurie McGuire's garage, where he interrupted industry beneath car bonnets and chassis to serve Atlantic petrol at the bowsers at three shillings and sixpence per gallon of Super, threepence less for Standard. He'd pluck a patch of filthy towelling from his grey coveralls and wipe his mitts before hooking the nozzle to the car tank. In the early 1960s, he shifted across the road—'Atlantic' was rebranded 'Esso'. Mr Dyson built his jewellery shop on the vacated ground.

Dyson's windows displayed necklaces, bracelets, watches, glassware and two reproductions, the sole examples of public 'art' in Boronia. One on black velvet was an emerald, bikini-clad island beauty, fronting a sunset from the bough of a palm. The other, paired horses romping along a beach, a pale wave breaking at their rumps.

The hairdressers' was west of the rail crossing. To undergo a shearing was to submit to the footy and horse-race parlance of the two barbers. The air was a confusion of Californian Poppy, and Straight Eight hair oil. Waiting my turn, I'd study the scissors and combs kept in the sterilised glass cabinet emblazoned with a red cross.

'Who's next?' bespectacled Freddie Tyers would call, shaking the white cape free of hair, his own raked vigorously back, high and wavy, an advertisement for his trade. 'Short-back-and-sides is it, today?' he'd add, tucking the coarse-fibred towel beneath my collar as he slipped fresh gum into his mouth. No matter the answer, this would be the result. Tyers and Henshaw resumed their sports' talk as my hair slipped to the linoleum. It was the same green, orange and beige gridding of our kitchen floor. But home was sadly remote.

I was immobile beneath the sheet, imprisoned, glancing in the mirror at my disappearing crop as electric clippers thrived about my ears, leaving a mere tuft on top. As the shameful end drew near, Tyres would ask, 'And which side are we parting your hair today, Roddy?' I detested that royal 'we' given through his minty breath with its implication of willing collaboration. Then followed the spike of aromatics as he self-congratulated, clapping cologne between his hands and dowsing my neck, followed with a dusting of talcum. I'd grudgingly thank him, slipping from the chair and avoiding his gaze in the mirror, as he searched for my approval. Paying my two shillings and sixpence to Mrs Tyers at the cigarette counter, I'd duck between trees, hiding from the community's mocking eyes. Dad would gloatingly enquire, 'How was your visit to the tonsorial artist today?' pleased to be no longer shouldering haircutting duties.

The fire brigade was opposite the hairdressers. Tuesday evening, volunteers were summoned by the siren that, in summer, sounded trouble, but mostly their practice drills. Laurie McGuire was head honcho. Younger brother, Don, married into the Chandler clan, captained The Basin Brigade. November 5th was cracker night and the brigade, concerned at a previous unauthorised bonfire on Chandler Park, hosted the Guy Fawkes celebration next to their small fleet of red trucks. We knew nothing about the failure of this Catholic terrorist to ignite the English Houses of Parliament in the 1600s. If the few Catholics in town were present, they weren't letting on. Such nights were wonderful. Luminous corollas bloomed in the dark. An array of sparklers and rockets fizzed to airy extinction against the starry sky as the scarecrow of the infamous Fawkes, mounted on a tall pole, disintegrated in flames.

Crackers were confined to Guy Fawkes Day. One November, with dad on night shift and rain bucketing down, we talked mum into allowing us a limited show in the kitchen, however—just sparklers and a few belts of the tiny green crackers. We'd store the fountains and big three-penny bangers until next year. But there was a new item we were keen to see, a white, peg-shaped, jumping thing. As mum was too frightened to ignite it, Ian stepped up. The lights were switched off and away it sprung, manically, around the linoleum floor, causing us to flee to chairs in excited terror and leaving its black prints for dad to harangue us about in the morning.

West of the rail crossing was foreign country and why I suspect my grandma dream was set there. Apart from the football ground and hairdresser, we stayed east. Those serving in the shops were like extensions of family, more familiar than putative 'aunts' and 'uncles'. My picture preserves the 1950s' ambience and appearance of our village. Its horse paddocks and lanes are now car parks for charmless shopping marts, replicated in most suburbs. As the decade closed we acquired an electric washing machine and other kitchen gadgetry. A vacuum cleaner replaced the manual one and the infrequently used telephone, requiring the assistance of a telephonist in the Ferntree Gully Exchange, was automated.

There were scalloped pits beneath the rail line either side of the pedestrian and road crossings that dad called cowcatchers, though cows never strolled the streets. To lie in them when a train crossed was an act of bravado highly esteemed by a certain bunch of boys. Once Ian had proved himself, he urged me to do likewise. Several times I watched him before submitting to the ordeal. The rails trembled for several minutes before the terrible power of rolling iron rushed overhead. The train activated a sudden and violent gale, forcing me to tighten my eyes and clap my hands over my ears, involuntarily lining my nostrils with specs of metal. I much preferred placing bronze pennies on the tracks above the pit prior to the train's advent, admiring the resultant misshapen oval discs, the profiled head of our monarch and kangaroo pummelled without depth or texture, to outlines. These I collected in my cigarette tin of valuables along with a Blood Bank badge dad gave me, two blood-red marbles and a blue wren's feather, to bury at the base of the *Faraway Tree*.

New enterprises sprung to life in the 1960s. Dutchman Jack Van Gene, repaired shoes in a shop near the station where a short mall bisected Jack Ewison's sports shop and the newsagency. Repairs were confined to a space cordoned off at its rear, just sufficient for burly Van Gene and his industrial sewing machine. Out front, the shelves were choked with an eclectic range of leather goods and memorabilia: a mounted tiger head, facsimiles of medieval armour, imported Buddhas and whatnot. Icons unknown in Boronia, these Buddhas gathered dust during lengthy shelf lives despite Van Gene's enthusiastic sales' pitch. 'If I not got it for you, I can get,' he pleaded when not rueing the misfortunate choice of a mail-ordered Amsterdam bride, a tiny hunchback whose agreeable visage he'd hitherto proudly produced from his wallet.

On one side of Fred Tyres' hairdressers was Harold Page's Real Estate agency. On the other, the State Bank of Victoria opened a branch. Next to it,

Ray Barclay, selling and servicing white goods and a small selection of vinyl records, opened his doors.

A cluster of shops also grew opposite the mouth of our avenue. Most substantial was the tall green edifice of the Commonwealth Bank, catering for a population beyond the capacity of the post office, which shifted to new premises next to it. The Rose brothers opened a menswear business, and facing our avenue was Behan's Fish and Chips, whose greasy products we partook of most Fridays with gusto. We'd sit with a fragment of the white wrapping for a piece of battered flake, bickering for equal shares of chips and potato cakes.

***

I was unaware of the existence of First Peoples until five Mornington Islanders visited school during third grade. We had no idea where their island was or why they'd come. Nor had there been reference to the Wurundjeri that once occupied the ground on which our school and house stood. Bare-chested men, painted and feathered in silky white down, danced before us mesmerised kids. The Islanders performance broke the boredom of assembly, anthem singing, flag worship and marching. They were full, handsome, and flagrantly free of the school's bidding, making a lasting impression on us, inspiring boys to strip to the waist at recess and lunch, improvise spears and boomerangs, and roam the school's scrubby acres, playing blackfellas.

In what we imagined to be Indigenous practice, Peter Spooner and I firmed our allegiance by scraping the backs of our wrists with wire, smearing them together and swearing blood brotherhood. Despite the daily dishonour of being hauled to the flagpole before assembly, and the continued confiscation and destruction of arsenals, we persisted for months. This instinctual embrace of being closer to the world was more intense than sitting in desks reciting tables, alphabet, and poetry.

I see now how our weedy torsos and tribes, soon to form into football teams, translated our diet of Westerns at the cinema. We never registered the faces of native Americans attacking settlers and cavalry. Nor was it clear what motivated the outrage of these anonymous hordes; their war against prospective white settlers actually being a defence of their lands against the invaders. Scripted Wild West shows of the 1880s, acting out the sorry saga of Manifest Destiny, had been the progenitors of the movies. Like Aboriginals, the Indians obstructed development, were 'other', wild, and feared. In play, however, we put faces on them, embodied them, had them corresponding with our outdoor world.

We studied Egypt that year—its Nile River and mud-brick buildings with flat-topped roofs where Egyptians slept on hot nights after building pyramids. Maps showed the delta's blue fingers of water that seasonally flooded and enriched the soil for wheat, corn and barley crops; and date palms fringing oases. These water havens were particularly alluring and where I'd be sheltering from the eye of the permanently shining sun. Tanned Egyptians walked everywhere in profile, communicating through an intriguing pictograph language Miss Hoff called, hieroglyphics.

She sported a short Hollywood hairstyle, wore scarlet lipstick and her cleavage looked inviting in her sky-blue dress when stooping over my work. Teachers were never seen smoking, but her breath carried the forbidden scent of tobacco when she lent close. She may not have been a goddess but as the lone female staff member our side of fifty, I worked hard for her approval. Our first and only assignment for the year represented the stark and curious culture of these ancient people on a large sheet of Manilla card. Night after night I scrupulously toned palm leaves and the sacred ibis and gods, Nut and Osiris. Dad advised to draw light pencil lines that could be erased after guiding my script. In large shadowed letters, he titled the card, **EGYPT**. Hoff approved.

She was less generous with 'Stinky' Frank Wright, forcing miscreants to sit next to the otherwise shunned boy. He was sockless, unwashed, incontinent and doubly shamed by her unpardonable cruelty. He hailed from neighbouring Bayswater that I'd associated with dairy and poultry farms, and thereafter, added poverty. The only shame Hoff visited upon me occurred on Parents' Night when the class assembled on stage to sing *The Happy Wanderer* in the school hall. For months we'd rehearsed the one song and were designated boy and girl roles to chime in rounds. Mum had been apprised of our progress as we built towards performance. Stepping onto the bleachers, Hoff pulled me aside and whispered that I should mime. The awful truth of my loud, tuneless voice hammered home. The pleasure in mum's eyes as she ran to embrace me off stage was stifled by my sobbed confession.

That same November, Ian and I took the train with dad to the city. Determined to abate tensions among European nations, and the jostling between USA and Soviet Union super powers, Melbourne promoted its 'friendly' Olympic Games. Other than a bloody fracas during the Hungarian and Soviet water polo teams, the media reflected a successful campaign with people of all creeds and colours competing and intermixing. While excited by the day's prospects I knew little about the events other than road cycling due to the prominence of champions, Sid Patterson and Russell Mockeridge.

Dad's interests guided us to the velodrome. The stalling, then sudden bursts of speed on the weirdly warped surface, not to mention the men's massive thighs, was enthralling. Ian was delighted with our high jumper Chila Porter's silver medal. Yet it was sprinter, Betty Cuthbert, together with swimmers, Fraser, Crapp, Devitt, Henriks and Rose, that put Australia on the world map.

We were very proud of Australian achievements. And I was proud to present my report card to dad whose judgement always exceeded that of my teachers. Healthy scores in all subjects and no absences, save the unexplained half-day us liquorice-lovers spent in the bush. Common colds had struck everyone but scrupulous me who'd dodged coughing classmates whenever possible. Unfortunately, Miss Hoff was the last female teacher until high school. Men assumed the mantle of upper primary, suited in dull greys, browns and blues, with white shirts and muted ties.

Having recalled Nicholls and Wright, the full cast of third-year names and faces float unbidden before me: Glenys Russell, April Steele, Nonie Sinclair, Robyn McGuiness, Mary Wilcox and other girls I had nothing to do with; with Spooner, Johnny Milne, Kenny McMullan, Keith Turpie, Alan Worrall and the rest I'd played footy, Releaso, hopscotch, or marbles. They're all there. Just mug-shots, passive and glum, their eyes devoid of spark. None have I seen or heard of in sixty years. Yet they're archived, as none from subsequent years, have been. Was I more attentive then? Did this mark fuller embrace of my social world? Maybe the morning's roll call preceding our sing-song tables and alphabet embedded them.

As with my Egypt project, dad often took over projects I'd started, cutting paper shapes or making model airplanes, finishing them with perfection which, given he was uninvited, honed a feeling of incompetence in practical matters. This plane or ship was his, not mine. Rather than emulate his skill, my interest shut down. But he also taught me how to draw ocean liners in raking perspective. My renditions impressed schoolmates and teachers. I developed them to a degree that kept dad at a distance. Diesels were also subjected to perspectival laws, the gentle arc of their carriages tapering to merge with the rail tracks.

Once a month dad dressed in a tuxedo and crisp white shirt to attend Lodge in Belgrave. When I asked mum where he was going, she'd reply, 'To see a man about a dog'. I anticipated him returning with a pup, but that never happened. When I asked him what he did at Lodge, he gave a sly grin and said he rode a goat. I imagined his florid cheeks swelling over the tight-fitting collar as he gripped the mane of a formidable Billy like that custodian of the orchard. Freemasonry was secret men's business to which we uninitiated had no access.

Several experiences encouraged trust in my imaginative faculties. I dreamed I was in the bush next door standing beneath a large stringybark surrounded by cherry firs. Growing in its leaf litter was a circle of mushrooms, a phenomenon unknown to me. At breakfast I recounted this to mum, then excitedly crossed the sceptic tank, hopped the fence and visited the tree. There was the circle as dreamed, parent mushroom in its midst. I began seeing familiar faces slip into strangeness then resume their former identity. I'd behold them with novel lucidity, aware of the space separating us. As much as I was thrilled, I could neither invoke nor cultivate this split state.

Did it result from the earaches that plagued me? Mum ladled warmed olive oil in both ears plugging them with cotton wool. The pain persisted and eventually, she called fleecy-haired, Dr Merry to my bedside who referred me to Melbourne's Eye and Ear hospital that I anxiously misheard as the Iron-Ear hospital. A tonsillectomy was recommended, and I returned to the bush hospital of my birth in Upper Ferntree Gully. Sweet chloroform swilled me to sleep. When I woke to a soothing bowl of ice cream, I was earache free, forever.

***

Mum rented out grandma's home until the Parkers purchased it. The three kids were much older than us and we saw little of them or their mum, Edna. Ex-butcher George Parker, an alcoholic and conspicuous oddity in our sober streets, was dropped each afternoon outside their gate by Mr Fellow's taxi, returning from Vass's Ferntree Gully pub, singing and muttering with a brown paper bag of bottled beers under arm. He habitually sat in the outside toilet facing our house, door open, trousers at his ankles, singing about racehorses he'd had tips on, and extolling the quality of sausages, prime cuts and mincemeat that he'd somehow sourced from Pinnock. Neither mum nor dad drank, so George's random antics drew both pity and fascination.

Within a few years he was banished to a weatherboard room built by son-in-law, Tex, where grandma's washhouse once stood. I saw him through his open door, standing only in pristine Chesty Bond singlet, legs like peeled leeks. Square-faced with bristled mole on lower left cheek, he was remonstrating with the empty beer bottles on his shelf. The shelf, a glass, the bed and laminated stainless-steel table, comprised the furnishings. Other nights I'd pass him lying in a puddle mid-track beneath the great messmate, bottle by his side, undeterred by mizzle or attempts to rouse him.

With the sale of the house, we purchased a car. Dad laid a slab and built a fibro-cement garage, blocking access to Parker's and the two holly trees framing it, but not George squatting astride his thunderbox. The lumbering, blue-grey Wolseley 6/90 was slow of acceleration but a workhorse on highways. So began drives, almost exclusively east. All week it sat waiting for Sunday's excursions, its maroon leather upholstery oozing toxins that it belched as the doors opened, causing squeamishness in us kids. First up, we pressed our eastern limits with a trip through Buchan, its caves and on to Butcher's Ridge where we suffered chickenpox and calmed our irritations in the creek. Dad was bent on visiting reservoirs; mum packed picnics to eat at Yan Yean, Eildon, Maroondah, and Silvan Dams. 'We drink the purest water in the world,' he'd proclaim, the dammed water looking anything but clean.

We'd drive over the drained flats of Koo Wee Rup, when his aunt Gwen shifted there; and he'd remind us that as a teenager, he'd often cycled there from Ferntree Gully. Heading across partly cleared farming land in Lysterfield, he'd remark on the stands of trees lining the road through rural hamlets, Narre Warren and Berwick. These, he said, were to commemorate young men who died in the Great War. Were they buried beneath these trees? Dad clarified that they honoured soldiers from those communities; I visualised the avenues as men standing proudly at attention. We accepted the names of these places and neighbouring towns like Nar Nar Goon and Lang Lang without questioning their strange departure from standard English.

We frequented the 'ghost' village of Walhalla, its mining tunnels and overgrown hill-top cricket ground, the valley being too steep and narrow to fashion a field. There was paltry evidence of its productive gold era, but photos in the general store and cemetery, with alarming disclosures of infant mortality, confirmed otherwise. We often camped: by the Buckland River near Porepunkah relatives, with a drive up Mt Buffalo, Cape Patterson and its lighthouse, Phillip Island and its koalas, Rye and its back beach. Returning from Phillip Island, we invariably stopped for fish and chips at Tooradin, devour them on the banks of Sawtell Inlet midst bickering seagulls and ducks.

Half buried in the sand dunes of Phillip Island and Portsea's ocean beaches were strands of rusted barbed wire. Dad told us they were protection against a possible Russian invasion during the Crimean War. When was that and who were they? Why would they come here? Even had dad known of Europe's nineteenth-century colonialist enterprises, his explanations would mean nothing to me. Maritime records did, indeed, reveal Russian ships had appeared in Australian waters since the nineteenth century's outset. An exploratory contingent had been first to circumnavigate the Antarctic in 1821 and had re-stocked in Sydney, as was customary for ships traversing the Pacific. The Crimean War intensified The Bear's rivalry with Britain. Weakening its enemy's dominion by cutting wool and gold wealth flowing from its prized colony would have inflicted serious damage; by 1854, fortification of the southern colony had commenced in earnest.

Most exotic and for extended holidays was Wilsons Promontory. Its granite boulders invited anthropomorphic interpretations. Armour-plated Mt Oberon seemed in silent communication with a leviathan-like island slumbering a few kilometres offshore from pristine Norman Bay. Sassafras and lilly pilly trees were novelties as were the multitudinous March flies. Wombats waddled and rooted around the picnic grounds day and night. Rosellas landed on our shoulders and fed from our hands. The truly wild was enhanced whenever blasts of Antarctic air whipped the place. Protruding into rugged Bass Strait where a chain of islands marked land once connected to Tasmania's chillier latitudes, the 'Prom' invited its own weather. Salt air suffused everything, blasting rocks and wafting traces over dewy leaves and grasses, and beading spider webs. Clouds would spring from behind Oberon, bunch together and hurry east, leaving rainbows as evidence of torrential havoc. We'd either tent or take the log cabins dad said were built for commandos. I later learned these commandos had been trained in guerrilla tactics to defend our northern shores from Japanese invasion in the Second World War. Ethnologist, Donald Thompson, had also trained local Aboriginal people to protect their coastline.

Highway tedium on these outings was broken with games of I Spy with My Little Eye and being first to identify the brand of approaching cars. We'd pester mum, 'How much longer before we get there?' and get her infuriatingly vague, 'Not before too long'. Half an hour on, I'd naively pipe, 'Have we passed Toolong yet?' Wherever our destination, dad read as much signage as attention permitted. Our objections to his readings only encouraged him. Town cemeteries, he called 'bone orchards' or joked that the 'dead centre of town' lay on its outskirts.

In our front garden: Ian, Marilyn and me.

Us on the beach at Seaford.

Now too, we could drive to the beach at Seaford or Black Rock where dad spent his infant years before shifting to Ferntree Gully. He'd point out the *Cerberus*, first iron-clad ship of the Victorian Navy, that he'd seen scuttled in the 1920s to become a breakwater. Before that, the resurfacing of Russia's malignant intentions in 1882 had prompted both its rejigging and the construction of a fort at Queenscliff. Hitherto, Black Rock existed only in mum's recitation about a child accompanying his mother in a train sitting opposite a bald man that I took to be the train dad travelled on as a child. I loved the progressive annoyance of the child's questions about the likelihood of his own baldness and, having been given sixpence by the man to shut-up, if he, too, will one day have 'bald-headed money' to give boys like himself. Mum's voice and face inhabited each character with enchanting conviction, transforming the couch at her side where I sat, into the train carriage. This, and other stories she'd performed before the community in Boronia's Progress Hall, in the early 1930s.

Seaford's summer sands were a trial by fire. The exposure to sun and salt, the six-bodied competition for shade beneath the beach umbrella, the burned skin during the cramped slog home in bumper-to-bumper traffic, and the swabbing with calming pink calamine lotion. I didn't know whether to believe dad's take on the Navy's means of taking the heat from sunburn—the crew would strip and piss on each other. We declined his offer to demonstrate. Until the Wolseley visits to bayside foreshores, we had been restricted to a couple of Church picnics benched beneath the tarpaulin of a truck belonging to one of the congregation. This grudging acceptance of torture, of blistering and peeling skin was the competitive means to browner bodies. We toughened and darkened ourselves to be like Indians and Aboriginals.

Dad's sallow complexion kept him under the umbrella so if we arrived ahead of other beach pilgrims we'd covet the shade of one of the brightly coloured boatsheds. Dad never entered the water and mum couldn't swim, restricting herself to only floating in the shallows between the first and second sandbanks. We were warned not to venture beyond the second. We wandered the shoreline where jellies, periwinkles, weed, clams and crab claws were deposited. The flat bay's energy arrived from some distant elsewhere, slapping, sighing and sucking at our ankles. To avoid the congested Frankston Road, we sometimes lingered until the day's hostilities dissipated, feasting on flake with chips from the Seaford shop.

When the tide slipped mysteriously back through The Heads, Ian hunted. Torch protectively sheathed in rubber and fitted above the fencing wire he'd filed to lethal perfection and fitted to a broom handle, he waded. Across the ribbed sea bed, he scanned for the shudder of flounder whose binocular eyes hinted at primeval origins. When dad bought snorkels and masks, Ian delighted in the sub-aquatic world. Enclosed by water, I would become stressed. Nor was I enthralled by the sea's regular beat, its advance and retreat, the ticking of the clock. Sand irritated my toes and salt tautened my skin. Summer's furnace was intimidating. I had no passion for the sea, and though preferring estuaries, never enthused about swimming.

Though Ian pulled leatherjackets and parrotfish from the Mt Martha rocks, his exploits weren't confined to the bay's shallows. Occasionally dad dropped us for the day at Woori Yallock and Olinda Creeks, arranging to pick us up at sunset. We'd root for earthworms and dragonfly larvae. In magpie mode, he'd cock his ear to the ground to hear them moving under earth. While he lured blackfish and eels from tannin waters, I roamed the paperbarks and ferns, hoping to sight platypus, echidna and wombats. Attenborough's film crew was decades away and no school lessons hinted at the marvellous means and purpose of the case moth's silky, stick-crusted encasement, or the magnificent earthworm Ian chanced upon Woori Yallock's banks. Though dad had shown us a giant specimen enclosed in a glass display case in Ferntree Gully's National Park, it was an immeasurably richer experience to lever a specimen, thick as a cigar and twice as long, from its comfy habitat. After a few minutes in its thrall, Ian segmented it in hefty portions, sufficient bait for the day.

During summer's furnace I did my best to avoid the glare. I often lolled in a cold bath as I'd done in earlier years in the concrete laundry trough. From there, I'd watch mum feed the washing machine and wringer set above it. The rancid scent of Velvet Soap Powder filled the laundry. Beside the soap and corrugated washboard were a few Reckitts Bluebags for whitening the wash and dousing ant and bee stings. In the bush I'd smear bracken fern juice on the bite, following mum's advice.

Sundays in summer, were often faithful to their name. The hills cringed in the heat. Saps ran and eucalypt oils simmered in the leaves while ants dozed underground. Twice, Ian cajoled me into trudging seven kilometres in searing heat up Old Olinda Road, passing the Salvation Army and Chandler's Como Nursery, halfway to Mt Dandenong's summit. Cicadas blared from the gums even as birds ceased singing. An unattended creek-fed pool in the grounds of the Seventh Day Adventist Camp, built just prior to World War II, promised relief. We had it to ourselves, stripped and dipped in its algae-rich waters, snakes of moss frilling the crude concrete perimeters. As our bodies broke the green veil, swarms of tadpoles nibbled our legs. For half an hour Ian stroked 15-metre laps while I struggled with breaststroke, less efficient than the frogs fleeing to the sides. We dawdled home, burning within minutes, lips cracked, sticky and smelling of sewerage.

Spring, and all sorts of plums ripened in orchards. Ian and I rushed supper for a prompt getaway, codifying our targeted patch, be it 'Niven's', 'Convent', whatever, to elude our siblings and stuff ourselves. The season's speckled spiders rolled nests in gum leaves, clotting the tracks. Stealthily, we'd creep to Blind Creek through Chandler's daffodils, hoping to avoid his eye and the weave of golden orbs spanning the trumpet heads. Ian reckoned the fields were under surveillance from Chandler's towered residence though I never heard of apprehensions. The creek is now a grey-water gutter crawling through remnant Koolunga Reserve, so titled in the mid-1990s to acknowledge prior Indigenous occupation.

Magnificent stands of conifers formed windbreaks between the fields. The pines' balmy perfume and concert of sighs were exalting. Under their shady cover I luxuriated on needled floors, admiring mushrooms and booting the boletus with their curry-coloured underbellies from which armies of black beetles fled for cover. Cones littered the floor in pale greens, browns and decaying greys, with wings splayed like spent grenades.

Thrush, firetails, bellbirds, magpies and kookaburras thrived around Blind Creek to which Ian and I, as we grew, had ventured from the bush next door, and where mum's gentle 'cooeeing' couldn't reach. Engaged in bush chatter, I felt liberated and expansive, as I never was at home. Wanderer butterflies idled in the breeze above parrot pea and kangaroo grass. Swamp gum and grey wattle numbered there. The bush was the place of unreflective sensory excitements as I fingered its barks, bit into its fruits and grass-heads and buried maps and small troves of personal items as messages to be discovered by my future self. Here, the clear and continuous thronging of insect and bird fleshed as one. Time ebbed forever as we played hide and seek until dad hollered our names for 5 o'clock supper. He could be heard over distant kilometres even when, having arranged after-school matches, we'd be punting footy at the oval.

The six Turpie brothers, who lived next to the oval, formed a side, and the rest of us were their opposition. For a few years the Turpies drove doomed petitions for a local swimming pool. The family had long left Boronia by the time an Olympic-sized pool was established. The eldest of the clan, Ian, took the lead role in *Wind in the Willows*, staged in the Progress hall. Later, 'Turps' career path centred on hosting game shows on daytime television, but for me he would always remain 'The Toad'. Hearing dad bellow our names embarrassed us in front of friends, though we dreaded his anger if late. As car numbers grew and the road noise increased, a bell replaced his call, though its clanging still wrought derision due to what those remaining regarded as our absurdly early supper.

***

Mum's piano, polished bi-annually with heady claret-red Marveer, sat in the lounge. I savoured her *Für Elise*. She knew other pieces, but this one always transported her, making her somehow more 'present'. She was attuned, and I loved her more for this. The piano's whorls of cherry-wood laminate fascinated me just as my failed efforts at the keyboard did not. I was sent for lessons with widowed septuagenarian, 'Toots' Willoughby, who lived in the street below. Her bemoaning my pathetic progress further dampened interest. My hands travelled separate ways from middle C, the left soon losing direction, timing and touch. Scales were excruciating. The keyboard was dead beneath my fingers and sheet music remained a foreign language.

The other prized furniture was an oak dining table that we dined at twice yearly. Two elegantly fluted muscular legs supported it, curving graciously into stands placed at each end. Chocolate and beige felt upholstered the seats. Mum was furious when toddler, Colin, took the bread knife to a chair leg which was swiftly healed, however, with dad's deft pasting of plastic wood. Perhaps this was Colin's light-bulb moment. Undeterred, thirty years on, he was chain-sawing red gums for his firewood business.

Our literary stocks were unexceptional—a set of *Newnes Pictorial Encyclopedias* and some *Little Golden Books*, whose glued spines I nibbled.

'Prince Destruction', dad called me, 'Devourer of Literature'. Rather than fostering literary interest, he'd infuriate us by reciting: 'It was a dark and stormy night and the King said to Antonio, Antonio tell me a story, and the story ran thus … It was a dark and stormy night' and so on. Or, 'The boy stood on the burning deck, picking his nose like mad'. Mum read Blyton and Ballantyne's *Coral Island* at bedtime. But there were 'heavies' that thrilled and terrified in equal measure. A book celebrating Elizabeth's Coronation reproduced Charles Dixon's 1916 painting of the slaughter at Anzac Cove. The contorted bodies of the beach dead were too much to bear more than a peek before I slammed the covers.

Mum's edition of *Arabian Nights* bore images of deceptive malice. The end pages featured an old man clinging tenaciously to Sinbad's back. Jackson's turbaned and veiled figures in robes and curly-toed slippers were disturbingly exotic, a quality enhanced by their marionette stiffness. Louis Rhead's engravings in dad's copy of *Kidnapped* also frightened me. A fight in a ship's cabin showed Alan running his sword through the stomach of an intruder. A forlorn leg dangled through shattered glass above. Rhead favoured spatial congestion and highly animated figures. Elsewhere a malformed man, dirk drawn, tumbled in deadly embrace on desolate highlands.

There were a few copies of *The National Geographic* with richly coloured pictures of strange lands, animals and people. One featured Renaissance painters: Giotto's halos and angel-infested heavens, Mantegna's rocky outcrops and granitic figures. Orpen's *Outline of Art* also counted among our stack. Between drawing pictures of birds and footballers from the *Sun News Pictorial*, I copied Michelangelo's *Head of Adam* and Titian's *Sacred and Profane Love*, bemused by the woman's preternaturally long arm. *Coles Funny Picture Book*, less funny than puzzling, showed a Whipping Machine that I imagined in use at the Salvation Army Boys' Home. Modest though our library was, it provided windows on a wider world.

✸✸✸

Dad was permanently occupied with projects being capable of constructing and repairing everything—electrical appliances, shelving, the radio and the car. He had a cast-iron cobbler's last bolted to the garage bench on which he resoled our footwear. With due polishing, the life of our boots might stretch over several years. Bitter winter westerlies released rains that paved our muddy street with puddles. Home from school, we'd remove our boots, stuff them with newspaper and place them on the hearth before the fire.

Socks and laces were squeezed and folded over a brass fireguard featuring an embossed reindeer, frozen mid-leap.

We older boys took turns gathering sticks for winter fires and fetching briquettes stored in the garage, washing and stacking dishes, and scything the knee-high grasses. A few years on, we lumbered behind the manual mower, up and down our quarter-acre, heaping the cuttings to compost. The arrival of a Victa motor mower rekindled enthusiasm for the chore. Dad also had a government-issued manual on gardening, promoting post-war self-sufficiency. For several years we grew greens and tomatoes to supplement store-bought produce.

He'd built the garage as well as the cupboards and drawers in our bedroom and, with our assistance, laid concrete footpaths, girding the house. There was no council rubbish collection so the chooks got the kitchen scraps and dad dug pits behind their yard to bury cans and glass. This predated plastic containers and packaging. Milk was bottled in glass and congested cream in the bottle's throat was prized by us kids.

***

Twice we visited mum's friends, the Emersons, who had a cabbage farm in Werribee. Her friendships, as with Joyce Barker, commenced in Ferntree Gully's maternity ward and June was another. It was a rare venture west of the city. Just before Werribee we were slowed by an accident. Two wrecked cars were splayed across the tarmac with the flashing red lights of ambulances and the blue of police, who were herding traffic into single file. A bloodied body lay motionless in the gravel, at awkward angles. Another was being stretchered to the rear of the ambulance. I'd never seen police cars or ambulances, let alone a dead person before. I couldn't banish the image until we passed through the farm gates and were ushered into June's kitchen, livened with fresh scones and tea while a leg of lamb, spuds and pumpkin roasted in the oven.

At lunch their disabled five-year-old, Neil, startled me, dribbling, grunting and shitting his nappies as he crawled around the house. In hushed tones Mum told me not to stare. Something was wrong with him, but no one told me what. The house was adapted to his undisciplinable ways; breakable stuff was set beyond his reach. I kept my distance, bewildered and wondering what human aspect moved in him. But he was not lying dead on the Princes Highway or carted off in an ambulance. June was extraordinarily patient, and I was impressed with how his siblings waited their turn for her attention. I was glad none of us were afflicted or needed to make such sacrifices. What relief to hurry from the table and sit on the big red Massey Ferguson tractor in the bleak fields where cabbages and the city's sewerage soured the air.

Later that year they visited in their Bedford farm truck. Besides Christmas and Easter visits from Aunt and Uncle, we didn't entertain, and it was unusual for us to have playmates at our house—should they visit, they weren't allowed inside. Mum's rule wasn't explained but we intuited she didn't want her home ruffled. The clock ticked past the anticipated hour of the Emerson's arrival. Then there was a knock at the front door. It was Bruce, about Ian's age. Their truck was on fire. Dad grabbed a blanket and we headed down our track to the truck which sat limply beside the lamppost. Farmer Perce folded the blanket in two and dashed to and fro with it until the flaming motor flamed no more.

Neil never left June's watch and was the subject of the women's small talk. Dad and Perce chatted about the drive through the city and the fire. Perce light-heartedly dismissed the event, though lunch done he was keen to get back on the road for the cautious slog home. Though mum and June corresponded, it was the last we saw of them.

Joyce Barker invited mum to accompany her for a kid-free week in Adelaide. It was her first break from us and both women trusted their spouses could manage. I don't know how the Barkers were fathered, but we were fine with dad's minimal culinary skills. However, the evening after mum returned an almighty row started. Dad pursued her down the passage from their bedroom to the kitchen, where we'd gathered for supper. He was fuming. Swearing, he cornered her and started belting her to the ground, kicking her against the chrome stool as we kids stood, stunned, helpless to defend her. We'd never seen him enraged with her before. Ian had felt his full force, for sure. Me, to a much lesser extent. But not mum.

'What's his name?' He yelled repeatedly, face reddening around his clenched jaw. He'd threatened Ian and me with spifflication if we caused trouble. This was it. And as he kicked her in the ribs a final time she squeaked, 'Mullins'. 'Mullins!' he echoed derisively. 'Mullins. So that's his name.' What satisfaction he got from her confession, I didn't know. Anger spent, he backed away up the passage as we waited for mum to rise and regain composure. Mum sat staring at her untouched chops while we ate in silence. Dad remained in their bedroom. It would be more than two decades before mum ventured on a husband-free Mildura holiday, this time with Marilyn.

His cowardice when grandma came to say goodbye, together with this violence, surely scarred mum as they did me. For all the multitude of things he did for us, the distrust these acts engendered was permanently engraved.

***

Radio serials gave way to television, coinciding with the arrival of the Bourne family from the Gold Coast who settled on the wooded block at Number 1, Hastings Avenue. Shane and Dannie became firm friends. Their dad, Stan, was a big-name entertainer and hadn't joined them. As soon as we acquired a TV they'd huddle with us around the fireplace, entranced by black-and-white episodes of *Life with Elizabeth*, *Life with Riley*, *Leave it to Beaver*, or *Liberace*. Dad showed no interest in television though he parroted Riley's 'what a revoltin' development this is' when passing through the lounge. Black and white TV continued into the 1970s. For a brief time in the 1960s we flirted with a coloured transparent sheet we taped across the screen, sitting in hope for occasional alignment between the moving images and the colour embedded in the sheet.

The Lone Ranger, *Hopalong Cassidy* and *Texas Rangers* cemented my passion for Westerns. Cassidy astride his nag, Topper, with dispassionate hard voice and foreboding black costume was not a man to meddle with. The siren call of *When You Wish Upon a Star* summoned us to the 'box' Sundays at 6 o'clock. *Disneyland* was mandatory as much as anything for gorgeous Annette Funicello beaming beneath *Mouseketeer* ears. *The Tarax Happy Show* hosted by moustachioed, if mistitled, 'Happy' Hammond, ventriloquist Blaskett with doll, Gerry Gee, Princess Panda, and 'King Corky' also transfixed us. We were so proud of Shane when he made his screen debut on Happy's show with his *Miming Prawns*. We had a celebrity in our midst!

Shane joined my play in ways Ian's dominance didn't permit which helped break my brother's hold over me. Now I had his company on the walk from school, someone to guard my trepidations at the halfway rise where a surly black dog sometimes sprang from sleep to busy itself at my ankles. Black lips curled back over sabred incisors, its chunky 30 kilos presented lethal menace. Mostly, he slept inside the gate, docile and unperturbed. If he lay outside the gate, I'd edge along the opposite fence, or turn and walk an extra kilometre on a parallel street. He'd tasted the flesh above my ankle once; I'd hoisted my sock over the throbbing pain, incommensurate with the blood beads blooming there, washed the socks in private, and hung them out of sight to dry. Wary of fuelling Ian's allegations of timidity, I told no one.

One wet afternoon our viewing was interrupted with the slamming of the wire-screened front door. Again, dad was meting out hefty slaps to the back of mum's head as she tried to escape him. She halted in full view, crouched to weaken the blows from behind. None of us could hear through the lounge window if the dreaded word 'Mullins' was at issue as mum cowered in the rain. We sat mute, staring at the TV when they came inside, knowing it was best to say nothing. Sometimes, when dad targeted us boys, Marilyn would run to her bedroom and press herself against the door in the unlikely event he'd turn on her. Beatings were less frequent as we grew but caution governed us in his company.

***

December meant Christmas holidays and heat. Ian and I would creep among the windbreaks at the daffodil farm searching for a suitably sized and shaped conifer sapling. We'd drag it home and plant it in a red and green crepe-papered pot of soil by the lounge window. The box of decorations would be brought from the top shelf of mum's wardrobe and draped or pinned to the tree, star atop, with rare devotion. And though Bing Crosby's crooned carols filled the air, little credence was paid to Christ. Apart from the symbolic star crowning the tree, it was all about the man in red and his troop of Scandinavian ruminants.

Christmas was eagerly anticipated as much for our parent's gifts as the arrival of Great Uncle Hughie and Aunt Chris in their Citroën Goddess, seemingly floating up the drive from another planet, but actually from Port Melbourne. Port Melbourne, where Uncle's grandfather had settled in the mid nineteenth century and launched a steerage company, with nineteen boats, on Hobson's Bay. They also visited at Easter, bearing roast chickens and large chocolate eggs wrapped in iridescent emerald, gold and magenta foil that we carefully unwrapped for re-use.

Uncle's spinster sister, Gwen, would have arrived earlier, cream or caramel-suited, striding imperiously in her scissory gait from the station. Having moved from Koo Wee Rup to Belgrave, she took the train to Boronia fortnightly, for mum to enliven her helmet of steel-coloured hair. Off came the straw bowler. Off came the tortoise-shelled rims housing lenses that owled her eyes. She'd toss her head back into mum's soothing palms for a rinse clasping hers on her lap. I knew the comfort of mum's hands, one cupped under the fall of hair while the other poured warm rinsing water from the jug. Hers were the fingers of love. The old lady's left wrist was cuffed with a bore's tusk, relic from an earlier century. And finally, there was the ammoniac reek of the dye.

Uncle Hughie and Aunt Chris, 1989.

It must have been the thing, this colouring. What remained of Uncle's oasis of thinning hair was rigorously parted and tinted a pale russet. His wife's rufous coif was swept from her brow in a steep and startling wave. From them, we children would each receive a fresh five-pound note. And then the two roast chickens, purchased en route from Myers: we'd convene at the oak table and fidget as the plate of roast vegies, the re-heated chickens and jug of mint sauce were served. I fingered the rarely seen embroidered flowers and crochet trim of the tablecloth Gwen made for our parent's wedding gift. There were matching doylies. I'd play with the perimeter of the table with its intimations of entwined vines.

Gwen wolfed down her meals with canine enthusiasm. 'That was bonzer, Beryl. I'm full as a goog.' 'Would you care for seconds, Gwen?' 'Don't mind if I do,' she'd reply as if famished since Easter, as she pushed her plate at mum, mopping gravy from her mouth with serviettes also of her making. Uncle ate with elegant indifference, dicing his spuds and chicken in dainty morsels, knowing what his dentures could cope with. Each mouthful was sipped and slowly minced, unlike his older sister's shovelling and sucking. He paused between swallows whereas her fork was loaded even as she chomped.

This was ceremony. Who'd get the wishbone and who the sixpences and threepences deployed in the plum pudding? The anticipation of these prizes equalled the relish of the pale meat. Whether the bone delivered my sibling's wishes, secrecy denied my knowing. Though none materialised, hope never died. Finally, there was the fruit-and-nut-rich cake encased in a centimetre of tooth-challenging sweet marzipan. Was this barely nibbled crust some feeble allusion to the snow-covered fields evident in TV movies programmed during the festive season?

The old couple was childless, and we assumed they were wealthy. Chris shared ownership of a scrap metals business with her brother in Port Melbourne. They had an imported car. While the women nattered over the dishwashing one Christmas, I heard Chris tell mum the old man had 'outlived his usefulness' and worried this might be the last such Christmas. But the ceremony endured until, aged 94, Uncle no longer challenged the roads.

Most years on the weekend preceding Christmas Day, dad took us to his work's party. At Wattle Park fat men in red suits simultaneously arrived at a dozen small festive gatherings. No reindeers were on deck but the place was breeding the Big Boys. One landed by helicopter on the cricket pitch. One came in a truck. Several arrived in limousines and one, less grandly, by horse, a bag of goodies slung over his shoulder. I was confused about which group to attend and claimed a gift from the neighbouring man in red. The spell of the benevolent man from the North Pole was rent. This attenuation of Christmas was compounded when mum opted for a collapsible plastic tree that was packed away with the decorations before the New Year. Scented pine had been the real deal.

***

Blind Creek remained our favoured playground until one fateful June day in 1958 when Ian crashed five metres from a cherry fir's brittle branches, ingesting his front teeth and leaving his kneecap dangling by a tendon against his shin. His glassy eyes rolled back, and I saw his body's workings. Blood wept over the white bone and gristle. I sped home with the news. Dad drove as close as the bush tracks permitted and carried the semi-conscious Ian to the car, before rushing to Ferntree Gully Hospital. The wound was well beyond the curative powers of mum's acriflavine and mercurochrome.

The accident prevented him joining our mid-year holiday at Healesville's Cascades Guesthouse and cut weeks from his schooling. We cut around the foot of the ranges through Lilydale, joining the Maroondah Highway that ran beneath the rail bridge to Warburton. Scrawled in large white letters on the bridge were the words, **PIG IRON BOB**, which dad said referred to wartime Prime Minister, Bob Menzies' willingness to export iron reserves to Japan. 'Helped the Japs build the ships, planes and bombs they used against us,' he said.

Nearing Healesville he detoured to the cemetery of the abandoned Coranderrk Station whose Indigenous occupants had been shifted to Lake Tyers Mission in the 1920s. The place had been set up in early 1863, led by petitioners, Barak and Wonga. Despite successfully adapting to the coloniser's farming lifestyle, the Aboriginal Protection Board undermined Coranderrk when the Half-Caste Act was passed in 1886, effectively initiating assimilation. It halved the workforce on the eve of the Depression, crippling productivity and self-determination in the process. This was my first awareness of local Indigenous occupation. Woori Yallock, the Black Spur, Narbethong, Wonga Park—places we'd played in and considered to be untouched ground, had been trampled for centuries.

It was a ten-minute drive from the guesthouse to Mt Slide whose trees were the largest I'd seen. The track to Murrindindi Falls was framed with a cathedral of Mountain Ash resounding with lyrebird calls. 'Listen,' said mum, 'their songs are stronger than those they imitate'. Amidst the repertoire was the sound of chainsaw and axe. The intrigue of this was clarified at the crest when we passed acres of immature regrowth. There were piles of branches ready to be torched. This was a logging track. No longer were we beneath the ancient trees' protective umbrella. On the dry northern flank, trees surrendered to scraggly bush and small gums, interspersed with vast heaps of muscular granite before the sawmill and emergence of pasture at Glenburn.

Dad did the 80-kilometre round trip each day to check on Ian. We bunked in a cabin and romped in the surrounding damp, fern gullies. Meals were taken communally in the guesthouse. Lunch offered silverside with mashed spuds and peas, steaks and roast lamb lathered in gravy, followed by sticky date cake and ice cream. Salty silverside, with its suggestion of mineral wealth, had neither appeared on our plates at home nor been sighted at the butcher's. That week's treat was so successful we repeated it the following winter.

Determined to restore and strengthen mobility, Ian improvised a lead boot strapped to his foot and flexed his suspect cartilages. This led to weightlifting and an obsession with high jumping. Was this genetic? One of the few things we knew about Aunt Gwen, improbable as it appeared to us, was that she'd once been the state's champion jumper. Dad built a box from car crates and brought a bar and set of steel gears from work. Both sides of the crate were notched to house the resting bar. Ian knitted a maroon scarf to cushion the back of his neck and grunt through repetitions of 'squats' to empower his thighs. Russian athlete, Valery Brumel, was world news with his Straddle technique. He and American, John Thomas, battled for supremacy, echoing the Cold War tensions between their nations. Ian forsook the Scissors while dad sourced asphalt and lay an all-weather run-up in parallel with the pittosporums. Soon, Ian was school champion, and would one day represent state and country.

Foam landing mats, indeed most miracle plastics, were unheard of. Sawdust had to be sourced to fill the landing pit, and Ian knew where a mountain of this lay at Richie Nottage's St Elmo Road sawmill, backing onto Blind Creek. He promised me two shillings to accompany him there, wait as he slipped through the wire fence, where he filled the burlap sack. Together we hauled it home. The resins swam in our nostrils as the bag bobbed over the tracks. This, we repeated half a dozen times over several weeks until the pit was topped. Two shillings, he then said, didn't extend to the extra loads.

***

During the year, a score of German-speaking students proved an exotic addition to our school. They were Templars, dressed in leather pants and lederhosen. Not knowing they were children of a Lutheran sect transported from Israel at the beginning of the Second World War, we regarded them warily as enemies whose fathers our fathers fought. The Templars had fallen foul of mainstream Lutherans in the mid nineteenth century and left Germany to settle in what for them would have been the Holy Land of Palestine. With the start of war, the British, who controlled Palestine at the time, declared them enemy aliens and deported the majority of them to Australia. These new bods on the block were no more connected to the war than us. Unsurprisingly, our taunt:

Hitler has only got one ball,
Göring has two but very small,
Himmler is somewhat similar,
But poor old Goebbels has no balls at all...

fell on deaf ears and was soon dropped. By year's end, they'd been absorbed into the larger mix and proved to be superior academically. Though not adept at football they excelled at marbles, causing skirmishes and a re-ordering the playground's pecking order. Indeed, Ian was the cause of one incident.

To avoid walking home with him, I'd usually give him a five-minute start. Nearing the crest where my dog foe reclined, the Germans, on bikes, were circling Ian. They insisted he'd cheated them of marbles. Ian called to me to run home for help. I backed away and took the longer route for help. Before I could utter a word, Ian was through the door, looking dishevelled but breathing not a word of his encounter. I understood from his glance to keep it hid, that the incident would invite dad's wrath.

The Germans also joined games of hopscotch, foursquare, rounders and cross-ball whose rules were simpler. If Germans were baddies, why, for several months, did dad drive once a week to Armand Kraft's house to learn German? Years later, he told me Richmond power station had just imported dynamos from Germany. Their installation instructions needed translating, so he'd volunteered to get a handle on the language. I wasn't convinced. He'd once brought German workmate, Hans Otts, home for supper; he could have helped. And surely it was simpler to have Kraft spend an hour at Richmond's substation.

Similar racial and social ignorance circulated through jokes about the Italian Army's cowardice. We knew nothing about Fascism or the Partisans opposing it, and though no Italians graced our schoolyard, we were content to idly ridicule the mythical Italian Book of War Heroes that lacked an entry.

Despite my being dux of Grade 6 and captaining sports teams, it was Year 5, impounded with 'Fungus' Neil, that proved more vivid. His leer and hunched deportment intimidated even the most insolent of us. Neil's rubicund face, saliva webbing the corners of his thin blue lips, was omnipresent. Lead pencils were supplanted by pen and ink as we were introduced to cursive script. Coloured pencils enhanced drawings. We envied the few students with expansive sets of *Derwent Lakelands* housed in tin boxes featuring an attractive landscape that suggested skilful use of their contents.

'Get into the little room, Pritchard,' short-fused Neil exhorted; the little room with its bodeful scents of ink, stationary, chalks and clag, this last so reminiscent of mum's gelatinous desserts. Here in the storeroom bisecting the two class fives, Neil dealt his leather strap. That he dealt it often suggests it was more stimulant than deterrent. We teased from him his tantrums. Paul Pritchard, son of the local cop, and feisty Russell Conway were regular clients of the leather. So much so that one morning in his role as ink monitor, precocious Pritchard cut the strap in pieces and hid it beneath Neil's Akubra.

Undeterred, Neil stalked the aisles, whacking his wooden yard rule on the knuckles of unsuspecting students whose writing wavered from the statutory

75-degree angle. Left-handedness added to Conway's frustration, and often landed him in the little room where he toyed with its contents until Neil's arrival. Ink and blotting paper, from which Conway crafted aeroplanes, would be superseded by biro at high school. By then plastics had arrived with the advent of Altona's petrochemical complex. Then Tupperware opened in Ferntree Gully. Packaging and food storage would never be the same.

One gardening session while weeding roses, I accidentally uprooted a plant. Neil went berserk, grabbed my fork and thrust it through my day-old rubber boots. My toes were spared but my left boot ruined. I was devastated, less by Neil, than by having to report the damage to my parents. Though I hid them as soon as I got home, all-knowing mum guessed something was up. My tearful confession relieved me of punishment. I'd have to wait till next winter for replacements.

Pommie brothers, Roysten and Phillip Larkin, arrived mid-year and, perhaps for their Cockney accents and Phillip's prodigious overbite, the ready-formed cliques ostracised them. Sensing their misery, I took them under my wing; part conscience, part curiosity, I felt helpless to do otherwise. They need-ed protection and security in an unfamiliar environment. Their parents rented a cottage in the orchard behind Bourne's and the brothers started visiting our house straight from school, perching on the banister outside our kitchen when we went in for supper. Their hungry eyes followed each mouthful through the window. Mum urged me to send them home while we ate, conflicting my wish to please both parties. They shifted elsewhere at the end of the year, freeing me to romp once again, with Shane and Dannie.

Whatever afflictions Neil suffered, or fears he engendered, something in his mania inspired me. Craft took on new dimensions: raffia was woven, cane baskets made, footballers jig-sawed from ply, a rose garden was planted. I won a John Gould state-wide prize for a drawing of a wedge-tailed eagle and, catching Ian's passion, made several plaster-of-Paris budgerigars which I painted and lacquered. For weeks during recess, I wrote of an adventure about marauding blackfellows while holidaying on a cattle station in Central Australia. It was inspired by Chevraul's, *Jedda*, and Indigenous actors Rosie Kunoth-Monks and Robert Tudawali. Dad had it typed at work and submitted to 'Corinella's Sunbeamers' centrefold in the *Sun News Pictorial*.

It was also the year of the plastic yo-yo, a retractable twin-disked toy housing white, waxed string. Like marbles, they arrived and disappeared from the schoolyard unannounced. Most illustrious was the gleaming red Coca-Cola offering. Like all things Coke, it was glamorously labelled, thus granting it unrivalled allure. Kids competed at various tricks, though the one I strove to master, without success, was a double loop and spin back into my pocket.

To ingrain a sense of post-imperial national unity, the tale of *Simpson and his Donkey* was trotted out over the PA each Anzac Day. The tragedy gave small change to the beach bedlam at Gallipoli. We didn't know where Turkey was or that the British High Command bungled the Anzac Cove landing that cost 8,000 Australian lives. It was intended for a nearby, more accessible beach. Why did we celebrate such a humiliating defeat? And if 'Fungus' knew Simpson wasn't Australian but illegal immigrant, John Kirkpatrick, who'd volunteered to gain free passage back to England, he wasn't saying. Uncle Hughie had also served in the Ambulance Corps, but never alluded to the donkey man.

I really knew little of death's reality or grieving. Sacrificing one's life for one's country was an abstraction. The following year, Robyn McGuiness and I, as school captains, represented our school on the 11th November at the Shrine of Remembrance on St Kilda Road. We squeezed into fifth-grade teacher, Mr Evan's car, and headed to the Shrine, noting a sculpture of the donkey man in nearby gardens. The Greek-inspired building, with its strange stepped roof, stood solemn and aloof. Hundreds of students from suburban schools attended the sweltering ceremony, standing with bowed heads in the forecourt as the Last Post bugle released its mournful cry, followed by a spritely Reveille. By and large the sense of dealing with communal wounds, and the folly of war, flew past me. Perspiring in that tiny car, the sun grilling us while corralled into regiments on the hot paving, the officer's dour recitation, these trivial sufferings were our sacrifice.

***

Sometimes dad jousted with us, bare-knuckled in the kitchen, correcting our pugilist poses, instructing on how to maintain balance, which fist parried and which defended. His sleeves were rolled to reveal his Navy tattoos. On his leading arm a whiskered cat with cap grinned when he flexed his bicep. On the other was an anchor. Perhaps this was where he learned to box. There was no way we could seriously challenge him, and perhaps that was his point. But he wanted us readied for contest, and football and cricket were where we matched our fellows and found our feet.

He took us to several Collingwood games at Victoria Park, and once we'd taken the Geelong Flier to witness a trouncing by the 'Cats' at Kardinia Park. Through a friend, Keith Roberts, he'd managed to obtain standing tickets to the 1960 Preliminary Final match against Fitzroy. So my first experience at football's Mecca was a slugfest in the rain, less memorable as a spectacle barely visible from my vantage between gabardines and brollies, than for dad's first encounter with canned beer. I'd never seen him drink alcohol. Most men within sight were quaffing. At quarter time he must have felt the urge to meld in; he slipped off to the bar beneath the Southern Stand. Fifteen minutes later he squeezed back through the crowd. Keith handed him his church-key opener and dad punctured the top, surprising himself and drenching the immediate circle of supporters. I shrunk beneath their hostile stares. Dad grinned sheepishly while Keith sprung to his defence, lamenting the loss of the beer. We rejoiced in our narrow victory, a short-lived reverie given the total humiliation at the hands of arch-rival, Melbourne, the following Saturday.

Before graduating to the junior footy team, I served as an enthusiastic scoreboard attendant. The playing field spread behind the barber's and Progress Hall. The scoreboard sat between massive pines on the railway flank. I had my six times' table down pat to account for goals and caressed the black tin plates with their broad white numerals, feeling that in responding to heroics on field, I was participating even at a distance. I could hardly wait to be eligible to play. After Thursday night's training we'd trudge home and the coach picked the team. The team sheet appeared in the barber's window the following day. We budding lads mulled over positions, inclusions and omissions.

Saturdays, we'd join with lads desiring the spoils of victory: perhaps kick a goal or take a 'mark of the day'. We blackened our boots with Kiwi boot polish whose white laces mum laundered as well as pressing socks and shorts to perfection. Raw-boned toothless elder, Frankie Wyatt, distributed team jumpers from a hessian bag. He'd call our names and anxiously scan the benches to confirm our presence. On the many wet days, he'd doll out an amber ball of rosin to coat our fingers and help us grip the sopping ball. We passed it between each other like some sacred object before it circled back to Frankie's pocket. Pre-game, the umpire visited the rooms to have our captain decide which of two balls we'd use, then he'd inspect our boot studs for protruding nails from leather stops and our fingers for rings.

A hard-wired hierarchy asserted at the quarter-time break when we huddled in a lose circle, vaguely attending to the coach's clichéd ranting. The older and more deserving lads swigged from a flagon of lemon squash while we saplings patiently awaited the dregs of spittle-diluted flecks of fruit at its base. Halftime, and the communal ritual repeated in the rooms. Then at three-quarter time, sitting on a groundsheet to insulate us from the usual wet turf, we sucked slices of orange while the coach berated us and advised of the stiffening breeze at our backs that would carry us to victory.

We had an old ball to punt on our dirt road. No cars interrupted our flights over imaginary packs to mark 'screamers' as there was no through traffic. Dad had sourced it from our beloved Collingwood club at whose playing field in 1929 he'd witnessed, with Great Uncle, the immortal 'Nuts' Coventry kick 17 goals against Fitzroy. He earned sixpence for each goal, a pre-match promise honoured by Uncle Hughie, the equivalent of a day's wage in the Depression. My heroes had punted this ball, their actions captured on cards I collected from Greg's cereal packets.

I was besotted with Collingwood, so on noticing an ancient laced-up Melbourne guernsey in a chest in the garage, asked dad why Uncle Hughie, whose father played for South Melbourne and Melbourne in the competition's infant years, supported the Black and White. Apparently, he'd courted and married the daughter of a Collingwood committee man and collected rent for the club's notorious sponsor, Jack Wren. Though she'd died early in their marriage, Uncle's passion for the 'Pies' was fixed. We were third generation 'tragics'.

I proudly bore the plastic number 17 of my idol, Thorold Merrett, which mum had sewn onto my footy jumper. He'd starred in our 1958 premiership win. Dad and I, absenting ourselves from the family, had viewed the last quarter telecast in a packed room at Melbourne's Royal Showgrounds. My exultation even surpassed the fairy floss, greyhound racing, and calf with two hindquarters. On the coldest of days, my plastic number still exuded a sweet dioxin perfume from my sweaty exertions. Dad reckoned Merrett perfected his 'stab kick' by kicking the ball through a car tyre swinging on a rope. A commentator joked that his stab was so accurate it could penetrate a chicken's arsehole. I emulated his left-side skills until they were indistinguishable from my natural right.

We lavished our ball—affectionately dubbed 'pig'—with mutton fat to preserve its leather from puddles, pressing it into the stitching and laced cap. Eventually the bladder punctured, so we stuffed the ball with newspaper. When it landed in the blackberries Ian would demand I retrieve it. Though we tossed planks over the prickles, scratches couldn't be avoided. This power play was a source of tears until I realised that swift compliance without protest gave me a freedom he couldn't violate.

Dad brought a yellow foolscap pad from work to record the commentary and scores of both football and cricket games. I would often play alone in the backyard, enacting all thirty-six players in a league game, knowing their numbers and mimicking their kicking styles while calling the game in the dulcet tones of sportscaster, Norman Banks. At the end of each quarter, signalled with a throaty trumpeting, I hurried to record the game in a style adopted from the pink-paged *Sporting Globe*. If it rained, I reconvened in the lounge room, using chairs rather than trees as goal posts and a balloon as a footy.

Falconer's Grocery offered a stocking of foodstuffs to the person who most closely guessed the scores of the year's Grand Final. I coveted that stocking and rehearsed the game in the backyard in my customary manner in time to make a submission. With uncanny prescience, I was point perfect and prize-winner even with the quarter-by-quarter scores and goal kickers.

Winter Saturdays, we rose early to test the weather. Football was best on cool clear days. Wind and rain hampered skill, and though the great cypresses encircling the Boronia ground reduced the impact of Antarctic winds, the surface was often soggy, our boots drenched in ankle-deep mud. The Yarra River, when flooding, wended its way to the Bay across the lower half of the Warrandyte ground. After the ball was heft skywards to commence each quarter, it was rarely airborne, being soccered end to end with barely a score. East Ringwood's black Merri Creek topsoil caused abrasions and infections despite Frankie Wyatt's Dettol daubs. On one occasion, snow covered Olinda's patch and ice coated the One-in-Twenty road up Mt Dandenong which challenged George Nicholl's dawdling Bedford in whose tray we huddled for 'away' games. Several of the home team squibbed the encounter, so we lent them players to make up numbers, before flogging them in the fog.

Summer Saturday afternoons, we retreated to the Electra Cinema, built to serve the region's expanding post-war population. Its cavernous confines were the coolest in town and showed images rather in the manner of my mind. Had my ancestor's dreams unspooled so cinematically? Neither the national anthem, for which we stood before musty maroon seats, nor the *Movietone News*, possessed narrative power. We were there for the serial. As the gangsters' Chevrolet forded a bridge, police in close pursuit, they'd crash through the guardrail and fall to the torrents below. Or did they? Be watching next week. Out front during intermission, we'd crowd Ferrari's milk bar.

Pint-sized Ferrari, the town's first Italian so far as I knew, had moved next to old Morcroft, and limped along Hastings Avenue's clayey soils. His built-up boot seemed more handicap than assistance, severely testing his skewed hips. We'd queue before the glass-fronted counter. There was the burring blender frothing milk and breathing malt as it topped our glasses. We sucked hard, competing for the loudest intestinal rattle at their base, then return to the feature film clutching bags of Jaffas to flick at the screen if some event or star earned disapproval.

Next door was Joyce Barker's toyshop against whose windows I pressed my nose, pondering games to be had, with lead armies, cowboys and Indians, tee pees, and a wonderful silver pistol with silver bullets. Plastic copies of those warring platoons came on the market but lacked the gravitas of their leaden forebears. I was the outlaw or Indian in the Westerns running in our heads, firing rounds of caps at Shane and Dannie, repeatedly copping a fatal cartridge and falling hysterically to ground. There was a rail circuit winding through the display around which a locomotive, lugging four carriages, made steady progress. If I pressed an ear to the glass, I could just hear it buzzing. I envisaged it spread across our lounge's floral carpet. Perhaps a birthday or strong Christmas wish would deliver these. Ian got his meccano set which kept him busy for hours. Though the model of Sydney Harbour Bridge on the packaging wouldn't be made from the contents of a single box, he engineered cars and structures with an aplomb I neither shared nor strove for.

We joined cubs on Friday nights in the Scout Hall on Chandler Road. Dad completed a leadership course on the Yarra River's Herring Island and mastered the senior scouts. When he took them on bush camps to Mount Martha and Healesville, we happily trooped along. Most scouts were stars of our junior footy team. The Mount Martha camp took place on the Lawadorn family's Ti-tree acres, overlooking the Bay. Lawadorn's had twin 14-year old girls who, while not fraternising with the lads, were a lurking presence and keen to accept dad's invitation for a week's holiday.

Janet and Ray were devotees of Elvis and wore peg-legged denims, lime-green fluorescent socks, leather jackets, short greased coifs, and surreptitiously smoked in the bush next door. They urged us to take a drag, aware our complicity came at the cost of not 'dobbing in' to mum or dad. They were widgies, they said, and liked bodgies—names new to us. There was an alluring sexuality in their company, verging on ostentation when they strolled the streets, hoping to be spotted by some of the senior scouts they'd seen during camp. The summer streets however were scoutless. Only 40-year old Bert Coma, who was a little slow, was there, propped on the post-and-lintel pedestrian rail crossing, waiting for an approaching train to ignite the clanging bells and red lights.

From the rear, his fashionable crew cut and checked sports coat measured well. How could the twins know of his scabrous skin, or how he backed up

Boronia Hill tugging his mother's shopping jeep with the clatter of empty jam tins trailing on a string hitched to his belt—these, his insurance against missing action at the crossing. We could have told, but did not destroy their flirtatious intentions as we held to the shade of the grocer's veranda. As they closed on him, he swivelled, flinging spittle from his ropey lower lip, his glazed eyes and furry mono-brow causing them to back away as he drawled his customary, 'Giddaay'. He rose to face them, his ungainly stoop thrusting his head forward eagerly, causing them to hasten their steps. A certain satisfaction stirred in me, seeing their shock and shame as they shuttled towards us. For all their verve, their fags, their leather jackets, their 'cool', traits presumed as passports to adulthood had been unravelled and reduced.

The girls departed, but Elvis remained in the air and the hair. Barber Henshaw adopted Elvis's quiff, now acknowledged as the 'rocker' look, and the fad was in full career. Vinyl record album covers had fresh-faced Elvis, Jerry Lee, Johnny Horton and fellow rockers grinning beneath pomaded waves. We persuaded our parents to go some of the way with semi-crewcuts, and felt acquiring Canadian jackets, flecked with green and pink Lurex, to be party to the trend.

Neither of us proceeded from cubs to scouts. The Explorer's Club at the Church of Christ commenced under the stewardship of Henry Chandler. He was closer in age to us than bow-legged wolf man, *Akela* West and large bear, *Bagheera* Laird, and enjoyed our zestful games in ways alien to the restrained Pack leaders. Though we'd long quit church, having renewed association via the club, we felt obliged to a final devotional act. We took the train to the new Myers Music Bowl one sweltering February day and endured the ranting of American evangelist, Billy Graham. The assembly far exceeded our village population, though none of us were inclined to join the troops accepting baptism.

The same games were played at Explorers as at cubs, including tug-of-war, but without the stress of badge-striving and knot-tying. I'd happily donned my navy uniform, peaked cap, toggle and garters with green tabs, and enjoyed its militaristic mode. I loved the memory tests, rowdy evasive games with a sand-filled, leather medicine ball, and Shipwreck, on the dusty floorboards. When fund-raising newspaper drives were invited, the Moss brothers were keen contributors. But dibbing and dobbing had run its course.

We also joined the church's cricket squad. Porcine 'Dobbo' Dobson, butt of cruel jokes and inevitable twelfth man at cricket, was first pick as anchor in our tug-of-war tests of might on the long rope. The Dobsons had been in the area since the 1870s. Dobbo's enthusiasm never waned and his claims on our attention were often heard above the din.

We were mid-rank performers. Better teams usually had one or two stars good enough to play with the men in the afternoon. For three hours each Saturday we pounded up and down the matted concrete or fetched the 'pill' in dewy grass. The one dreaded encounter was with The Salvation Boys' Home, the place of our potential incarceration. For reasons unclear at that time, all the Salvos' contests were on their lushly grassed paddock trimmed by cows, ousted while the matting was unrolled. Avoiding manure pats provided additional challenges to fielders. The Salvos' batting was not so strong but they had two bowlers with such stamina and destructive skill we were never introduced to other talents with the 'cherry'. They were Indigenous brothers with men's physiques. Apart from the Islanders' school visit, the bowling brothers were my only experience of First Australians. Their 'cannonballs' had us ducking and dodging in fear. Few teams topped 100 runs. Had they misbehaved at supper, taunted siblings, been thieves or orphans? Only they presented as 'other', with institutional livese we neither knew nor wished to delve into.

The sporting world was enthralled by the calypso brand of cricket Frank Worrall's Test team introduced from the West Indies. They'd played an unprecedented tie in Brisbane; hulking bowlers backing their batting flair. I'd never witnessed before the ease these dark bodies deployed, exemplified by Garfield Sobers, who I tried to emulate by switching sides from my natural gait to his loping left-handedness. Dobbo asked if I'd join him at the Melbourne Cricket Ground on the second day of the Fifth Test. Though wary of his lack of social graces, my enthusiasm triumphed.

We were soon snared in the passion of the 90,000—none more than Dobbo. It was a partisan crowd but most, like me, were thrilled by the West Indians' fluent athleticism. Dobbo, though, remained a fervid patriot. After the tea intermission, he suggested we jump the fence and sit beneath the sightscreen. He'd been making loud ball-by-ball commentary and continued to deride West Indian fieldsmen even as we sat their side of the fence. I warned him to shut up as he baited supreme speedster and imposing athlete, Wes Hall, whose run to the crease started only metres from us. Dobbo persisted. 'Bring him on both ends,' he shouted. Hall, a man neither of us would dare confront anywhere, let alone exposed before such a vast public, fixed Dobbo with a glare. I felt the multitudes follow his line of vision and wished in vain to shrivel to the size of a cricket ball, be hit over the fence and lost in the crowd.

A few days after Australia won the Test, we undertook an odyssey to mum's paternal aunt in Brisbane. The car was packed with the spacious canvas tent and its poles strapped to the roof rack. We headed off along the Hume Highway around midnight to avoid city traffic. Colin slept curled on the front floor at mum's feet. As the day gathered heat and we crossed the Murray River, we encountered a locust plague south of Gundagai, where we verified that the dog, did indeed, sit on its Tucker Box. In Sydney, Dad copped abuse from angry locals for driving against the traffic in that city's ubiquitous one-way streets. Ian and I slid in shame from the sight of remonstrating drivers. Repeating the confusion in Newcastle caused him to switch inland through Griffith and Armadale before re-emerging on the Pacific Highway.

Snakeboy in Brisbane, 1959.

A hundred or so kilometres south of the Queensland state line, dad erected our tent by a swollen river while mum pan-fried some chops on the primus. We older boys took a dip, unaware its placid surface bore no hint of what swirled beneath. I was instantly out of my depth, fighting a strong undercurrent and gulping mouthfuls of water when Ian pulled me to the bank as I was about to sink a third time. We kept my misadventure hushed, not wanting to add to mum's harried state. Whenever bickering broke out between we three in the back seat, dad berated her for not dealing with us, and threatened to turn the car around.

After supper, we retired to lilos but a feral cat came and pawed a cradle amongst our sheets. Having settled herself, she gave birth to a litter of six, one by one clamping them in her jaws and returning to the bush. As this birth miracle revived us, dad, obsessed with driving, packed and gained Indooroopilly inside a remarkable 48 hours from Melbourne.

We detoured to Toowoomba and purchased souvenir canned mountain air that we boys ridiculed. South of the Brisbane was a suburban resort with multiple swimming pools and enclosures housing koalas and pythons that we cautiously nursed for photoshoots. A few days later dad turned for the enormous drive south around the coast. Aunt Chris once told mum: 'If a man is in the car, Beryl, he should drive'. Dad assumed this mantle; although mum was licensed, he never asked her to take the wheel.

Fascinated by history in general, he was bent on visiting the War Memorial in Canberra. This sandstone bunker enclosed a narrow strip of water where I lingered, finding the relics and walls commemorating the dead overpowering. A brisk tour done, dad found his way through Canberra's maze of roundabouts and headed for the new Tumut Pond Dam, keen to see the Snowy Mountain Hydroelectric Scheme.

Having been interstate, where I had half expected to see some equivalence to the perforated lines of my plastic Australian template, I was almost disappointed to find that people in different states looked, talked, and ate the same food as us. I'd ventured over the Harbour Bridge, Brisbane's Story Bridge—illuminated during the State's centennial celebrations—and boarded car ferries across the Clarence and Richmond Rivers. Few of my peers had travelled further than the Dandenong Ranges, and none had been interstate.

Now I had to put away the lead armies that had clambered the humps of my eiderdown, quit playing Cowboys and Indians, and face the rigours of high school. The school had only recently shifted from The Progress Hall where it commenced in 1957, to the new Tormore Road buildings on the former estate of old Zeising.

4

High school

Assay from the Crowded Plain, Rod Moss, 1984.

The threat of bushfires is a summer constant in Australia's eucalyptus forests. The dominant species of the ranges provides the perfect fuel and, in certain conditions, self-immolate to stimulate reproduction. Each year warnings are broadcast. There are days of total fire ban and metal roadside rainbows registering the degree of hazard: low, moderate through to catastrophic. Driving to Healesville, dad had indicated the antlered, Mountain Ash old-growth reaching above its smoky green descendants, relics of the devastating 1939 Black Friday fires. Seventy deaths. Thousands of homes destroyed. Livestock, native animals and vegetation obliterated.

Heavy winter rain that year had thickened ground cover on the ranges. A spring dry spell primed them for fire and an arsonist was busy keeping the brigades on red alert. In January 1962, the mercury hovered around the 40s. Serious heat so hot, possums in the bush next door dropped dead from the trees in their dozens. It was a pitiful sight. By the 14th the hills were ablaze. We stood in awe in our backyard watching the glaring night sky crackle, fearing drifting embers might ignite trees close to home as the evening news reported was happening in Blackburn, 12 kilometres closer to the city. The rim of the range was a crimson necklace. McGuire had the 1942 modified Blitz truck in overdrive and was in full command of volunteer fighters; Red Cross ancillaries were catering and treating heat exhaustion. The volunteer firefighters fought day and night to defend homes and towns, contending with heat, exhaustion, the gullied terrain and quirks of wind, until rain late on the third night extinguished the fires. By morning the mountains brooded in smoke.

After school, I joined Ian on One Tree Hill, mopping up with wet hessian bags tied to sticks, issued by the Brigade. The soil was sooty and warm. Ashen stumps and stripped trees stood as sorry sentinels to disaster. Near the peak were three houses, one slightly lower and separated from the others. Inside it a man could be seen in his armchair watching the fires on TV. He could have fought the previous hours, for all I knew. But as I stood at his charred fence quenching posts, his experiencing the drama on TV while it smoked at his door was strangely discordant.

Out of the blue dad's stepmother phoned to check on our safety. Thirty years and there'd been no contact. She lived with dad's father in Croydon, a mere seven kilometres distant. What the quality of relationship between them was, I didn't know. Dad regarded Hughie as his father, though his grandmother and Gwen had raised him. Fortnightly visits commenced to their house adjacent to the Croydon Market, for a couple of years. Dad brought them to us a few times, but his father had little to say and his wife's gaiety felt contrived, as much as anything, to fill the space he left vacant. Perhaps they were sick, disappointed or just old. When they wanted to shift to Richmond dad bought a cottage in Cremorne Street, five minutes from the power station, and saw them each day, either coming or going to work. They died soon after this arrangement, without us seeing them again.

I commemorated the disastrous fires in a painting, and exuberant young art teacher, Royden Irvine, chose five lads to develop the theme into a mural on the art-room windows. He submitted the original painting to the *Herald* Art Show and took me to see it. Peggy van Praagh, artistic director of the Australian Ballet, purchased it. My first sale! Riding the success of the windows, we painted a three-metre panel depicting sports activities which Irvine mounted next to the staffroom. His response to my art grew my confidence, and my perfect score at year's end was rewarded with Ernest Norling's *Perspective Drawing* book and a van Gogh monograph.

Irvine's impact was phenomenal. His six-foot frame bounded throughout the school. Wiry, red hair, centurion profile, he seemed tireless, his tone oscillating between playfulness and stern enquiry. He energised his House competitiveness, designed a logo for their football vests, trained the school swimming and athletic teams, and staged the musical, *South Pacific*. Some of us had seen the filmed version, but any sense we might have made of its anti-racist statements surrendered to drooling over the unattainable older beauties swaying in raffia skirts.

During Christmas holidays he took several dozen boys on excursions to Wilson's Promontory and the Hawkesbury River. Colin Turpie numbered among us. Blessed with his family's vociferous self-confidence, he commandeered the megaphone at Albury while we changed trains for the New South Wales' gauge and, mimicking the stationmaster's announcements, advised it was time to board the train. It proved difficult to relieve him of the thing throughout our holiday. First, he'd strolled the carriages, blaring features of the rural pastures we could see for ourselves. Then in the lift of Sydney's YMCA, he did much the same, informing of goods available on each floor as in a Department store, until Royden confiscated the thing.

Dad and workmate, diminutive Ivan Dukic, veteran of the Snowy Scheme, helped captain the 36-foot cruisers that were hired on the Hawkesbury while Royden and friend, John Evans, captained the other two. When piloting Halvorsen cruisers from their Bobbin Heads moorings upriver past Trollope Reach to Windsor, Turpie again pressed tour guide claims, despite unanimous displeasure. When the megaphone's batteries were removed, the irrepressible Turpie was finally silenced. Overnight, the tide at Windsor dropped several metres, tipping boats, bodies and crockery to the floor. We were amused as much as surprised.

We were further surprised by Dukic's offer to spit a sheep, something none of us had witnessed. With dad assisting Ivan's uncertain English, they bought a dressed lamb from the Windsor butcher. We ate it that evening, much of it half-cooked due to our impatience, but savoured nevertheless, and were entertained by the chef's handstands and backflips that none could emulate.

There was a fabulous all-night torch game inspired by TV's *The Untouchables*, between Elliot Ness's cops and Capone's crooks on Bar Island. Capone's mob hid on the small island, but half an hour later, with muffled oars, the cops rowed ashore and crept through scrub, springing mob members with torch beams. Some of us hid in trees, others crouched in the ruined 1876 chapel. Most kept moving, as much to elude the resident goats as the probing beams.

Our exhilaration extended to an athletics meeting with Manly Boys High School after returning to Sydney, where we acquitted ourselves handsomely against much greater numbers.

Royden Irvine, 1980.

Stan Davey, 1984.

Royden, single and new to Boronia, befriended our family, often sharing in our meals, watching TV, and with dad on night shift, bringing playful unity; fussing over us with concern, not part of dad's kit. He escorted Ian and me for a sex education slide talk held at the primary school. This was no more illuminating than the transparencies of the body I'd pondered in *The Britannica* that had recently replaced the *Newnes*, and failed to explain how a man and a woman actually negotiated this preposterous act. I couldn't believe what classmate, Keith Turpie—boasting insider knowledge—had confided. Did my parents commit such things beneath their sheets?

Apart from struggling with Tibor Bedohazy's French classes, I enjoyed success in all subjects and had plenty of friends. We boys had already formed associations when bully, Paul Dodd, another descendant of early settlers, hit upon my little mate, O'Dowd, one recess. I didn't see who provoked who, but our combined strength wouldn't topple the bullocking Dodd. As I intervened, Dodd turned and instantly pinned me to the ground. The fetid breath of cabbage rose through the earth into my grass-stained shirt. The chant, 'fight, fight, fight', gathered lads in a circle. But it was no fight. A few pathetic wriggles and I knew it was useless. The bell saved further humiliation. In their eyes Dodd was victor. But I had my victory. Until lunch I could feel the imprint of his knees, see his black cap of greasy hair cropped at the brow, his dark eyes blistering with contempt, hear the obscenities frothing from his lips. But I'd diverted his attention from my friend. The incident hadn't escaped Irvine's attention. He'd noticed me comforting O'Dowd as we arrived late to assembly and mentioned it in my report card.

***

Fitness fanatic and coach of world champion runner, Herb Elliott, was billed to speak near the bakery one Saturday morning. Celebrities were unknown in Boronia. There, wily 70-year-old Percy Cerutty stood on the back of a truck, ranting about our moral duty to be fit or be dammed. He advocated a wholefood diet, including something called muesli. His tanned skin, shock of white hair, and conviction that resistance running on sand dunes and in headwinds, struck a healthy fit with the advert for Morse's Indian Root Pills staring over his shoulder. Cerutty's elixir was 'just what the doctor ordered', quipped Ian at my side. It was a small crowd gathered at the foot of the Spartan master, and I doubted converts to any of his regime numbered among us. Ian, however, kept with the weights.

Year 9 often proves a watershed for teens. Our maths and home teacher was Stan Davey, another significant male model. He was a lay preacher whose profound commitment to Indigenous injustice stirred him to join forces with Pastor Doug Nicholls and form the Victorian Aboriginal Advancement League. Both worked for the Church of Christ. Davey was the most political non-Indigenous activist in Australia and brought former Fitzroy footy star, Nicholls, to school. Until then none of us were aware of Indigenous inequality. Davey's calm and compassion impressed me with how discipline could be maintained, without intimidation or anger, rather, appealing to our better nature.

Perhaps on the back of Nicholl's appearance, sportsmaster, 'Nobby' Clarke, introduced a faux Indigenous warcry to inspire our interschool representatives. The infamous parody, *My Boomerang Won't Come Back*, may have contributed to its creation. Sport, being so popular, 'Nobby' was a regular at the assembly microphone, of similar height and vintage as Nicholls, his wispy moustache struggled to conceal a harelip. He insisted we follow his lead as he chanted: *Arra-gingey yah. Kot pot nah hah. Ninny go wah hah. Anthragoppa guy.* Within months we'd left mirth and shame behind and proudly encouraged our athletes at Olympic Park—the only school offering choral support—and we thrived in our uniqueness. Waddling Clarke's portly demeanour and nicotined fingers were hardly prescriptions for athleticism, but he talked like an insider and had befriended several league stars.

Davey also introduced schoolmate, Noel Price, and me one Sunday to environmentally concerned artist, Neil Douglas, at his Research home on the Yarra River's Bend of Islands midst the scrub and red box gums featured in his paintings. The place had been modelled from scrap materials and clay by partner Abbie Heathcote, seeming to rise from the ground on which we sat. I was amazed at the proliferation of figurines and walls chocked with painted canvases. The countryside was drier than home albeit only half an hour's drive north, and retained the ambience captured by the Heidelberg Impressionists who camped in the vicinity during the 1880s. Tea and biscuits done, Douglas toured his block with us. He was savvy with its botany, birds and insects and passionate about his art. A knowledgeable gardener, his ecological understandings influenced Permaculture guru, Bill Mollison, and enlivened my interest in the art of his neighbour, Cliff Pugh.

Pugh shared Douglas's environmental interests and had been influenced by Indigenous painting. Royden had also gifted me a monograph with reproductions of Pugh's work. While Douglas's work was derivative of those Heidelberg artists, Pugh's palette ventured stronger contrasts, and his canvasses were staffed with children, menaced by birds and thorn thickets. Claws, beaks and twigs were hyped at savage angles, acknowledging nature's inherent danger. Pugh's paintings evoked the darker side of the country we'd experienced during bushfires.

***

Sealed roads marked the newly subdivided daffodil fields. The bush had been reduced and the creek now trickled along a concrete storm drain. We noted with disappointment the construction of the first two-storey house, blocking access to our haloed playground. The closest casualty was the old maids' cottage. Though the precious fruit trees in their yard had been uprooted, by some unresolved legality, the lane remained, totally embowered and accessible only on foot. With new houses sprouting around us, dad purchased a light calibre gun to cull domestic cats that lurked in our backyard. We hadn't sighted a bandicoot in ages, and most of the smaller birds resorted elsewhere. Though mum was stressed about the falling bird population, it seemed an excuse for dad to peel off a few rounds. He hated cats. Once, he'd returned from work with a hessian bag of kittens and had us watch him drown them in the laundry sink, bubbles ceasing to float from the bag after a few minutes. We knew he could annihilate without remorse.

He drew no sympathy, however, from what eventuated as his last nocturnal sortie. We were engrossed in TV thriller, *The Innocents*, when the back door clicked. Dad was off to the lane and pittosporum hedge where cats hunted. There was a shot. The door was flung wide as he burst up the hall to the bathroom. He'd been resting the gun on his shoe and in his excitement had fired a round. 'Beryl, come here, quick,' he yelled. Mum reluctantly interrupted her viewing to drive him to hospital. He limped around the house for a couple of weeks, object of our supressed laughter and his work colleagues' mirthful card that read, *Get Well Soon, Hopalong*. Given he'd recently given Ian and me lessons, the mishap eroded his authority about gun handling. It was too painful, in all respects, to mention the accident in his company, and we were relieved when he sold the gun some months later.

Over the hills and far away. With our bush no longer the place of old, some Sundays I packed dry biscuits, cheese, and a bottle of cordial and roamed the ranges—Colin and Marilyn in tow—telling stories and investing rocks, trees and gullies with personalities. Often, we made for the old goldfield headframe serving as a lookout on One Tree Hill. I goaded my flagging siblings to continue up hill and down gully with tales of mythological marsupials, presided over by a cigar-smoking, furry-bottomed snake. I wore them silly, and almost insensible, with fatigue. But the promised stories of the elusive snake never failed to get them out of the house. In the manner of mum's reading to me as a child, I enacted the seductive elixir of tall tales.

But it was the Prom where Ian and I did our first serious hiking. The place had gained dimension after old Niven and Thomas recounted adventures to Darby River in the early 1920s. Out came an album of faded sepia photos to help prod memories. They'd driven from Fish Creek to the Yanakie isthmus, then continued on a plank road along the beach at ebb tide. They'd turned inland at the mouth of the Darby River along a track embowered with banksia, sheoak, teatree and honey myrtle. A kilometre upstream was a chalet. We'd noticed its remaining slab when driving to Tidal River. All this, I told dad. 'What would those two old lesbians know?' he sneered. Two what? 'Oh, Geoff, don't be awful,' said Mum, rising to their defence. 'They're just friends.'

Before daybreak, we set off for the southernmost tip of Australia's mainland, aiming to return by nightfall. That was, for us, fifty uncharted kilometres without preparation! We'd recently read *The Lost World*, about an Amazon adventurer and lampooned dad's prancing some distance ahead as the pompous Percy Fawcett. We respected dad but feared his flights of temper. Noting his Chaplinesque footprints, I pigeon-toed mine in undetected defiance as we paced the compacted sand of Norman Beach and trudged the Little Sahara.

Predating the Hawkesbury venture, Irvine had brought school lads to these dunes and encouraged the collection of driftwood that we later sketched in white and sienna conte on black paper. The Halfway Hut, with formidable ascent at its rear, Roaring Meg where we sipped brackish water: these we conquered, lunching on a solitary tin of Tom Piper Camp Pie within sight of the lighthouse. We did a rapid round of the headland and lighthouse while dad watched from our lunch spot. He lagged an hour behind us on the return, limping over the shoulder of Mount Oberon into our Tidal River camp after dark. Blisters carpeted his feet. We, too, were exhausted but not blistered, and quietly considered this a double triumph.

If the inclement weather kept us in tent or cabin, we'd play Monopoly, Scrabble or Cluedo, the latter my favourite as it circumvented Ian's customary dominance. He thrived on competition and winning, often fudging rules to that end. I was helpless against him playing 'hands', piling them upon each other until mine couldn't budge from the base. 'Knuckles' and Rock-paper-scissors were similarly humiliating. My favourite was Test Cricket that I played alone and preserved competitive temper within myself.

Irvine introduced oil pastels, assigning us to evoke images of our Christmas holidays. I dived straight into picturing Mt Oberon and Little Oberon, delighting in the vibrant hues of the pasty medium that relegated our poster paints as pallid cousins. He then gifted me sets of acrylics and oils whose clayey sensuality enabled greater expression.

He lent me Griffin's *Black Like Me*, my introduction to racial prejudice, though I didn't know about the gathering Civil Rights Movement that prompted the author's investigation. To uncover prejudice existing in the southern states, Griffin ingested Oxsoralen and sat beneath a ultraviolet light 16 hours each day to change his skin colour. On his month-long travels as a brown version of himself, he endured hate stares from whites and conversed with blacks and whites on racial matters. He glimpsed how African Americans regarded segregation and discovered ways in which they assisted and supported each other against racism. Elsewhere blacks, ashamed of their race, denounced other blacks for their darker skin or derelict clothes.

Griffin's encounters were confronting; the rudeness of a clerk when he tried to pay for a train ticket with a big bill; the difficulty he had in finding someone who would cash his travellers' cheque; a bus driver who wouldn't allow blacks off the bus to use restrooms; a white man who followed him at night and threatened to mug him. I wondered how his Caucasian features and weirdly dark skin went undetected. Within days of starting his experiment, he seemed to inhabit a black mindset and speak for black men. Though I remained unaware of Australian racism, the book served as a brutal record of the indignities suffered by black-skinned citizens in segregated America.

***

Homework increased and each subject had its spring-loaded folder and reference texts. The friction of my weighty Gladstone bag wore the side of my trousers thin and caused a limp from which I never fully recovered. Calluses gloved the inside of my knuckles. Dad bought and painted an old fixed-wheel bike that took some adjusting to on downhill corners. I started a paper round, earning five shillings a week and drawing dad's taunt that I was 'the last of the big spenders'.

When ancient 'Aunt' Ida needed a minder, while her orchardist son enjoyed a fortnight's vacation, mum volunteered my services. The prospect of accessing coolstore apples was an added incentive. It was only four kilometres from Wantirna to school, but a challenge living with the old lady whose sharp tongue and passion for euchre ruled our evenings. 'Bowers' and 'Trumps' became familiars, though I shared neither her enthusiasm nor skill.

Her granny flat was sufficient for wheelchair-bound activities. Though it had that stale old-people aroma, she eschewed the black attire of her ilk. Cardigans, be they mauve or fawn were preferred, and dresses of similar hue in delicate Liberty prints. Behind thick rimless spectacles, her blue eyes gleamed with rock-splitting intent. After our hour of cards, she hobbled from her chair and crawled beneath her eiderdown. I'd retire to the divan and read myself to sleep.

Other than my questionable progress with euchre, or the way I brewed her syrupy tea or tended lemon-iced biscuits, I couldn't think what passed between us to cause her parting quip: 'You're very particular, young man. Your wife will need to meet very high standards.' I'd never been critiqued in matrimonial matters or placed myself so far into the future.

***

As Uncle Hughie and I had birthdays two days apart, he invited us to celebrate the dual event at Melbourne's magnificent Menzies Hotel, one of

65

the few icons remaining from gold-rush days. We were guided through the royal red interior to the reserved table. Vast mirrors reflected our shy entry, dressed as mum still referred to in our 'Sunday best', which for me were pressed school pants and shirt with accompanying tie.

We'd never been inside any sort of hotel, and only once eaten in a restaurant—a subterranean Chinese den in Russell Street, serving gob-full bowls of greasy rice. This was five-star service we needed coaching about, and to have our napkins tucked in by waiters. I waited to see which cutlery should be picked up first, to avoid embarrassment. It was all 'does sir require this or that' obsequiousness from men many years my senior, making me uneasy. The adults toasted champagne in elegantly stemmed glasses, kept topped by the waiter from a bottle swathed in a straw cradle. We, kids, had raspberry cordial with soda water. A wonderful chocolate cake capped the event though. Not wanting to disturb our salubrious surrounds, we skipped the candles and song.

We always dressed up for our annual visit to Uncle's Port Melbourne digs in Bridge Street. We'd arrive around 11.30. There, the Citroën would be slouched beneath a puny canvas shelter in the narrow front yard; one never intended for the automobile era. Aunt Chris would answer the doorbell, looking somewhat distracted, and call over her shoulder to Hughie, buried somewhere deeper in the house. Their passageway featured a water-coloured coat of arms of the House of Boscobel. Dad told us we were descended on his father's side from the Pendrill brothers who'd hidden Charles II in an oak tree when he was pursued by Oliver Cromwell, in 1651. The coat of arms, featuring the oak, was conferred in appreciation. Dad was proud of this lineage and had the husband of one of mum's friends make a copy.

Mum's single ancestral knowledge was that one side of her mother's family had landed at Robe and, like thousands of prospective diggers in the 1850s wishing to avoid Victoria's poll tax on immigrants, headed across land to its Ballarat and Bendigo goldfields.

We kids would file into the lounge and Chris would invite us to help ourselves to the bowl of muscatels and sweets, centred on the small cherry-wood table. The room also accommodated a Pianola at which I discovered novel keyboard expertise. Half an hour on, we'd retreat for lunch. That done, Uncle would lead us to his quarters at the back of their small yard where he spent most of his days; self-sufficient with TV, mini fridge, porta stove and ready access to the pigeon loft abutting his bungalow. Chris customarily pressed more sweets upon us as we left despite our unconvincing denials and mum's disapproving frown.

Uncle Hughie, attuned to my adolescent needs, suggested I join him to be fitted with my first casual strides with his tailor at Fletcher Jones Menswear in Flinders Street. We scanned the racks and I selected cuff-less, hickory brown woollen pants with fob pocket. 'And on which side does the young sir dress?' the tailor asked. Uncle whispered I must indicate which side 'my equipment' hung. 'Just measuring the inside leg, sir,' the man added before dashing off to the cutting room, a number of steel pins pursed between his lips. 'Your trousers will be ready within the hour, sir,' he assured us.

No sooner having escaped this embarrassment than Uncle insisted we add a pair of leather gloves to the outfit, so we wheeled around the block to Buckley and Nunns. Dad used to joke that Collingwood's chances of another premiership in his lifetime were 'Buckleys or None', citing the popular and amazing restitution of escaped convict, William Buckley, a century earlier. How far from Buckley's bush life was this salubrious department store! First, we chose a pair of black kid leather gloves. Finally, a belt to halter my herringbone pants. Not that I had as yet an appropriate occasion to parade my finery.

***

Dropping by on his twice-weekly round to Dandenong market, Daryl Martin invited me to spend school holidays on his sheep and cattle farm in Yea. A few Hereford yearlings usually jostled in the back of his truck. His wasn't a big outfit, maybe four hundred acres of good grazing on the confluence of the Yea and Goulburn Rivers. We called Daryl 'cousin', though it was his wife, Mary-Joy, who was mum's first cousin. He was the same stocky 170 centimetres as dad, though a dozen years younger. Both had powerful forearms, although Daryl was a tanned picture of outdoor robustness, with a ready laugh glinting his blue eyes.

Alluding to his vitality, dad called him 'The Mallee Bull' which Daryl wasn't flattered by, knowing the lean fodder available in that arid zone. 'Poor buggers are so thin they can't attract females,' he winked, imputing his own roving fantasies. 'Too busy searching for a decent feed.' My parents exchanged playful banter about the fortunes of their footy teams. The Wesley College 'old boy' supported the Carlton 'blue-baggers', derided for their middle-class pretensions. Collingwood, on the other hand, was thoroughly working-class—both its players and its supporters.

The Wolseley climbed the dirt track beyond Yarra Glen over the forested Divide, through Glenburn to Yea. There the land was rolling hills and pastures, bereft of trees save those fringing waterways. This was the sunburnt country we feigned affection for via Mackellar's oft-recited verse, an abstraction for most coastal-hugging Australians. Nineteenth-century gold-mining tunnels were noted from the car window. Dad said the Chinese had dug all over the country, not just Ballarat and Bendigo, but north as far as the Buckland Valley, and east beyond Walhalla as far as Butchers Ridge, Bonang and The Snowy. Cockies and crows interjected the silent stanzas of the rural airways.

For some reason, Daryl called farming neighbours 'cockies'. Perhaps he was referring to their persistence. Or was it those chats from tractor seats along adjoining fences with 'Knocker' McKleish or Ronnie Drysdale when they broke from fieldwork? Talk of weather, of the river's height, of some heifer struggling with its first calf, what a yearling fetched at market, or the return on the wool clip. This was men's talk about elementary things—slow and studied—given through cracked lips. They drew out the leave-taking, delaying the tweaking of throttles that signalled departure. But it was the crop that had them there. One way or another, cockies, both bird and man, depended on the seeds.

Their farmhouse had been built as part of the World War I Soldier Settlement scheme. Some of the original pear, apple and apricot trees struggled in the house block. Dad helped Daryl renovate the house's rudimentary wooden structure, sharing carpentry and welding skills. The rickety shearing shed, where the tractor sat midst myriad farm gear, was as old as the house.

Daryl drove the four kilometres into Yea to see Pat the Beeman, two-metres tall and drawler of bee-centred concerns. He received honey from Pat in exchange for shifting hives. Talk was that Pat never removed his wax-encrusted hat even when asleep. Who had witnessed this? Above the hatband was a medallion-sized hole issuing a steady traffic of bees about which he was unfazed. He retraced our path along the front yard, fence-to-fence with busy hives, and filled a pail with liquid honey he'd saved for Daryl.

'Too wet last year, mate. Just like mead, this one. You'll love it, mate.' He related how his 'little friends' set just out of town, would fly to tell him when besieged by disease, bee-eaters or when bereft of water. 'Them critters keep the country healthy, mate. Swarming time comin' up. Red gums flowering down the river an' 50 hives to truck there this week, mate. Bit of yellow box flowin' round Bonnie Doon, mate. You up for a run?'

There was grass to be cut and baled. Daryl cursed the cockies, pointing to their outrider sitting in the upper reaches of a river gum a hundred metres from its flock-mates. It filled the air with its agonised shriek and flapped away to join them, rising from the field in one great cocky cloud. Copperhead, black and tiger snakes wriggled from the tractor to take refuge on the riverbank as the crop was trimmed.

'Tigers're the ones t'watch for,' he yelled over the grunting tractor. 'Might turn an' run at yer if yer not careful.' The sweet scent of fallen grass flared in my nostrils. I felt very adult when asked to take the wheel. Graduating from opening gates to hauling baled hay to the lower pastures, I was enhanced.

He also his cursed the cows when they damaged fences. Neither mum nor dad swore. But this seemed a manly thing to do. Without pliers, he twisted and snapped the heavy-gauge wire with his fingers to mend breaks. He lifted a ram into a holding pen the better to douse its damaged horn with disinfectant. Such mundane duties accomplished without fuss. The Corriedales were mustered by his dogs and dipped besides the shearing shed. Lanolin perfumed the air. I noted their nervous eyes, bitter-smelling shit and the rams' large scrotums, about which Daryl passed lewd remarks.

Together with the herd, breeding and selling rams provided most of their income, but the clip was a useful supplement. Now and then the dogs bestrode their backs to hasten passage up the ramp and meet the clippers. Once shorn, they'd rush down a chute at the other end of the shed and be stamped with Daryl's teal-blue moniker. Pristine white and freed from burrs, they looked no happier than I did with short-back-and-sides.

Weekends were no different from other days. Load the haycart from the barn, drive to the cows herded on the river flat, cut the bailing cord and toss their feed, a bail at a time. They bunched at the gate, big-eyed and bawling, then dropped behind in dribs and drabs as the necklace of broken bales circled to the gate. In a few months, calves would be separated from mothers. Now, they stooped with their mums, forgoing caring licks and comforting mewing, their pink mouths roped with slobber.

Then we were home for breakfast: toast, bacon and eggs. Mary-Joy had stirred the wood oven back to life while nursing baby Mark on her hip. Bacon frying set my kidneys on edge. I'd told mum it smelled like dad's armpits, and she let me go without, whenever my siblings gobbled it at home. She'd said it was rude to protest food at other people's houses, so I kept a poached egg back, allowing it to drench the toast and drown the bacon's saltiness. Daryl broke from his Coke regime for a cup of tea, afterwhich we'd return to bailing, our lamb and pickle sandwiches packed for lunch. He was legendary for keeping a crate of the Coke beneath his bed from which he'd swig throughout hot nights. We'd eat beneath a river gum and flush the bread with tea from the thermos. Food had never tasted so good or been so anticipated.

In the evening, the dogs, all heeler derivations—mottled grey Toohey 'Red' housed in his 44-gallon drum and 'Bluey' in a hollowed log—were fed freshly butchered sheep shanks. No mince or canned food for these hounds. They strained at their chains, yapping frantically as I approached their kennels, saliva dripping from dark lips. 'Bluey' eyed me studiously, giving encouraging yelps when I split wood from the pile near his kennel.

Daryl suggested I take his .22 and reduce the rabbit population from surrounding hills. He showed how to load and flick the safety catch and spent a few rounds on some tins lined up on a post, while adjusting the sights. 'Practice,' something we'd not done with dad, 'makes perfect. Just keep an eye out for me cows,' he said. Big deal, this gun with its copper-tipped bullets, small and deadly. I stalked the bald, domed hills besides the Yea River then sat concealed midst bracken ferns waiting for quarry. My few shots went unrewarded. I was crestfallen, returning at dusk, the barrel warm and smell of hot oil lingering in my nostrils. He suggested that fumigating warrens with larvicide was more effective, but it was good to try my hand. 'Ask yer Uncle Hughie. They used that gas in the trenches during the Great War,' he said. 'Great War'? The slaughter of nearly ten million young men on battlefields resembling gargantuan abattoirs wasn't my idea of greatness. Great was the waste and great the loss of confidence in mankind.

The only horse I'd ridden gave birth to a foal that was christened after me. I'd been early to the shearing shed, rising before the household, wondering what the groaning was. There, standing in the near paddock was Cavil, straining this bubble of baby from her rear. Her tail was lifted straight out, her eyes dilated and nervous. Her nostrils pressed deep snorts of hot white air into the chilly morning. Within half an hour the baby dropped to the frosted grass. The sun peeped over the hill, gradually gilding the grasses. The household, higher on the gradient, slumbered in frigid shade. Cavil sniffed and roused her offspring, licking clean the afterbirth. Soon, the baby staggered to his feet; a miracle, especially staged for me.

I sparkled with this independence from family and welcomed Daryl's rough-edged, manly banter on stints at the farm. His was dependent on what the land could produce, and his language and behaviour was at one with it. Weather talk, for instance, was not some incidental small talk to pass the day. Working holidays on the farm in varied seasons flexed my muscles and grew my confidence in new skill sets.

I was unaware of how dad regarded Royden's presence in our family, or his influence on me. But my father was happy about my relationship with Daryl and harboured dreams of running livestock on a few acres. Sensing Daryl and bucolic life were challenging, and perhaps undermining his influence, Irvine slipped me copies of Stone's *Agony and the Ecstasy* and *Lust for Life*. The energetic scale of Michelangelo and Van Gogh were impressive, though the political intrigues of Renaissance Italy slid by me. Van Gogh's turmoil was more gripping in Graetz's *Symbolic Language*; he also pushed my way. Letters from the artist to his brother on one page faced paintings made the same day. Graetz's case for Van Gogh's valiant struggle was compelling and caused me tears in their reading.

***

We adored sport. The few who didn't were non-entities. The playing fields in our high school were formerly a cabbage plot that emitted a foul odour after rain, though weather rarely deterred our exploits. At lunch and recess the grounds were crammed with footballers in winter and cricketers in summer. House rivalry was fierce, encouraged by housemasters for whom the annual fete, in particular, was of great moment. Senior Science teacher, Jack Arscott, headed my house, Chandler. Disinterest in sport intensified his hunger for success at fetes. With a blend of cynical encouragement and threats, he was intent on maintaining Chandler's fine record. Stockpiles of canned fruit, meat and vegies, a sausage sizzle, coconut shy, raffles, games of quoits, Hoopla and Tin Can Alley, kept our unblemished rating and helped swell school coffers.

Interschool sports were also keenly anticipated, if with less passion. We excelled at athletics despite a much smaller population than established schools at Lilydale, Upwey, Croydon, and Ringwood. Lacking access to a pool, our swimming performances were abysmal, rarely troubling the scoreboard, and our somewhat ironical cheers were reserved for those brave contestants who swam in a lap behind the rest.

Perhaps old Ida and Uncle Hughie sensed my hormones were kicking in. Apart from football and cricket, the main topic of conversation amongst mates was girls, whom none had so much as dated, and rarely spoken with. A year ago, they were from a different planet, but now the universe had inexplicably contracted. Five of us commandeered the sports storeroom through whose venetian blinds we overlooked assemblies at recess and lunch after checking in cricket or footy gear. From here, we rated the girls. It was a challenge for them to look sexy in their uniforms with headmistress, Marion McGibbon, invigilating over an undone top button or earring, a rolled sock, a glimpse of sexy black petticoat beneath shortened hems, and the appearance of flagrantly promiscuous fingernail polish. Still, no uniform could subdue our imaginings of those curved bodies dwelling within.

We passed comment on grooming, deportment, and the one zone of available flesh, legs. Mind you, we were attentive to our own appearance also. I was up well before breakfast, renewing the crease in my grey strides and pressing my tie. And there was the usual self-scrutiny of worrisome acne that needed tending before the bathroom mirror. While I doted privately on copper-tinted brunette, Gloria Tully, the unanimous, uncrowned queen was blonde Patty West, whose shapely calves and what was visible of her tanned thighs caused us to salivate. Her group sought semi-seclusion in September's long grasses to sun their legs at recess and lunch. We were too timorous to infringe their circle, holding to our own, while envying the intimate exchange of daisy garlands the girls wove and draped around each other's necks. They remained tantalisingly aloof, grooming and gossiping, none more than Pat. Ever aware of probing eyes, she kept a disdainful distance, comb propped in her breast pocket in a silent ploy of cat and mouse.

Our contingent comprising Worrall, Cromarty, Price, and Braden met on Fridays to watch *The Twilight Zone's* half-hour episodes which disturbed our sense of the world as we dined on new-fangled Rice-a-Riso. Grimacing Rod Serling treated us to an eclectic range of social, psychological, and futuristic themes, shot under lamps that gave granular definition, sets that declared their artifice and were recorded with vertiginous angles and close-ups.

It was Worrall who organised a date-matching meal at the town's new and only restaurant, one Friday. He was the most gullible regarding the *Twilight Zone's* fictions, genuinely believing on one occasion, the smoke rising from a burned valve in the TV was the work of extraterrestrials. But he had no qualms fronting the girls. He'd canvassed us for our preferences and, as we lacked courage, acted as our intermediary. Over the months I'd shifted attention to a tall, honey-blonde girl two years below me, though as mature-looking as girls in my year. It was an evening about which both the *Britannica* and I were clueless.

Some evenings, evangelist Garner Ted Armstrong, kept me company on the bedside radio. Though I'd missed the plot at Sunday School and been bemused by Billy Graham's ranting, I now sought explanatory powers beyond our daily grind. For a few months I subscribed to Armstrong's message through his *Plain Truth* magazine. Its cries of imminent catastrophe and salvation failed to console my pubescent pangs, however. His fulminations were bookended by Pop music that stimulated fantasies. I was tongue-tied around girls and loathed my whippet-thin body. How would I ever attract the girl of my desire?

So here was Kerry who I'd admired from afar—buxom, brown-eyed, and of regal bearing. She embodied calm. But what was suddenly ignited when her eyes returned my invitation? To touch her body and to be touched, lips and fingertips. *Do Wah Diddy Diddy Dum Diddy Do*, I chanted Manfred Mann's ditty as I walked home, having dared my first date. We'd kissed at the edge of the field bordering her parent's block. Don't come closer she'd warned. Father's pigeons would stir and set the two Dobermans barking.

The Twilight Zone had never been this luminous. We'd meet in the bush halfway between our houses, settling in a glade, conspirators in the amorous dark, spilling into each other. She provided a rug and me what talk there was besides that of our exploratory fingers and tongues. To hear her breathing against my chest while fingering the resins in her scalp, instantly hardened me. At dawn we pinched cream from milk boxes, nursing and cuddling the glass bottles to our cheeks. Membranous clouds smeared the bird-free sky, mute witnesses to our passing pleasures. Eyes still shining, we'd waltz the silent streets, giggling at languishing lounges, leftover kitchens and imagined bedroom music, then slip back to respective beds. We were newly created, as was the world.

She had a reassuring slow, deep voice. Her pace and purposeful stride were the measure of mine. Our laughter erupted simultaneously. It was a classic case of mirroring; I saw in her the female image of myself, at least the gentle and considerate side. I started writing love poetry, more precisely, the angst our awkward avowals and mutual stripping aroused, and how the love of her body grew into the love of her entirety. I didn't understand this feeling of being more completed when with her nor the abandonment when apart. Mum had married at 16, a 'war bride', and I sensed how she might have wished in those tender years to be bound to another.

I ducked school one day with fellow prefect, Noel Price, who knew of an Ingmar Bergman movie in the city. Ingmar who? We took the train in and slipped into the cinema beneath the Australia Hotel in Collins Street to watch the subtitled, *Through a Glass Darkly*. I'd never experienced anything like it. An eerie northern light permeated the 24 hours the four characters spend in a cottage by the edge of the Baltic. The teenage brother's consciousness organises the film. The psychologist father is morbidly curious with his daughter's descent into madness, noting it with criminal objectivity in his diary. He's helpless to assist his wife and was racked with guilt about this loss of empathy.

The chilling climax is the daughter's illusionary encounter with a 'Spider God' appearing in the patterned wallpaper of her bedroom.

It was the brother's struggle with emergent adulthood and his desire to create a bond with his father that spoke to me. Not so much his tormented sexual awakening. I'd emerged from my chrysalis with Kerry. But the lack of guidance from his emotionally distant father and being left to handle the transition from puberty to adulthood still rankled. Climbing the stairs into Collins Street buzz, I felt the world had tilted several degrees.

I resented being questioned about my new love. Ian showed no interest in girls, and I was chuffed to have skipped ahead of him, regarding myself as more mature. He'd gradually ceased antagonising me. Boronia High had yet to deliver matriculation subjects and Ian chose Upwey to do his final year so was largely out of sight and mind. Dad was concerned I'd be distracted from study. But my grades held, despite evening phone calls and frequent letters. I phoned from a public box, not wishing family to be privy to our intimacies, or mum's concerns about phone bills. Kerry was welcomed on our weekend drives and much loved by mum. Her father, Willy, in his late sixties, rarely drove other than to his pigeon races, and he and wife, Florrie, happily conceded to our family excursions.

Early on, matchmaker Worrall and I would team up, me courting Kerry, and he, her girlfriend, Jan Gill. We'd yet to dare the privacy of bedrooms for our couplings. Once, I'd snuck out of bed, and as planned, met the others outside Jan's Ferntree Gully house. It was midnight when the last train passed and we'd settled in the long grass by the train track, midway between Boronia and Ferntree Gully. The ringing in the rails had no sooner subsided than we heard a car cruising the road parallel to the tracks. It was the Wolseley! Dad passed, and we split our separate ways. With utmost caution, I opened and shut gates and doors, then crawled beneath my blankets. Suddenly, the bedroom lights flared and mum and dad stood at the foot of my bed, fully clothed.

Without prying into our sexual activities, dad made it clear I was not to get Kerry 'in trouble' or I'd be banished from home: his sole contribution to my sexual education. Though I attributed all my happiness to our relationship and sex, her affectionate fit with family and friends made her more like a sister. In fact, we were occasionally mistaken as siblings because of similar body language and demeanour. To ward off enquiry and keep our capsule inviolate, I became abrupt with mum. I felt helpless to stem it and usually regretted my rudeness. I was her son, not her little boy.

For pigeon racing reasons, Willy shifted their family 12 kilometres closer to the city. I'd study until 11 p.m., catch the last city-bound train, run three kilometres from the Laburnum station, and hop through her bedroom window, careful not to disturb the dogs. We'd canoodle an hour and I'd hitchhike home. If I slept beside her I'd rise before dawn to catch the first Belgrave-bound train. When she shared meals with us we'd catch the train to her station, rampantly fondling throughout, then speed to the grassed lane abutting the cemetery containing my grandparents, and satisfy our lust. Reaffirming infatuation replaced thoughts about transcendence and things metaphysical. Were sex and love one and the same? What were her needs? Was my universe centring or de-centring?

Sex and study pulsed through my days, their ardour encouraged by taking up Toots Willoughby's offer of a vacant bedroom. The months of piano struggle had long receded. She'd shared her residence with her daughter, son-in-law, and granddaughter. Bert died five years before. Eryl had left home, and the previous year, 'Toot's' only daughter, Frieda, succumbed to cancer. The room was more comfortable than the bathroom bench I'd commandeered to exclude sibling voices and enjoy its fluorescent lighting. I'd not factored in 'Toot's' nightly prayers, sobbing through the thin wall. But I could slip away undetected with a ready excuse, if found missing. Our literature teacher, Joy Planten, had recommended the State Library's holding of secondary texts, and I had sourced its sanctuary by train after school, an hour each way. More often though, my research was in Kerry's bed.

Fortunately, the radio delivered consolations other than the pious doomsday of the good Garner Ted Armstrong. There were the soaring lamentations of Roy Orbison and Gene Pitney pumping two-minute epistles of obsession's tension and release. I aspired to the latter's adenoidal falsetto and clean-cut look with dubious success. And then there was Dylan. What antithesis! While the aforementioned alluded to rebelliousness, Dylan embodied it.

There'd been a positive music review of *Another Side of Bob Dylan* in the recently launched *The Australian* newspaper. I'd been perusing its literary pages since its inception to supplement those of the *The Age*. Enquiring at the local record shop, I was told it wasn't in stock. But his most recent release was. I forked out two pounds two shillings and ran home bearing the vinyl, adding my first LP to a small pile of 45s. Unbelievable! Thrice, I moved the cumbersome record player's arm to the rim of the disc, flipping it as it moaned to anchorage.

Here was an irreducible 'I' that rendered other voices as cliché: one with narrative wordplay, glorying in itself rather than pandering to mass legibility.

Here was fearlessness. All other Bobbies—Lind, Vinton, Vee, Darin, and Goldsboro—were discarded in Pop's dustbin. I hovered above the turntable that summer Saturday morning, entranced, as *Highway 61 Revisited* spun its web.

The healthy hate and blasphemies of the title song and *Tombstone Blues* were alien to mainstream consciousness, questioning as they did received history and the institutions supporting it. How thrilling was the outrageous blast of the Claxton horn introducing *Tombstone Blues* assembly of absurd characters. This sneering tirade changed the face of Rock and Blues lyrics, savaging the tame clichés on which they'd been based.

Breathless short and middle-length songs with explosive, electrified arrangements were sandwiched between the seemingly endless *Ballad of a Thin Man, Queen Jane, Like a Rolling Stone*, and *Desolation Row*. No one in my circle had an inkling of the civil unrest inspiring Dylan's protest songs, or awareness of the suffering feeding the Blues. Nor did I. Australia's experience of war, the Depression and pioneer tribulations were expressed through anodyne Country and Western twang. Dylan didn't really cut it with my friends who were divided down the Rolling Stones and Beatles' axis.

I wore his songs into myself through mimicry, carried them wherever, unapologetically unleashing them on friends. Mimesis emboldened me, giving me permission to be who I wanted to be, a rebel with cause to break family shackles. No single song was more resonant than *Desolation Row* whose melancholic flood of despair spoke truths about which I was hitherto inarticulate. My pubescent brain was in overdrive as Dylan's cinematic vision unwound. Adopting his stance and affecting his accent, I positioned myself with the dispossessed, the losers and outcasts. Without sharing my obsession, Kerry, like my mates, either tolerated or was entertained by my antics.

I gravitated to her as much as possible, hitching rides on the dark roads, or risking ticket inspectors on ticketless train trips. On weekends when we weren't together, the village streets beckoned. In company with Dave Morgan or Shane, I'd ramble about, laughing, comparing insights and adventures; in short, hanging out. Despite the advent of new shops, Boronia's sole nightlife remained the weekend cinema.

One Saturday night during interval at the *Electra*, Shane and I were caught in a feud between local 'Rockers' and their Ringwood counterparts. Rockers comprised lads attending Ferntree Gully Tech, a male training domain for 'tradies', the legendary toughs who caught the 'red rattler' to school and hung from its open doors and dared to 'surf' between carriages—at least until one fellow fell to his death. High school students were aspirant white-collar workers, a division clearer than that between Catholics and Protestants. If high school lads could be said to follow a style, we'd be 'mods'.

Rockers' gang leader, Stan Barton, and sidekicks Noddy Mason, Bazza Hosking, Chopper Binding, Fatty Fuke, and the lanky Hutchisons, regularly haunted the crowd as they poured into the dimly lit lane. They sported leather jackets, pointed shoes and coifed hair with duck tail. During the week, Barton's finned Dodge idled by The Basin bus stop at the end of the school day, prime zone for parading and checking high school 'chicks'. He would drape across the bonnet, smoking and drinking beer, emulating Marlon Brando 'cool', envy of his fawning cronies. Though Brando was my film god, Pitney's pretty-boy looks were more easily emulated than my dangerously elusive star.

The lane's dynamic suddenly shifted when the Ringwood hood's Chrysler turned into the lane beside the theatre. Shane saw a gun glint in the back seat. They taunted Barton's crew who, accepting the challenge, heaped abuse on their foe and fled to the Dodge. Having circled the block, they headed for the hills. We scampered along the lane behind the theatre, seeking the police station, and flattened ourselves in someone's garden until the Chrysler slunk past and turned up Boronia Road.

We'd forgotten Sergeant Pritchard locked the cop shop at 5 o'clock. This was an unusual event. If the village had been a hotbed of civil disturbance riddled with hoodlum anarchists, the cop shop would have been on 24/7 red alert. But there was no local pub to encourage unruly dissipation. The fact that Shane, Ian, Dannie and I had 10 p.m. shopping trolley races down Boronia Road hill without fear of cars, spoke otherwise. We'd punt the 'pig' around the new Safeway's flood-lit car park in scratch matches of football or reconvene for sham Olympics on playground equipment at the footy ground. When police did pull up a mate for running his pet goat in the streets at midnight, or apprehended Shane and Nick Ouchtomsky for laughing uncontrollably on someone's grassy verge, it was Pritchard's Ferntree Gully brethren from their more formidable station that dealt justice while he dozed.

***

I was oiling my cricket bat Saturday morning on 22 November 1963, when news broke that President Kennedy had been assassinated. Until Kennedy, leadership had been in the hands of old men. Why was I shocked? I was barely aware of our Prime Minister. Yet this distant power-possessor must have inspired my parent's generation and carried my country's hopes with it. Now they'd been dashed. If the head of the world's dominant power, and our ally, was so easily eliminated, were we as vulnerable? Kennedy, and his assassin's murderer, saturated the news. Inevitable reviews of his time in office, his massive commitment to put a man on the moon, his botched invasion of communist Cuba, and increased military spending, drew America closer. Though its conflict with Vietnam was gathering momentum, our involvement in a war seemed far away.

Dad never raised the prospect and rarely referred to his Navy years, though once or twice we'd attended annual RSL picnics and shared pride in Great Uncle's annual fronting of Anzac parades. Dad joked about contracting measles when inducted and spending weeks quarantined at the Flinders Naval Depot playing Monopoly. The local RSL sub-branch, started before the World War II held no interest for him. There were war souvenirs in his cupboard: a US Air force jacket and a sheathed bayonet that filled me with awe. Yet, he'd produce a felt-lined case of medals and polish them during these commemorative times, together with odd-shaped foreign coins with undecipherable script, collected from various ports. Pennants of the ships he'd served on, principally the destroyers *Napier*, *Bowen*, and *Norman*, he'd pinned above our bedheads along with a model sailing ship stuck in waves of putty, housed nearby in a shallow glass case.

Mum and Dad, 1942.

He'd once sung, so tunelessly as to seem a parody, *Take Me Back to the Old Transvaal* as the family strolled the hills. Its unheralded emergence drew no applause as birdsong happily reasserted. Was he recalling some wartime dalliance? Mum had mentioned a post-war letter from Indonesia with a woman's signature. Other than accounts of shore leave in Capetown, Mombasa, Borneo, Ceylon and a journey up the Congo River, we heard nothing of combat, what led to it, or its resolution, though a shipmate reckoned dad had been on *The Aranda* in the Pacific Ocean's final battle. The photo of him in uniform had prominence on the mantelpiece taken the same day as the one with his bride and sharing the shelf. He smiles, as well he might. Of medium build, high cheekbones and carroty curls bequeathed from his mother's Nordic stock, he'd secured this brunette beauty. She's slim and though shorter than grandma's 170 centimetres, shares her gentle mien.

Other than the fact that Australia was to follow America's invasion of Vietnam, I had no idea why our lives were being risked, or the economic and social conditions motivating mass destruction. Details were sparse about the century's conflicts; the reparations demanded of Germany after World War I, the renaming and realignment of Middle Eastern countries that ignored Arab advice. We never heard of the Treaty thrashed out at Versailles.

We knew art school reject, Adolf, was the century's bad boy who'd sent millions of Jews to death camps. None of us had ever encountered a Jew, and we knew nothing of their beleaguered history or why the culturally rich and advanced German nation, with a fine record of assimilation, would tolerate the ranting Fuhrer's policies of exterminating ethnic minorities. Drawing innumerable maps, I learned only the shapes and whereabouts of countries, their climates and produce. There were dates of events, their heroes and villains, but no discussion or debate.

Lessons were spent copying script from the board about Mao Zedong's Long March, and the battle with Chiang Kai Shek. Communist leader Mao was presented as the bad guy, and Nationalist Chiang Kai Shek, the good. Neither Marx nor his work was mentioned. No mention was made of Western intellectuals' disillusionment with capitalism's failure to cope with the economic crisis following World War I, which fed into the Depression. Nor had our parents mentioned the harsh realities that encouraged the emergence of communist parties. I didn't know how communism or socialism differed or even that I lived in a capitalistic democracy, and how it had arisen.

Nor was there reference to battles that occurred when settlers conquered Australia; and reprisal killings that continued on the frontier until the 1930s. Eureka was mentioned without elucidation of unjust licences and taxes that caused conflict on Ballarat's goldfields. Or that Chartists on the fields had encouraged Australia's nascent democracy. The birth of labour unions, and the facts encapsulated in our familiar song about a dead swagman following a shearers' strike in the 1890s, remained hidden. What racist attitudes fed our new Federal government's White Australian Policy? We were taught the succession of English monarchs, but little sense of its religiously based Civil War that caused Charles to scramble up our ancestor's oak.

We focused on America's War of Independence and Civil War, though these were only vaguely alluded to in our rich diet of TV Westerns like *Wyatt Earp, Gunsmoke, Rawhide, Bonanza* and the rest. Richmond, Virginia was as real as Richmond on the Yarra River where dad worked. We'd not fought for independence from England; our governance and legal system were inherited from our 'Mother'. I never knew that the Japanese bombed Darwin in 1942 with intents to invade, or that First Australians regarded us as invaders. While entertainment was prized above understanding, I remained largely ignorant of the power structures governing town and country.

The rules I knew and obeyed were those of home and school. In all lessons we simply copied notes from the board to memorise for regurgitation at exams. This was how curriculums were delivered. We neither questioned nor considered if we had anything but excellent tuition. Indeed, we felt privileged to enjoy Boronia High's best years, with teachers acutely attuned to the necessary preparation for scoring well in the externally set memory games comprising state exams. By the time younger brother Colin, entered the system, nearly all those staff had moved on. The town and school's altered demographic contributed to its decline.

Our Year 12 of 1966, was only the second year of Matriculation classes at Boronia, a year of considerable responsibility for me aside from study. I was elected captain of the school footy team, made deputy head prefect, and cast as the Jerilderie bank manager, Tarleton, in Douglas Stewart's *Ned Kelly*. Noel took the lead. Bold and talented, though no felon, he was an obvious fit. Kelly's hoodlum gang had been venerated in song. They were the subject of Australia and the world's first feature film in 1906, and a succession of dramatic re- enactments. All made less of Kelly's treachery than his heroics. Decades after that first film Mick Jagger, rogue Rock n' Roll celebrity, was recruited to this end in Tony Richardson's film, much being made of the home-tooled armour that delayed his capture. The energy demanded of working a script through to the stage was a fresh and challenging experience. Projecting myself into nineteenth-century bank manager mode was an imaginative exercise, and collaborating with a sizeable cast, an opportunity to expand my repertoire beyond Dylan.

I also jumped at the offer to edit the school magazine, design its cover and negotiate printing. In appreciation, home teacher, Chris Dyer, gifted me Xavier Herbert's *Capricornia* and Trotsky's *My Life*. Trotsky was born to a Ukrainian Jewish family in 1879 being one of eight children, although only four survived infancy. As he tells it, the deaths of newborn children were regarded with no more emotion than the survival of others. High infant mortality and maternity rates were accepted facts of life at that time in Russian Ukraine. Educated in Odessa, he started involving himself in trade union activities which led to his arrest and exile to Siberia. He escaped this fate and somehow managed to reach London where he encountered fellow revolutionary, Lenin, and began their troubled association. Imprisonment continued intermittently in consequence of his pamphleteering and speechifying. He organised the October Russian Revolution of 1917 and created the Red Army in the ensuing Civil War.

Herbert's book had plenty to say about race relations in the frontier town based on 1930s Darwin. I'd never heard of his support for a mixed-race Australia, or the sound of his character's Aboriginal English. Nor had I known that thousands of Chinese and Malays were recruited to pearl diving and the goldfields of the North before Restricted Immigration and the White Australia Policy were instated.

***

Dad started back at Swinburne Technical College to complete Matriculation English denied by his war service. He intended upgrading qualifications to move into administration with the Electricity Commission's at their Flinders Street headquarters. Mum was cobbling dollars together from chiropody with instruments inherited from grandma: clippers, forceps, scalpels, probes and the ancient piece of pumice. How I loved that old hand-held foot vibrator with its rubber suction cap! I was pleased to see mum carry on the tradition and have our lounge filled with those antiseptic aromas and gossip.

I matriculated with honours in Economics and Literature that gave me options for tertiary study. My success in Economics was due to Johnny Willis rather than genuine interest. He was more interested in Art than Economics and told us of his pilgrimage to eccentric painter, Ian Fairweather, on Bribie Island. On a semester break, he'd made an equally epic journey west to Port Hedland to visit miner and activist for Aboriginals, Don McLeod. This was the first I'd heard of these men. McLeod had helped organise about 600 stockmen from Pilbara pastoral stations in an historic walk-off for improved conditions in 1946. It was Stan Davey, I heard later, who'd introduced McLeod to Victorian Indigenous communities.

Though art had taken a back seat, that's where my heart was. It was the first time any of us had openly tested wills with dad. An Art Diploma was the path of prospective artists but required self-funding. An Art and Crafts Teaching Bursary paid tuition and dad, though not concealing his disappointment, conceded. I'd be indentured for three years. That was the deal. And I could start paying board.

5

The Big Smoke

Nijinsky Box, Rod Moss, 1984.

The dilemmas of my working life would be determined by accepting the Teaching Bursary. I didn't believe I could sustain myself by making art or develop a career from it. Yet teaching Art required presenting ideas and advice. I had little confidence that anything I said mattered to others. What training might redress these deficiencies?

It was a relief to have graduated and sensed nascent manhood. Academic study would never again present such stringent demands. For decades I'd occasionally wake from sweaty dreams having forgotten something in an exam, or having failed, needed to sit again. Those who shared the year's stresses I'd not see again. Noel was headed for Monash University with film directing in mind. Any spare time had been devoted to Kerry. It might have been good to leave home and shack up together but we lacked the means. She'd completed Business College at her father's insistence, leaving school at 15, and now had a secretarial position in the city.

I was closer to friends in the year below me who were all within walking distance from home. All were on deck to stage Dylan Thomas's *Under Milkwood*, co-directed by Planten and Willis and staged at the George Maddocks Hall. Thomas reportedly wrote the play as a riposte to the atomic devastation of Hiroshima. I attended rehearsals and performances, enchanted by my mates' acting and the musical language. The metaphoric reach of both Dylans opened in me the wonder and power of words to steer lives. Daily banter was peppered with rehearsed lines.

Jill 'Polly Garter' Thompson's mellifluous singing turned us on, not to mention her coy smile. Nick Ouchtomsky and Shane were the first and second voices. Kenny McMullan was Captain Cat. Jack Adams was the Reverend Jenkins. The play's nostalgic reveries, both celebration and condemnation of small-minded village life, translated easily into our experience. Realising the play's *Llareggub Hill* inversed was 'buggerall', united our sense of the ridiculous with the author's. Willis's 1954 BBC vinyl recording guided my mates' delivery. The performance was recorded, and Dave Morgan designed the sets and album cover. When Mrs Organ Morgan rebukes her husband, 'It's organ, organ with you all the time', Dave inevitably wore the double entendre jibe.

***

I, alone, had chosen art and travelled by train the hour and a half to Caulfield Technical College. No one from Boronia High had ever pursued any sort of art career. Art school provided gratifying freedoms. As the train approached Caulfield on my first day, I saw a massive red-brick edifice and mistook it for a penitentiary. I was soon told it was the racecourse. But the wire-caged balconies of the campus did feel like gaol. The studios had an institutional indifference that permeated most staff. But we students were immersed in Pop culture, adopting bohemian garb, and enjoying the collegiate feel of a shared language that differed radically from the tradies attending the college, keeping us polarised from them. The aspirant women artists and teachers were the only females in the place. For all its conservatism, staff treated us as adults. Bob Dylan was my model, more so when he arrived mid-April to perform at Festival Hall boxing stadium with an unknown backing group of Canadians.

Kerry was more into Donovan and The Stones. I'd tagged along with her to St Kilda's Palais Theatre the previous summer to hear 'her' Rolling Stones and the incomparable Orbison, whose stony stance belied his vocal flights. Though reluctant, she rugged up for Festival Hall and whatever revelations Bob might deliver. He was smaller and paler than anticipated, pursing his lips at the microphone with intimate intent. His enunciation made a ghost of his studio-recorded voice. His guitar and harmonica were sharper. I was entranced as he crouched at the piano for the last of his acoustic set, unwinding *Desolation Row's* improbable scenarios.

After intermission the Canadians wandered onstage, one after the other, to pound us with the electrified second half. It was a blitzkrieg of unprecedented intensity. Lead guitarist, Robbie Robertson, later fronting these guys in The Band, darted between verses with whip- cracking glee. He and Dylan stood either side of the mike gyrating in sync like lovers. Bearded keyboard genius, Garth Hudson, sat in semi-darkness, extending the chords with whimsical accord. *Like a Rolling Stone, Just Like A Woman*, and *Ballad of a Thin Man* hovered in the air between stage and the enthralled, entranced crowd. I had been immersed in a timeless dream. Was it *All Over Now Baby Blue*? Far from it. Kerry was a fresh convert.

My Dylan was electric Dylan, not the guy who'd recently betrayed legions of acoustic guitar-carrying folkies with their investment in authenticity. After the show I dug into his early albums. But they and his avowed references— Lead Belly, Brownie McGee, Big Joe Williams, and Robert Johnson—barely registered. So what if he filched from old Bluesmen and folkies. Dylan's Beat-influenced bricolage was what I inhabited.

We, students, led double lives. That's how I regarded the dichotomy between making and teaching art. Teaching methodology required attendance twice a week at the Department's 1880s city campus where artistic instincts were thwarted. Teachers' College requisite jackets, shirts and ties, disrupted our pretence. Then again, pretence was rife midst the condescending male staff we regularly ridiculed. Twinkle-eyed Dave Newbury, painter of gentle nudes in bush settings, delivered Design sermons, rolling his vowels, punching the air with pugilistic gusto, a prime candidate for mockery. Suave Lou Senini swept through Art History, projecting images of himself before Greek temples and pyramids. Most ridiculous was Chalkboard Cunningham, imparting a mode already superseded by whiteboards and marker pens. It was impossible to believe the loon cramming the board with his loopy left-handed script and infantile icons took himself seriously.

Not far into the year, students were presented the option of donating blood. Dad had taken me as a three-year-old, somewhere near Essendon Airport to a Blood Bank and afterwards, we watched planes in action. A donor's badge was always affixed to his lapel, joined later by another acknowledging his 100th visit. I made no pretence of making noble contributions to my community. Mike Cuthbertson and I, alone, rolled up at the Blood Bank, agreeing our donations offered a break from Cunningham and crew. But the habit stuck, and I continued to sign on in later years with a keener sense that my pint might save a life.

Dad fashioned a cottage for Ian in the backyard from car crates. He'd struggled through high school since his fall. As well as his absence with a ruined knee, having a December birthday meant he was twelve months younger than his peers. He'd clawed his way through each year until finally failing English. Having repeated, he now excelled in Science at Monash. On one wall he pinned rat skins dissected during Biology, for which he was dubbed, 'Rat', thus joining our coterie of recently coined animal monikers: Shane 'Tadpole' Bourne, Tony 'Loupas, The Wolf' Lintermans, Nick 'The Russian Honey Bear' Ouchtomsky, Rod 'The Tassie Devil' McMillan, Dave 'Ant-eater' Morgan, and Kenny 'The Aboriginal Dog' McMullen. Michael 'Jack' Adams wore his father's moniker. Given my gliding footy style and slow arousal, I was dubbed, 'Snake'. Although 'Ratty' was a footy teammate, he eschewed our social pranks, preferring to hang out with 'Tadpole's' younger brother Dannie, in the 'Rat's Den'.

We heard Stan Davey had returned west and was teaching English with Nyangmarta people in their Pilbara mining camps. Again, I heard of Don McLeod, who'd earlier organised their walk-off from cattle stations where their labour had been exploited. The 1946 May Day strike lasted three years, the longest in Australia's history. This 'Strelley Mob' were fighting for independence, equal pay and rights. McLeod had been introduced to Stan in Melbourne in the late 1950s when invited to share the Nyangmarta's concerns with Victorian Aboriginal activists.

Soon after, Davey's name cropped up in the news sourcing support for the Gurindji who'd also walked off beef baron Vesty's cattle station at Wave Hill, in the Northern Territory. Vincent Lingiari was the group's spokesman and beacon for emerging Land Rights. Having seen the degradation of their land, endured generational disrespect from non-Indigenous workers, suffered appalling living conditions and pathetic or no payment for their labour, they wanted a small parcel of their land returned. The plight and lack of rights for

Indigenous Australians was regular news after the Freedom Rides to Walgett and Moree in northwest New South Wales led by Arrernte man, Charles Perkins.

By second year I'd purchased a 1952 green Austin A40 for 50 dollars, started drinking beer, and felt the world at my feet, the accelerator at least. Dad had chaperoned my driving lessons in Policeman's Paddock behind Rowville's Drive-in. Though he knew the army had trained there during the Second World War, he'd not alluded to its function in the 1830s as the site of Native Police and their horses. There was no evidence of either activity as I motored the dirt tracks and managed the footwork needed to balance clutch and brake on steep hill starts.

Dominating the estate were pairs of gigantic, steel transmission towers bearing heavy cables, swathing up hill and down dale en route from Yallourn to the city substation where dad worked. They chomped through forests and farms on their march with unalloyed power I associated with him. He was keen to instruct, but bumbling his advice could ignite his unpredictable temper. He'd taken me on a tour of his workplace several times when I was eight or nine, delighting in the dozens of dials indicating pressures, wattage output, and whatnot in the elevated, glassed-in, control room. It mercifully muted the appalling din and stench of rancid oil on the shop floor where boilers, generators, turbos and dynamos clustered. And once, detouring from a Walhalla weekend, I'd accompanied him around the Yallourn complex where he pranced around affecting a superior air with staff.

The day of my eighteenth birthday I earned my licence under the watchful eyes of seasoned tutor, Don Pittard and Sergeant Pritchard, and immediately drove solo to the city centre to assert independence and memorise the route. As Pritchard signed the documents, he eyed me sternly and added, 'It took your parents 18 years to get you to this stage. Don't blow it in a moment of stupidity.' Perhaps dad sensed a rising vanity with this burgeoning independence. I struggled to decode his new greeting: 'Did you see anyone today you liked better than yourself?' I passed by in silence.

The A40 was crucial to my mates' pleasures as I, alone, had a licence and car. Weekends commenced Friday evenings, appraising which party offered the best possibilities for picking up girls. I'd earlier teamed up with mates who'd opted for courses at Monash, for 'sippies' in the student crush at Nottinghill pub. We, self-titled 'Neo-Diggers', reassembled at 'Tadpole's' whose single mother, Pixie, tolerated our gang in her large lounge. Tall and elegant in her forties, she retained the glamour of her modelling days. She was a reader, too, and we enthused over Schweitzer's, *Philosophy of Civilization*, and Dag Hammarskjöld's, *Markings*. Pixie's lone parenting status and sophistication cut her apart from other mums.

In the event of no party being on offer, we indulged poker nights that I observed from the sidelines, topping bottomless teacups and revelling in the comic atmosphere. As with chess or Cluedo, to be successful at cards required strategic thinking and logic I lacked. I was ill-equipped for games demanding a nimble mind and degree of bluff.

With Saturday's footy finished and post-match drinks priming our mood, we'd pursue the night's promise. This, Tadpole termed 'Mighty Stuff', or MS, and comprised of parties and flesh spots like the Thumpin' Tum and Sebastian's discotheques. Chances of picking up girls were compromised by our Op Shop attire. Sporting cast-off jackets, waistcoats and Cuban-heeled boots with elasticated sides, puffing MacBaren's Dark Twist or Blend 11 tobacco, we looked absurd. We heralded each other, opening our tobacco pouches to inhale a fresh 'batch', thinking our pipes and antiquated apparel granted us respect and wisdom beyond our years. After all, hadn't Dylan imitated the worn tones of his much-travelled elderly folk hero, Guthrie?

By mid-year the news of Dylan's motorbike accident cast a pall leaving questions about his health and durability. His favoured trilogy, *Bringing It All Back Home*, *Highway 61* and *Blonde on Blonde* were in my keeping. I remained a devotee of his swagger and hoped his neck injury wasn't permanently debilitating.

The pear-shaped A40, whatever its failings as a slick fiat, facilitated solo trips into the mountains beyond Warburton, Healesville, Cockatoo—places familiar from our Sunday outings. An hour or two from home I'd pick a spot to explore. Birdcalls certainly featured, but the undisturbed immersion in the rich ferment of scents and rustling leaves was what I sought. Closest to home was Doongalla Forest in The Basin, once the site of a magnificent 1880s Swiss chalet whose destruction by fire in the 1930s dad recalled. It was near the Adventist Camp Ian and I had trudged to as kids and a ten-minute drive from home, making it a frequently accessed place to park and read. Mt Slide presented another venue. I could spend hours in these places, far from human affairs.

One warm afternoon, 15 minutes north of Gembrook on the Launching Place road, I crossed an unprepossessing trickle of water signposted, McCrae's Creek. The sign halted me as much as the need to pee. The creek was barely discernible amidst reeds. But while spraying a patch of fern, I heard water thundering somewhere west of the dirt road and went to investigate. Fifty metres down a gentle slope was a massive granite boulder which, years later, I discovered was Ship Rock from which the falls, 50 metres further on down a steeper incline, took their name. Shaggy-barked grey gums, blackwood and tree ferns jostled for space in this precipitous gully that had likely spared them from loggers and the ravages of bushfires. Mosses and lichens had colonised the lower trunks. This became my new special place. I'd revisit to lie alone and be pummelled by the torrent before retreating to dry off on the flanking boulders. An epidermis of variegated emerald and jade lichens clung to them, their puckered flakes resembling in plant form the crystals of their hosts.

The icy refreshment was a lure. But it was the unique morphology of those grey rocks that struck accord. Largely ignorant of geology, I felt befriended by their size and scale. I'd been similarly impressed by such monoliths at Wilson's Promontory; Tidal River, Pillar Point and, of course, the Oberon mountains I'd celebrated in pastel. The meeting of water and rock invariably issued an agreeable frisson. But seas were endless and left me encrusted in salt. They lacked the claims of intimacy that Ship Rock Falls held over me. These were purifying.

***

Our government's commitment to follow America's invasion of Vietnam triggered reappraisal of World War I trench warfare. Bravery, stoicism, sacrifice, mateship; the mantras were trotted out. My buddies were enrolled in liberal arts courses at Monash, the university named after Australia's heroic World War I military commander. Ironically, the most vehement anti-war protests were staged there led by communist activist, Albert Langer, who featured regularly in the media. Caulfield was just fifteen minutes down the road. Some lunch breaks I drove across to catch up with Tadpole and the crew and sniff Monash's radical air.

The morality and legality of invading the small Vietnamese nation was deeply divisive. But our coterie of poet-philosophers must have counted amongst the least likely military combatants on any campus. The depraved shadow of war spoke through our 'neo-digger' humour. Half-formed men, we were by name and costume, unwittingly echoing our grandparent's generation.

Our clothing came from the Op Shop next to the Fire Brigade, and Saturdays, Tadpole and I trotted down, pre-match, to check the stock. His flare exceeded our Digger code and Pixie's tolerance. The showman lurked within. He prized a fox stole that he flaunted on select occasions. Such sharp snouted glass-eyed grotesqueries, crouching on the shoulders of visiting 'aunts', alarmed me as a child, but had since fallen from fashion. Taddy joked he was extending the life of this mouldering pelt. A woman's royal blue frockcoat was also a must buy, an item befitting a Gainsborough portrait. Never mind it was tailored for a frame far smaller than Tadpole's 190 centimetres. He squeezed into it and we headed to Number One. Pixie saw us dawdling up the front path and was incensed. She charged at him screaming, 'Shane! You didn't wear that through the streets on a busy Saturday morning? Tell me you didn't,' as she wrenched it from his shoulders. Though I'd never dare such extravagance, I joined Tadpole's gaping silence before Pixie's rare rage as Shandy, their Airedale hound, nuzzled the remnants at his feet.

Pixie sold half her acreage to make way for the Boronia Telephone Exchange. Its imposing crude brick edifice split their magnificent sloping garden in half. The subterranean vault to house cables lay vacant for several months while interior fittings were finished. Tadpole and I would lower ourselves into this echo chamber and imitate Sam Cooke's, *Change Is Gonna Come* and The Righteous Brothers', *Unchained Melody*. The changes Cooke intimated were far from our doors. Our plaintive tones may well have been dedicated to our street. The Exchange signalled the end of its rural condition, further disrupted by Hoag and Bosch's Real Estate Agency and a Dance Studio, eclipsing the street's post-and-rail entrance and dad's signage. Suburbia was upon us.

Dave Morgan, having dropped studies at Monash, then Art at Caulfield, went to work at the National Museum of Victoria in Swanston Street. He re-vamped the Indigenous displays and showed me the upstairs' studio where taxidermist Mike Trainer, and diorama artist George Browning, created their *trompe l'oeil* illusions of bird and animal habitats. The diorama's arced worlds had entranced me since childhood and were still my favourite section of the museum. The seamless transitions from animal tableaux to painted backdrops challenged my eye, hermetic museums within the museum, and in some ways, prototypes of late twentieth-century installation art.

He took me beneath the building to look through archives. The stock below ground far exceeded the public displays as I trailed Dave along dim tunnels crammed with tigers, bears, shields and whatnot. In his workroom he opened draws of Baldwin Spencer's astonishing glass photographic plates. Spencer had accompanied the Horn Expedition into the Arrernte country of Central Australia in the 1890s. Groups of proud muscular men, wielding weapons, glared at the photographer. Women holding babes and surrounded by kids, squatted before humpies. Stacked on shelves were string bags, coolamons, spears and woomeras, that in all probability were those recorded in the photos. Their immediacy caused me to tremble. Like people in any photograph they were ghosts from another era. But the power of those presences thrust itself into my space and remained through the years.

Having blown a third head gasket, the Austin was towed to the wreckers. Dannie sourced a 1948 Rover P3 75. It was a superb replacement sharing my vintage. 'The poor man's Rolls Royce,' quipped college mate, John Anderson. Leather upholstery, walnut-veneered detailing, a sliding tray of dedicated Rover tools beneath the glove box, semi-automatic free-wheel, a trapdoor in the rear floor to jack the car without leaving the cab—these and other features were a far cry from anything we'd encountered in the automobile world. It would be my lone love affair with the wheeled world, the only one I've ever bothered to polish. No subsequent vehicle would elicit pride and quicken my heart when its kind appeared on roads or English movies.

Rover P3. 75, 1968.

The lads competed for the bucket seats of this gangster-style Black Mariah, though if Kerry was on deck, she had unarguable privilege as the lone female and essential group member: the 'snake-ess'. After dark the roof was retracted, so roof-bound passenger's legs dangled on my shoulders. Another might squat in the trunk to and from parties. We vetoed the practice after losing 'Tassie' as we slowed over a bridge in the small hours one pitch-black night on car-less Colchester Road. We feared him dead or injured, but backtracking discovered he'd voluntarily alighted. The car's pre-war feel complemented our Image as Neo-Diggers. Its sluggish engine and gearbox barely enabled it to overtake trams which, in pre-seatbelt days, likely saved many a disaster. What a far cry were its soft-edged panels from the gas-guzzling Yank tanks, those menacing road-missiles declaring post-war supremacy, and heightening the *Twilight Zone's* surrealism.

I let my hair grow despite dad's snide comments. Aping Dylan's unruly mop, Cuban-heeled boots, work shirt, anything approaching the star's image sufficed. To keep the peace, I took up the offer of mum's new German stylist, waspish Jan Wagner. Wagner, apprised of the situation, cut to satisfy both parties, chain-smoking as he raved about art, politics, and women's issues. Stylishly long Kent cigarettes smouldered simultaneously in trays as he moved between clients. He'd stoop to pet his poodle and gush his 'darhling' this and that over their confessions. It was a vast gulf between his mercurial sensitivity and the conservatives plying short back-and-sides west of the rail crossing. Declaring vanity, our unruly long hair crept over collars as it hadn't in a hundred years. We deemed this the age of the ugly man and were compliant candidates.

The Art course demanded space away from the house and my eighteen months at Toots' ceased when she was found curled and cold in her chenille dressing gown on the kitchen floor. Dad cordoned off a narrow section of the garage to accommodate me; grubs in respective cocoons, the hulk of the Wolseley slumbering a metre from my bedded shoulders, separated only by sheets of Masonite. It was literally a bedroom with uninsulated walls, freezing in winter and a sauna in hotter months. The walls were soon papered with photos cut from popular magazines and book reviews that nabbed my attention. Written assignments were researched in the State Library and concluded sitting in bed. As painting on stretched canvases demanded a space-hungry easel, I scrounged off-cuts from the wall, primed and propped them against the bedhead to make landscapes composed of entrails and cellular life.

At least with a car I wasn't jostling paintings and a heavy bag of painting gear amongst peak-hour train commuters. Any discomfort seemed small sacrifice to retain independence and court the company of mates at will. I suspect mum and dad worried though they never questioned my night hawking. Dad's sole rebuff was to start the lawnmower next to my louvred window way too early Sunday mornings. Even after big nights on the tiles I resisted giving him the satisfaction of complaining. Behind his back we retitled him, Thor The

Thunder God, acknowledging his Norse blood and middle name Thorwald. The Wolseley became The Chariot and Dannie, who'd earned dad's wrath more than once, delighted in deriding the activities of the man and his machine. Dad banned Dannie from the house after he backed into and smashed mum's prized Japanese weeping maple, a gift dad had presented her when establishing the front garden. Dannie continued to sneak after supper to Ian's shack to chat over a pipe. But his censure confirmed our house as a no-go zone for our crew.

Marilyn left school to work in the photographic department at Channel 9 and Colin quit high school soon after, taking on a sales job at Jack Ewison's sports shop, while promising to conclude studies at night school. He wasn't enamoured of school and teachers returned the compliment with occasional suspension. He was confident, quick-witted, and had better truck with the consensual world than his shy siblings.

Mum never alluded to the feral reek that must have affronted her nostrils when stripping my sheets for their weekly wash. Imagined sex was private business. In the swaying train crowded with commuters, I was helpless to conceal the swelling in my pants whenever mini-skirts retreated over glistening hose. Maybe it wasn't a joke that men were given insufficient blood to serve brain and penis simultaneously. I'd hurry up the ramp of Flinders Street Station, passing the **Do Not Spit** tile marking tubercular times, hoping the changed rhythm would set my little fellow at rest. It was a mark of our fraternity's intimacy that we started comparing fantasies and competitively ranking the number of nocturnal emissions, goaded by 'Jack' Adam's quip that masturbation was the thinking man's TV. And when Tadpole trialled several weeks of abstinence Loupas and I tempted him back to the fold with our centrefold collections, my cherished Kim Novak among them.

Each day I took the train to college, I saw this stocky gentleman suited in crumpled grey standing in Swanston Street bent over an exercise book, rapt in some writing project from which he rarely raised his head. Though curious, timidity had prevented me from approaching him for more than two years. He had shoulder-length wavy white hair, tanned skin from outdoor living and a fulsome buff-coloured beard. His demeanour, broad forehead and high cheekbones conjured Latvian fellow student, Imants Niedra.

If fronting Darrell Lea's Chocolate store on my way to college, on my return to the station he might have sought protection from winter's westerlies in the mouth of barrel-vaulted Cathedral Arcade. His seasonal concession was to add a tattered tweed overcoat to the suit. He needed the crowd. It was a performance. Though I never saw him talk with anyone, he joined the city's mass exodus after 5 o'clock. Was he mute? Nearing the conclusion of the course I was emboldened to ask him what he was writing.

At close quarters his eyes were pale winter blue with pinprick pupils. In thickly accented English, he told me Christ walked inside him, and he was writing down what he dictated in Aramaic. He'd written to the Pope seeking counsel regarding these scripts. At the rate he wrote, none of it decipherable to me, I envisaged daunting volumes confronting Vatican staff. He added he'd been attacked a few years before near his Prahran flat and had both palms pierced, 'Just like Our Lord'. He prayed, and overnight the wounds healed. Sensing my incredulity, he tucked his notes under an arm to show me the scars. Then he told me his wife had passed on after a 'grave illness'. In empathising with her pain over the years, he'd consumed her medication, thereby unwittingly hastening her death. These facts he gave without sentiment or regret. Finally, he invited me to his flat but I'd delved sufficiently into his domain, and hurried to the station.

***

Painting's pre-eminence in the visual arts was challenged by the moving image just as photography had done in the nineteenth century. Surrealist painted dreams looked quaint beside the cinema's representations of the subconscious ensuing from Dali and Bunuel. All of Tarkovsky's *Mirror* resembled stream of consciousness. Realist painting, under siege since photography, took another hit. Pop Art and Abstraction rose to prominence, but general opinion insisted painting was on the skids.

Having tasted European cinema, I hungered for offerings from Pasolini, Antonioni, Bertolucci, Bunuel, Bresson, Kurosawa, and Nemec, against which American and English film seemed juvenile. Pasolini's raw edge particularly won me and I devoured everything he did, most memorably the urgency and anxiety evoked in *Medea* and *Gospel According to Matthew*. We shared atheism and fascination with Christian art, evident in his hilarious spoof, *La Ricotta*. Two or three times a week, I watched films in Carlton's 'flea box' in Faraday Street, or Melbourne University's Union Building.

Diamonds of the Night by Czech director Jan Nemec unnerved me. Nemec follows the vicissitudes of two Jewish teenagers who escape from a Nazi deportation train and attempt to survive. The opening images show them sprinting desperately through a field fleeing a pack of invisible pursuers whose gunshots echo in the near distance. It's as if the film has been playing for an hour already and we are snapping back into focus as the jittery hand-held camera provokes dreams and visions of their semi-feverish state. For the first time I was convinced of cinema's capacity to replicate consciousness. On one hand the film seemed to be playing out inside their heads; on the other, the present dangers were poignantly real. The near total absence of dialogue accentuates the sound of their footsteps and heavy breathing. We trek with them through the forest, have run-ins with local farmers, encounters with childhood sweethearts, discover a swarm of ants crawling on an eye socket and hand—some events present, some past, some real, some imagined. A housewife betrays them when one youth steals a loaf of bread. They're captured by a coterie of Home Guards and sentenced to a firing squad.

These old degenerates burst into a song-and-dance routine in the presence of the emaciated teenagers, collapsing the boundary between their inner and outer lives. They enact a mock execution. The film concludes, more or less, where it began, only now the forest has been transformed from a site of literal, life-or-death struggle to a kind of shadowy mental theatre. Most troubling is the banality of evil brewing in those wizened faces, veterans presumably of the Great War, mindlessly rekindling violence.

The Prague Spring? For me this meant the flourishing of Czech cinema such as Nemec's. Kafka, I was just getting into. Decades would pass before encountering the literature of Kundera, Kovaly and Havel. I knew nothing of Czechoslovakia's oppressive post-war communist regime, the Soviet tanks that suppressed their Dubcek-led retaliation, or the tenuous relationship between Slovaks and Czechs. I walked from the movie house devastated by the boy's mental torture. I was their age. I, too, might lose my freedom and perhaps my life, if summoned to National Service.

After this, I suffered murderous dreams. Like the Czech youths, I ran from assailants, hiding behind trees, ducking them and their bullets. In some dreams I enacted revenge, turning the tables when I was armed. I shot a passing stranger without compunction. I lived two years undetected until caught passing counterfeit money at the local grocery. Some confusion with my identification allowed me to be discharged. In the dream I confessed these crimes to Kerry, but she didn't believe me. In other dreams I stuffed old men and children down street gutters, or drove them to ocean beaches, locked the doors and waited on the incoming tide to finish them. I'd wake shivering with paranoia. What was this violent tit for tat? In Asian paddy fields and jungles 6,500 kilometres north of my bed, others were doing the real killing.

With our government's troop commitment to America's war with North Vietnam, males of 21 years were conscripted by lottery. Approaching our twentieth birthdays, Ian and I were galvanised to the TV when the wheel spun. About the war, dad spoke not a word of encouragement or discouragement. He reckoned that whenever America's economy stagnated its munitions industry ratcheted up. If it wasn't at war itself, it supplied armaments to whoever would pay, in some instances to both conflicting sides.

Neither Ian nor I were summoned to service though dread drew me to Sunday's stuttering black and white footage of Great War atrocities on the ABC. If this was to inspire patriotism, it failed. The devastating imagery had me considering conscientious objection. Remote Turkey, France, Germany, remote Vietnam—what sense could I make of these? Apart from Test Cricket where the English were enemies, I had little sense of patriotism. Those far-flung theatres of war were too abstract, and their industrial might too awesome. I'd yet to kill a rabbit for the table. Killing a 'faceless' man was preposterous.

Earlier that year we'd changed from pounds, shillings and pence to dollars and cents, which felt like a concession to the American way. Mid-October, Prime Minister Holt invited American counterpart Lyndon Bird Johnson, to Australia. It was a ploy to bump up military alliance with America. *All the way with LBJ* was anathema to many students, and Johnson's limousine received a pelting with paint and toilet paper when his cavalcade broached Melbourne's main drag. I observed these anti-war demonstrations on TV, unsure of what the scourge of communism signified or why America invaded Vietnam. As the death toll mounted so did anti-war resentment and anger.

***

It wasn't all doom and gloom. Far from it. *The Mavis Bramston Show* breathed local humour into our home and was a welcome relief from the likes of *Steptoe and Son* and *Til Death Do Us Part*. But it was satirists, Peter Cooke and Dudley Moore's, *Not Only… But Also* that inspired Tadpole and me to conduct mock interviews between each other. We emulated *Poets Cornered* and its Vat of Foam for failed rhymes, imitating Cooke's upper-crust idiot, Streeb Greebling. Having refined our lunacy, we'd front unsuspecting peak-hour commuters on their way home from Boronia station. And as was our practice, bunch a fist to simulate a microphone and request comments on the day's events.

When Tadpole quit his Economics course at Monash and I'd completed the requisite number of Friday teaching rounds, we chose suburbs on unfamiliar train lines and searched out a pub, hoping to engage gossip, perform our Pete and Dud routines or converse entirely in Dylan lyrics.

***

With expensive art materials and cars to service, the need to fill our coffers was ever more pressing. Over Christmas, John Anderson and I launched into sledgehammering re-enforced concrete kiln trolleys at Scoresby Brickworks. John and I gravitated to each other during the year, sensing parallel intents in art. He was the most gifted student whose easel we gathered around during breaks in life drawing to admire and be inspired by rather than the inept guidance imparted by the various lecturers.

We kiln-demolishing novices were sent into the 40-degree sun to hack the trolleys that, when cleaned and re-stacked, were rolled through the ovens. They were reinforced with steel girders. On such days we wondered at the need for ovens. Graduates of this labour, employed elsewhere under shade, offered superior approaches during 'smoko'. Sun-blasted, blistered and fatigued, we blew our first pay at nearby Vass's pub, and opted to pack overnight freight trucks at Reg Ansett's Footscray depot. I joined Tadpole, Jack and the Tassie Devil picking daffodil bulbs in Chandler's Colchester Road fields; and later, 'Abo Dog' and his younger brother, 'Pup' in the Dandenong Ranges on the strawberry slopes of Silvan.

***

Not until second year did I meet lecturers that left indelible impressions. Dutchman, Bill Pepperkamp arrived at College, in suit and tie with Gladstone bag at his side, approaching Drawing with business-like ethic. He conveyed the intensity required to interrogate the model and drive at its essence. Relieving students of their charcoal to demonstrate, his eyes drilled the model and crisp gestures emerged on the newsprint. It seemed as if he had X-ray vision. The model's warmth related to us in a way still-life subjects didn't. Pepperkamp resisted shapely contours, prioritised structure and cut to essentials.

Initially, I'd rhapsodised line work, using the curvaceous model as an excuse. Mastering this abstracting applied to all subjects. By squinting and reducing the light striking my retina, forms became patterns of light and dark. Pepperkamp taught how weight was distributed, where the head was positioned above butt or foot, and where to fix the centre of the image on the paper; encourage the eye around the model, feel its third dimension. He sensitised us to the qualities of charcoal and graphite.

I'd not thought of stance before, to maintain balance and keep as much of our bodies open to the model to access data. No Drawing lecturers had committed more than a few months. They seemed to regard us Education Department bods with disdain, despite surpassing in number our Diploma coevals. That we weren't regarded as art careerists perhaps caused bias. Pepperkamp bore none of that. He was a stayer and made every minute meaningful.

Warwick Armstrong, 1988.

The second, Shakespeare authority Warwick Armstrong, lectured Painting and Art history. Warwick was as far removed from the archetypal Aussie as I'd encountered, and his sensibility immediately grabbed me. For decades he'd been a stage designer in London theatres. No other lecturer made such sense of Europe's visual history. His erudition and belief in art emitted breadth and understanding I'd found only in books. Unlike Senini or Graham Hopwood at Teachers' College, Armstrong seemed to have integrated art into his belief system. His lectures privileged the humanist lineage from Michelangelo, Velasquez, Rembrandt, through Goya and Manet to Modernism.

As an exhibiting painter, his work acknowledged Klee, Picasso and Francis Bacon; a curious mix of moderns encompassing the linear approach at one end and the painterly at the other. In the linear tradition he cited Paul Klee, whose work he emulated in a series of delicate pastels, *Flying Machines*, alluding to Mozart's *Cosi Fan Tutti*. He regarded Bacon's stark and violent canvasses as the greatest contemporary examples of the painterly tradition. He explored this tradition in themes devoted in turn to emblematic *Chairs*, the *Titanic*, and lastly, *Adam and Eve*, for which I modelled the First Man in his Mt Macedon studio. Warwick was insistent about purity of gesture, and laid emphasis in the hope of one's first stroke being the final one to transmit emotion. Several times he cited, with a smirk, the case of a child who, when asked how he drew replied, 'I draw a line around my think'.

He noticed Aldous Huxley's pacifist essays, *End and Means* in my grip, and lent me transcripts of Krishnamurti's Australian lectures he'd attended in the 1930s. The guru insisted on separation between the observer and the observed. How this was to be achieved eluded me. Platitudes about living without fear to enable love or living without comparison were well and good, though remained aspirational for me. Lust and bloodlust, attraction and repulsion, love and hate, war and sex; the polarities seemed inextricably bound. Philosophically, Warwick was indebted to Heidegger, reckoning the German made sense of life without resorting to the notion of god. He lavished interest in our work, the significance of our mark-making, flattering efforts where warranted. Projects no longer seemed like dull exercises.

During lectures, his entire being exuded an enthralling theatricality. It was a romantic approach that, as with his Van Gogh lecture replete with a slide of Vincent and Theo's headstones orchestrated with Don McLean's pop hit, elicited student sobs. Though indebted to Graetz's *Symbolic Language*, Warwick made it something of his own. He dwelt on Graetz's definition of the ancient tradition of the symbol. Two men break a bone and share the halves, vowing that should their descendants chance upon each other, by producing their piece of the bone, they could be identified and reunited. Graetz insisted on reading the paired objects in Vincent's paintings as a dialogue between Theo or Gauguin, and himself.

No artist was presented simply on the basis of some technique or personal problems. Of greater significance was how particular sensibilities deepened and expanded our cultural vision. In the darkened lecture theatre, Warwick's cultivated tones rose and fell with dramatic flourish, as if on stage, which in a sense he was. He made sweeping gestures, his tenor voice stretching for emphasis, his spectacles periodically flickering when caught in the projector's beam. He lived what he meant and meant what he said.

He placed before us the central argument of Twentieth-century painting between abstraction and figuration. On the one hand, the shortcomings of mimetic realism had been exposed by photography. On the other, the weakness of so much abstraction tended towards mere coloured surfaces and geometry. Referring to an image of Cezanne's interlocked hands, he suggested narrative content should be at one with the chosen materials, technique, and style.

I thought of how Caravaggio's embrace of darkness sheltered his impoverished subjects. And how Dylan's voice was at one with what he sang, nimbly skipping from lazy indifference, to relaxed pleasure, to painful separation, taunting and raging: 'a flute that tutes and a bee that stings'. It's strangely beautiful the way disappointment in the human condition inversely increases a love of humankind; that love can be born through the nature of suffering. When Warwick drew attention to personal crises, as he did with Rembrandt and Goya's late work, he clarified this connection with pain. In their cases, Warwick gave us to understand that personal hardships simultaneously limited and crystallised vision and technique. Something in us recognises our sufferings' increase awareness, that insights hurt but make us more sensitive. The tone of his voice made us feel he'd suffered with them.

The National Gallery shifted from the State Library and Museum to St Kilda Road. Water cascading down its large front window earned its derogative 'fish shop' title. It was inaugurated with a major exhibition entitled *The Field*, a bold gesture confronting Melbourne's figurative tradition with exercises in abstraction. I understood the emphasis placed on the materiality of paint and the affirmation of the picture-plane's flatness, though few works engaged me. I needed stories and was no more interested in white on white canvases than the blank screen before movies. Finer minds than mine could rhapsodise the subtleties of purely white or black paintings.

While lecturing on twentieth abstraction, Warwick suggested Mondrian's grids echoed Vermeer's organisation; how Pollock's vegetable tangles resembled bacilli colonies, that Rothko's mauve and purplish rectangles, which he regarded as enhanced wallpaper, absorbed their subject. Nevertheless in citing Rothko, he avoided the artist's claims for the spirituality of his art as postulated in Kandinsky's, *Concerning the Spiritual in Art*. My Dover edition helped unlock symbolic colour theory as well as imputing links between sounds, shapes and emotions—echoing Baudelaire, Rimbaud and Blanc's ideas. The Russian eased his way into non-figuration via bright landscapes, retaining links with the recognisable world. Subsequent geometric abstraction had no more appeal than the Bauhaus exercises we replicated in Newbury's Design class. In the same bookshop as I'd found the Kandinsky, was Whitman's *Leaves of Grass*, whose celebration of the senses had more appeal than notions of synaesthesia.

Warwick presented four basic compositional modes that could be described as curvilinear, all-over, symmetrical, and asymmetrical. Baroque artists favoured the curvilinear to express abundant vitality. He cited the regular pulse operating through Persian carpets as 'all-over'. Most portraiture was symmetrical, and Tintoretto's plunging diagonals exemplified the asymmetrical. Much art combined modes. Bacon slapped his dominant images symmetrically, yet they writhed in curvilinear discomfort. Bonnard's paintings satisfied the all-over and asymmetrical.

John and I were among the handful accepting invitations to join him at his home, *Solly*, on Mount Macedon. It had been the gatekeeper's house for Alton, a 1870s retreat modelled on Indian colonialist, hill stations. George Nicholas of Aspro fame owned it. Warwick walked us around its gardens whose rare exotics, he said, were planted by von Mueller, designer of Melbourne's Botanical Gardens. Drink, fine food and talk ensued around the dinner table, coupled with long walks on the mist-enshrouded mountain. Whatever the allusion to Greece the mountain's name incited, Warwick re-enchanted it by spinning local lore and grafting Bartok's *Bluebeard* opera onto a nearby artificial pond as *The Lake of Tears*. Later, he'd dim the house lights and Jerome Hine's bass and mezzo-soprano Rosalind Elias, would storm through the speakers. The weekends were an introduction to privileged society that, together with his invitations to Exhibition Openings, gave us a sense of belonging.

In a confidential aside, he reckoned art was about love. Love chooses its subject. Greatest of its manifestations is care. He slowly moistened his lips with the tip of his tongue before qualifying his claim. 'Love consists of caring for one's materials, in what one chose to paint, pre-eminently, touch. An artist is not so much interested in things as in their relationship to each other. It's the space between objects that concerns the artist. The greater the work, the more complex is the system of relationships. The artist abandons the stream of life to reconstruct and organise systems of relationship.'

Our respect for Warwick encouraged us to entertain art careers. Entertained for sure, but I was no more confident about being an artist, than I was a teacher.

✳✳✳

The sculpture department boasted two young men who helped establish and shape the Mildura Sculpture Triennials. Elwyn Dennis was freshly graduated from the University of California. John Davis, a willowy graduate of the course we were undertaking, was fascinated by Indigenous modes of expression. His work matured into environmental landscape works made onsite, fragile wrapped twigs and logs subjected to weathering. Towards the end of our course he organised an excursion to the Triennial, my first flight. Despite Davis's enthusiastic guidance, the sculpture show had less impact on us than the excursion to Lake Mungo, our winery visit, a riverboat trip, and our various amours. But his allusions to Indigenous artefacts and archaeology expressed emerging concerns for land, culture and what was starting to be identified as Environmentalism.

***

The last of my Fine Arts essays on William Blake returned me to the State Library's archives. How wonderful were these public institutions conceived during the cash-rich Gold Rush, which also included the Royal Melbourne Zoo and the Botanical Gardens. Housed in the Library was the Museum and Art Gallery in whose gloomy corridors I communed with el Greco's *Portrait of a Cardinal, 1605*. I knew nothing about its provenance and little about the artist who'd worked much of his adulthood in Toledo, Spain. Before research sessions I'd regularly detour to pause and pay homage to the Cardinal. His pale, lugubrious gaze spoke from its small frame with a dignity absent from more ostentatious neighbours.

***

Another Kennedy was assassinated. Martin Luther King, too. Demands for Black American Civil Rights tipped past crisis point. Fires and looting scarred American cities. Though our student campuses were disrupted by demonstrations, nothing approximated Chicago's violence. On Australia's door, the referendum agreeing to recognise our First Peoples in the national census had just been passed without bloodshed. Whatever racist attitudes persisted, murdering protesters advocating Indigenous rights, was inconceivable to us.

The Mexico Olympics dominated October's news in unprecedented ways. There were threats by African Americans to boycott the Games. In the build-up, Mexican students also demonstrated against inequality and racism but no word was broadcast of the 2000 killed during the protests.

American Bob Beamon's stratospheric long jump grabbed my attention, while Dick Fosbury's triumph with his 'Flop' high jump technique excited Ian. Both events took a back seat when, standing on the podium after the 200-metres run, Tommie Smith and John Carlos thrust their black-gloved fists into the air, symbolising Black Power and Black Union. Australian silver medallist, Peter Norman sympathised with their courageous stand for human rights. Heads bowed in memory of the many violent and unjust African-American deaths, their defiant gestures were witnessed by a world audience. The simmering continued.

***

The distinctive scent of eucalyptus smoke was in the air as I neared home during the last week of the Christmas holidays. Against a panoramic blue sky, a great auburn and purple cloud billowed over One Tree Hill. I accelerated the final kilometres and picked up Tadpole from Number One. We queued at the Brigade where Laurie McGuire was directing traffic. We were given water backpacks and told to join fighters on the Old Olinda Road. The fires were raging right across the Ranges. On and on we worked up, the gullies surrounding the Adventist Camp. In the small hours of the following day we headed back to the station, passed in our gear and flopped exhausted on our beds. There would be other fire events on these hills for sure. But I wouldn't be there to share the fight.

It was time to quit the nest and commence my career in an alien environment. I'd been placed in the extreme northwest corner of the state not far from Mildura. All I knew about Ouyen was its notorious reputation as the state's premier summer hot spot on weather maps. Not wishing to be separated from friends, the most remote destination I'd gallantly nominated was Bacchus Marsh, half an hour from the city. No assurance was given about granting preferences, as vacancies needed filling wherever they presented. Was this exile punishment for my rebellious attitude to the Education Psychology and Theory lecturers?

In a second-hand Swanston Street bookshop, I'd chanced on A.S Neill's reflections of the Summerhill School he pioneered in Suffolk during the 1920s. It countered the teacher-centred, hidden curriculum being endorsed by our training. In my essays, I championed Neill's 'freedom rather than coercion' philosophy and was slapped with a lowly 10 percent. I shouldn't have been surprised, but in my eagerness to elucidate an alternative, I was barking at the wrong masters.

I showed my essay to Royden who'd proceeded to teach at University High and Melbourne High, where I'd spent the third term teaching round. He'd recently run an experimental course at the school's Tecoma bush camp in Sherbrooke Forest. He loved the essay and duplicated it to share with friends. At Sherbrooke, his Year 10 groups had a week immersed in contemporary politics, where their sense of entitlement was challenged. Marshall McLuhan's ideas on media were aired. History shrank to the beat of Baba Ram Dass's *'Be Here Now'* dictum and the school's arch-conservatism was all but abandoned.

Each student had copies of the daily papers, access to *Time* and *Newsweek* magazines, and issues of radical Left magazine, *Ramparts*. Guest writers from *The Nation Review*, including cartoonist, Michael Leunig, attended. Leunig's laconic imagery spoke to and for the little man: tender washes and fragile lines footnoted with koan-like commentary. A cast of humble folk with tippler's snouts inhabited sparse rooms and topographies beneath a sickle moon.

Royden sourced films from Melbourne's International Film Festival. Swami Vedenanda and filmmakers Arthur and Corinne Cantrill gave talks, as did political columnist and editor of *The Australian*, Adrian Deamer. Parisian student protests for education reform were prominent in the media at this time, inspiring Royden to make slide transparencies of students posing in coat lockers that evoked the harrowing photos of Communard victims in their coffins during the 1871 revolt. These were projected into dry-ice smoke, wafting over the forest canopy to the amplified sounds of Pink Floyd's, *Careful With That Axe, Eugene*. It was intoxicating stuff.

However, such intoxication was unlikely in remote and arid Ouyen. Family, girlfriend, mates, the momentum of weekends—all my intimate relations would be distanced. The damp fern gullies, crouched beneath the Mountain Ash with their fund of lyrebird, kookaburra and magpie songsters, would be mere memories.

And what was it I could teach? My paucity of experience and knowledge seemed unworthy of transmission to people only a few years my junior. My uncertainties were legion. I was confident with football, paints and pen, but little else. I was a good listener but not a talker; a witness rather than a judge. My opinions remained in utero. My knowledge of people and the world was scant: in short, this child was now entrusted to act as an adult in the adult world.

6

Across the Great Divide

Fragments of After-earth, Rod Moss, 1977.

The Rover was in dry dock. Its side valves needed replacing and no mechanic in Boronia would take it on. It was a February Friday 1969, and two mates offered me a lift north to Ouyen. We headed over the Great Divide. Beyond Bendigo, the country flattened with occasional small lightly wooded hills. The highway had few bends. A wisp of smoke sprouted from the old eucalyptus distillery on the northern edge of Inglewood and there was a taste of the low forest feeding the enterprise. Then sheep. Then wheat. After the shorn hills, their scabs of granite protesting the heat, the land opened, visible for miles. Sheep flocks huddled beneath the occasional tree in bare paddocks.

Our first stop was 245 kilometres up the track at the Charlton pub, right on 10 o'clock opening. Two stocky men were propped at the bar, sipping schooners. They were from the quarry south of town where work ceased when grader cabins topped 40 degrees. This had happened an hour before. I was shocked to discover they were only 19. The Mallee could radically accelerate ageing.

The Tassie Devil's venerable Plymouth scored its two hundred thousandth mile on the leg north of Wycheproof. The *Bluebird of Happiness* may have whistled a celebratory tune had he not cut the engine, rewarding his trusty ally by gliding through the milestone in silence as the western sky degraded into purple greys. Forked lightning jabbed six fingers across the horizon into the endless plains of wheat. Rain burst upon us. Great gobs obliterated vision. The car stuttered over the hot tar through rising steam. At Sealake, we were forced to a garage and placed a protective plate between the engine and fuel line to hinder evaporation. The town's male population assembled in the street outside the pub, silently grinning over frothy beers. It was the first substantial rain in three years.

Having driven into the dark hours, we pulled over out of town. I woke in the back seat of the car. Jack and The Devil dozed up front. There was the sun blooding itself at the end of the Mallee highway towards Manangatang. Flatness announced itself in each direction. Wheat shoots at 6 a.m. already looked defeated. The lads had come for the adventure and to deposit me so I could fulfil my pact with the Department.

Oke Street as Uncle Hughie saw it, 1919.

Oke Street, 2014.

Great Uncle came here soon after World War I to inspect the soldier settlement block he'd been assigned at Walpeup, 30 kilometres west of the Ouyen railhead. He overnighted at the ten-year old Victoria Hotel and visited the real estate purveyor next morning. Can I inspect my lot, he queried. Just step back on the street, was the reply. In an hour you'll see it blow past the door. That was enough for uncle to catch the next train back to

Melbourne. The great red dust storms assailing Melbourne over the decades would continue to issue from this marginal country.

We roused ourselves, breakfasted on pies from a roadhouse and headed the extra hour north to explore the river town, Mildura. The lads intended leaving me after we'd returned that evening to the hotel. We skirted the tree-lined town. The only familiar locations from last year's excursion were The Wintersun Hotel, Art Museum and the riverbank on which we lounged and demolished a six-pack each. A day of drinking found us back in Ouyen bracing the Saturday cricket crowd in the bar when we entered carrying the last of our canned beers, an unintended gesture of bravado in these parts. There was a hushed pause at the bar as heads pivoted in our direction.

We were soon invited to test our strength at arm wrestling on the bar. The contests evolved into 'charging' where we three pitted ourselves against the might of the Walpeup eleven, lining up at each end of the long barroom and running full pelt, cannoning into each other's flanks like bull elks. The Tassie Devil, whose football exploits featured an unruly raised elbow, was in his element. When ushered from the hotel at closing time, we agreed to resume the contest beneath a peppercorn tree at the town's western perimeter.

Having proved our manliness, we settled into camaraderie. A Walpeup man, a Blandthorn, insisted we needed smokes. He and I headed back to The Fairy Dell Cafe, where the crowd was spilling out from the Roxy movie house. Blandthorn, who years later would shoot his estranged wife and family then himself, beckoned me to the female toilet on the dark side of the theatre. I was unaware Blandthorn intended tripping those leaving it until the first girl fell across his foot. She recomposed herself on a bench besides a scruffy pimple of a kid who blew cigarette smoke in my face. I would meet Margaret Smith and Daryl Pettit in my first class the following Monday.

My fellow Arts and Crafts teacher had three years' experience and knew this class too well. Fifteen-year-olds now, they were the bane of school, at least the boys, whose antics were orchestrated by weedy class clown 'Rocky' Manley, and Brian Lewis who was about my size. How my mentor disciplined them the previous year was not in any book I'd consulted on the course. He'd had them for woodwork and advised on how he'd handled miscreants.

Alan was large of girth, slow and deliberate of speech. On first entering the craft room he'd approached the chisel rack, took from it a 50-millimetre tool, switched on the grinding wheel and sharpened it. The lads were quiet, glued to his voiceless manoeuvres. He turned and said, 'So which one of you is Lewis?' Lewis mumbled, 'Me'. He tossed him the tool. 'Want to try me on son?' Lewis demurred and was tamed for the remainder of the year. These salutary means were confided in the staffroom during morning recess after Rocky and crew who, apprised of the cinema performance, had derailed my first lesson.

'Try the hair twist if you're worried about leaving incriminating scars,' Alan suggested with a smirk. 'Just grab a sprig of hair at the back of the scalp, twist and lift. Never known to fail. Get in early and establish who's ruling the roost.' Fortunately, I didn't need to resort to this, instead gaining their confidence by inviting them to paint a three-metre mural prominently set above the covered way to the craft room. Its theme was animated woodcraft tools floating in abstracted space. The lads were chuffed at being selected for this after-school collaboration and Lewis displayed surprising design and colour sense that he never replicated in class.

***

Here I would teach for two years and attune to the climate bleaching the continent. I would experience small town prattle where private and public life fused, and my smallest actions were scrutinised and rebounded before I realised their newsworthiness. First term I lodged in a room above the hotel bar. Strident disinfectant couldn't stifle the cigarette and beer fumes clinging to everything, creeping upstairs as I rested on my steel-frame bed wondering if the place had seen repairs since Uncle's departure. The ceiling fan wobbled noisily on its axis. Beetles battered the bare bulb. A frayed, floral maroon rug was worn thin enough to detect the floorboards. Beside the veranda exit squatted a three-ply wardrobe whose doors no longer aligned, and a chipped, laminated desk.

Weekends were focused on football. The clubs in the competition—Tempy Goya, Speed, Tiega, Patchewollock, Murrayville, Kiamal, Galah, Underbool—were unfamiliar names. Indeed, when I visited them I wondered how they managed to field teams, or have pitches to play on. Ouyen's well-grassed oval was distinct from the undulating, sporadic tufts of grass and prickles on other ovals. Most had no more than a general store and some a mere silo and rail siding; place names only.

In an era pre-dating the mega-blocks and heavy machinery, these pastures were inundated with labourers and horse teams. Jack, with historic bent, had pointed to an eight-horse team just out of Wedderburn, slowly gouging furrows in the terrible morning heat. 'Probably the last of its kind, Snake. You're witnessing history here,' he'd grinned. The 15 and 20-kilometre distances between towns reflected horse travel rather than car mobility. Ouyen wasn't even a one-horse town; the great bay-coloured Clydesdales were long gone.

I'd not anticipated students watching my every move on the field. How did they measure me against their fathers and older brothers? Footy banter rolled its course throughout classes. 'Sir, I reckon if you'd just kicked the pill to Barney in the last quarter you would've got over Murrayville.' 'Sir, d'you reckon Skeeter Kaye'll be fit for the finals? That tackle ya laid on 'im was a little bewdy.' So, went the cynical baiting and flattery. Several players were students I initially felt would compromise my teacher status. They sported facial hair declaring masculinity I couldn't match with twice weekly shaving. One was already a supporting parent.

Registration at the hotel was contingent on agreeing to play for the team the hotelier's son supported. Glen signed me in, squinting through bloodshot eyes, relating that last season the club, hearing of a likely colt, hijacked him from the train at Birchip, 120 kilometres south, to secure a signature before a rival club. I was flattered and keen to reveal my innovative ankle-cut boots with moulded soles, and mastery of the drop punt, now vogue in the city.

Glen was thirtyish and had seen action on Vietnam's killing fields, which probably explained his starting each day behind the bar with a shot of this or that. 'Hair of the dog,' he grinned nervously at old barflies seeking morning solace. After five, bar habitues reassembled on self-appointed stools with well-rehearsed spiel. I was an avid sponge for these larger than life characters: larger than mine, that is.

Though no sportsman, Glen was one of the first into the change-rooms to lavish our thighs with oil pre-match. After the game we'd reconvene at the pub, and at closing time drink by the reservoir below Tickle-Belly Hill, or any number of lanes defining the wheatfields. A stumpy eucalyptus was uprooted and burnt while men, and the occasional girlfriend, stood around 'the twig' quaffing until dawn. Glen usually arrived late with wounds stitched from mishaps that the players reckoned, behind his back, was self-harm.

I wondered what scenes of wartime carnage he re-invoked when confiding his voluntary service on ambulance call-outs to road accidents. Most recent was a collision between a car and freight train at Mittyack, half an hour south on the Calder rail crossing. There was an adrenalin rush in his recount of bagging body parts scattered over two kilometres of track. Whatever, having access to beer after the bottleshop closed, his late arrival was always welcomed. We huddled together offering our bodies as primitive rotisseries, our eyes roving between faces, flames, and the million stars above.

Sunday's recovery sessions, referred to as 'church', were held at the clubrooms, a disused shearing shed on a farm just shy of town, where we gathered around a fire in a 44-gallon drum kept alight purely from the plastic ring-tops of Vic Bitter. Our inebriated brotherhood relived the game and surmised the possibility of useful rain. Such weather reportage was exchanged in casual tones, concealing its critical significance. Their language was polished by overuse, muting anxieties vital to their existence: whether or when not to sow a crop or cut back on sheep stocks. Its shorthand suppressed something too big to define. Desperation hummed beneath their flat syllables as the drama of the two-hour game wrestled the boredom of the long week in the tractor saddle.

These male gatherings deserved their reverential status. Despite the church retaining regular devotees what other institution had such communal magnetism? What other domain rivalled its passions, or lifted folk from the tedium of their days?

***

I befriended 19-year-old farmer and team mate, Stan Sleep. To supplement incomes, we picked Mallee stumps on weekends from his father Harold's freshly ploughed paddocks west of town, in Galah. 'Can't beat a good root by the fireside in winter,' was the local refrain. I admired Stan's practical aplomb tending farm equipment or de-balling a brood of piglets, and the way he rucked on game day with unfettered transition. Stan's methodical, purposeful days contrasted with the irresponsible carnival of my work.

At night we'd often cull more than 100 rabbits, earning in a single night as much as my paltry, fortnightly teachers' salary of 98 dollars. The paddocks were riddled with the pests whose eyes pinked in the spotlight as they sat waiting the whistling .22. A bullet across the ears was best as it kept the carcass from bruising. Off the tray-back one of us jumped before the rabbit regained its senses. Stoop, snatch the back legs, and crack the neck. Unzip it down the middle with my blade, flick the innards into the furrows and peel the skin while warm. Initially, I studied these parts that seconds before maintained life. Kidneys, intestines, liver and heart—smaller versions of mine, but lacking the symmetry of *Britannica's* transparencies, whose printed inks failed to capture the pulse of these dark juices. My fingers were wet with rabbit. The ammoniac stench of rabbit shit permeated my body. If I farted, the surrounding air filled with the story of carnage.

One night I joined a 'roo hunt and witnessed a big doe fling its joey aside, hit a fence then turn and rip out the guts of the pursuing hound. The farmer bemoaned the loss of his favourite 'roo dog. The doe had ruined his fence and broken her leg, making her skull a simple target for his rifle butt. Both animals were left where they dropped; the joey's fate remained unknown. The violence deeply shocked me. So, too, did the farmer's blithe indifference to the suffering.

Some Sundays Stan and I wallowed in the shallows of small, kidney-shaped Lake Walpeup, half an hour southwest. Wading in knee-deep we fingered yabby holes, groping for purchase behind the pincers, plucking and chucking the crustaceans to the bag carrier on shore. We filled half a hessian bag to boil at home as squabbling babblers and bronze-wing pigeons hovered overhead.

We'd usually skirt the sanctuary of Hattah Lakes and camp at Fireman's Bend, on the Murray banks, above the flood-zone and clear of 'widow-makers' that dropped limbs unannounced. These river gums were remnants of extensive bands felled by settlers but spared to stem erosion. Though the sandbars were covered with foul carp carcasses, the aquatic pleasures of the Big Muddy more than compensated. Once, close to camp, a wedge tail wheeled, then dive-bombed to snatch a rabbit in its talons, a thrilling sight of sudden destruction. I'd snuggle in my swag after dusk, accompanied by the continual plopping of carp snapping at the swarming midges.

Save for the hurly-burly of footy, Mallee tempo differed radically from Melbourne. Speech was indicative and nowhere more evident than the president's post-match address. I hung on Frank Healy's lilting drawl with as little hope of untangling sense as the cockies had of winter rain. During his speeches, the earth moved on a slower axis and threw his inflections into exaggerated off-beat rhythms. Stan joked that the gist of Frank's brogue was easier with a few beers under the belt. Perhaps, but matters agreed upon when inebriated eluded me the following day.

Our team featured in grand finals in successive years, winning the premiership in my second year. Football was where I excelled and proved myself: we, local gods garbed in sacramental red and white 'Vs' blazed upon our chests. On the eve of a final between Tiega and black-and-white-vested Kiamal, some prankster sabotaged the milking cow of Kiamal's club president. All its black patches were swabbed in livid red paint. It was a squaring up for the Tribunal that suspended our champion rover earlier in the week. Their president had cast the crucial vote and though his presence on the judging panel was questionable, it made no difference to the game's result.

* * *

I turned 21 while domiciled at the pub. My parents and estranged girlfriend visited, gifting me a portable turntable on which I exhausted the vinyl of The Band's brilliant Americana albums and Dylan's *John Wesley Harding*; the lyrics through which I envisaged this community. Who was this strange crew fronting Dylan's cover in the Woodstock hills? Surely not The Band's members we'd seen at Festival hall? Shorn of choruses, Dylan's austere sound was all backwoods biblical language, and I sang the album start to finish until I had it down pat. Not much of a challenge as the songs, by comparison to earlier work, were as brief as Pop tunes.

I was riveted to a song situated in the late eighteenth century. Singing *As I Went Out One Morning*, I embraced the air on Tom Paine's turf, pamphleteer and author of *The Rights of Man*. He'd been a crucial advocate of American and French Revolutions, protesting that wars were burdens that reinforced powerful autocracies. A girl walks the field in chains. I gallantly offer my hand, but enslavement forbids her to respond in kind. We enter a compact of power and powerlessness as I insist she depart while she pleads she'll secretly accept me and fly south. I insist she has no choice, when Paine arrives to take control of the situation, addressing me with deference and claiming responsibility for her actions. I am free while she remains in chains. This theatre of desire, freedom, authority, powerlessness, subordination, and order restored, is achieved in 24 incredibly concise lines.

What South was he proposing? I wondered if Dylan was invoking Paine's relevance to Civil Rights issues and disturbances in the warm Gulf States. In my South, where Antarctic winds gusted, Kerry had relocated to a city flat and was accessing urban nightlife with increasing frequency. Just as the surreal flights of his mid-1960s anthems had nourished my transition from Boronia to the city, these discs welcomed rural existence with simpler, doomed and flawed desperados in a voice freed of the neurasthenic stoniness of those hyper-tense electric albums. The harmonica snorted and the drumming aligned with my heartbeat.

My parents sat with Kerry in the Wolseley—an oddity wedged between Ford and Holden pick-ups ringing Blackburn Park's boundary—to watch the game. Tiega won despite my inauspicious performance, still feeling my way into team strategy and my mates' idiosyncrasies. The parents booked a room at the Victoria while Kerry squeezed into my single bed. Glen was all over my parents and invited us to his room, two doors along the passage. He wished to show them his impressive gun collection.

His suite was four times the size of my room. Hardware glistened behind glass cabinets on the feature wall. Dad's fascination with the small arms drew an immediate response. Out came a Browning Hi-power handgun whose slick loading he demonstrated before passing it to dad to admire and check if his loading lesson was successful. This much weaponry housed only metres from my door by a man of suspect stability, was cause for concern.

***

Given their unavailability in Ouyen—which also explained their absence from the streets—Stan and I purchased motorbikes in Mildura. Obtaining a learner's licence was a cinch. When I stated my business, PC Bradley simply requested I ride a few metres up the road to the Fairy Dell Cafe and fetch some smokes. He was still wearing facial lacerations from the weekend's match against Walpeup—one of the Blandthorns had shirtfronted him at the opening bounce. Bradley had demanded the Blandthorns get petrol and erase the tyre 'donuts' they'd left on the Mallee Highway the previous week. Tit for tat, the ledger had been squared, as had the licence paperwork when I returned with the smokes.

We rode the hell out of our 250s up and down the Calder Highway, giving ourselves to the wind and tarmac. Thus, exposed and vulnerable, the machine's sudden bursts of speed demanded constant vigilance. Occasionally, we made it to Mildura on post-match jaunts, looking for parties Stan heard of in the pub, wary of kangaroos crossing the highway. By our 2 a.m. return, it was too cold for them. We alternated the lead to stay awake. He'd flag me kerbside to jump up and down until the blood was running in our feet and fingers. Sometimes we'd light a twig and thaw out before proceeding to the recovery session at the clubrooms.

So, I was somewhat hardened for the 300-kilometre exodus to surprise Kerry. We'd exchanged letters each week and I rang evenings from the post office. Not often though. Her distant voice and silences only primed anxiety about imagined nocturnal activities. While her voice was better than nothing, telephone intimacy couldn't give engaging glances, linked hands, or her hair's perfume. I set off for St Kilda. At Woodend, an hour north of the metropolis, I no longer felt my fingers on the handlebars and, removing gloves, called a halt. Uncoiling my spine, I entered the toilets of yet another Victoria Hotel where, fortunately, a fellow pisser warned against dousing fingers under hot water.

'Cold enough to freeze the balls off a brass monkey,' he cackled as I returned to the hubbub in the bar and thawed by the log fire. I resumed riding through Diggers Rest, Sunbury and the western burbs, hoping to surprise my lover in her flat just before midnight. But the surprise was just as much mine.

Tiptoeing the passageway and prising her door open, I found her in bed with a stranger who immediately dressed and fled without word. I eased into his bed warmth, suppressing adrenalin and humiliation and fell asleep, utterly exhausted.

Come the morning, I ducked downstairs to the corner milk bar for fruit and yoghurt, and whipped up breakfast. There was tentative banter but no word about what should have been said. It was like being captivated by a crab nibbling your toes, oblivious of a whale romping offshore. Friday's interception was a threshold moment. Sunday's return up the Calder felt twice as long. We corresponded and saw each other during school vacations but the letters lacked heat. Our five-year affair ground to December closure.

***

Teaching was not as onerous as anticipated as I acted a role based on edited highlights of Royden and Warwick, kidding myself I was a bastion of culture to untutored country minors. Yet in worldly wisdom and responsibility, I deemed many of them my superiors. I juggled the need to discipline with that of being accepted. It was mostly a matter of inspiring imaginations. How would my material relate to their farming lives? The van Eycks and van Goghs: how did these translate to the Mallee? Did I really understand the culture that produced these geniuses? I ran some of Warwick's tack on the greats past Alan who scratched his ear and dismissed both Warwick and his ideas as 'bullshit'. But students rose to my ideas, some of the more fantastic, inherited from Irvine's early years. As often as possible we'd use the immediate environment for observational drawing, both the natural and man-made ready at hand.

Of the 15 or so staff, all save three were in their first or second year of service. The turnover was rapid as most served their indentured span and returned to the city. Thus, young teachers were welcomed but remained guests who would soon depart, the bonds of intimacies withheld. One or two staff, by marrying a local, demonstrated commitment to the place and gained trust. Male staff—save the principal and his deputy—attired in shorts, long socks and ties, contrasted with the town dress code. We were a brood apart, suspect university types and, sporting prowess apart, unassimilated into Ouyen's farming community.

***

A lean, grey stranger of middle years, one J. D. Lobascher arrived in town and set up business as watchmaker and repairer of same in one of several vacant shops in Oke Street. His room was a few doors along the corridor from mine and he was always sitting in the dim corner of the dining room, studiously working through his eggs on toast, when I arrived. If his 200-centimetre height and shiny scalp didn't distinguish him, then his navy suit and tie surely did.

Uncle Hughie had recently bequeathed me his dysfunctional pocket watch. Not that I intended to wear it, being averse to men's jewellery. Anyway, the surrounding world was clothed in clocks. It was a memento; its open face and clear numerals recalled Uncle's unperturbed beaming. I tended it with the tall man's expertise. Measuring me eye-to-eye, he reassured me it'd be ready within the week. It was still unavailable after a month. Other things had cropped up. Another month elapsed. He had to see a sick friend in Mildura. He was waiting on a part from the city and wouldn't show it to me when, with rising anxiety, I requested it fixed or not.

During these weeks, JD, who kept his name locked behind initials, had opened a Tourist Agency in a shop across the street, and taken out a double-page advertisement in the town's four-page weekly. He criss-crossed the street throughout the day.

His targets were couples, honeymooners or pensioners, and he asked for the bucks up front before delivery of tickets. It said something about Ouyen's isolation and its good folk's ignorance of overseas travel matters. JD cashed in on four or five likely couples and fled overnight. Luckily, I'd retrieved my watch the day before. And it worked!

***

On July 20, Principal Joe Skeehan, with a befitting sense of occasion, stopped the school to watch Neil Armstrong on TV trudging through moon dust. That night I walked to Tickle-Belly Hill and gazed into the lustrous ebony with its staggering stellar profusion, humbled and wondering. The moon, a citrus giant, bobbed above Manangatang. How astonishing that this disc now bore man's imprint. What would flow from information gleaned from its soils? What knowledge might alleviate the suffering of we creatures beneath its uncompromising indifference? That man and camera had bridged the stupefying space between the moon and us justified our term 'astronomical'. Science fiction was now science fact.

The epic bike trip also marked the end of pub residency. I boarded with three other young men in Mitchell Street on the eastern periphery. The house owner was septuagenarian farming widow, Mrs McLean, who'd left their Mittyack property in the care of her son. I shared a small bedroom with mosquitoes and Bob, the Elders Stock Agency rep. There was Russell, a fellow teacher and Graham, a clerk at the post office. I heard her ask Bob how he wanted his breakfast cuppa and he replied, 'Black, Mac,' a name that stuck.

'Mac' never rested until the day's dishes were dried and returned to the cabinet. Then she'd remove her wiry small frame to the lounge, prop both feet on her pouf, and puff on a rollie before the glare of Bob and Dolly Dyer's quiz show, *Pick-a-Box*. She lamented the recent departure of encyclopaedic marvel Barry Jones who, she reckoned, was the cleverest bloke she'd known. Above her was the framed, yellowing photo snipped from the *Sun* of her other hero, Aboriginal bantamweight Lionel Rose, who'd wrested the world title by beating Fighting Harada the year before.

Across the road and next door in this low end of town were families whose tin-clad houses and dirt floors I'd not seen the like. Kenny Davis and his mother could be seen after school tugging a shopping jeep of discarded roadside beer bottles. On weekends they might traipse ten kilometres along the highways. Their bounty was stashed on a semi-trailer which when topped every two months was hauled away by a contractor. It was a thirsty climate! The two Eastwell lads living opposite, shared Kenny's hunted look. They hung in a tight threesome at school, ostracised by knowledge of their dirt-floor commonality and conspicuously sporting the same crinkled winter duds throughout the year.

Although my drinking was confined to post-match reveries it was becoming boring. The city's multiple distractions, not least being nightclubs and girls, made drinking less of an end in itself. Colin Tucker and his Owltones did their best for the dance crowd Saturday nights in the town hall. But Old Time and Country with a touch of Elvis, couldn't appease a man who was living Dylan and had imbibed throbbing discos.

A teammate celebrating his buck's night was stripped naked, one leg chained to the town's war memorial, the other tethered to an engine block. If PC Bradley was amused, he didn't admit it when taking bolt-cutters to the chain. Another player, sozzled on his twenty-first, was driven comatose to the cemetery, lowered into a freshly dug grave, and had a sheet of roofing iron enclose him. His mates drank through to dawn and waited in hiding to cheer the disorientated 'Skeeter' Kaye as he emerged, to be confronted and confused by the phalanx of tombstones.

I was party to such events, and when dozing amidst post-match revellers on Tickle Belly Hill one night, 'Sards' Jardine parked his car over me. I woke bewildered about the chassis inches above and there and then, decided the booze had outlived its usefulness.

***

Reading *The Brothers Karamazov* provided the key to abstinence for several months as I ventured to write. In Ivan's atheism I heard a more erudite version of dad. He elucidated the opposition between Protestantism and Catholicism, and claimed that the choice was between freedom and misery under the one, or happiness as slaves under the other. Which left no choice but atheism. Such religious divisions might have served as a template for Ouyen or Boronia. But Dostoevsky was inside the consciousness of fictional characters at depths I'd yet to extend to actual people. Yet I persisted weaving a tale about the town based on personalities from the pub and footy club.

Part-Aboriginal Bimbo who slept atop the hotel's wood-box or under his 'mother peppercorn tree', had cornered me with a rambling discourse on the discovery and the benefits of 'tongs'. It took 15 minutes to figure the subject of our discussion was thongs. I described his invariable toothless grin and novel, dead-fish handshake, whose grasp was at total odds with the rigorous, macho Aussie grip. Bouncy, garrulous Stan MacDougall, also a featherweight, demonstrated the skill of rolling a smoke in one hand—useful during spells of truck driving. He related incidents where he'd outwitted road inspectors and occasionally diddled people he was subcontracting for.

Our captain-coach and ruckman, Bricka Weir reputedly earned his name by uncoiling his manhood on the bar and lengthening it with a brick before admiring teammates, presumedly post-match. There was Indian hawker, Fred Runga, camped in a shanty near the Catholic Church. Old Cliff Carol, who'd made and lost fortunes in the halcyon crop days of the 1930s, was another daily pub client. Preferring the company of fellow railway workers at the far end of the bar, slouched lugubrious Jumbo Mills and pugilist, Jimmy Burns. I'd see these fettlers pumping their hand trolley on the line north to Kiamal and as far south as Mittyack. Of mottled puttied features was Burns, permanently primed for fisticuffs. Compliance with, or evasion of, his opinions was no protection, especially for novice me. Hands that fondled beer pots might pounce upon me unannounced and fostered mutual distrust. Mills wore a beery film on his upper lip; tall but bent beneath the weight of elephantine ears and nose, his gaze was never raised above my chin.

Another pair of sozzled regulars, Bernard Latouche Millen and Roy McGregor, was returning through Roy's wheatfields after closing one evening.

They believed they'd spotted an intruder. Stalking from opposite directions, they'd thrashed each other near senseless before realising their mistake. I would snack on such raucous tales pre-supper when the beer worked the men to their animated peak.

Two cyclists in their sixties who avoided the pub also fascinated me. Window-cleaner, Flash Coleman, unlit rollie permanently perched on his lip, another tucked behind one ear, had appeared in court on bestiality charges. Flash may have desired carnal knowledge with warmer species than milking cows, but his rubbery features and bloodshot focals were an unbreachable deterrent. The magistrate had let Flash off with a warning but fined the guy who'd filmed him in the act, 50 dollars. Prints had been passed around the Ouyen Club.

And there was Overcoat Joe, gaunt occupant of the town tip, seen in winter wearing an additional sports jacket over his customary couple. On pension days he rode to town to indulge a bucket of vanilla ice cream. I plucked the courage to bike out and visit. He was squatting over billy tea but didn't invite me to his fire. Grey-bearded and held together by his wardrobe, it was hard to ascertain his age. I told him my name and that I was a fresh teacher in town but this drew neither his name nor any response. He harvested drinking water from the roof of his tin humpy and stored it in dozens of scavenged wine flagons, protected with a ground sheet. Though he professed ignorance of the townsfolk or their doings, he knew birds by names he'd given them. A dozen improvised bikes were neatly racked beside his tin humpy in a superior shack. Did his reticence hint at profundity? Wouldn't he be pleased having a visitor? I pressed on.

'Overcoat.' I was wary his nickname might offend or that he might be unaware of it. 'How long have you lived here?'

'Left the city in '32. Depression Days.' Silence. 'Tried Swannie Hill, you know,' he continued. 'You know that big gum where the Murray curls north?'

'No. What then?'

'Five summers there until Council pushed me on. Cheeky mob they got there.'

'And then?'

'Arh, that was Piangle. Had a peek then at Nyah West. Nice little tip they got there, sonny boy. Very nice tip.'

Silence.

'What happened then?'

'Police get onto me after only one summer. Same again, Robinvale. Council come again. Been a Mallee man, though, ever since the 30s. Mallee, right through to the bone. Town mob here is nice an' quiet. No worries here, y'know.'

I wondered where he did his ablutions and laundry. Swarms of curious flies feeding at my eyes, nostrils and ears showed no interest in Joe. I'd expected him to be on the nose. Not so. Was the great outdoors a purifier? He waved in the direction of a muddy dam I hadn't noticed until he too glanced through the eucalypts beyond the tip. He was concerned about snakes, rising to show me fresh tracks from early that morning. But that was it, and given his cautious reserve, would remain so. Here was a man living as close to nature as I could conceive. I'd expected him to be some oracle, a fount of fundamental laws that had shaped an elegant and articulate language. He was open to the natural world in ways I was not, but socially a closed shop.

***

Apart from Art essays and a Dylan Thomas-like elegy honouring Toots, I'd written very little. It was far harder than the reading of books suggested. Making a convincing parallel world was easier with paint. I failed to articulate rural ambience. All these hardened men appeared to have emerged from the bowels of the ochred earth and were fluent in a vernacular foreign to me. Unlike them I did not wear the weight of the summer sun on my back or do 24-hour shifts on the tractor during harvest. Rain or its absence did not alter my fortnightly pay. As a soft city slicker I couldn't compete on their terms. I tried to get inside their voices. Crucially, I tried to recreate Kerry's manners and talk, with no more success on the page than in life. I constructed conversations we'd had and should have had, fleshing out unfulfilled ambitions. My artifice was transparent and cumbersome. Forty pages on I realised I lacked understanding of the drives and power shifts of relationships worthy of fact or fiction. So, it was back to art, fiddling within the confines of the shared bedroom.

***

I filled watercolour pads with lightly brushed pastel washes and fine black lines, inspired by Klee's luminous palette and Blake's *Songs of Innocence and Experience*, weaving text amongst images. I dived into Klee and Kafka's diaries, following their acute perceptions and self-scrutiny. Klee's range was prodigious; beguiling abstracted figuration matched by meditative writing. If his questioning led to a radiant touch, Kafka's doubt led in the other direction. And I enjoyed his incisive conversations with Gustav Janouch.

Klee's revelations in Tunisia as the First War erupted, revealed how foreign cultures stimulate creativity. At a time when Western Art was looking beyond its accepted canon to revivify itself, he found inspiration in carpets and brickwork. His gridded patterns could be quotes from Tunisian rugs and mud-brick walls. He confessed that he wanted 'to be as though newborn, knowing nothing, absolutely nothing of Europe,' which unlike me, implied he knew too much already. He was inland at the hot and dusty, holy Islamic city of Kairouan when he had his revelation about being at one with colour. I gazed into the wheatfields from my window hoping for such realisation. Here, the light and air had affinities with North Africa. But Mallee trees, bordering gridlocked fields, were not in conversation with Ouyen's architecture as palms and flower heads had been abstracted on Kairouan's patterned walls.

Joyce's *Ulysses* and commentaries by Anthony Burgess and Joe Campbell's were inspirational, too. I was looking for systems and patterns, slogging through Spengler's *Decline of the West* to wrest order from my shambolic life. In books, I buried myself. I checked out Gandhi, Schweitzer, and Bernard Shaw biographies, and decided vegetarianism might order my behaviour. It wasn't about gaining some moral high ground, though I was aware of environmental damage caused by sheep and cattle. Nor was I making a stand on animal cruelty, though the rabbit culls had ceased with the onset of winter. Would a change to vegetarianism, by some act of osmosis, confer similar distinction upon me as these luminaries? Perhaps, but health was the real motive. I felt that by removing meat, I'd detoxify. A balanced diet? Who needed a dietician to know intoxication caused imbalance.

Black Mac had never heard of vegetarianism. She simply removed meat from my supper which meant that I got progressively leaner on peas, mashed spuds and boiled carrot. She had electric and wood-fired ovens, preferring the latter and blaming the former for cakes that failed to rise. I split some of her woodpile though her aplomb with the axe shamed me. Breakfast was honey on Wheat-Hearts cereal with cream. On weekends it was poached eggs on toast.

Book learning was balanced with bodily discipline. I started running the dirt tracks around the great wheatfields at sunrise, dappled by Mallee-tree shadows, like the gums fringing the Murray, they were survivors of former extensive forests. I was far from factories and furnaces. Taking succour from pungent eucalypts cured any congestion. For several hours I belonged to air, filled with pellucid light, my shoes striking the sands in time with my pulse. Mile upon mile to a cocky chorus, running until my brain and body nearly jelled. Previously, running had been at the service of football training, the school cross-country and Kerry's bedroom window. Now I volunteered my body to this communion with nature before human action and flies sullied it.

Occasionally, I ran barefoot circuits on the couch grass and bee-kissed clover at the footy oval.

***

The following year I rented a railway house with fellow teacher, Paul, opposite the terminal's wheat silos. Shunting trains hammered through the small hours. Come harvest time, tractors groaned across fields all night. Cockies—the human variety—commenced queuing before dawn, 20 to 30 of them most days. They stood beside their truck doors, puffing rollies and nattering about footy, wheat prices and overseas markets, their voices carrying 100 metres in the crisp air.

On one side, in an identical structure, lived our landlady who we saw only on rent day. She had backyard lawn, flower garden, and veranda with hanging pots of ferns that mitigated the afternoon sun. Unlike our clothesline, propped on poles midst the dust, she had a Hills Hoist with canvas covering to save clothes from fading.

On the other side in a house akin to ours was affable Harry Lauder, his wife and kids. I never got hold of a head count, but all were pre-schoolers. And, as she confided from between multitudinous nappies on the line one evening, she was 'up the duff again'. On another occasion, in the gloaming, I heard the kids bawling in their backyard. Fifteen to twenty minutes passed before I poked my head over the fence and saw four of them huddled around the flyscreen door. When I went over and called for the mum, there was no response, so I unlatched the door, startling her from sleep in the sudsy tub, wet fag floating between her fingers. I backed away into the kids clustered behind my legs, mumbling my apologies.

Harry was a train driver whose night duties beyond the connubial couch rattled in the railyards across from our front door. Over a weekend I helped him pick and shovel a cesspit. A few weeks later he passed a generous steak of Murray Cod across the fence, flashing a photo showing him resplendent with the shoulder-height monster on the banks of Fireman's Bend, his 'tinnie' rowing boat, beached on the bank at his rear. 'Not so many of these big buggers around, mate, now. Them river rabbits, them carp, have got the run of the place.'

Summer heat lived like a separate entity in the house, mostly hot and dry. The brittle air vacuumed the mucus in my nostrils. No sooner had we finished pegging the last shirt or sheet on the clothesline than we could remove the first. Out west was what locals called 'Sunset Country'. One evening, the last hour of light was spectacularly flamed, ominously so, had we known. Oppression set in, the heat doubling and re-doubling. The door handles were too hot to touch even at breakfast. Suddenly it was preternaturally dark. Dust followed silently, fine and red, initially making an apparition of the clothes on the line and each other as we dashed about retrieving them to save a second wash. Thus far, dust had rolled slowly through town. Then it gathered momentum, sucking up twigs and loose litter, thrashing them against the timber walls.

Standing at the front door stuffing scrolled newspapers beneath it, I turned to see Paul, in mere outline, doing the same up the back. The dust was so fine it made mockery of our struggles, entering through the smallest cracks and filling the house. When the hour-long storm abated, we swept the floors of their sandy centimetres. At the same time the following day a second storm arrived, and we repeated the process.

I decided to paint my bedroom black, scribing its walls and ceiling with charts of the digestive system and enneagrams describing the process of laws three and seven, discovered in Ouspensky's, *In Search of the Miraculous*, which Dave Morgan had posted on request. Blackening the room suggested the infinite pitch of space. Those childhood dreams and premonitions stirred my interest in commentaries on time and space. Ouspensky had been quoted in Priestley's, *Man and Time*, that I'd seen on Royden's shelves. Were my childhood experiences better dismissed as occult superstition? Scientists scoffed at Priestley's inferences, reckoning coincidences were explained by statistical probability. What, they asked, about the multitude of things that slid past our attention?

I was perplexed by Ouspensky's terminology but determined to push beyond its seductive title. He recounted teachings gleaned in Moscow from Georges Gurdjieff, just prior to the First World War. Thus, the mysterious Mr Gurdjieff entered my world. Ouspensky, as his title declared, was searching for keys to unlock a reality lying beneath the pointless absurdities plaguing mundane existence. Like Klee, he'd been disillusioned with Europe. And the religious schools of Egypt and India failed to provide satisfactory answers for him. Here was Ouspensky describing an inscrutable man in possession of understanding more profound than his own eminent rationality.

Gurdjieff emerged in Moscow as the edifice of European culture was crumbling. Much of the esoteric revival of the late nineteenth and early twentieth century was based on a revolt against insignificance. The need to re-assert the primacy of humans had been dealt a serious blow by scientific method. Established religions were questioned, as was the role of the mind's unconscious behaviour. Steiner, Blavatsky, and Krishnamurti were amongst those re-evaluating European decline. Just as Indian gurus challenged overripe materialism in the 1960s, holding similar appeal to those of the educated middle-class grappling with the sciences' ever-shifting disclosures. Artists, Malevich, Kandinsky and Mondrian, amongst others, found promise in their teachings. Their abstractions were regarded as expressions of inner selves. Artists also embraced the art of so-called 'primitives', children, the unconscious, and the insane, as alternatives to academic realism.

Ouspensky alluded to cosmic governance by a law of 'vibrations', and insisted humans were sleeping creatures of habit. Was I no better than an automaton, with little power of decision-making? Mass production was stirring in and on the ground. Mice were on the move.

✳✳✳

I'd driven through devastating locust swarms but never seen mice in comparable numbers. The rodents crossed highways to raid the silos. Humps of carcasses caused cars to skid from the highway. The sandy Mallee soils and freshly sown fields were conducive to breeding. They holed up all day in wait for the ravenous night. I slowed over a hump, thinking of mum plucking snails from her plants after rain, crushing them on the concrete path, her jaw bent on death; and how we distanced our murdering selves, relegating them as pests.

Mice had been observed forming pyramids to access silo ventilation holes set a metre from the ground. Frank Healy invested in a mouse-proofed silo with ventilation just beneath its lid. Still the levels dropped steadily each day. Returning late from the Ouyen Club, he wondered why the 30-metre power line from house to silo hung so low. High beam revealed it was beaded with mice that had scanned the yard until hitting on this lone access.

I tested these reports, driving to nearby Kiamal silo and training the high beam at the steel ledges girthing it. Their appetite was boundless. They fled the beam and fell in torrential millions. I was too stunned to get out of the car and trust my feet on the turf. I reversed over the moving ground mincing mice. *Time* magazine jested in a footnote that the town boasted a golf course of over 10,000 holes!

Cliff Carol suffered a stroke and was found dead on the kitchen floor of his farm, the palms of his hands devoured by rodents. Dairyman, Pedro Shaddock, casually mentioned this at footy training, how he'd noticed three days of uncollected milk and rapped on the flyscreen door, entered, and found the old seed. Cliff had once boasted such riches that he'd left his duplicate T Model for years roped to the limb of a tree when the hauler had forgotten to bring a loading ramp. 'Kept it for spare parts. Collectors' item, now,' he'd told me one long afternoon at the bar. 'What about rust?' I'd asked. 'Don't you worry yourself about that. Bet that old donkey ticks over first nudge. Chassis would be worth a mint too, these days. Don't make them like that anymore, young fella.'

Some farmers on tractors circled their silos with plaster-of-Paris that mice, maintaining impeccable cleanliness, licked from their pads and solidified. The bodies were raked into pits, often twice a night. We fitted our bed legs with old baked bean cans of water to hinder their passage between our sheets. It was a strategy the hospital adopted after patients had been disturbed by mice grazing on hair and stubble.

Lucid dreams delivered European cloud ships, disgorging swollen mice that scurried over the new lands, immigrants in the dust. Roused from sleep and half-awake, I tried figuring if the patter I heard was rain? No. It was mice nibbling studiously in the wall at masonry and insulated wiring.

Paul filled the kitchen sink and balanced beer bottles with bread stuffed in their necks. Mice slipping to watery deaths had to be scooped from the sink throughout the night, several dozen at a time. In the morning he pegged them by their tails on the clothesline for the crows. Fat cats had mice fatigue.

'Griff', a scientist from Walpeup Research Station, estimated mouse density in the vicinity of 3000 per hectare. If disease didn't halt their tide they'd reproduce until no holes were left. Fighting over diminishing resources, they'd cannibalise down to the last mouse. Within the month they disappeared as quickly as they'd come. I took little joy in the destruction of mice, yet I'd been keen to join Stan on rabbit culls. Why this distinction? Was it the respective size of the species? Both were imports that ripped the country's fragile soils. I knew too, that deforestation had caused the dust storms, and horse, cattle and sheep had pocked and hardened the earth's crust in ways unknown prior to settlement.

Earth engineers and croppers of wheat, rabbits and mice taken individually, I bore you no malice. Holding your furry bodies in my palm, I felt your pulsing sentience. Perhaps it was my enthusiasm to ingratiate Stan with preparedness for rural activity, protecting his crop and earning a few bucks, rather than murderous delight. Whatever, the transformation of the pretty individual into a destructive mass dissolved sympathy: the perfect mammal weighted against the perfect plague. How arbitrary were my attitudes.

***

Success with last year's delinquents was based on confiding in their better nature and devoting after-hours to a mural which received accolades from their fellows. No such joy attended the two Aboriginal Clarke brothers who appeared during the plague in my woodwork class. I heard a family in Underbool was fostering them. Older brother, Joe made slow progress but was no bother. Little Freddie was beyond my control. His electrified movement around the room interrupted students. He switched on the grinding stone, hid beneath workbenches, and when spotting mice in the covered way, was out the door on frantic hunting expeditions.

I couldn't bring myself to hair twisting, and haranguing utterly failed. Last resort was to pass responsibility to senior master Denis Niall, imposing ruckman of our Reserve team. Though the truths on his acid tongue would have eluded the sulking midget, their tone complemented his strapping. Much to everyone's relief they moved on, leaving me wondering to where, and to what fate—the one whose boundless curiosity and zest exceeded school parameters, and the other who fell so far beneath them. Where had they come from, and where were their actual parents, questions I'd not seriously considered with those Salvation Army lads back in Boronia. The Clarkes were exotics, even though possible descendants of the people who once roamed the estate Great Uncle neglected to take up.

Close to concluding this memoir I flipped on the TV at random and was jolted by the face staring at the camera. The same Freddie Clarke, fidgeting, darting eyes, whose fate I'd wondered about forty years ago, and again, while penning this script. Bald Freddie, prematurely aged, alcohol-ravaged, was admitting his suffering and lack of parental love as one of the *Stolen Generation*, and of his years in the Ballarat Orphanage. I was transfixed by his tale, familiarised by the *Bringing Them Home Report*. And to think I, too, however minimally, had added to his woes.

***

During Christmas holidays with family I'd enjoyed a fling with Margaret, a girl Dannie Bourne had introduced. My confidence was re-ignited with her interest in me. He who had sourced the Rover for me, and now an attractive consort. How fortunate the advent of new love just as my first concluded. How easy to fall in love, as falling it surely was. She was pretty, petite, and porcelain pale with short-cropped blonde hair that looked and felt like teased cotton wool. This strong electricity rendered me defenceless before her doe-like eyes and caressing words. I met Margaret's large Catholic family in neighbouring Ferntree Gully, not 100 metres from the field where I'd first kissed Kerry.

Before returning to Ouyen, Tony 'Loupas' Lintermans presided over a mock marriage beneath the stars in the car park of what became Mt Dandenong's Ski-High restaurant. We celebrated our parting with drinks the following Saturday evening at the Mt Dandenong pub and were enmeshed in the general reverie. A gay guy, charming people as he moved from table to table, noticed our mooning. Thinking to avert rather than encourage his enthusiasm, we said we were honeymooners. He hushed the crowd, drew attention to our status, and called for celebratory champagne for everyone, drinks on him. We felt hopeless to refuse his offer of the guest suite at his nearby mansion. His buddy gave a disgruntled greeting at the top of their drive as we slinked off to the fabulously fitted bedroom. Trumpeting cupids danced across the bedhead and a silk quilt with Arabic throwover gave a hint of harem. Off we crept down the looping gravel driveway before dawn, hoping not to disturb our hosts and compound our mischief. I hadn't seriously considered the repercussions.

During the next months she urged we marry and make a life together in the Mallee. That seven of her letters arrived one day should have served warning. Her mother had died when she was 12 and by her account as eldest of eight, she'd helped her grieving alcoholic father care for her siblings. She wanted out of the family arguments and self-pitying dad. Flattered by her need, I felt I could protect and help her esteem. That I was more together than her was self-deception. I, too, needed to be needed.

The Rover, which I'd just managed to save enough to return to the road, was sold to cover costs of the reception, to be staged at my parents. I received instruction from the Ouyen priest in Catholic matters and we married during April at her church, St Josephs in Ferntree Gully. How bizarre this marriage thing, this voyage into imponderable commitment. Yet, like many of my peers, we regarded this as the natural course of events in our early twenties. I'd not lived in constant company with her or Kerry. Coupling commenced at Railway Terrace. Housemate Paul, moved on.

Mere weeks into our marriage, nuptials my parents had pleaded to reconsider after meeting her, I recognised my idiocy. In part I'd reacted to their interference in my decision, though I was too proud to admit this despite stressing over her paranoia. She wouldn't leave the house and remained in front of the television behind sunglasses.

We got a sturdy green-eyed, ginger mongrel, Emil, with a lot of Weimaraner about him. He was a loveable hound and joined my morning runs, tail wagging and biscuits deferred until we returned. He was to be company for Margaret but shadowed me wherever I went. He'd sit on the doormat anticipating my return from work, nuzzling under my wrist, demanding a few strokes as soon as I came through the gate. Then he'd roll on his side and, with sideways glance, plead for a belly scratch. That done, he'd retire to one of the dust bowls he'd dug beneath the house where he dozed most of the day. I didn't have a strong dog history. The Boxer, Pekinese, and Foxie hadn't enjoyed long tenure at Hastings Avenue. The first had been taken to an animal shelter, having proven unmanageable; the latter two succumbed to misadventure and disease. We had mutual affection, but never developed strong bonds.

Maybe Emil was a one-master dog. Having sourced him from an animal shelter, I didn't know his background and, already adult, he resisted my feeble attempts at training. As company for Margaret he was a failure. Then one morning, way before traffic hit the roads, I was running five kilometres south of town with him at my heels. The school bus from Mittyack suddenly turned the only corner of that stretch of the Calder. Emil bolted after a rabbit on the other side of the highway and was crushed beneath the wheels, instantly dead. I was shattered. Here we had been at the peak of expansiveness, our blood hot, our pads pounding, with apparent perfect understanding of each other. Then following instinct, for I did not deem it a decision, he bolted after potential quarry with no sense of self-preservation. Instead of killing, he was killed. For all our undeniable bonding, his action in that instant showed how far apart we were.

The driver stopped and the few kids alighted. There was nothing we could do other than drag him to the side of the road. I declined the offer of a lift and stayed a few minutes before completing the run. At home I couldn't speak to Margaret but borrowed Harry's car to fetch him. I replayed pointless scenarios that might have prevented his death. Sorrow at the loss of my companion burned in my gut. I dug a hole near the clothesline. Tossing dirt directly onto his fine mottled fur was rude to the point of obscenity. Margaret stood clutching a handkerchief to mop tears as I wrapped him in an old towel and lowered him. His tongue hung long and flaccid between his jaws. She placed a few pebbles on the mound and I went to school. By recess it was impossible to concentrate. I told the senior master what'd happened, though by then half the school knew; and I went home. Not until supper when, out of habit, I went to fill his bowl, did I weep. Margaret suggested we get a replacement. No more dogs for me, I thought. Not then, at least.

I started to dismiss her monotone whine of complaint. I no longer considered the constant fingering of her kiss curl cute, but rather, neurotic fidgeting. My infatuation had misread her convalescent nature as delicacy. I was not pleased to chart my uncharitable response but was helpless to stem it. How quickly her beauty conceded to a miasma of demands. I lacked the capacity and desire to be her carer. Our sex lost its mystery and grace. I was disappointed, having determined, like my parents, to sacrifice conflicts and difficulties and remain loyal to our vows. Self-interest reigned.

***

Ian returned from representing Australia in the World University games in Italy where he'd shone. After a dozen years of grunting beneath those weights, even some sessions of hypnosis, he'd been amply gratified. I invited him up to the school to demonstrate his straddle technique. The students crowded round the sandpit during lunch as 'Ratty' limbered up and thrilled them with a leap just shy of two metres.

The other great leap came courtesy of a mate of Colin's. How come I hadn't heard of Van Morrison? I knew the great anthem, *Gloria*. Was this the same guy? *Astral Weeks* broke aural boundaries. His rolled vowels evoked a world soaked in nostalgia and hope, exaltation and abandonment. His back lanes, eccentric personalities and yearning for love, conjoined Ouyen and Boronia.

Soon after, Dave Morgan passed through town with taxidermist Mike, from the museum. They hoped to trap quail, Mallee fowls, wrens, honeyeaters, tree creepers and teal to replace tatty specimens in the century-old display cases. Dave mentioned that he intended quitting his post and heading north to Darwin—north into Xavier Herbert country. I was already as far north as I could imagine. On arrival, Dave found work in the Indigenous community of Milingimbi and, during his eleven years there, learned the printing trade. Together with school principal, David McClay, he helped curate The Milingimbi Collection, intended as an extension of the school's bilingual program.

Early December 1970, Joe Skeehan called me to his office to tell me I'd been posted back to Maroondah High School in the eastern suburbs. Anticipating that I would have to serve a three-year sentence, I hadn't actually applied for transfer. Some football scout with links to the Education Department, however, had reported my on-field successes, having been selected in the inter-league team and polling second in Tiega's best and fairest. I was to present at VFL team North Melbourne's pre-season training sessions. The news pleased Margaret who was missing her family.

At her insistence, we relocated in the vicinity of our parents. On the one hand, I felt somewhat defeated, returning to Boronia. It wasn't as if I was the prodigal son. I couldn't wait to be out of home. The thought of returning there was as remote as Ouyen had been. What independence had I established? Yet I was happy her five sisters and two brothers could provide comfort when my misgivings short-changed her.

We found a flat in Cypress Avenue, heavily lined with the conifers from which it took its name. Had Van Morrison's song of that title been personally addressed? Those pines protected the playing field of my childhood, whose great interlocking branches provided passage for our monkey selves as we braved their heights and hollered our Tarzan cries.

It was only seven kilometres to the school, close enough to regularly run to work. My parents never visited or enquired after us, which, I assumed, expressed their disapproval. We saw a lot of her family and I learned from the sisters that they'd been the ones who cared for her rather than the other way around. Indeed, the older girls were her lone confidantes. Whenever she approached her father with advice on handling her younger siblings or his drinking, he brushed her aside and she'd return distraught. I was inexpert and lacked the courage to discuss our issues, often resorting to the wood heap to express frustrations with the axe, or to the easel in the spare bedroom studio.

Though fit as a proverbial Mallee bull. a few weeks' training with the 'Roos' at Royal Park convinced me I wasn't built for the rigours of elite performance. Running and vegetarianism had my 68 kilos stretched over 188 centimetres, more snake-like than ever! I had speed and endurance sufficient for the minimal physical contact of the Mallee but not the mongrel courage to put my body on the line for North Melbourne. The money footballers earned was no inducement in those days, either. Perhaps, if Collingwood had called, as it had for teammate O'Callaghan, I might have persisted and done the weight training the big time demanded.

Needing to increase my earnings by upgrading teaching qualifications, I opted for further art studies at Caulfield and worked through the Christmas vacation to cover tuition and material costs, doing a stint of life modelling followed by night shift at *Baker Boy Bakery*. I reconnected with my cronies. Alerted to the timing of the various bakes, Tadpole and Loupas slouched in Taddy's Volkswagen, waiting for the midnight raisin loaves to cool. A tub of butter rested on the dash to lavish on the warm dough. Management was smug about having secured a revolutionary yeast-free recipe from the United States. It was some type of cost-cutting acrylic that quickened the rise.

There was also casual work at Camm's Monbulk canning factory for which, a few years earlier, I'd picked berries for their jams. This time when I met the manager at the delivery door, he handed me an apron and hairnet then led me past women engaged with sweet-smelling fruits to a room at the far end of the building. Camms had contracted to export canned meat to troops in Vietnam and it was in this subsidiary department I'd be toiling. It was filthy work and not what this recently converted vegetarian anticipated. The grease steaming from the vats of navel and cheek gristle converted into so-called A Grade canned beef was deplorable. We used pickaxes to break pallets of frozen meat into chunks manageable for a three-minute dunk in vats of boiling water. The conveyer hoisted these into a stainless-steel mixer where taste, if not quality, was enhanced with caramel. This was siphoned into cans and stamped with its questionable grading. Despite washing my hair and clothes daily, the stench was beyond the power of detergent to remove.

Money was still short when school resumed and younger brother Colin, who'd taken weekend work at landscape gardening supplier, Big Rock, threw occasional Sunday jobs my way delivering rock, sand, or soil by tip truck, to suburban homes.

Given the momentum of the pre-season at North Melbourne, I forsook cricket in preference for running before breakfast with Boronia High old boy, Bill Scott, on the soft tracks of Sherbrooke forest. Bushfires forever threatened this haven but right then, it was thriving. Bill was bent on breaking into the Olympic squad as a 10,000-metre runner and excelled at state and national levels. Lyrebirds shattered the crystalline air with powerful, liquid voices and we startled them into low flight as they scratched the tracks. They were descendants of one of the planet's oldest species of songbirds and I would slow my pace to immerse myself in their astonishing repertoire of mimicry of kookaburras, yapping dogs and more. We would commence downhill towards Kallista, then returning to Sassafras, Bill would dash the final 100 metres to the car, doubtless imagining a finishing tape he would breach as I would never do.

Ian encouraged me to middle distance running with his Box Hill Athletics Club. The day prior to Saturday's events, I fasted, to sharpen mind and body. Several weekends of competition and shin soreness though, were sufficient for me to drop competitive athletics, but had been excellent preparation for football. My body said those weekly 100 kilometres were unnecessary for fitness. So, I squeezed football into my work and study schedule, playing for the first time with Colin in the black and white stripes of Scoresby. No other football code offered as comprehensive and expressive choreography. It challenged men of speed, strength, and agility to instinctive decision-making that frequently defied spectators' eyes. Body contact was part of the contest and fatigue earned from playing was deeply satisfying. Bumps and bruises caused from accidental circumstances I'd usually mope over, were readily accepted in football.

My sister Marilyn, had married Andre and started a family in Selby, little more than a general store, post office and charming stone Anglican Church. Colin remained with my parents but was rarely home. Mum was a shop assistant at a pharmacy where Pinnock and Simms's butcher shop once stood. Dad had shifted to the Camberwell offices of the Electricity Commission, advising heavy industries on appropriate power sources.

Uncle Hughie sold me his EH Holden station wagon so I could commute to Caulfield after work. Warwick welcomed me to his Art History sessions, enquiring after my painting and startling me by saying I was 'probably a painter and nothing else', which buoyed my confidence. Some evenings, I took promising students, Martin King and Jan Fleming, to his lectures. Martin was sufficiently impressed to later enrol at Caulfield and later base a career on his printmaking expertise.

Warwick mentioned Pierre Bonnard's show at The National Gallery. Bonnard extended Impressionism's ruptured surfaces with the most expansive palette I'd encountered: vermillion, violets, saffron yellow, and a range of whites. Fresh and literally illuminating, these blobs of coloured sensation conveyed lived experience teetering between joy and sadness, certainty and ambivalence. Odd perspectives and indefinite outlines conveyed life's uncertainty. I wondered why Warwick, earlier, had never made more than passing reference to him. Here, sight and touch embraced with what I regarded as love, exemplified in the tender images of his wife bathing. His palette and Klee's, became enduring influences.

He invited me to his friend, Kristian Fredrikson's South Yarra flat for a series of Sunday philosophy sessions. Warwick was unpicking Gelven's commentaries on Heidegger, who he deemed to have restored Mind to the Universe. Revelations of Heidegger's Nazi association, as far as Warwick was concerned, neither damaged nor detracted from his propositions. Fredrikson's costume designs for a ballet were scattered across several desks, stoat-like androgynous figures resembling him. Following a discussion with Warwick about Hamlet, he made himself scarce.

At one of these small gatherings, another attendee, hearing of my interest in Ouspensky, recommended John Bennett's *Witness* which I was able to track down in the *Theosophical Bookshop*. He was born June 8, 1897, of an American mother and English father and spent early childhood in Italy, learning to speak Italian before English which groomed a facility with languages, later enabling him to talk to spiritual teachers in their native tongues, and to study original Hindu, Buddhist, Islamic, and Christian sacred texts.

In the First World War, Bennett became a captain in the Royal Engineers, with responsibility for signals and telegraphy. Lying unconscious on an operating table with a head injury, he experienced an out of body state that convinced him there was something in humanity that could exist independent of the body. During convalescence he was invited to join a course in the Turkish language because the army needed intelligence officers in the Middle East. Committing to the task, he found himself in Constantinople (now Istanbul), holding a very sensitive position between the British and the Turks. Fluency in Turkish made him the confidant of many high-ranking political figures.

The city was a bustling centre of change and conduit for many displaced persons passing to the West. One of Bennett's charges was to monitor their movement. Among them were Gurdjieff and Ouspensky. Duties completed by 1923, he reconnected with Gurdjieff at his institute, the Prieure, near Fontainebleau, an hour's drive southeast of Paris. Here he was shown things that convinced him that humans are capable of transformation and that Gurdjieff had knowledge and understanding of techniques by which this could be attained.

Back in England, he joined Ouspensky's groups studying the 'system', or Work, as outlined in his *In Search of the Miraculous*. Bennett remained with Ouspensky for 15 years, during which time his professional life involved various brown-coal mining ventures in Greece and Turkey that gave him expertise in mining and coal chemistry. In 1938 he was asked to head the British Coal Utilisation Research Association. With war imminent, a coal-based alternative to oil was needed. BCURA developed coal-gas-powered cars, coal-based plastics, and efficient fireplaces that gave more heat for less fuel.

After World War II, he renewed contact with Gurdjieff in Paris. This brief period preceding Gurdjieff's death in October 1949, was crucial to Bennett's sense of mission in transmitting Work ideas and techniques. His more digestible prose encouraged my further reading.

Growing awareness of environmental degradation also led me to Schumacher's *Small Is Beautiful*, which proposed a reappraisal of earth's energy supplies given diminishing resources and a rapidly expanding population. He'd collaborated with Bennett at BCURA on coal research and Bennett happily endorsed his friend's ecological arguments when they were published in 1973.

***

Unlike Ouyen High School, the staff at Maroondah were predominately middle-aged mortgagees. Fortunately, there was a fellow-traveller and poet assigned in his first year to teach English. John Scott shared my love of Dylan and would strum an air guitar while quoting the bard—I caught him mid-act when we first met in the staffroom. *That Million Dollar Bash* and *Tiny Montgomery* hovered in the air between our desks. Scott had bootleg discs of Dylan's *Basement Tapes* and live concert, *Great White Wonder*. These went some way to explaining the hiatus between *Blonde on Blonde* and *John Wesley Harding* recording sessions.

With John Scott (Michael Peters, partly obscured), 1971.

Soon we were rounding up student teams at recess to contest volleyball. We co-ordinated pranks lampooning the institution, which attracted the ire of the principal and senior staff. Some of this material ended in cartoons I inked across the rear wall of Scott's classroom. Although students enjoyed our impromptu Pythonesque interviews in class, other staff were less impressed. The earth sculptures students mowed from the long grass behind the boiler room weren't endearing me to older staff; nor the death masks students queued to have cast. And in our reveries, we were occasionally joined by, surprise, surprise, the Tassie Devil who, having just graduated from Monash like Scott, had been assigned maths and sciences classes.

Some weekends Scott and I collaborated with word and picture, filling broadsheets with cartoons and caustic speech bubbles. I valued his grasp of popular culture and the musicians and writers he introduced. He alerted me to the avant-garde music show, *Room to Move*, hosted by mellow, Chris Winter. It was in this forum that I was swept away by the deep melancholy of David Ackles and the symphonic majesty of John Cale's, *Paris 1919*, which used the Peace Talks of that year to riff on events flowing from their failure. Further, Scott told me about import record dealers, *Euphoria* and *Gaslight*, where their material could be sourced. My vinyl collection swelled with artists linked to artists and their obscure backlists, with richer cover art than Australian companies would print under licence.

We endured the years, and later, I would visit him whenever I could—in Canberra, Thirroul, Bowral and Trentham—wherever lecturing work placed him. He was the first writer I'd befriended and admired for his sharp eye and elegantly written intimacies of heart and body. Scott added novels to his poetic achievements and adapted, *What I have Written*, for screen, filmed by friend, John Hughes. 'N', his political thriller, charted Australian responses to an imagined Japanese invasion during the Pacific War. In crisis, we see how rapidly democracy can be replaced by fascism, how history can be rewritten, and dissident voices suppressed or annihilated.

College friends, John and Leonie Anderson, married after graduating from our course and, after a year teaching at Rushworth High School, moved to Mornington High. Then John resigned. At this point they'd purchased a house in semi-rural Merricks North with access to a shearing shed he converted to a studio. They had a son and infant daughter. He had a crack at carpentry and fish mongering while Leonie bought into *Ramshackle* craft retailers in Mornington.

Then with fellow disillusioned teacher, Jim, he bought a cray boat and licence and spent the small hours in swells between Flinders and Cape Schanck. I joined the crew at four one cold April morning. It was heads down and bums up for them as I watched the sun break through grey skies and wink blearily over Bass Straight. Heaving cray baskets aboard while balancing on the wonky craft fighting seasickness, soon crippled this landlubber. But John, sucking seasickness pills, soldiered on for several years, keen to get home late morning and face the easel and kiln he'd fabricated to cast bronze sculptures.

✳✳✳

Our marriage stuttered to dissolution after three years. Marking its nadir, Colin a speedboat enthusiast, invited Margaret and me to his annual Christmas camp on the Murray at Yarrawonga. Amazingly, she agreed to go camping on condition that younger sister, Jo, accompany us. While I enjoyed waterskiing with Colin, she met a guy fishing an irrigation channel. When she brought him to our tent late one night to break the news, I was mightily relieved. To the young dude's astonishment, I expressed my happiness and wished them luck.

Bill was an apprenticed car mechanic who soon shifted from his parent's urban digs to our house in the eastern suburbs. I was so grateful he'd rescued me that I welcomed this move, remaining in the rear sleep-out for a few weeks until finding alternative lodging. What I didn't know was that in leaving Preston Motors he'd helped himself to spare parts and tools from the garage. Police arrived the day after and when they knocked and enquired if the apprentice lived at our address I said, yes, and invited them in. When they asked who paid the rent, I said I did.

'Where does the apprentice sleep?'

'In the double bed in the front room.'

When I admitted my wife cohabited with their suspect, there was a rolling of eyes and no more questions regarding house politics.

He was charged with appropriating goods, and a date was set for a hearing at the Collingwood Courthouse. I felt the same shy tentativeness of that moment in the tent at Yarrawonga, when they asked me to serve as character witness. Had they no options? We'd known each other only a few weeks. Well, they knew no other irreproachable schoolteachers. I'd only observed his courtesy, straight talk, and responsibility. The theft was a hiccup in an otherwise unblemished career. Moreover, this blossoming relationship ensured my liberation. Of course, I would testify! The magistrate gave him a warning and direction to donate to the poor box. Though the Catholic Church frowned on divorce, the prevailing social stigma softened when the No-fault Divorce Law was passed in parliament in 1975, easing my conscience about our separation, later that year.

7
Rubbernecks

Abandoned Trophies, Rod Moss, 1977.

Several months after separating, I fell in with Jan, a vibrant graduate from Ouyen High School, now studying Economics at Monash University. We'd kept intermittent contact since leaving the Mallee, and I filled my neediness in her company. Her vitality, art smarts and thirst for adventure contrasted with Margaret's retreat from the outside world. Robust and athletic, she wished to travel, and I happily accompanied her over Christmas, rejoicing in the potential of a new start when I'd thought obliged to endure a life sentence.

Once more life seemed uncomplicated, trustworthy and good. Again, I felt swept up in my body's sway. What could we develop in addition to sexual attraction? Might adventure reveal this? I hoped for inseparability without conflict or loneliness. We shared interest in the arts, movies, and literature. Before travelling I moved into her shared student accommodation opposite the Monash University gates in Wellington Road.

We took advantage of university-discounted fares that encouraged swarms of students to holiday in Southeast Asia. The Tullamarine airport was full of students, like us, on their initial overseas adventure. First stop, Singapore where, at gunpoint in the terminal, I submitted to the shearing of my shoulder-length hair as the condition to reclaiming my confiscated passport. The conservative government of Lee Kuan Yew was wary of hippie drug traffickers, though draconian censorship of long hair was unlikely to apprehend serious offenders any more than its death sentence would deter trafficking.

The dank air was rich with the scent of decaying fruit and vegetation, a faintly disagreeable smell that persisted throughout the archipelago, and to which I never accustomed. The city had a thriving sense of industry that ratcheted up after dark. When did these tireless labourers sleep? What a change from home. Melbourne emptied of its citizenry after 6 p.m., deserving Ava Gardner's alleged remark when filming nuclear flick, *On the Beach*, that it was an ideal location for a film about the end of the world. Singapore's days ceased between 2 a.m. and 3 a.m., burning more energy daily than Melbourne did in a week.

On The Beach reflected our fears of holocaust. Though the Vietnam War avoided nuclear bombing, its spectre loomed. I didn't know of Britain's nuclear testing in arid Australia during the 1950s with anglophile Prime Minister Menzies's compliance. But high-profile British author Shute, with his military history, surely knew of the Maralinga tests as he sat at his Melbourne desk penning the script. The chilling final scenes showed deserted Melbourne streets with bits of newspaper tossing about, its printed warnings unheeded.

Singapore's streets were anything but deserted. We wandered the night markets; in the hubbub of a downtown lane a young Chinese couple beckoned us to their table to share some wanton soup. I'd never eaten chilli so when the first mouthful exploded, they found my spluttering hilarious. It was no act. Realising this, they apologised and insisted that we join them for a feast when we next returned to the city. 'You've tasted the volcano,' the young guy said. 'Now for the fire extinguisher,' he added, passing his bowl of smashed cucumber and yoghurt.

We caught the train to Kuala Lumpur. Our hotel's cheap rate there was due to proximity to the airport, though we were unaware of this. We unpacked in the mildewed room, also ignorant of the phenomenon of bed bugs. Between arrivals and departures at the airport, we detected chitchats feasting and copulating with noisy celebration. The next morning, we walked blearily into town for breakfast, determined to avoid the decrepit hotel's English fare. Vendors sold tiny bananas the size of my pointing finger and giants of such magnitude one would suffice for a meal. We tried the segmented, 'toilet fruit' durian, sold on skewers, though pegging my nose, as advised, failed to enhance its appeal. Rambutan and freshly juiced coconuts were scrumptious chasers.

Before taking a bus to Butterworth and Penang, we visited the Batu Temple. Sculpted Hindu gods and overly inquisitive monkeys populated the cave. I'd never seen carving directly into a mountain and marvelled at the skill and the scale of this undertakng.

We'd learnt at school that rubber and tin had been economic drivers of this nineteenth-century British colony, but nothing of the racial divisions employed in these industries: of how Chinese were introduced as indentured tin miners and Indians as labours in rubber plantations. After the British withdrew, Indigenous Malays, less educated than those growing urbanised minorities, resented their lack of representation in professional tiers. I was vaguely aware of interracial turbulence between Malays, Chinese and Indians and of the street violence between Malays and the wealthier Chinese in 1969.

Was I witnessing this resentment when a blind Malay, pocked-face enflamed, and donned in white *songkok*, fumbled through the bus back to KL, singing for a few miserly coins? The Indian conductor shoved him to the rear, threatening his removal if he didn't shut up.

We took the train to Bangkok, but desperate for passage from Butterworth, and discovering our ticket didn't entitle us to seats we resorted to the livestock carriage whose window vents were near the ceiling. The menagerie had degraded the air and we slept restlessly on the floor amongst crates of frenzied, chirping chooks. Only hours into our overnight journey I'd sensed an invasion of my sinuses and the unaccountable 'high' that, for me, now signals 'virus'. On arrival, the virus fastened me to the terminal bench, too feverish to find a hotel. From my resting place there, at least one mystery was solved. As the train had slowed through the suburbs of Bangkok, we'd been alarmed at the sight of elderly women haemorrhaging by the track. Spotting the floor around the bench were gobs of beetlenut emissions.

The virus was short-lived, fortunately, and we found lodgings the following morning on the second floor of a nearby hotel. By lunch I was sufficiently recovered to hit the streets. Glancing at a tray of sandals a few doors away,

I was taken in hand by the cobbler, and led to the rear of his shop where the shapes of both feet were stencilled on card. He assured me, mostly by gesture, that they'd be ready by evening. English signage was non-existent throughout the city and the Khmer script unintelligible to us. We walked and gawked. Our few enquiries with tentative English speakers were met with baffling, vowel-rich phonetics.

If the two lanes fronting the hotel thronged with bicycles, scooters, *tuk tuks*, cars and buses, a vehicular tsunami confronted us as we swung onto Phra Ram concourse. A traffic cop, mounted midstream on a concrete dais, gesticulated wildly and blew his whistle, barely discernible from the din. His cap was fitted with a feather and his feet with cowboy boots. Was he an imposter masquerading in borrowed costume? Despite his uniform and holstered firearm, commuters on foot and in cars paid no more heed to him than to the lights. Chaos reigned. Pedestrians, singly and in pairs, gathering wits and courage, plunged forth, darting between oncoming cars, motorbikes and people. We gritted or teeth and did likewise.

Bangkok's air was challenging. Motorbikes and *tuk tuks* coughed carbon clouds over the streets that some commuters filtered through surgical masks. Others adopted the full ninja job with slits for sight, giving them the look of some strange sect. For a while I wondered if we were not ambling the same set of streets as at many corners, a similar scrawny, toothless ancient sat in the limited shade. The formula encouraging my confusion was thus; singlet or shirtless with baggy shorts, one thong removed to fondle the sole placed beside a retracted umbrella, and cigarette either in use or in waiting.

Politeness ruled, at least to us visitors. Everywhere, palms were pressed together and smiles offered. The clammy air soon got to us. We were tempted into an impressive cinema complex by its huge, hand-painted hoardings, art on a scale and with realism rivalling Pop artist, James Rosenquist. The airconditioning was welcomed too. We were surprised initially that the audience, apart from Jan, was entirely male, and that smoking was permitted. It was soon evident that this martial arts flick, wedded to a chaste romance, satisfied everyone but us. Subtitles, had they been available, wouldn't have enhanced the banality. We left the theatre bemused, and joined the bustling streets.

Though the sun had disappeared the heat hung, bottled in by smog. People sat eating at small, improvised cafes open to traffic. One thing I enjoyed about the ocean was its product. This was a fish lover's paradise: an astonishing variety of crustaceans, grilled and fried mackerel, golden snapper, salmon and butterfish, fishcakes, curries in coconut, as well as fresh juices of guava, limes and oranges. We'd never eaten like this; Chinese and Italian tucker offered Melbourne's sole exotic dishes: dim sims, mung beans and sliced chicken on soy-sogged rice in the first instance, pizzas and pasta in the second.

More by accident than anything, we found the cobbler's shop, rather the shop owner spotted us as we were passing. He'd honoured his promise and was keen to get me inside to close our deal. Fitted in fresh leather, we found our way to our nearby hotel and collapsed in a sodden heap, taking showers at midnight to cool down, flipping the fan to full bore. Rather than mopping ourselves, we spread the towels over our sheets before lying down, maximising our chilled interlude by allowing the moving air to dry us.

The city had many channels from which enthusiastic boys netted small fish. In Lumphini Park they darted about giggling, tethered to kites that danced wildly in the high thermals, trying to cut their mates' missiles from the sky. Hundreds of vanquished kites rotted in the surrounding power lines and trees. Lads also grouped in circles with a cane ball, keeping it aloft using elbows and feet as in Thai boxing. Squirrels, with equal finesse, twitched nervously in nearby stands of bamboo, dropping furtively to ground to vie with mynahs for discarded scraps.

Foreign currency had interested me since watching dad arrange his collection. He was much the same with stamps. Queen Elizabeth passed from pocket or purse on our coins reminding me of my purchasing power, out of sight and mind, and certainly not as revered as King Bhumibol. His portrait was in shops, on billboards, hotel lobbies and on every form of denominational tender. He was as much on people's minds, or in their faces, as Buddha. Everyone we spoke with declared him a great and good man who worked very hard for his people. Commissioned portraits gave no sense of the joys of office, however: the queen occasionally cracked a smile, but her king looked variously forlorn, disengaged, even startled.

Fellow tourists were easily identifiable. Many were young twosomes like us but a few guys courted Thai girls, but were far outnumbered by older men dallying with local dames, causing me to reappraise presumptions. My relationship was based on shared enthusiasms and though sex was one of these, it was not alone. The stark imbalance of age, appearance and status stripped relationship to its transactional essence. What if children were the outcome of these couplings of beauty and beast, svelte girls with guys whose heads look to have dropped from the gables of gothic cathedrals? Might I, too, in senior years and still in thrall of physical beauty, place my foot on the accelerator and dash to Bangkok to join this troll line, money belt wobbling at my buckle?

Were I to reduce these female faces to essentials I'd start with a heart shape swelling from the forehead, tapering to a delicate chin. That's the love-heart, not the veiny organ with ventricles that might better serve the troll's visage. Unlike the festering bulbs of the old men, the women's noses never disturbed the balance and proportion of their faces.

As every Thai male submitted to a stint of monkhood to better appraise Buddha's life, there was a sizeable population of young saffron-robed, shaven-scalped guys fronting the streets. Did this, in part, account for the aforementioned incongruous couplings? Over 30,000 monasteries and temples were scattered throughout the country. Flower power, rather than the passing phenomenon of the 1960s Peace Movement, was literally enshrined here. At domestic-scaled shrines in homes, shops, and parks the Buddha-besotted made daily flower offerings of bougainvillea, orchids, camellias, jasmine, frangipani and roses. Flowers were depicted on ceramics with meticulous delicacy. One-haired brushes were used for the initial gold lines, later to be filled with infinite combinations of the five colours used in Benjarong cups, plates and vases.

Similar care applied to food presentation. Each dish presented complementary cooked and raw stuffs, flesh and plant, sweet and savoury, dowsed in delicate dressings.

***

A few older and grander buildings conformed to Buddhism's curved roofing spines. Apparently, the cute lick either end of the spine was not a flame but the rearing head of the snake, protecting the meditating Buddha within. It followed that the roofing tiles were its scales. Close inspection of exterior embellishment revealed ceramic floral motifs repeated *ad nauseum*. Repetition, by definition, thwarted innovation and had its place. It applied to chanting, naturally, wresting order from chaos. Cranking out my monotonous times tables and alphabet each morning had also hard-wired them for life.

This attention to detail wasn't shared by most of the built environment, where the concrete trade thrived. Office businesses, hotels and apartment blocks abounded, cubed monoliths rising a few levels above the hovels and dowdy shops. Some were painted in pale pastels long overdue for rejuvenation. But the dominant theme was black mould streaking buildings top to bottom which resulted in a careworn complexion.

Both locals and fellow travellers advised us that the *Wat Poh* temple was a must-see. If your taste was for big, bold and gold, then the reclining Buddha provided pleasures aplenty. I'd been corrupted by Disney and the mega-scaled excesses of Pop Art that rendered the palace as a Buddha theme park; too gaudy for my tastes save the costumes in the textile museum and the subdued murals depicting the Ramayana. The reposing giant seemed to have emerged from a mindset at odds with the refined paintings surrounding him. Delicate he was not.

We headed to the river the following morning to catch a ferry to Chinatown. The queue extended 200 metres. I thought there'd been an accident. But the accident was us. We were too many. When we reached the swaying pontoon, a porter greeted us, asking which country we were from. On hearing its name, he took pleasure in repeating it, jubilant in his English mastery. He turned to the river and set to welcoming us Australians, presenting us to the waterway.

'Kangaroo,' he chanted, and started hopping, his arms tucked in the marsupial's fashion. 'Welcome, kangaroo Australians,' he called, bowing to the river, hands joined in prayer. Boats came and went as we waited, his voice rising above the cacophony of whistles, moans and engine farts, thrilled at outbidding their might. He alone was worth our ticket upriver.

Since the gold rush, Melbourne's Chinatown occupied a short strip of Little Bourke Street devoted to restaurants whose shellacked ducks and aquariums of crustaceans and grinning catfish promised cuisines unavailable in the suburbs. For us suburbanites, Little Bourke Street was a rare hundred metres of exotica. Bangkok's Chinatown looked to have predated Australian settlement, an intenser world within the city's intensity. Sandals, guns, jewellery, bike parts, clothes, tools and kitchenware were literally hammered and cut into shape before our eyes for ready sale by men and women who worked, ate and slept on the spot. What we couldn't see had probably not been invented.

Food was available in many forms and outlets: poultry, crabs, squid, prawns, noodles, tubers, and greens. And fruit: paw paws, guavas, melons, mangoes, strawberries, cherries, oranges, bananas and pomegranates—whole or pieced, or grated and iced for drinking. Shops selling similar products were clustered for convenient consumer comparison. Cars squeezed through the crammed streets. There were alleys and even darker tunnels given over to ever smaller cells, each occupied by a man or woman squatting over their tray or two of knick-knacks; thirty T-shirts, fifteen transistors, a few boxes of combs and hairpins.

There was order, deep order, as there must be to conduct such immense commerce: an order legible to locals but opaque to we rubber-necking tourists. Motorcyclists forded the paths, obscuring the distinction between road and pavement without advantaging speed. Collisions were rare and harm more likely from suffocation. Bells tinkled the presence of vendors, pushing barrows through the crowd with fruits ready to be crushed and iced for the crowd's ceaseless thirst.

On the tarred ground of a dark alley a man lay motionless, prone, one arm at his side the other extended above his head just shy of his begging bowl, a sundered coconut shell. One leg was lopped at the knee, the other above his ankle. He could have been dead, comatose or asleep, exhausted from the struggle to his bowl. His plight was all the more pitiful for occupying this zone of plenty where goldsmiths toyed with their metals, electricians fused wires and tailors snipped. A palpable silence orbited his startling configuration. I was pressed past him by the perpetual masses, noting the stark disinterest of shopkeepers at his body's borders. We had never seen the likes of this in Australia then, neither the suffering nor indifference to it.

Returning downstream, we hired a small craft and detoured along an anabranch west of the Chao Phraya River to visit the king's Royal Navy, docked in a large hangar. Apart from a couple in another small boat, we had the place to ourselves. What a peaceful alternative. Maybe it wasn't on the tourist itinerary. Six superbly painted teak barges with ornately carved prows were dedicated to his ceremonial passage; virtuoso work that shook me from pettiness. Of course, we hadn't seen Bangkok in full, but we'd seen enough for now and anticipated relaxing in less populated places.

***

Hearing of the Koapoon cave temple near Kanchanaburi, we booked train tickets northeast to the Kwai Yai River. Several times on the train, local commuters proffered home-brewed whisky, but as we weren't drinkers, considered this wasn't the occasion to break with habit. The rural city's air was lighter and the breeze carried a soothing whiff of jasmine; exactly what we needed. Birds of greater variety than Bangkok's pigeons and sparrows, fluttered around our feet at roadside meals. Warblers, thrush and bulbuls, previously unsighted, bobbed about the low branches and leaf litter. A massive tree dominating the garden gave the hotel its name.

The *U Inchantree's* lush garden ran to the river. On the opposite bank, 50 metres distant, egrets and herons waded, disrupting the near perfection of reflected pines, palms, poplars and the distant range wherein the temple lay. By our hotel door half a dozen monstrous bees hovered before plunging into the purple petals of vine clinging to the wall. What manner of hive did they command? And what of their honey? Who would approach and rob such a

143

hive? They were, I heard, Carpenter bees, nesting singly or in family groups in shafts of hard wood or bamboo, an association giving them their name. It was Chinese New Year and crackers erupted at 7 a.m., flushing birds from trees, even drowning the siren calls of rainbirds as they fled above us.

Otherwise this peaceful setting made its wartime history impossible to conceive. Here was the legendary bridge and infamous railway Australian prisoners laboured on during the war with Japan. Burmese armies had also invaded, centuries before. There'd been wars too, with Cambodia, a country several Thais advised against visiting.

We taxied the half hour to the temple. The place softened my jaded attitude towards Buddhist monuments. The grounds were dominated by the monks' terracotta dormitory. Despite the gold Buddhas peppering its edifice, it was remarkably restrained. In other temples the urge to occupy all available space with imagery was stifling. So, I welcomed the minimalism here. Steps led down into the womblike cave complex, kept immaculate by several white-robed nuns. There were perhaps a dozen naturally formed niches within the greater space, each with a sitting or reposing Buddha. So ingenious was their proportion, so graceful their placement that, had it not been for contemporary electric light fittings, their coupling with eternity would be complete. It was a marvellous coalescence of effigies, stalagmites and stalactites, a peaceful approach to rock enhancement bespeaking the mystery of creation rather than, for instance, Mount Rushmore's proclamation of presidential power.

***

We returned to Malaya by train through Hat Yai Junction, having overnighted in what was, we discovered to the detriment of sleep, a paper-thin-walled brothel in Songkhla. We kept the window open, hoping the Gulf air might drown the smell of stale piss, and its crashing waves to counter mosquito music. Yelps and hoarse male tones issuing from rooms flanking ours sounded anything but pleasurable. Pity, as our day on the beach riding ponies and dining on grilled mackerel exceeded the expectations we'd nurtured on first sighting the dismal place.

Southeast towards Kuala Baru and Kuala Terengganu we headed. The train dithered on its single track to the border, often stopping between stations where sidings allowed trains to pass in the opposite direction. Bandito-styled men shouldering sashes of bullets unbuttoned their shirts to compare wounds. What conditions had created this struggle? Our ignorance again prevailed. We'd never kept company with the trappings of violence so openly displayed.

Here was the Muslim south, with separatist ambitions from the Buddhist-dominated, central government. This, we learned from one of the two Indians sitting opposite, the first we'd seen in Thailand.

Paul, the younger, shorter man, was accompanying his Sikh friend, and waxed lyrical over the riches and delights of his country. 'Oh India, very wealthy country. Much gold.' I was surprised, having only heard of the survival struggles of its impoverished rural multitudes. 'Oh, India enjoyed nearly one quarter of the world's trade before your Raj reduced it to nearly one third. Sure, they built railways, but these were primarily to extract the very materials they exported to Europe for their benefit. For instance, they took our excellent cotton to their mechanised looms and sold it back to us, using our designs. They stymied our wonderful shipbuilding and metal industries. But we have returned with force since independence from the coloniser.'

Paul, I learned during his brief lecture, was a schoolteacher. Though not devout, he admitted he was a Christian, another revelation for me. I'd regarded India as the province of Hindus, Moslems, Sikhs, and sects that swept the ground of bugs and wore masks to avoid swallowing them. Finding me a captive audience, the pitch of his rant elevated. 'And how do you think Singapore was built?' By Chinese, I supposed. From our scant observations, they had the run of the place. 'No. No. No, my friend. Indian labour. Oh, yes. After slavery was abolished, we Indians were indentured workers in British Colonies of the Caribbean, Fiji, South Africa.' Gandhi's courageous stand for Independence flickered. The Indian Mutiny protesting the occupying British in 1857 was a distant footnote from high school. The appalling Amritsar massacre of 1919 propelled Gandhi's passive resistance. And, fearing mass organised revolt, the Raj set about dividing Muslims from Hindus.

The older man's creamy white beard cascaded onto his buff, buttoned cardigan. He was journeying south to see his son for the first time in four years, and smiled gently when Paul referred to him, holding to his silence.

I shared my paper cone of cashews with them. The elder, Kavi, carefully split each nut prior to eating; I wondered if this was some religious etiquette. Having scoffed more than my share, I questioned Paul. He turned to his senior and passed on my concern. With a tilt of his head and flashing a smile, the Sikh took his last nut, bisected it to reveal a weevil.

Having befriended them, we decided at the border to share accommodation at nearby Kuala Baru, hailing a taxi to town. Two single beds with two bodies per bed in a thick-walled room, never mind the wiring sprawling nomadically from bedside to the globe dangling above. We'd been sleeping less than half an hour when Jan complained of being nudged by Paul. I was annoyed with being woken and dismissed her complaint, insisting he wasn't serious, and to go back to sleep. A second disturbance and I switched on the light, catching him looming above her. This time I warned him to stop or get out. Back in bed, head poking apologetically from his sheets, he claimed, 'In India, one man, many woman'. 'Not in Australia. One man, one woman,' I chastised.

We slept fitfully, not hearing them quit the room before dawn. They were breakfasting on monstrous cones of pink, yellow and green ice in the market when we sought a feed. Taking care not to engage further, we slipped by and succumbed to ice-cream temptation. Impossibly sweet! Had chilli-infused foods scoured their taste buds?

A two-hour bus trip had us in Kuala Terengganu. Its markets had richly coloured batiks—trendy items amongst our peers back home. We were enthusiastic consumers. Not so happy though with some food, or drink, from which Jan contracted enteritis. Was that lurid ice cream the culprit? Bananas failed to firm her gut. Boiled water ran through her. We hired a rickshaw for the half-hour ride to hospital. After a brief consultation in full view of the waiting public, we joined a long queue to the dispensary. I was alarmed, on nearing the window, to see medicines poured into unwashed bottles. More so, when I noticed people must provide their own bottles, accounting for the boys touting them up and down the file.

In the hotel lobby, the one battered book in English was Jarvis's classic, *Folk Medicine*, a tourist donation, perhaps, left by someone with Jan's complaint. I found a shop selling local honey and heated it in water on the ring burner in our room. Whether it was hospital medicine or the honey and vinegar concoction I spoon-fed her, was debatable. Possibly involuntary starving did the trick. She was weak but up for travelling a few days later.

Across the spine of the archipelago we bussed, the driver careering with homicidal speed. There were terrifying switchbacks on a single lane and sheer drops to the jungle where several buses lay cartwheeled far below. At each sighting, most passengers on the leeward side stood gaping and adding to the unnerving sway. Undeterred, the driver was bent on keeping his schedule. Had he factored in the likelihood of collision? He tooted an oncoming car that refused to back up on a bend and then rammed it. Everyone alighted while the two drivers spent half an hour settling matters. A seasoned commuter muttered that this was the way of things without insurance and the bus company's unwillingness to foot repair costs.

Unwilling to repeat the experience, we opted for a taxi from Kuala Lumpur to Singapore, slouching south in the security of an old Mercedes—through Malacca—for little more than the train fare. Back in Singapore, the Chinese couple kept their word and escorted us to a Chinese restaurant high above the city. Jan's appetite had revived, and we relished sumptuous, chilli-free dishes. Corn and asparagus soup, squid, mackerel and crab were served on a Lazy Susan, another contraption new to me. The dishes kept coming. Centre-point sat a spittoon. I was shocked when our elegant hostess at the meal's conclusion cleared her throat and spat into it, an image lingering long after the taste of those culinary marvels.

***

Later, in Bali, I too fell ill, poisoned from a liver-coloured fish in a Kuta Beach open-air restaurant that turned me like-wise and my heart aflutter. The receptionist at the nearby clinic told us the doctor slept at lunchtime and was not to be disturbed. It was a long lunch. The thought of hiring a *bemo* (van) into Denpasar was too arduous to contemplate. For 24 hours I lay groaning, barely able to crawl to the drop toilet. What should I have expected? The previous evening at a similar lamp-lit restaurant we'd ordered fried frog's legs. Awaiting desserts, I needed the toilet and was directed through the kitchen where the chef was fishing frogs from its effluence, draining beneath the preparation bench. Toxins clustered in my gut.

Weakened through the experience, we stayed in our immediate environment for a couple of days. Pigs, or what I took to be pigs, scrounged about the market gutters lining village streets. But it turned out they were hairless dogs, 'leatherbags', a fellow-traveller chortled, as we sorted through batiks. Monkeys joined these 'leatherbags' in the hunt for banana, papaya and coconut scraps. I'd had no joy seeking medical help and these dogs seemed similarly fated.

Lumbering Aussie that I am, the contrast with lithe Balinese was conspicuous. There was a feminine aspect to the men strolling in pairs, arms slung across shoulders, hand-in-hand, or fingers interlocked—public displays of camaraderie our protocols frowned on unless intoxicated. By feminine, I don't mean effeminate. It was embodied in their lightness, erect deportment; at variance with our round-shouldered slouch, clothes hanging haggardly as hasty afterthoughts. Ah, the Western male body. Ironic wisdom, the business of T-shirt slogans, was tested by a young American breasting, *Let the Great and Good Rule, The Rest Can Desist*; his greatness and goodness was evident in his expansive waistline.

Our *losmen* (accommodation) was one of several in a Kuta compound. All the compounds adhered to a code that acknowledged the human body and generational hierarchy. Eating, cooking, sleeping, toilet and relaxation: each had dedicated structures. Across a grassed courtyard, an older man spent his days beneath his veranda, sharpening adze, chisel and plane to hone a sizeable slab of teak. He was up and at it before we breakfasted on fruit, yoghurt, coffee and eggs. He was still bent over the wood when we returned after lunch, planing with unhurried dedication. Only late afternoon showers persuaded him to down tools and squat at the perimeter of the protected space, whereupon he produced a clove *kretek* to puff in rhythm with the pattering rain. He seemed less to be observing rain than allowing its beat and weight to inhabit him.

The hour's shower done, he packed tools and wandered to the beach, joining a line of village men squatting on its upper rim, and smoked once more in silence, before the setting sun. Its yolk bled across the sea as the black dots that earlier had beaded the horizon sharpened into a fleet of fishing boats returning with the day's catch. I asked the gent what he was making. It was a table tennis table for his grandson, using teak, as he'd done with our *losmen*. As we stood to return, a young man and woman, the latter with towel wrapped about her head, approached and asked if we'd like a massage. Sure, but not right now. We booked the following afternoon.

It wasn't the beaming nymph who had accompanied the tout. But the experienced hands of a wrinkled ancient more than compensated for my fancied intimacies. She unwrapped heated towels from her bucket and doused me in coconut oil, tinged with ginger and lemongrass. Cloves rode there too. Without word from me, she detected lingering gastronomic issues. 'I scrape you, okay?' Not knowing what she meant, I nodded. Out came a coin which she ran across my back. It was far from the soothing muscle-relaxing session I'd envisaged. I clenched fists and teeth to suppress exclamations of pain. But my head cleared, and I told Jan I had been purged. The woman waited for me to leave our *losmen* before starting on Jan who, noting my raised and pulsing flesh, declined the virtues of the coin.

***

We purchased a motorbike licence at the Denpasar Police Station. No testing was required. A wall poster displayed two-dozen mugshots of recent, mostly Australian, fatalities. We commented on it, confident of our invincibility. Accidents surely resulted from reckless novices; I'd served my apprenticeship on the Calder Highway's hard yards. In Bali, however, the few narrow, tarred roads were severely potholed with perforated edges dropping perilously into gravel. As with Malaya, we soon discovered that might was right including that of animals. Pigs wandered freely as did chickens and goats.

I was startled one day to see the bike rider in front of us suck a snake from the tarmac into his rear guard, another time a helmetless infant, losing grip of her father, dropped to the road in a motionless bundle. To leave the craft-busy village of Ubud coincided with leaving bitumen. It was a rocky track through terraced rice fields all the way to the summit. The poster at the police station continually flickered into focus as my shoulders tightened from the challenge—no doubt Jan shared my thoughts.

We gained Mt Batur around sunset, encouraged by mirthful children who, at each village, responded to our enquiries by pointing uphill. The lake squatting in the dormant crater was spectacular. It was too late to explore Kedistan village but the restaurateur encouraged us to witness 'boxing cocks' in the courtyard. First, we were expected to inspect the contestants in their domed, cane cages. This grisly combat, cocks with razorblades strapped to their claws, inevitably concluded with a victor. We felt obliged, enduring 20 minutes of squawking combat as feathers and blood flecked the pavement. The loser was dispatched for plucking, probably accounting for the stringy strands of meat in our soup, soon after.

Next morning we hired a boat and relaxed in its bows while the oarsman headed it across the lake towards Mount Agung, which rose from the rim of the caldera. I'd dipped in volcanic lakes at the dormant mounds of Mt Eccles and Mt Gambier, back home. This, however, was an encounter with an active volcano, a mountain large enough to determine weather and for locals to deem it the earth's navel. We'd intended to sight Agung's workings but were too tired, instead we lolled in a hot spring at its base, while thunder clapped across the summit and threatening clouds rose on its shoulders.

***

Though the gut was settled, my immunity had been damaged. An earache's mounting case drove me to a toilet-sized surgery occupied by a Chinese doctor whose great girth hampered his groping for tools. Lee Chew Fat swivelled in his chair and grasped my hand with surprising force. Squatted on the stool, I winced in his anchovy aroma and offered the offending ear. Midst his multiple chin folds, a long hair prospered from a plum-coloured mole. Was this some good luck charm, as with the long nails men cultivated on their small fingers? Between it and the bristling black toupee sitting alarmingly askew above his snowy brows, I had difficulty concentrating.

'What your name?' he rumbled while letting rip a whopping burp. My reply set him in raucous mirth which rocked the room. The light bulb flickered. My thumping ear impeded conversation as I teetered on the cusp of consciousness. Throughout his probes, he repeated my name with increasing volume, 'Roord Moorse, Rooord Mooorse, laughing and elasticising the vowels so ludicrously, I forgot my pain. Yes, this was a fungal infection. He felt the pulse of both wrists and declared my immunity was low, my blood acidic, prescribing forty sachets of what looked and tasted like finely powdered dirt—a herb to be mixed in warm water, and that proved most efficacious. I asked what I owed, but he waved me away with a final volley of, 'Rooord Mooorse', and a round of laughter. I wasn't laughing. A reflection in a shop window en route to the airport later that week, showed a gaunt, emaciated stranger, like a survivor of a prisoner-of-war camp. My stomach was weakened for decades.

In the Denpasar terminal, we gathered midst a hiatus of Darwin residents who anxiously awaited news of the devastation wrought by Cyclone Tracey. Most of the flight home was across the great dry interior, seemingly void of habitation. Tucked on its southern fringe like some maritime misadventure was our city, so isolated, so far from anywhere. The plane's wheels surfed the runway. As we halted, a squad of quarantine lads entered to decontaminate the cabin of its microbes with aerosol, stripping layers from our nostrils. A few appreciative travellers kissed the tarmac at the base of the exit ramp. Fumigated and bug-free we submitted to a drug search, removing our shoes after a thorough shakedown.

Sure, there were no threatening guns as in Singapore, but this re-entry, replete with surly sniffer dogs, surprised us. We bussed to the city a little after 6 pm, bewildered after weeks of travel in populous environments by the inactivity. Had there been an emergency evacuation? Ava Gardner's remarks resounded. Within the hour of the working-day's closure, Melbourne's millions were happily tucked indoors, watching television.

A small sea separated us from our more colourful, industrious South-east Asian neighbours. We'd kept much to ourselves on our travels, skimming the surface of cultures, like extras in an exotic movie. Clearly, religious beliefs moved these communities with greater impact than at home. I was touched by simple acts of devotion witnessed in domestic settings, and by courtesies exchanged between individuals. Would some foreigner say the same of us?

Linking hours, Jan and I learned how each other handled challenges, what tastes we shared, our tolerances and enthusiasms. Not least was our preparedness to help each other while ill. Would Jan's exuberance and my quietism serve a long and kindly companionship?

8

School's out

Defying Gravity, Rod Moss, 1977.

We soon shifted from Clayton to the lower end of Milton Street in Canterbury, a five-minute walk from my new workplace. I'd been asked to join the staff at an alternative school, annexed to Camberwell High, called Brinsley Road. Jan was in her final degree year. We rented two rooms behind an elderly couple's house that had the feel of the aunts' dark Edwardian dwellings. The neighbourhood seemed the province of retirees. No children pranced the streets. Lawns and hedges were immaculately clipped as pensioned occupants, having tended morning domestics, were devoted to their gardens. If their well-groomed pure breeds toileted on nature strips, it'd been removed before the deposits calcified or troubled footwear.

Wattle Park was within walking distance. Also nearby was the infamous Surrey Dive where, as teenagers, Kerry and I idled on the quarry cliffs before plunging recklessly into its turbid waters. To think that young Roberts, Withers and McCubbin once roved the nearby hills to paint the bush *en plein air*. Would McCubbin's *Pioneers* have despaired over this tamed suburbia? I envisaged them posing on the grass strip out front. His schmaltzy themes were dated, and perhaps his saccharine palette was a foretaste of anodyne suburbia.

The invitation came from Royden with whom I'd kept contact. Strings had been pulled with Harry Fletcher, Principal at Maroondah High who wasn't enamoured of Scott, the Tassie Devil, or me. While observing the curriculum, we had always extended its boundaries, as well as encouraging familiarity with students that challenged his conservatism. Like many of the students, I regretted the loss of Scott's creativity when Fletcher dispatched him to nearby Norwood High. 'The Devil' had already departed after altercations with Fletcher. Now I followed suit. Scott was writing poetry and scripting a comedy for radio; he and his wife had shifted to the southeast suburbs where I now saw less of him.

A unique and trusting relationship had formed between Royden and Director of Education, Bert Schrumm, to pilot a vision of education within the ultra-conservative state system. One of their agreements was that he could hand-pick staff. Most of the dozen were under aged 30. Melbourne had sprouted a handful of small schools that countered prevailing education. Community Schools, as they were tagged, indicated shared values that might never be expressed in the large state schools.

Each Community School had agendas inspired by young, charismatic men. They captured the heightened feeling of social reform accompanying the newly elected Whitlam Labour government. Brinsley Road, housed in a former hostel of the Salvation Army, was a revelation to me, being a development of Royden's Tecoma program. The school was comprised of disillusioned students from the upper levels of MacRobertson Girls' High, University High and Melbourne Boys' High that had been inspired by Royden. These closely associated urban schools were elite performers.

Radical educational texts abounded. In addition to Neill's *Summerhill*, other reformers had recently published: Paolo Freire, Ivan Illich, John Holt, Jonathan Kozol, and Marshall McLuhan, among them. Pop cultural studies were to the fore. Humans are born free but everywhere, are in chains. Populist philosopher, Colin Wilson, recycled Rousseau's phrase in his work, *Outsider*—

another contemporary author on Royden's shelves. When Royden had rung Neill early one English morning, Neill asked him what age his pupils were. On hearing they were senior secondary, he responded that 'they are too late for freedom'; presumably this was the freedom, with accompanying responsibility, he'd engendered in his democratic nursery since the early 1920s.

Many of our students were from privileged middle-class families who would likely have succeeded in industry, commerce and the arts had they never attended school. Their urging, together with their parents, had been crucial to Royden's confidence in petitioning Schrumm. These young people would have sat through well-informed table talk and accessed substantial home libraries— from birth. Among their parents were members of the new State and Federal Labor parties, heads of business enterprises, barristers, doctors, psychologists, university professors and scholars. Influential leaders and thinkers such as Moss Cass, Cairns, Rector, Holding, Saffir, Feith, and Lowenstein featured among luminaries that believed in revitalising public education.

The grounds and two-storey mansion, built by the Baillieu family in the 1880s, suited our amiable enterprise. Senior Art students took possession of outhouses and stables for studio work. Royden's office housed a marvellous library of contemporary Art books that they regularly accessed. Their end-of-year folio results figured at the top of state awards. No students elsewhere demonstrated an equivalent grasp of what generated from Christo, Oldenberg, Rauschenburg, Jim Dine or Kaprow's documented 'Happenings'. Overnight, one student wrapped all the objects on staff desks with silver foil and documented it. Another constructed an environment incorporating a recycled Hills Hoist. Photomontage also had its exponents, and those few opting to paint, aped the loosely brushed and splashed abstract canvases of The New York School.

I was way out of my depth. There was no school uniform. Everyone was addressed on a first-name basis, distancing strategies that assisted law and order in the state system. Smoking was permitted and popular. The curriculum was infinitely mutable, determined by highly articulate students as much as staff. In good weather Drama and Literature were taught under the great oak, evoking images of Tagore's Shantiniketan School we'd witnessed in Satyajit Ray's documentary.

Yoga and film were also on the agenda. I soon found rapport with filmmaker John Phillips, and several times helped ferry students to shoot scripts around his Research shanty. He organised an excursion to his painter mate, Piers Bateman's rambling mudbrick dwelling at nearby St Andrews, a window for our middle-class students on the earthy lifestyle I'd witnessed the previous decade at Neil Douglas's property.

The entire school resolved philosophical battles and day-to-day operations consensually; crowding into the carpeted ballroom, crouching on the floor, and sitting on windowsills. Minutes weren't kept but Royden's rhetoric established order and direction. He had the orator's gift of changing the pace and direction of meetings. With an ironic aside he'd lighten the mood with a personal anecdote, his left arm pumping the air for emphasis. Turning to field questions from his side, he'd twist stiffly from the hips rather than simply turn his neck. It added gravity to his pronouncements, that the subject of his attention was fully considered. Perpetually tense and doubting, Royden's antenna registered the school's moods shifts. Debates challenged my instinctual avoidance of argument. Empathising with so many voices, I was emperor of ambivalence, drifting on the tide of other opinions.

We were renegotiating rules we'd accepted from our parents and the state system. Students gravitated to favoured friends and teachers on a popularity basis, substituting institutional authority for charismatic authority. Through questioning and respectful listening, self-esteem, and care were nourished. Our million words, shared and spoken, shaped the freedom we felt we'd found.

Following Neill's edict that students learn only when they really want to, attending classes was encouraged but optional. Few opted out completely. One student, when not socialising, spent much of the year reading, in a broom cupboard. Others pursued gardening and animal husbandry.

The timetable advertised the staff's talents and availability, as it did for students inclined to share their skills. Classes were negotiated with teachers usually on a short-term basis. Those sitting Matriculation (Year 12 exams) heeded the state curriculum. Rivalries, jealousies and ambitions were sorted between students and staff, though Royden ultimately counselled the more intractable ones. Regular lengthy consultations took place in his first-floor office regarded as the inner sanctum by a select number of senior bods who gathered there in support. Detention and strapping were from another place and era.

Royden's load was massive; I wondered how he carried the anxieties of so many parents who, entrusting their progeny to his experiment, were in regular contact. Their children questioned them as much as they did we staff, and there were no guaranteed outcomes. Staff also needed his support; we shared our vulnerability during long evening meetings at various staff residences, where student and staff issues were thrashed out. A definite energy emitted from this transparency, a feeling that honesty and openness would stimulate self-awareness and productive action. Authority and respect were earned rather than assumed. Would this situation suit students less secure about their place in middle-class lives—those less disciplined or motivated?

The friendly rivalry between Carnivores or Vegies stirred daily when meals were cooked, exposing food's central role in our lives. To supply the kitchen and food co-operative, rostered staff and students shopped at Footscray Road's Wholesale Markets in the small hours.

Singer-songwriters, guitars tucked under arms, sat in the mansion stairwell or beneath shady trees wooing prospective partners at will. I was inspired to learn guitar and be added to the burgeoning numbers of aspiring Cohens and Dylans. John Scott had introduced me to Jesse Winchester, exiled in Canada to dodge conscription to Vietnam. His early discs, without mentioning war, reflected the crisis he'd endured. His pure tenor elevated sentiments with serenity—at odds with Dylan's world-weary grooves—and was the first whose basic chords I emulated. The likes of students, Steve Connolly and Ronnie Reinhardt, later members of Paul Kelly bands, were on hand to guide my fumbling fingers.

At the end of six months, Royden, exhausted by the pressures of inexperienced staff and anxious parents, took indefinite sick leave and went into retreat. During this time his marriage crumbled. I visited his secluded lodgings where he told me that he was undergoing counselling with a guy called Thomas who, at least, was holding him from falling further. He was disillusioned with not having brought the school to its creative and artistic possibilities and developing a post-secondary model. Broad though his shoulders were, and broad his freckled face, he admitted defeat. The chemistry of his leadership and charisma were unlikely to be replicated; momentum lulled in his absence. His creative imagination and uncanny understanding of adolescence had ridden the aspirational wave of the late 1960s' cultural reformation.

At year's end the lease expired so new premises were sought. The Department tempted us with portable classrooms in Camberwell before we settled at Argo Street, Prahran. This building had also begun life in the 1880s, but as a Quaker institution for female prisoners. Its redeeming feature was a giant fig tree occupying most of the small grounds. During the Second World War it catered for 'wayward girls and friendless women'. Though these weren't propitious antecedents, the choice between Argo Street and portable classrooms was a no-brainer.

A few streets south was hip Grenville Street; home of a cobbler, baker, funky clothes, bookshops and an import record store—the height of 'cool'.

Inner city suburbs like Prahran. Carlton, Fitzroy and Brunswick, attracted New Age enterprises. There was an influx of therapies, many asserting legitimacy through claims to ancient traditions. Reflexology, Aromatherapy, Dowsing, Tarot Reading, Bach Flower Remedies, Acupuncture, and exotic forms of massage were marketed to a willing audience, prepared also to indulge ginseng and Oshawa's macrobiotic diet. Yoghurt and sourdough were cultured in home kitchens.

Astrology hadn't enjoyed such popularity for centuries. Homeopathy returned after decades of obscurity since the advent of penicillin derivatives. I was curious to try some these but was never ill enough to truly test their efficacy. Specialist bookshops catered to Numerology, Crystal Power, Pyramid Power, Colour Healing and whatever. Not Aversion Therapy, though. The piped song of whales and stench of incense gusting through their doors kept me on the pavement.

Health shops appeared, selling bulk product in paper bags, much as in my childhood, but now boasting credibility with 'organic' or 'free range' labelling. It was odd, this health business, this ethical consumption. Talk of health foods and lifestyles hadn't figured around our plain tucker upbringing. Besotted with footy in winter and cricket in summer, there had been no cause to promote exercise amongst our peers.

Domestic TV was enlivened by comedians, Paul Hogan and Norman Gunston. Hogan's swagger traded on clichés milking easy laughs that helped popularise the national ocker image of beer-swilling mateship that countered rising feminism, environmentalism, and Aboriginal rights. Gunston burst out of the box, taking satire to unprecedented levels; mocking talk-show hosts in the guise of a pathetically aspirational celebrity. Dressed in an appalling lurex tuxedo, fly at half-mast and sporting a comb-over and conspicuous shaving mishaps, he careered guilelessly through his sets singing toneless versions of popular songs and appearing unprepared for the guests he interviewed. This feigned sincerity was disconcerting and all the more liberating for its subversion.

Royden's replacement was unsympathetic to our program, sitting alone in his office dissociated from staff and students. The latter now comprised mostly disaffected teens falling through mainstream education and referred by Education Department psychologist, Betty Murphy. The ideals piloting the original charter were significantly compromised and few of the inspirational senior students made the move to our experiment, preferring to sit Matriculation at mainstream schools.

Vertically structured classes survived the transition, however, so older students mentored younger ones, coaxing those who'd rejected adult authority back to class learning. Still, the tension with the principal undermined our confidence. Only the previous year, I'd experienced the disorientation he was enduring. But we were on different trajectories now, and I couldn't abide his resistance to our ideology so was unable to offer a consoling aside. We sensed his unease with students interacting with staff and their open affection with each other. What authority he tried to impose derived from old-school thinking we'd tried to bury. Staff in meetings and individually had attempted to bring him on board, but without success.

I was sitting in my car at Canterbury station waiting for Jan to arrive from university when the 6 o'clock news reported John Phillip's drowning at Port Campbell. One minute here. The next gone. John, so vital and attuned to others. We'd taken an immediate liking to each other, both bemused by Brinsley Road's rollercoaster dynamics. I readily assumed his invitation to help student-initiated film projects, helping to scrounge cedar planking from a defunct coolstore to build his shack. John and his wife Marie, lived an alternative life with their sons at Research—the region continued to attract artists after the Great War, and was popularised in the 1930s with Jorgensen's Monsalvat colony, and the likes of Clifton Pugh and Neil Douglas. The boat with him and Piers Bateman, capsized in heavy seas. Bateman managed to swim the two kilometres to shore—four decades on, Bateman would be less fortunate in another maritime incident.

I was speechless when Jan opened the door; struck dumb. Death's great partaking, everywhere, continually and without discretion. Though there was no foretelling its advent, I'd associated it with old age, not a talented aesthete of 30, with beautiful Mexican partner and two tiny tots.

My grieving settled two months later when he visited me in a dream. We were in the hull of a sunken vessel resembling the theatrette we'd fashioned from Argo Street's first-floor dormitories. He tapped his forehead by way of explaining he'd been unable to swim to safety, having been struck by the oarlock. I woke in tears. I'd not recognised the stored tension but could feel my heart soften. The following weekend I visited his widow and two toddlers to share this dream. Marie had had a strikingly similar dream that week, as had three-year-old Jojo, who'd told her he'd seen his father during the night.

Science teacher, Peggy Cole, suggested we tackle a stage version of Edna O'Brien's, *A Pagan Place*. Enterprising student James Dean enlisted volunteers to demolish the small rooms of the former upper-floor dormitory to create a theatre. We took some of our frustrations out on the walls. A month on and many barrow-loads of rubble later, we had our theatre. Though John wouldn't see the outcome, my labours were dedicated to him. It was wonderful stepping from our selves into those characters, and rehearsals were welcomed for their collaborative power. The play proved the year's highlight, performed for parents and students, and repaying the volumes of dust we'd ingested.

Though Royden hadn't contacted staff or students, news he'd left for England added to the stress of students and staff; one of our 15-year-old students, Rudy, went on a rampage, breaking windows and smashing bottles. When I heard the breaking glass and his swearing, I quickly moved to where he stood, his arm raised with a bottle. Facing him to me with hands on both shoulders, I met his tears in silence. Without berating or restraining him, he let the bottle drop. With my hands still on his shoulders, I told him softly I too, suffered the loss of Royden. Many of us did. 'It's all fucked,' he said. I couldn't have agreed more. We shuffled off to our separate ways.

I took the semester break at Phillip Island in my parent's caravan, contemplating Janov's *Primal Scream* in tandem with historian of the West, Dee Brown's *Bury My Heart at Wounded Knee*—both troubling texts. Janov provided case studies of emotionally disturbed patients and claimed reliving birth trauma could cure any number of repressed behaviours. How repressed was I? Janov's revelations caused me to project my confusion and unhappiness on my parents. Was my abhorrence of caves and fogs, or the dread sometimes experienced on waking in blacked-out bedrooms traceable to some struggle in mum's birth canal? For all the author's claims I was not about to submit to unauthorised practitioners of his therapy. It seemed an overstated First Cause, akin to the significance of time and place of conception for astrologers.

Dee Brown's report of shameful depredations visited upon America's First Peoples by settler culture—serial betrayals, displacement, sickness and massacres—were a recipe for tears. There'd been recent news of a ten-week siege at the same Wounded Knee of Brown's book. Back in 1890 the US military massacred an estimated 150 Oglala Lakota. Once more, heavily armed military turned out in force. After a 71-day standoff and sporadic gunfire, the siege concluded after the death of a prominent Lakota man. Finally, in April 1973 after repeated failures to solve the Indian grievances, US Attorney General Kent Frizzell, and Indian activist Russell Means, signed a settlement. Clearly, the fight with the government to honour its treaties with First People's nations persisted.

Were there were parallels during Australia's colonisation? Henry Reynold's revision of Australian history addressing my question had yet to be published. However, Aboriginal voices via oral history projects were beginning to appear. In a Richmond bookshop, dedicated to Aboriginal Australians, I accessed Dave Morgan's recommendations: Elkin, Coombs, Rowley, and Stanner. Stanner's, *After the Dreaming*, was very compelling. I ruminated on something an Indigenous confidant told him: 'White man got no Dreaming'. Surely, he wasn't referring to the stuff of my nocturnal life, or the history of European Dreamings that Warwick's lectures elucidated. What was this Dreaming? I wrote to anthropologists Margaret King-Boyes—an Ouspensky admirer—and Nicolas Peterson, who clarified the unintentional confusion the term provoked between European notions of sleep imagery with Indigenous creation stories. In some parts of Australia, the creator was a dingo and in other sites a huge snake. Past, present and future co-existed in Dreamtime stories as life followed a cycle in which there was no real beginning and no real end. Stanner's claim that the culture of First Australians possessed 'all the beauty of song, mime, dance and art of which human beings are capable', was a departure from their usual museumification and an invitation to learn from living beings.

I took long beach walks in the blustery winter winds, worrying about Royden, but could do nothing other than write to him. Long letters arrived in black ink detailing his ideals and introversion. My chest and stomach were cold and dry. His correspondence didn't ease concerns. It was a dark, low time through which, on returning to city digs, I steadied myself, drawing a suite of images depicting domestic gardens with writhing vegetation and discarded artefacts. The eye view was elevated and close-up. I'd sit before an empty sheet and allow the initial marks to dictate development. Images poured from my mind's eye without error. I say mind's eye, unsure if this adequately captures the experience. It felt instead as if my imaging had transferred from head to hand, and my hand was sovereign of my thoughts. Having sharpened pencils for the following day I'd stand and walk the nearby blocks at dusk. Everything was washed and remade. Trees were groomed and moths swirled in fanatical hoops around street lamps. Pigeons settled in the eves, chortling two-toned lullabies to chicks. I drew myself from despondency.

The school's increasingly tenuous state totally preoccupied me, gradually superseded my relationship. I sensed that Jan realised my drifting, but lacking courage and clarity, I called a halt to our intimacy, without explanation. Rather than allow sufficient time to clear my head, I soon transferred my murkiness to Gina, older sister of one of the students, whose fluid, relaxed movements were those of a dancer. What trust could I fathom in her lake-blue eyes? Any fibre of rationality succumbed to flattery. Yet again, I was at the mercy of my hormones. Drifting. Very much my condition.

When maths teacher Alla Marshall, offered me residence in her ex's Armadale studio, I gratefully accepted. I'd been granted 0.5 study leave to pursue further painting studies at Caulfield, just five minutes' drive from her door. Mostly, though, I rode my bike to Prahran, Caulfield or Gina's North Balwyn home.

Still emboldened with Janov's newfound psychological wisdom, and veteran of failed relationships, I fronted mum while dad was at work, suggesting she quit the family home. In tears she admitted deep unhappiness and, I assumed, was convinced she should separate. When I returned the following weekend prepared for the fallout, they met me at the door and told me I wasn't welcome. Weeks later, again in tears, she told me she had nowhere to go. I was in no position to offer help and regretted having exposed her.

Mornings at school were spent with my home group around an old door rescued from storage in an outhouse. Inspired by master of animalian hybridity, Hieronymus Bosch, I sketched animals frolicking around its edges, and encouraged the group to carve them in low relief. The absence of a singular focus in Bosch's polyphonic compositions reflected my inner state. Bosch had begun his artistry decorating a table with circular designs of arcane icons, though recent awareness of this congruity humours no one but me. We did this while chatting and reading *Cat's Cradle*, savouring 'untruths' penned by alluring rebel, Bokonon.

Catch 22 was our other text. Both Vonnegut and Heller's farcical works reflected their experience of war's absurdity. The humour of *Catch 22* resided in the price we placed on freedom by passively trusting and obeying rules we assumed our institutions made to ensure our happiness. The distance between our professed ideals and the policies we accepted were manifested in sinister, Milo Minderbinder, representative of globalised capitalism gone berserk.

We needed legs for the table and heard that Brinsley Road was being demolished. I drove with Mauritian student Jack Curé, to the school the following Sunday, intending to dedicate four banister posts to the table's corners, thus incorporating some school history. The heavy front door Royden had restored was gone; so, too, was lead from the shingled roof. We hacked away at the staircase and were celebrating our haul at home with a cuppa when police rapped on the door. Had we been at the Brinsley Road premises and removed something? Its parlous state and my fantasy of fixing bits of our former abode to the table had muted my faint sense of criminality. The police reminded us we were trespassing, and theft was not to be taken lightly. Having revealed the contraband stacked in the boot, they escorted us to Camberwell Police Station. I clarified I was Jack's teacher. 'And, Mr Moss, what exactly do you think you are teaching Mr Cure?' The constable phoned The Salvation Army boss. Though upset at the loss of roofing lead, he didn't wish to press charges. In fact, he was pleased the banisters suited our project.

Late July, I submitted to an operation on my nose that had been broken during football some years before. It hadn't been attended at the time and my sinuses had begun bothering me. Back to the Eye and Ear Hospital I trundled, for the first time since my troubled ears and rotting tonsils. Though I'd not been hospitalised since my tonsillectomy I trusted the anaesthetist, doctor and nurses implicitly. Things were explained carefully, including the anticipated outcome of the surgery. I didn't finish the countdown to oblivion after the needle's contents flooded my veins.

I returned to consciousness in an unfamiliar public ward with tingling in my fingers and toes advancing along my limbs. My nose was packed with cottonwool. I panicked. There was only one patient in the eight-bed ward, lying at the far end of the room. I called feebly but my tongue froze. Was I dying? Here I was, comfortably tucked up in crisp cotton sheets after a minor nose job, consumed by my absurdity, petrifying in the 'Iron Ear' Hospital— death, so quick and painless, and not on Asian roads or killing fields. In the midst of vigorous health my lights could be switched off as swiftly as a roach squashed underfoot. But it was not death at all. Someone responded to my agitation. A nurse appeared and pressed the emergency button. A doctor came and covered my mouth with a paper bag. Within minutes the oxygen balance was restored. I'd hyperventilated. Never had I swung so swiftly or tenuously between desperation and gratitude.

A month later I re-joined the footy fray. At the first bounce the ball fell into my arms. An opposition player charged through the centre circle and, with no intent of dispossessing me, smashed my nose. I plugged it with cottonwool and continued playing, realising I'd ruined the surgeon's work. Repeating the procedure was beyond contemplation.

***

Some albums have particular resonance, striking accord with one's sensibility and sustaining hope. As *Astral Weeks* once added value to my circumstances,

162

studio days at Alla's were guided by David Forman's eponymously titled album, caressing wounds, inspiring romantic attachment, and stirring sentiments. Lost then found. For months it was the first disc fitted to the turntable and the last to be slipped in its cover at night. I knew nothing about him either before the recording or subsequently, but an entire era was articulated in those forty-three sublime minutes. Here was the vulnerability of a Vietnam veteran voiced without irony or self-pity: perfectly weighted and without cliché.

Other musical events marked the year. Little Feat, arguably the best live band at the time, played at Festival Hall and I was exhilarated by lead singer, slide guitarist and writer, Lowell George. *Dixie Chicken*, the band's release that year, was rollicking good time 'swamp' Blues. Bruce Cockburn's solo concert in the Camberwell Town Hall was of a different cloth, however, underpinned with religious associations. While his nasally voice had none of George's sensuality, he accompanied folky hymns to nature with deft guitar picking. If Little Feat thrilled my body, Cockburn's musings were cerebral pleasures. Celtic music was also new to my ears and Alan Stivell's harp at Dallas Brook's Hall roused much of the packed audience to its feet.

***

In November, the school camped in cabins on the grounds of the former Lake Tyers' Mission. During supper on our last day, news broke that Governor-General John Kerr had dismissed the Whitlam government. I doubt any of us realised that Kerr, rather his office, was empowered to do this. Together with the significant numbers of 'leftist' parents and kids in the school, I felt a curtain drop over the optimism Whitlam's government reforms introduced, and more that they promised. Gough, like none I'd heard previously, by addressing us as 'Men and Women of Australia', had made us walk taller. Young lives were no longer squandered on strange soil, since he'd returned the troops from Vietnam. His restructuring of the education and health systems was quite simply, revolutionary. And he placed the Land Rights of First Australians squarely in the public domain with the dramatic dirt sifting into Vincent Lingiari's hands at Wave Hill. It was a deeply dejected busload driving into Melbourne that evening.

Without our knowledge the principal had been in regular communication with the Department, so in hindsight his resistance to joining with us at camp wasn't surprising. Schruum the innovative educator and departmental head who had supported the Community School movement, had recently retired and was succeeded by Lindsay Thompson. Our untenable relationship terminated that December, at the end of the school year, when he closed the school. Allegations from the Department of student drug use were rife. I was unaware of any dealing or smoking of 'weed', though its presence in schools at that time was widespread. Staff were re-deployed at various inner-city schools, mine being Princes Hill in Carlton. Without teaching commitments, I was delegated to paint a mural in the stairwell of Princes Hill's old theatre. Former Collingwood ruckman and carpenter, Graham Jenkins was replacing its steps, so we fell into reminiscing about the Pie's regular, but abject, Finals' appearances.

Turning into Spring Street as we march on Parliament House, Melbourne, 1976.

The school's closure doubled our resolve. We were determined not to see our experiment quashed so over the Christmas break, we met regularly; and throughout next term, staff rostered in pairs, quietly absenting ourselves from our allocated schools to assemble with students at the State Library, the Botanical Gardens, the National Gallery, and elsewhere. Melbourne University Students' Union offered the use of their rooms. Buoyed by the success of recent anti-war protests, we realised that press coverage was essential to air our case. If it wasn't reported, it hadn't happened. We organised media coverage and, several times, protested on Parliament steps in Spring Street. Television and print journalists interviewed parents and the students we'd nominated, to plea for reinstatement. We lived our political freedom when granted a church hall in Fitzroy Street, St Kilda. Over three years we'd moved from the middle-class umbrella of Camberwell High, to hip Prahran, to the Wesleyan bluestone church in Fitzroy Street. The last location no longer the fashionable address of the late nineteenth century, but now notorious for petty criminals, prostitution, drugs … and us.

***

School re-opened in Term 2 under the steerage of veteran teacher, David Schapper. Early in his brief tenure he advised staff that what kids needed most was love. Ah, that troubled word that keeps the mind simple, flowing frequently from the lips of the flower power generation! It was the first and only time I'd heard a headmaster offering its palliative comforts as an educational strategy. When silver-haired Schapper slipped into his kaftan to relax, his espousals of love made New Age sense. He'd brought with him his son-in-law, Allan Tasker, with whom he'd taught in Gippsland and intended grooming as his successor. Allan was a highly motivated art teacher whose practicality and fair-mindedness re-ignited confidence and set a solid foundation.

There was much re-purposing of the building to do. Apart from sourcing discarded furniture from its Port Melbourne warehouse storage, the Department left us alone. Staff and students, with parents Allens, Ottos, Gregorys and Taylors, led discussions to develop a constitution. What we lacked in charismatic leadership was more than compensated by the strength of the parent body that was in closer touch with staff and students.

Prospective students were interviewed by students, staff and parents, to gauge each other's needs. The manse was part of the deal, and its small rooms were allocated for secluded study. My time was split between cooking, table tennis, reading with my dozen home group, woodcraft in a shed behind the hall, and footy in the park lining the opposite side of Fitzroy Street.

New staff members were inducted as we'd lost three able bodies during the period of uncertainty. There must have been some allure about the Northern Territory at the time, because gifted Literature teacher, Toly Sawenko, left for Utopia, 250 kilometres northeast of Alice Springs. He subsequently worked for the Central Land Council, featured as the pivotal character, Arkady, in Chatwin's popular book, *Songlines*, and was dedicated to Indigenous affairs. Science teacher, Peter McFarlane, joined staff at the Alice Springs High School, and. craft worker and basketball coach, Colin Wilson, travelled further north to the remote Numbulwar community in the Gulf of Carpentaria.

What motivated them? Was it the emerging sense of duty to our dispossessed First People? Perhaps some feeling lingered that Indigenous groups, having survived for millennia without recourse to Western technologies, were better informed to halt the ravages we visited upon our environment. These concerns were crystallising for me, too. Leftist social conscience was responding to Indigenous radicalisation, inspired by America's Black Power movement. Among guest speakers at St Kilda were Indigenous activist, Gary Foley, and social documentary filmmaker, John Hughes, who I knew through Scott.

Over many weekends, I camped with my home group. Our trips were predominately east, as it was easier to access and more familiar to me from childhood. We would commandeer the school's old Ford Transit and head to Phillip Island, Walkerville, Lerderderg Gorge, or Mount Feathertop, and rough it under canvas. These were big times for bush-starved adolescents who were predominately school 'drop-outs'—the camping really helped them. I, too, felt release where botanical coherence remained intact.

Gradually, the proportion of disaffected students from local schools, outnumbered the original cohort, placing increased stress on us all. Most were from single-parent homes, so staff agreed that to understand the family dynamic and convey our agenda to parents—who probably viewed us as a last resort—we'd visit their homes, on invitation, for supper. Staff were aware our guest appearance would not accurately reflect daily life in these homes, but there was no doubt our understanding of circumstances were enhanced and generated trust between home and school.

One weekend I ascended Feathertop with a student to witness a winter eclipse. I'd introduced 14-year-old student Don Campbell, to rabbiting in Ouyen and he'd taken to it with a vengeance, alleging man was a born hunter. Rabbits proliferated in the Mallee, at Bonnie Doon, the Howqua Valley, in fact, wherever we camped. That Friday we parked at the base of the path in the freshly minted air, delighting in an eyeful of the blue haze draping the ranges and spurs before they dropped into coppery twilight. Don was fiercely competitive and relished being first to Federation Hut, on the snowline, where we camped overnight. Rising at 'sparrow's fart' after a night disturbed by rats and possums, we walked the ridge in time for the event.

Five Melbourne Technical College students had braved the snowy ridge in a tent. They had set up a Super 8 video camera which was trained on a model globe showing Australia, and a bottle of champagne to uncork in celebration. The backdrop would be the eclipse. With interlocked arms, and camera on, we danced around the globe as birds disappeared in the darkening sky. I reckoned on a prompt descent straight after the eclipse, so had started along the precipitous ridge when brought to a sudden halt by an inexplicable phenomenon. There, on the snowy ground at my feet, was my shadow, ringed by a full spectrum; a thing to marvel. When I dropped Don home later that evening, a new book, *Alps at the Crossroads*, lay on his parents' the coffee table. When we moved upon its contents, it fell open on a photo and short description of what we'd seen, noting the rarity of it observation. And what of this chance confirmation on the heels of our experience? This feeling of being in just the place where certain elements coalesce gave rise to speculation of much greater coherence in all matter.

Another weekend, I walked to Lake Tali Karng to test my capacity for solo adventure in the wilds of the Gippsland bush. Dad had mentioned this 'bottomless' lake in the so-called Valley of Destruction but had never visited it. I was no stranger to the Wellington River but had never sourced it. My untried *Chippewa* boots bit my ankles and I abandoned them within an hour, stashing them in a hollow tree. The remaining rugged 15 kilometres, with river crossings, I trekked in socks. There was no signage but occasional forks in the track reunited after ten or so minutes of mild panic.

I had no map, had done no research, and was unaware that for the *Gunai Kurnai* people once inhabiting the region, the lake was sacred so camping forbidden. I had my survival kit, an old cigarette tin to reflect in the eyes of prospective aerial rescuers. It housed cotton thread and a safety pin for fishing, a shred of matchbox and a dozen matches. Wind roared suddenly up the narrow clefts of the valley and I steadied myself against a tree, flexing my thighs to hold ground, inclining my head to the bark to shelter from the swirling grit. Onwards up and down, up and down, I strode.

A couple of hours later the track rounded an ill-defined ridge which I took to be my destination. A steep path descended to the ink-black waters, my steps quickened by gravity and relief. Exhausted, I fell asleep on a mossy bed in the space provided by a fallen gum, protected from the starry estuary but not my dreams. I awoke before dawn, believing the log was crushing me. Pins and needles numbed my left side.

Peeling out of my sleeping bag beneath mocking kookaburras, I dipped my head in *Tali Karng* to shake the dream. I suspect it addressed anxieties that accompanied my walk and the urgency to return to safer realms. It wasn't a big body of water, so having circumnavigated its narrow track I started back, retrieved the boots and picked passage over the pebbles of the chilly river to relieve my tender pads. Curiosity was tamed and I never repeated such foolishness. Without a tent and carrying only a sleeping bag, sultanas and smoked almonds, and relying on river water, I survived by luck more than management.

On a long weekend, the Snowy River beckoned; I'd not been on the Gelantipy track since our family camp at Butchers Ridge in the late 1950s. Turning east on McKillops dirt road was uncharted territory. I set up beside the spectacular Little River Falls and dipped in the icy waters of the largest pool, slipping beneath the prominent overhang, and lapsed into a trance behind the torrent. Next morning the twisting dirt trail became narrower. There were no signs. Out of curiosity I detoured along a fire-track and chanced upon the vertigo-inducing Little River Gorge. I wasn't trustful of the rails on the overhanging viewing platform. Nausea arose as I imagined the risks made in its construction. Dropping on all fours, I crept forward and peered below: an eagle's vantage over the wooded gully with river cascading endlessly in lacy, lopsided veils gathering at 300 metres in fringes of spray, dispersing and dousing the mossy granite walls before gathering again for the last third of its descent to the valley floor.

Settling the vertigo, I stood and returned to the car and was soon cresting the range. The glistening Snowy snaked below the plateau. I was still literally on edge. One side was rock face. The other, sheer drops, causing a replay of the overactive imaginings back at the gorge. Great avalanches of grey shale gave voice to previous slippage. Fortunately, I didn't encounter a single car in the high country that weekend as there was provision for passing only on two bends of the seven-kilometre descent. I pitched tent within sight of McKillops Bridge and roamed both sides of the river, envisaging its depths prior to the hydroelectric power plant in headwaters upstream. Ten to 15 metres above the present level, branches had been snagged in tree forks. Cattle driven south to Victorian pastures had forded here since the mid-1800s until the bridge's construction during the Depression.

Noticing rabbit scats near the tent, I set a trap a few metres from the fly. The morning of my departure I heard it slap shut. I snapped the rabbit's neck, skinned and gutted it, and packed for home.

Jack Curé had recently demonstrated his mother's mode of preparing Creole rabbit: the carcass was peppered, salted and deep fried. So, having boiled a saucepan of oil, I submerged the rabbit and waited for it to crisp to a honey tone. On being cooked, I bit into the soft flesh of its back and swallowed a mouthful before realising I'd pierced a cyst. Could this be hydatids? I panicked and rang the Poisons Board in a sweat. A lab assistant came and collected the rabbit. I got the runs, imagining a slow debilitating death. That evening, I received a call: it wasn't the dreaded cyst, anyway, the technician casually added, I'd have been one stage removed from the cycle of contagion. So much for my recent lenience regarding eating only meat I'd caught myself. Was I carnivore or vegetarian? I was flexitarian, preferring not to draw attention in company and be accused of asceticism.

These flings didn't improve bush skills. Experiencing them alone, may have strengthened an illusion of independence but it was a romantic veneer at best, something I'd never contemplate without a car or secure food supply. Luck, rather than managerial skill, was on my side, and problems were rare. The co-operation with students, putting up camp and eating together, was sufficient to stand repetition. Health and Safety issues were a long way in the future. These days we'd never have got out the door nor have the Transit van pass a roadworthy.

Tasker's conciliatory nature was key to the feel of the place. Size-wise and with a consensual approach, we still owned community ideals. If anything, while lacking the glamour of its *avant garde* predecessor, the students' identification with school as refuge was more pronounced and crucial to their stabilisation. But the emphasis Royden placed on the creative process, indeed as he embodied it, had shifted to the periphery. I realised that the exceptional moment of the Brinsley Road School was just that. Though the school's dynamics had been constantly challenging, if not traumatic, I was satisfied with my contribution, attenuated though it was.

***

The drawings done the year prior to study leave underpinned my first exhibition at Hawthorn City Library's Gallery entitled, *Trophies and Abandoned Luncheonettes*. I had an understanding with lecturers that I could work at Alla's studio and attend Caulfield Institute, fortnightly. The creative thrill had been experienced during the drawings' moments of dislocation between conscious thought and expectation, and associated sensations. Like an orgasm, the moment when the conscious and the subconscious are opened up, the pores open simultaneously, sending messages into the nervous system. The experience of drawing didn't attend the paintings, though they were sufficiently competent to gain the diploma. It was good to have that first exhibition behind me and realise that art could transport me to more explorative places. Gratifying though the review and sales were, I felt empty, a disconnection between making and showing art. Me, the maker wasn't me, the friendly guy chatting away with people enthusing about art.

I desperately hoped the Gurdjieff 'Work' might improve matters. Bennett's books inspired my hunger for Being and mentioned a school in Gloustershire he'd modelled after Gurdjieff's experiment. Then I heard it had closed. A few months later, I was delighted to hear that in response to the growing numbers of American students willing to undertake the year's Basic Course, he'd shifted operations and purchased the 400-acre Claymont estate in West Virginia For me, that there was a school imparting practices geared for westerners was irresistible. It made no difference to me whether it was in England or the States. We were just as remote from both.

My application to study at The Claymont School for Continuous Education had been accepted by Director of Studies, Pierre Elliott. I enquired about Gina's suitability, given that she knew next to nothing about Bennett or Gurdjieff. He wrote that the last thing the Work should do was to separate couples. In addition to mental and physical well-being it would be appropriate preparation for her to earn the Course fees through her own labour. I purchased airfares for Gina and me, and paid my 5,000-dollars' course fees. Gina raised her tuition fees at the Camberwell Bowl snack bar. I resigned and planned to survive on my cashed in Superannuation and the sale of my car that sister Marilyn kindly marketed.

9

The New Age

Descent, by Rod Moss, 1980.

And so to our year on distant northern shores. I'd severed my umbilical cord to the Education Department. The sun arced in a different direction and cars motored the wrong side of the road. Weeks passed before my body adjusted to these elementary facts, during which time, instinctively looking to my right before crossing, I was nearly cropped thrice at kerbside. From Melbourne's winter we arrived, via London, to the humid Shenandoah Valley to spend the year studying the 'Work'. We had stopped a week in London with re-energised Royden who'd worked as a seasonal deckhand on a yacht moored at Dorset. He'd consulted with anti-psychiatrist Ronald Laing, who claimed he couldn't help him, so was currently seeing psychological astrologist, Liz Greene.

Royden recommended Jungian scholar James Hillman and, accordingly, was analysing projections he, Royden had made, and those directed at him. Jung's terms anima and animus regularly featured in his talk; anima being identified as the totality of the unconscious feminine psychological qualities a man possessed, and animus, the masculine ones possessed by a woman. These were our 'shadow' or repressed selves. I found Hillman's interpretations of archetypes a marvellous stimulus for imagery.

Royden hurried us around the Museum, the National and Tate Galleries, and to Watsons and Foyles bookshops. Numerous buskers worked the London Underground, both its corners and on trains; so many minstrels singing for their supper. John Martyn, Dylan, McCartney and Joni Mitchell were recognisable in the mix, all delivered with panache that shamed my mimicry. The rail tracks rattled 50 seconds before trains appeared filling our nostrils with flakes of steel and permanganate. Though the pandemic of singer-songwriters had spread to Melbourne, perhaps bylaws prevented them from performing on our streets. These drifting notes were welcomed in the dingy tunnels, each artist maintaining space sufficient to distinguish songs and compete for coins.

Having landed in New York and taken the subway to Central Park we were confronted by half-a-dozen mute, African Americans carousing the carriage, pestering passengers for money. Between gymnastics on the hand railing, they high-fived, something I'd regarded as a movie mannerism. I recalled Larry Peerce's harrowing, *Incident*, Royden had screened at Brinsley Road. And though nothing terrifying happened, we were relieved to regain the pavement and find lodgings overlooking Central Park.

A few days were spent at *The Museum of Modern Art*, where for the first time I could recognise the fuss made of paintings I'd seen only in reproduction. Books couldn't convey scale, touch and luminosity. At the Gotham Book Mart I picked up volumes on Duchamp, Duane Michal's *Real Dreams*, and Apollinaire's *Zone*, to gift John Scott. He was planning to translate *Zone* and like me, had affection for the Surrealist enterprise. Not all, or even most of it, though. Magritte's visual puns struck accord, and Max Ernst's *frottage* works inspired some of my experiments, as had Cornell's whimsical boxes.

The bus hove south along the eastern seaboard passing immaculate, unfenced lawns, and double-storey homes looking like the sets of 1950s' chaste TV families—the *Nelsons* and *Cleavers*. Here, the American Dream bourgeoned. Flagpoles bearing the Stars and Stripes proliferated, displaying a patriotism unknown in Australia. There was no evidence of Dylan's discontented land here. Swinging towards West Virginia, the Dream fragmented, though hovels and trailer homes still managed to hoist the flag. There were fewer well-kempt lawns, older model cars dumped on them, and houses crying for a lick of paint.

Claymont Court, 1979.

Claymont Court estate, also in need of a lick, was six kilometres outside Charlestown, a town of drab respectability, tidy without trimmings. We alighted for refreshments and work overalls at *Pennys*, and waited for Georgina, one of the residents, to give us a lift to school.

Bushrod Washington, nephew of President George Washington, had once owned the Claymont estate. The mansion he built, once the largest in West Virginia, was dilapidated, and our practical work was regularly devoted to its restoration. The Civil War had caused the family to divest itself of the property, so it had been through several hands and abandoned for many years prior to Bennett's acquisition.

Already I'd heard the word 'god' in common parlance invoked with reverence unfamiliar at home where his name, as mum might remind us, was mostly taken in vain. I'd not thought of God for years, but its prevalence here had me thinking. While gathering carrots in the kitchen garden that first week, I asked a fellow student and astrophysicist if he thought God was real. 'Is the Pope a Catholic?' he snapped, perhaps wondering what I was doing there.

There were a little over 50 students on the course. Five other Australians, a Danish family of five, a Danish schoolmistress, Danish actress Anne-Lise Gabold with infant, Gai, an Alaskan couple, three Canadians, and a German were the exotics. The rest were white Americans. All save Gina and I, had arrived from some grounding in Gurdjieff groups. Group work was recommended to assist in noticing personality flaws about which individuals were 'blind'. According to Bennett's educational principles, like-minded group work produced helpful energies no individual could build in isolation.

We all hailed from liberal democracies in search of some elusive thing that might underpin material existence. Yet it was savings wrung from capitalistic economies that facilitated 'dropping out'. There were no Third World representatives or anyone from a Marxist regime. No surprise really. Gurdjieff had fled Revolutionary Russia, aware his Work was antithetical to the Bolsheviks.

Though Bennett acknowledged Ouspensky and Gurdjieff's influence, he'd not confined his quest for meaning to them. After decades of tireless investigation, he felt impelled to help searchers with techniques to find their inner order. The techniques promised elevated creativity freed from machine-like slavery, to engage instinctive, motor, emotional and intellectual behaviour. The strengths and weaknesses imposed by our personality type would be discovered through arts, crafts, techniques of various kinds, and the effects they produced on consciousness. I was eager to press my body into such situations.

Bennett's aim was to prepare communities of people for the privations he believed were about to eventuate with the collapse of capitalism and environmental disaster. So education would require arrogance to submit to humility, selfishness to service, and expansion for its own sake to be replaced by acceptance of the quality that simplicity alone provides. Work on oneself was a complicated business because, while it focused on 'me', its striving for communal glue countered the surging individualism of consumer lives.

At the outset, Bennett insisted the question, 'Why are we here?' be asked. How must we contribute to conscious human evolution? His elucidation of energy levels was attractive, though the contention that a heavenly intelligence or Hidden Directorate surveyed our affairs, was a leap of faith beyond my grasp.

I wanted to be more patient with myself and overcome a host of practical aversions and incompetence. Gurdjieff's quip, 'Going faster than God's mother' definitely applied, in my case. I was careless with car maintenance, lacked monetary ambition and home ownership—those many things occupying my fellows. My little axe hands, apart from art, were often at the bidding of poor planning. Why did the language of user manuals and legal documents remain opaque? Had I no ear for foreign languages? Was I just lazy, lacking confidence, or desire? What other students aimed for, I didn't know: altruism, astral bodies, immortal souls, knowing the future, peace on earth—there were countless options. I wanted to be able to access at will the sublime state of rightness when painting, which Boronia schoolmate Tony 'Loupas' Lintermans, captured in a poem.

The pulse which is promise flowers into fact,
life takes flight like a bird in my blood,
love without limits falls towards the forms.[1]

Occasionally my artwork was 'on song' as if it had almost effortlessly completed itself. Decision-making on the way to completion seemed to come from somewhere other than my ordinary, thinking self. Indeed, thoughts were suspended. I wondered if this state was what Warwick referred to as pure consciousness, the quality he marvelled about in Picasso's late re-workings of European masterworks. Had this underwritten Klee's yearning to be 'as though newborn, knowing nothing, absolutely nothing?'

Such occurrences were the height of life. Tony's poem was inspired by a moment, after hours of rhythmically scything horehound in a stony paddock, when he looked up and saw the creek and surrounding trees and hills as a field of dancing atoms, a flux of colours. And I suspected that motivation to nudge the creative button accounted for the writers, musicians, dramatists and painters who subscribed to Gurdjieff's Work. Bennett's 12-tiered ladder of energies was a goad to develop sensitivity and access creative energies. The farming and house duties were merely forms in which our attention was to be tuned and my flimsy focus exposed. Gurdjieff's call for 'conscious labours and intentional suffering' was a lifetime's effort.

It was my first taste of a deciduous landscape. Corn sprouted above head height. Roadside stalls swilled with the scent of apple juices and ciders. The ranges sheltering the valley were a riot of red, orange and yellow-leafed maples, elms and poplars. I could have been standing midst the musical brotherhood of The Band as they posed before Elliott Landy's camera for their eponymous album cover.

Nearby, Harpers Ferry was so picture-perfect it was impossible to imagine it was where John Brown's small rebel army initiated a heinous war. The prim facade it presented to tourist flocks concealed the fact that masses of Civil War dead dropped throughout these forests. Primed with old-time religious fervour, Brown preferred action above rhetoric in his quest for abolition. He

---

1   Tony Lintermans, 'Falling Towards the Forms', *The Shed Manifesto* (Scribe, 1989).

had blood on his hands from a skirmish with slave owners in Kansas. The plans hatched with sympathisers to raid Harpers Ferry arsenal went awry. Yet his martyrdom proved the catalyst for the war he felt necessary to free the enslaved. 'The cries of the guilty land will never be purged except with blood', the prescient Brown pronounced the day of his hanging.

By coincidence, almost 120 years to the day of his utterance, we students assembled on the banks of the Potomac to present a public performance of our play, *The Christmas Key*, mirroring master-slave relations. Whether our theatre director knew the town's history or our play's parallel theme, I never knew. I did know that the war had touched Australian shores. Not only had four-score Melbournians been recruited by the Confederate Navy when its warship *Shenandoah* docked in Williamstown, Melbourne, but the cessation of slavery and the cotton industry driving the South's economy, prompted Queensland to fill the void, black-birding Pacific Islanders to bend their backs over Australian cotton and sugarcane.

Despite Civil Rights successes, I was struck by the fact that African Americans still did much of the heavy lifting and dirty work as garbage and petrol-pump attendants. I was shocked when converting a travellers cheque in Charlestown at the raging complaint levelled by a businessman at the black teller whose slow sums challenged his patience. The customer summoned the manager and heaped a stream of invective on the teller with a demand, if short of dismissal, then for him to improve his maths. The black guy's cowering face said it all. Racism was alive and kicking.

Later, there was snow, soft and flaky, unlike the occasional falls of compacted hail on the Dandenong Ranges. It fell silently one still night, and though the evening's mustard skies forewarned us, a buzz of delight swept the dormitory next morning. The white blanket sucked up sight and sound. Birds were nowhere to be seen or heard. Things seemed more distant and cloaked in a strange, immobilising lethargy. The sun peeked through the trees, shooting enamel-blue shafts of shadow from the feet of the forest. Apart from the disappearance of familiar objects with the first fall, snow failed to impress me—it meant cold and wet. I deplored working in such conditions and was advised by seasoned residents to procure silk-liners for my work gloves. Next opportunity, I headed back to Penney's Department store to equip myself for the challenge of what Bennett referred to as the First Liberation—freedom from our Likes and Dislikes.

Pierre Elliott, 1980.

One regime constant was cold morning ablutions each day in preparation for an hour's graded sensitivity exercises, performed in sitting positions in the octagon-shaped building. No one enthused about the showers. Yet I confirmed for myself that rubbing the skin with cold water cleansed it of accumulated waste energies and prepared a state of maximum attention. I found sitting cross-legged or kneeling was excruciating. During the first trimester, Director of Studies, Pierre Elliot, led these morning exercises which bore no relation to calisthenics but resembled mediation classes, aimed at inner rather than muscular work. He took particular care in the wording of these sessions, allowing adequate time to complete the relaxing and filling of sensation that were preliminaries to each exercise.

In this regime, relaxation was the turning point for self-observation with regard to tensions arising, as the ego defended itself from what it disliked engaging with—sitting still for example. At first, I noted how stiff I was before stilling and steadying my body. Ceasing the constant flow of thoughts that brought about total relaxation was challenging. It didn't take me long to be able to direct posture, to sit still in a cross-legged position. However, ceasing thoughts was tantamount to surrendering the very being I'd hoped to discover. Were not my thoughts what constituted and governed my self?

Pierre had worked with Ouspensky, Gurdjieff and Bennett, attending Gurdjieff during his final days in Paris, 1949. He also commanded respect because though 65, he was as fit and lithe as we students half his age, sitting the hour ramrod straight and motionless, without visible discomfort. Hair brushed back, he sported an Abe Lincoln goatee, and dressed casually in sneakers. Presumably, he exemplified the Work's creed, each breath taken consciously, a man liberated from the bonds of like and dislike and negative emotions. From the outset, he disclaimed he was a teacher, that he'd merely had the fortune to have benefited from the company of those he regarded as such.

When we met to review our work for the week, he waited for our circle to settle into a 'collected' state, gazing at each of us in turn, assessing our condition. He would pause before commenting, frequently volleying a student's observation back, to see if they could grapple for its essence. He'd gently purse the fingers of his right hand as if clutching the small egg of a rare wren when asking if we could search deeper for the essence of experience. Work on these themes set a tone of sincere self-observation that flowed through the course.

Of the many group experiences, the most impressive were these where personal insights were shared. They demonstrated how solutions to problems might be met without conflict in a setting privileging empathy above criticism. It was a reversal of any form I'd experienced, yet I had difficulty exposing the vulnerability of my ridiculous self. Even the free and lively questioning environment Royden had fostered in our staff meetings, was underwritten by anxiety that the school should adopt his vision. There was little time for pondering in those charged and reactionary gatherings. How could I encourage candid self-disclosure in my intimate relationships?

Pierre suggested we leave aside any reading, the better to attend the texts at the core of our study. If we must read, satisfy that need with comics. That we were advised not to take notes, challenged my well-grooved practice; I didn't relinquish my journal until Christmas. The hour prior to the evening meal, there were readings of Gurdjieff's magnum opus, *All and Everything*. The author recommended three readings of his text. Pierre would sit, book in both hands, relaxed on bended knees during group readings. Before commencing, he removed his glasses, thick as the base of a beer glass, and held them to the light to clean. No sooner did we struggle through one reading than the next ensued. As with the weekly group theme sessions, we learned how painful profound listening could be.

Most of us came to Gurdjieff via Ouspensky's, *Search for the Miraculous*. Yet if it hadn't led to Bennett's lucid writing, it was unlikely that I'd have journeyed to Claymont. Several students had read Gurdjieff's tome and declared it a work of genius, a contention my incomprehension couldn't challenge. Its obfuscating prose and parables were perplexing. Gurdjieff wished to mercilessly smash the illusory worlds of belief that people had cushioned themselves with and replace these with his 'objective' system. Though set in a more portentous key, his book reminded me of Mark Twain's *Letters from the Earth* that also employed Satan's wry commentary on Mankind's plight. Not that Twain proposed a salve for our shared ailments approaching Gurdjieff's, very saintly Ashiata Shiemash.

Curiously, given the era in which Gurdjieff wrote, little attention was paid by him to discoveries that were revolutionising Western culture: relativity, quantum physics, radiation physics, to name a few. And speculative ideas and artistic movements including psychoanalysis, existentialism, phenomenology, Expressionism, and Cubism gained no traction with Gurdjieff.

As with the readings, meals and morning exercises, we strove with varying intent for a 'collected state', not as a group but to individually focus attention without which our aims and endeavours were enfeebled. Most students dawdled to the octagon for the morning's inner exercise. There were habitual laggers whose shuffling of prayer stools and cushions disturbed the punctual bods. Pierre was among the early arrivals, slipping off his sneakers and adding them to the pairs at the door.

One morning he was sitting out the front long before anyone, looking as if he'd been there all night. He had yet to assume his rigid posture, intently studying his clasped hands rather than resting them on his knees. What was he thinking? Surely not 'mind-fucking' as a female student assured me occupied 90 percent of men's mental space. Nor would he be contemplating the fortunes of his footy team. Perhaps he was thinking about God, or blessedly, not thinking? More shuffling, and he asked us to stand and perform the crucifix exercise, with arms sideways at shoulder-height. I took it competitively, to stay the five minutes with Pierre. Certainly, this was a wake-up call, but were we now in a heightened collected state?

Considering one of my lures had been initiated by coincidences and pre-cognitive dreams, I was disappointed to be told that we should pay as little attention to dreams as possible; both those at night and daydreams. The necessary energy for transformation derived from stemming their tide. But some had such substantiality they inveigled my attention from the present moment, and returned me to other compelling accounts of coincidence, such as Koestler's citations in, *The Case of the Midwife Toad*.

One exercise to bring attention to daydreaming was the 'Stop exercise' that Pierre occasionally affected. We were caught unprepared at these moments, required to freeze in the posture we were in when the command was given. Fleeting thoughts, gestures, tensions and feelings were observed for a minute or so until Pierre cried, 'Continue'. It was discomforting to note that as I spooned porridge to my lips, or swept the reading room, there was no 'I' behind the driving wheel; that most activity drifted on automatic pilot.

I could buy into Gurdjieff's concept of reciprocal maintenance, that living things fed on one another, a pact between degeneration and regeneration that fitted Warwick's notions of metamorphosis. Herbivores munching grass clingers, moulds and aphids on leaves, our own decaying corpses fertilising the earth, all self-evident endorsements. But the scale of Gurdjieff's teaching travelled where I could not when introducing the appetites of cosmic entities. His report on human suffering was delivered from a distant spaceship, rendering us puny and pathetic. If earthlings were to rise above this state and cohabit harmoniously, we should recognise our blind spot. The *kundabuffer* organ, he said, had been implanted to prevent us from encountering the truth of our sad state that, if removed, would cause us to lose all hope. Was this, my conscience, the voice guiding decisions and actions, especially when no person was present to check on me?

Most enigmatic was his notion that the moon, a younger version of the earth from which it was catastrophically rent, required involuntary human sacrifices sustained by war. According to him, our souls could be transformed by opposing the moon's tug with conscious digestion, assimilation, contemplation and breath. Our persistent automatic passivity fed the moon.

I couldn't sort the literal from the metaphoric. Assertions of the moon's influence on the liquid lives on earth, on menstrual cycles, tides, sap and semen had been observed for millennia. I was unaware of its gravitational power fondling capillaries, moods, images and sensations, tugging my liquids back and forth. The dynamic duo, sun and moon, determined our days. But Gurdjieff's claims were linked to an all-inclusive notion of the solar system I couldn't accommodate. That the Work was directed at 'soul formation' demanding the cessation of dreams was already a big ask, despite its promise of alleviating suffering, illusion and potentially, war.

Each day commenced with the clanging bell just before 6 a.m. and terminated at 10 p.m. after two hours of sacred dance movements. Its tolling at meal times was unanimously rejoiced. I was dutiful with kitchen work, dormitory cleaning; and elected to join the handful of forestry workers keeping the wood supply topped during the winter snows. This was stacked on the outside wall of the boiler room, standing near the main building and providing the school's hot water. Pairs of students rotated shifts to feed the furnace, and it was a popular hangout for smokers gathering to gossip after meals.

Predominately we were urban professionals who possessed little muscle tone, few practical skills or initiatives. Years of running and footy training had me pumped for physical work though it didn't mean abandoning introspection as the weekly theme and sensitivity exercises which required my attention. Our group of five would halt on the edge of the forest to sense its energy field as we entered, my imagination diverting to those grey and blue-suited Civil War lads, ducking bullets between the birch and oaks.

When I raised the Civil War with other students, I was surprised to find my high school American history had been more informative than theirs. Morbid curiosity drew me one weekend to nearby Antietam where a staggering 23,000 soldiers had died in a single day. The field's sombre air was palpable; 750,000 died during that four-year conflict. And the region's prior occupants, the Shanantoa, Iroquois and Cherokee had been moved on long before, according to chilling accounts of ethnic cleansing by early settlers.

Claymont was a work in progress rather than a perfected model so provided dramas aplenty, notably practical incompetence where the blind leading the blind was frequently foregrounded. I was appalled with the unnecessary death of the community pig. A neighbouring farmer had shown interest in it. As its litter was now weaned the next chapter in the sow's life was about to start. Donning heavy rubber boots to combat the fouled mud, we quarantined the babes and pursued their mum around the pen for over an hour, trying in vain to corral it. Neither Gina nor I knew what we were doing. Nor did Sid, the resident charged with animal care. It fell exhausted, black eyes blinking at us through blonde lashes, before expiring.

We filled one of the bathtubs serving as a trough and hauled the poor thing into it, lighting a fire beneath to facilitate the skinning of its hide. Meat was a rare indulgence, so the prospect of pig was generally welcomed. Prospective chops and bacon had students licking their lips. How testing for my aversion to be on kitchen duty that day while it cooked. The reduced grey paste, referred to as 'brain food', didn't tempt me from the vegetarianism reinstated since my sortie with that rabbit cyst.

Another time, under the guidance of our practical-work supervisor, three of us spent an absurdly wasteful winter morning, each laying three cinderblocks with the assistance of copious anti-freeze. These were the foundation of the chicken enclosure that would replace their primitive wooden shack. What were the lessons? How common was our common sense? Here was another example of passivity before the assumed authority of the resident's instruction. 'Hutch' had left us after setting the task. For all we knew he was chuckling to himself in the warm Nissan Hut housing his worm farm. As it was, the chickens were content in their coop and still there when the course concluded, the building site much as we'd left it.

Chilean theatre director, Horacio Munoz, was putting our large cast through Shakespeare's *Comedy of Errors*. Like most Claymont residents he'd graduated from Sherbourne and worked in Denmark with *Teater Klanen*. It was odd hearing Shakespeare's musicality distorted through American intonations. Munoz allotted roles, casting Gina in the romantic lead with a New York Italian, spiking mutual affections that had been flickering. Rehearsals added conviction to the jealousy required of my role as Antipholus of Ephesus, uncomfortably blurring art with life. Perhaps Munoz derived pleasure in choosing a play whose title bespoke our endeavours on the course.

At every turn drama continued. Four enamelled steel poles supported the ceiling of the reading room. Informed of the imminent visit from a Turkish Sufi group I thought to enhance the uprights. In the half hour between supper and evening Dance Movements, I painted patterns from Keith Critchlow's study of Islamic designs. The month elapsed and the Halveti dozen were with us. I was in charge of the kitchen of a feast honouring their arrival. We'd decked the dining room with a Turkish ambience, so I considered the poles a suitable fit. Having seen to the serving and led the mandatory grace, I backed into the kitchen, careful throughout to face the sheik and bow thrice as instructed by Pierre.

At the time, my mind was racing with fears of my failing relationship. Rather than increasing our bonds through the Work as I'd hoped, Gina first needed independence from me. That was the stark reality I battled with, the letting go. I sought to shrink from sight, Gina's and the entire assembly, and was staring blankly at a wall when Pierre appeared unannounced through the door and asked, 'What's cooking?' He'd been sitting beside Muzaffer and surely knew. He raised his hand to halt my listing the kebab's ingredients. He meant my inner life. Having confided my turmoil and asked for advice, he suggested I paint out the columns.

The suggestion was vouchsafed by the Director, no less! I jumped at what might be an acute opportunity for self-observation, perhaps a revelation. My daubing might be the work of an inflated ego. Would I be liberated from angst, or recognise that time with the poles would have been better spent sorting through my expectations with Gina? Having been more invested in the creation of the designs than the result, I wasn't disappointed by returning the poles to their prime condition. Anxiety persisted. Were Gina and he at that very moment rehearsing lines from Shakespeare's *play*, her tenderness extending to him, not me? Perhaps I was meant to realise with merciless force Gurdjieff's quip that 'Man cannot do?'

The Sufis had accepted Pierre's invitation to share their practice of zikyr, or remembrance. Their sheikh, Hadji Muzaffer Efendi, conducted their ritual while incorporating we, students, with his followers. It was a concerted emotional event. Muzaffer stood midpoint of our circle as we contracted and expanded chanting throughout, changing the tempo and with it, our breathing. The duration of this ceremonial prayer was at Muzaffer's discretion. He, it was who sensed when appropriate energies had been attained, whether forty minutes or several hours.

There was a question and answer session at its conclusion late one night, and I asked Muzaffer why the Halveti favoured tobacco addiction yet censured alcohol. What nourishment did this chain-smoking Brotherhood seek that freely given air did not supply? He paused, 'Allah gave tobacco leaf for man to enjoy. Alcohol make him crazy. Man already too crazy.' Maybe I missed something in translation; so many Sufi tales were deliberately cryptic. While Muzaffer's explanation might seem self-serving and cheer the tobacco lobby, drinkers could argue Allah's benevolence regarding their addiction, with equal conviction. It was a cheap point but how would I subscribe to any devotional practice when such logic prevailed. Then of course, logic wasn't a necessary adjunct of devotion.

In collaboration with student and neurophysiologist Susanna Bloch, Munoz experimented with emotional states by altering breathing, facial expression and body positions to assist our acting. We stood with arms dangling, inhaling brief saccades through our nose, followed by a single exhalation through the mouth, then we were directed to drop heads and look at our feet. Within a few repetitions, we were enveloped in sadness, some of us on the verge of tears. This technique showed how we could induce anger, fear, joy, eroticism and tenderness. I'd never noticed that with both tenderness and anger we breathed in and out through our nose, while fear and sensuality are characterised by breathing in and out through our mouth. Happiness and sadness could be induced by breathing in through our nose and out through our mouth. Given the rapid changes demonstrated by these patterns, it was small wonder the Sufi chanting and dancing affected our state.

Munoz suggested Carlos Castaneda's *Teachings of Don Juan* had parallels with the Work. My trust in the author had been tempered by Richard de Mille's scathing revelations that his books were an elaborate hoax. Don Juan's tips on heightening consciousness were likely literary inventions. Initially, I'd gulped down his volumes as a true believer, grateful for their suggestions of expanded worlds, although his posing as an anthropologist did arouse caution. Munoz insisted that Castaneda, like Gurdjieff, pointed to the need to develop inner faculties to open us. Both insisted the ego should be our servant rather than our master; our 'ally', was Castaneda's term. 'Develop your own presence. Get a Life. Become effective in some way,' Munoz said, shrugging off my doubts with a polite smile.

We were in complete agreement though with Kurosawa's masterful, *Dersu Uzala*. A Russian captain leads a small contingent of soldiers into the Siberian wilds on a survey, presumably during the Trans-Siberian railway's construction in the early decades of the twentieth century. The centrepoint of the movie is his reverent and graceful friendship with old Dersu. For the most part this is intuitive and wordless, the Indigenous hunter notably forced to speak only twice, when saving the captain's life. The captain, with appropriate humility, recognises the hunter's unique authority in the land. He gradually learns how to survive near impossible weather and to act with dignity and compassion. We see both Eurocentric and First Peoples' approach to life: those seeking to alter their environment, and those striving to live within the given. Kurosawa's evocation aroused my hankering for a more connective life. Though neither captain nor hunter could exist in the other's world, for a brief moment they are brought together to show how and why we should.

***

I never fully grasped the exercises. Relaxation, okay. Sensing my body, yes. But checking the regions above my genitals, I failed to detect *chakras*. Nor could I locate the 'sacred impulses' of Faith, Hope, Belief, and Love transmitting from Lhasa, Varanasi, Mecca, and Jerusalem along an imagined thread produced from the centre of my forehead. The exercises revealed the paucity of my imagination and strength of my wishes. Far be it for me to dismiss their efficacy. Some people must have received something to be endorsing them. And whether Gurdjieff or Bennett borrowed, stole or invented these and the Movements, they were testament to capacities exceeding mine.

Ironically, for someone who had parted company long ago with alcoholic beverages, my sole 'spiritual' experience at Claymont derived from indulgence in high-grade alcohol added to cider. The students assembled one morning at a neighbouring apple orchard to gather windfalls. A copper cauldron, borrowed from a farmer in the adjacent hills, was propped over a fire set in the open between the kitchen and boiler house. Ten of us paired up for 48 hours, rotating stirring duties, with metre-long wooden ladles we'd fashioned, to reduce the fruit to pulp. Some men siphoned juice from the cauldron and converted it to alcohol. I bucked self-imposed restraint and indulged. Though the much-vaunted apple sauce was vastly overrated by locals, the brew rewarded our labours. A Canadian, Mark, hearing about the cider, tempered it with his 98 percent-proof alcohol. And with it me! Unfamiliar with alcohol of any description, I was still intoxicated the next day and unfit for morning exercise. I sat up and did a round of the breathing and holding pattern we'd been taught: my perceptions intensified dramatically. Crazy! The threads in my blankets, cracks in the wall, dust on the floorboards—all were massively significant. Aware of my state, Gina sent a student from the octagon, where morning exercises were beginning, to watch over me. I sensed, while trying to share this world, that each utterance cost me a grain of visionary power. I wanted to see how the fields and woods presented, so he patiently chaperoned me downstairs through the kitchen garden where corncobs whispered, and to the walnut orchard we had planted the previous week. Leaves, insects, their scents and sounds, shapes and colours, held me in a thrall of harmony I'd never before seen. Having rejoiced over the freshly turned clods of earth and seedlings, the intensity dissipated as the alcohol burned off. It was a wonder-filled world but not one I'd earned using the Work on myself. How could such sensate vigour be maintained?

The previous evening's events feeding this exaltation were less laudable and hazy, at best. Following rehearsal, Mark, clutching his supply, and perhaps a half dozen cast members, squeezed into our bedroom. Apart from Gina, the only other certain identity surprised me. Actress, Anna-Lise, not a cast member and with a toddler to care for, had minimal participation in the course. We hardly knew her. I wondered if her husband and director, Horatio, had sent her. Did I care? As the evening progressed, in the manner of my father I'd pontificated about American voices mangling Shakespeare's language and distorting the gist of his phrases. What would I know about Shakespeare? Virtually nothing other than what I'd heard and likely misheard of Olivier, Richardson or Gielgud in a few films. I was certainly no expert on idiom, cadence, or much of what my lines meant. How long I prattled on, I have no idea. Perhaps my learned discourse terminated with the single remembered event. At some moment amongst this unmooring, my lips closed upon Anna-Lise's, a contraction obliterating the rest of the evening, and possibly my last move before passing out on the floor. The others must have witnessed this, and surely Gina, who while possibly finding me entertaining, may have gained courage in her dalliance with my Syracusian namesake.

***

The sheikh of the Mevlana Order of Sufis, Suleyman Hayati Dede Lorcas from Konya sent his youngest son, Jalaluddin to the course. Part of his residency required him to transmit the 'whirling'. While wood collecting, I'd see him strolling the forest singing to himself and to the chickadees and cardinals, the Order's ritual chants. Only when performing *sema*, the whirling sufi dance—a form of physically active meditation—did his corrugated brows unclench. He built a one-metre square dais with a brass nail at its centre. We salted the nail and placed it like a thong between the toes of our left foot and slowly turned. We crossed our arms and placed palms on our shoulders, then, with the right foot perpendicular to the left, we turned our left foot to the right without lifting the heel from the dais. The left foot pushed, and the body turned with the right acting as a wheel. Arms outstretched, the right palm was turned upwards, the left on which we fixed attention, faced the ground.

The giddiness reminded me of our schoolyard game where with bending bodies, we rotated around a finger pointing ground-wards, laughing at our wobbly attempts to regain balance. The focus during *sema* gradually dispelled our giddiness, and its centrifugal action definitely effected welcome freedom from self-concern. The one caution given was that no alcohol should be drunk in the hours preceding zykr. Thursday evenings, Jalaluddin dressed in Mevlana-mode—dress, cape with 'tombstone' cap on his head— and led the sessions.

Jelaluddin Loras performing sema, 1978.

Come Thanksgiving Day, Pierre surprised the Americans by introducing fasting, an affront to their national day of ritual indulgence when God's help in slaughtering the Indigenous population and thieving their winter food supplies, was celebrated. After his breakfast announcement, a collective grumble floated through the corridors. He cited traditions that recommend abstaining from sex and lustful thoughts, and restraint from unnecessary speech, clothing and reading. It was not true fasting, he suggested, when one anticipated the next meal, or commented on the good or bad behaviour of others.

Indeed, at the time he was attempting a 40-day fast, that he terminated on the thirty-fifth day, in response to gossip about him having an affair with a visiting ex-student. He spoke of gossip's pernicious force and how subtle and oblique were its consequences. Gossip-mongers might have felt guilt over Pierre's aborted fast, but why had he not risen above this? The small school communities and towns like Ouyen were examples of how people oiled their moral machinery through gossip. 'What will the neighbours think?' was one of mum's main governances. Pierre carefully avoided the issue of the small talk. My lack of interest in his affairs didn't make me feel above those who'd participated in its dissemination. It was not his travails that rose before me but Doug Sanger, a lad from my third year of high school.

Big of body, voice and with acned visage, Sanger floundered through the days since his late arrival, hoping to impress, but only succeeding in keeping himself at odds with us. On this unforgettable day, he, inevitable butt of other boy's jokes, had detonated the last class with some failed witticism. There was a round of rejoicing at his expense at the lockers as we piled books into bags, freely mouthed we believed, behind his back. Hitherto, while noting what they'd said, I'd withheld comment. But now, though with less volume and vitriol, I added force to their talk and in doing so, I felt soiled even before I saw him. It was as though he'd waited for my endorsement to stand and slam shut the coat locker door that'd shielded him. Then, in the terrible woundedness seen in the rapid glance he tossed my way, I was again afflicted. Though my words were mild, I never apologised before he left the following year. My self-recrimination endured, even as his pain may have weakened.

***

Concentrated self-observation easily distorted into self-obsession. There was little spontaneity or laughter at Claymont. Work on one's self was dour stuff. In psychology classes, 'false personality' was highlighted. Our belief in a 'permanent I' was regarded as self-delusion; to think otherwise was a lie. Yet I regarded my multiple selves as my authentic, if unstable self. Witness the people who quickened my comic self, and others, my sorrow. Wasn't this empathy? Surely perpetual seriousness was counter-intuitive, another falseness.

We were presented with a surfeit of exercises to remember ourselves; stopping on the sound of the midday bell and sensing our hands and feet, inhaling before uttering the word 'I' in conversation, being aware of the food we ate as the initial mouthful entered our mouths, or noting changes in ourselves as we turned door handles and transitioned from the energy of one space to another.

Though we had little regular news of events beyond the Claymont property, the Jonestown mass suicide of more than 900 followers of Pentecostal preacher, Jim Jones, in their community in the Guyana jungle, filtered through. I assured my parents that the experiment here was diametrically opposed to the herd mentality of Jones's cult. Our process was aimed at encouraging us to stand on our own feet by developing independent thought. Gurdjieff himself had often discouraged followers when he sensed their dependence on him. It was an ideal sanctimonious Krishnamurti also espoused, despite decades of courting devotees at his seminars.

We were diligent and sombre about the Work. Exeats every few weeks—granted at Pierre's discretion—fostered relief, expectation and tension. Hitting food outlets was foremost. We could then forgo the lemongrass tea I dismissed as gnats' piss, and drink decent coffee. Vapid margarine on toast was substituted by a welcome spread of butter.

Our attention was drawn to the sensitivity required during food preparation and the importance of a balance of fresh and cooked food. Greens and root vegies came from the large kitchen garden, and tofu, yoghurt, porridge and bread made daily. Seeds and nuts, reproducers of new life, were occasionally available. And yeast's enlivening of dough, we were reminded, was analogous to the transformation we were undertaking on the course: the spark that refined energies. But not much culinary skill emerged from the kitchen. The predominately plain vegetarian meals had me snacking on peanut butter and dates, despite suggestions that eating between meals disturbed digestion. During our visits to town restaurants we anticipated richer, saucier, and varied food.

There were several young mums on the course and at a Sunday breakfast one time, the three-year-old son of one voiced what was occupying many heads: 'Pierre, when can we have an exeat?' American accents sprang naturally from these children, bemusing and exposing my pained adolescent attempts at Dylan mimicry for the affectation they were. But young Cero was merely mimicking his parents, as I once had. Mimesis had paved my progress ever since, affecting the styles of sportsmen, teachers, and now, spurred by dissatisfaction with my culture, the way of the exotic and humble Sufi. As if to reward the infant's fearless lack of pretence, Pierre instantly responded, 'Let's have one today'.

It was other cultures that spoke with accents, not Gina and me. Dining out, waitresses requested we repeat orders just to hear inflexions they couldn't place. From what part of England or South Africa did we hail? One waitress, perhaps thinking our population spoke only Indigenous languages, congratulated us on our English. A fellow student, equally ignorant of Australia, had laboured for months under the illusion that Gina had earned her course fees working at a 'snake bar'. We all hooted when clarifying that snakes were not on the menu of the Camberwell Bowl snack bar. But hey, Australia: anything goes!

The breaks were a valuable check on the outside world. Some preferred to stay on the farm and tend private chores. Most took full days in Georgetown or half-days in nearby Winchester. We were stunned that Washington's massive malls, dwarfing those at home, traded on Sundays. Each shop, it seemed, required an accompanying soundtrack to attract and boost sales, a ploy that gradually gathered favour on our shores.

A couple of times I chanced upon musician favourites. Doug Sahm headed a bill with Kinky Friedman at *The Cellar Door* in Georgetown. *Grateful Dead* songwriter, Rob Hunter, strummed and croaked through an acoustic set in a dingy movie theatre. And Norman and Nancy Blake picked their Bluegrass ways on the back of a truck at a Maryland fair.

Tensions escalated after Christmas. The cold temperatures, the communal life and the course restraints all kicked in. I responded to an outburst of tears from Anne-Marie with a consoling hug and sat with her in the emptied dining room listening through her sobs to her account of helpless struggle with our theme of Noticing. Later, I consulted Pierre as to whether I'd done the right thing. His blunt reply was, 'Did it help you?' which cast doubt on my ostensibly charitable gesture. Was I as benevolent as I thought? I felt an instinctive need to go to her, much as I had when mum wept at grandma's death.

Perhaps I had been flattering myself if I considered gentleness, courage, or honesty were impulses coursing naturally through me. It was a Camus moment, more precisely his narrator Clamence in *The Fall*, who unmasks the hypocrisy of his outward modesty, virtue, and generosity. Was I merely gratifying some lust for power but hoping Pierre would approve my kindness? We persistently lie to ourselves, he'd told us more than once—a fundamental self-deception.

After lunch, as several of us passed through the Reading Room to the foyer, we could hear thwacking and shattering of glass. Texan, Cliff, for reasons best known to himself, was smashing windows in the foyer. A blast of frigid air gusted against us spectators, paralysed by the violence. Pierre came past and, without pause or word, relieved Cliff of the offending club and punched out several more windows. Handing the club back to Cliff, he proceeded unperturbed as if the event had been scripted, Cliff's thunder stolen. He gave a hangdog glance at his weapon, then at us, who shared his bemusement. Pierre at play and Cliff, slumped in desolation, exposed again to the despair that instigated his outburst: the weather let in.

In contradistinction to Thanksgiving, on 13 January a feast was staged to celebrate Gurdjieff's birthday. Some students, unable to wait until official exeats, occasionally sneaked out on late-night grog runs to Charlestown, or across state lines where higher-percentage alcohol was sold. Otherwise, consumption was minimal. Following Gurdjieff's legendary meals in Paris, vodka, tinged red with capsicum, accompanied the feast. Throughout the meal, a toastmaster described, then called for endorsements of each of the 21 grades of idiot, thus honouring Gurdjieff's *Toast of the Idiots*; be they Ordinary, Super, or Arch, the truly Hopeless who sees his complete nothingness, a Compassionate idiot whose reason has opened to the sufferings of others, a Squirming idiot not yet ready for help, followed by a brace of geometric idiots—Square, Round, and Zigzag. There were Patented, Born, Doubting, Enlightened, Swaggering and the rest. Passage from one to another higher grade resulted from Work on oneself.

Diametrically opposite to our usage, according to a Sufi tradition, an idiot was one who sought not to live in the world of dreams and illusion. As no one could choose for us, we elected the idiot we felt most applicable when hearing the definitions. Alcohol, according to Gurdjieff, was intended to strengthen the power of one's wish for self-realisation. Muzaffer, strict adherent of caffeine, would surely not have approved. The women drank half-filled glasses. Toasting terminated at the discretion of the toastmaster who sensed the state of us drinkers. Full or otherwise, he deemed seven glasses to be our limit. Here was me thinking that references to intoxication in thirteenth-century Sufi poet Rumi were metaphors for states of euphoria, praised as the product of inward ferment resulting from inner effort. Abandon metaphor! Wish or no wish, the ritual rapidly produced euphoria in us serious idiots.

Gurdjieff's Sacred Dances or Movements, numbering over two hundred and fifty, exposed my stiff co-ordination. Me, who prided myself on my sporting prowess, was found frustratingly wanting. The Movements involved exquisite harmonising of the head-brain controlling intention and attention, the heart-brain of devotion and motive, and the body-brain's workings of the nerves between the spinal cord and the muscles. These were not the harmonious choreographies of classical ballet or modern dance. Loosely resembling folk gavottes and mazurkas, together with danced prayers of considerable gravitas, they challenged habitual gestures. With my head responding to one beat, arms and hands to another, feet and body displacements set to yet another, they demanded relaxed attention which I rarely achieved and certainly, never mastered.

Some of the students had familiarity with them or experience with other dance forms, but incidental nodding of my head to Bartok or Chopin was inadequate preparation for the Movement's dynamic rhythms, melodies and chords. We worked only with the piano although I believed Gurdjieff's music was intended for other instruments. Whatever, the hammering of the piano demonstrated the laws of vibrations more directly than any esoteric reading.

Pierre assured us that not being able to do the Movements immediately was part of their value. It was necessary to see how helpless we were, to experience our anger, awkwardness, or self-consciousness, and go past this phase of vanity. He reminded us that we had each other, grouped around, to help us struggle. The sensitive energy produced from struggling, yielded clearer insights, increased attention, and greater care about others and ourselves, in this philosophy. He reckoned the Movements profited practitioners for a year or so at most. De Hartmann's piano scores, ranging from serene yearning to sprightly marches, were an exquisite fit.

Easter, and Pierre reckoned it best to be with family; not an option for overseas students. Gina and I happily accepted the invitation of a friendly fellow student to his Dayton home, especially given the incentive that we'd tour Kentucky and camp in his parents' houseboat. There were two other considerations as well. Pierre had recently broken the interminable Gurdjieff readings to share with us a passage from his friend Thomas Merton's, *New Seeds of Contemplation*. I'd been excited by his *Geography of Lograire's* jaunty beat rhythms. Merton's verses, evoking colonisation and the Cargo cult mentality, inspired my lengthy poem written in the voice of explorer, Ludwig Leichardt. Both the Trappist monastery Gethsemane, where Merton had lived, and the *Stephen Foster Story*, were near the aptly named Bardstown and Green River Lake where we'd lodge.

En route, we visited our friend's relatives in the small coal-mining town of Hazard. 'Hazard', we smiled in unison, what an address! Bennett's opus *The Dramatic Universe* expressed the importance he placed on the nature of hazard. It was the fundamental situation of Life, of our lives: determining risk, opportunity and decision. Total certainty would be pointlessly dull. Dramatic tension is our lot, whether we chose to meet it or not. Life was certainly hazardous in these parts. Blood had been spilled in violent long-running disputes between striking impoverished miners and their bosses.

The relatives welcomed us on their veranda with mugs of tea and thick slabs of watermelon sprinkled with salt, a custom new to my buds and akin to gulping seawater. For their part, observing my preference for the unadulterated flesh, was a crime against the melon. When we rose to leave, I asked after the whereabouts of Kentucky's famous blue grass. They replied that I was unlikely to see any as cropping methods prevented seed heads developing.

At Gethsemane we were just in time to catch Vespers, the chants placing distance between daily work and the harmony of song. There were parallels between the Order's dietary, sleep, work and speech restraints and Claymont's. Outward restraints were voluntarily undertaken in the hope of achieving inner freedom. I wondered once more at the place of clockwork chanting.

Our repetitive morning exercises promised mastery and release, yet weren't they also endorsements of mechanistic nature?

Foster's story was enjoyable schmaltz, a rapid trot through the songwriter's short life. From childhood we'd been familiarised with his tunes. His nostalgic images of the Southern States brought Jesse Winchester to mind, whom we'd enjoyed at Melbourne's *Troubadour Club*. His breathy set had an intimacy impossible to replicate on a stage like Bardstown's. He seemed to search for each song, inhabit it and let it float. His idle chat between songs built such rapport that his act didn't feel like an act. The Foster bio was geared for a crowd that knew what to expect and expected to hear what it knew. Every inflection of voice and body ran with well-grooved predictability without a single transcendent moment.

As we returned to our friend's Dayton residence, we chanced on Miro's 1947 mural made for the Cincinnati Hotel, now in the city's Art Museum. I was blown away by its scale and intensity. It seemed as improbable to stumble on this masterwork as it might in an Australian regional gallery. His biomorphic figures, sprawling freely over nine metres of unfathomable night blue, were pure joy.

Our biggest break was a ten-day silent retreat with venerable Buddhist monk, Bhante Dharmawara, who taught *Vipassana* through meditation on green light. Green, he insisted, was the most harmonious colour. Like his friend Gandhi, his early working years were as a lawyer before he served as Nehru's personal physician. He was well into his 90s then, not passing away until he was 109. Apart from his glacial pace, he had the vigour and skin tone of a man half his age; a fine exemplar for the practice.

The retreat was held at one of the Reynolds' family farming estates at Long Creek in The Blue Ridge Mountains, North Carolina—Reynolds, of tobacco fame. They had established a self-sustaining community during the 1930s Depression, replete with mini Hoover Dam, stocked with trout. Butter, milk and grain produced on-site supplied the local area. Though descendants inhabited some of the houses, most of the property including the lodge and superb workshop, were rarely used. It once featured turkey and pheasant hatcheries, a movie theatre, dairy, powerhouse, even its own post office. All this in partly cleared land, ringed by verdant stands of maple, locust, oak, dogwood and pine.

We'd practised days of silence at Claymont, the better to observe inner states. Here, silence initially accelerated my mind, and dreams rioted. By day four, these states plateaued. The sensual beauty of the estate intensified; coral-coloured snakes squirmed in the frog-honking creeks, insects on grass, and budding leaves revealed their cellular properties. The guided group sessions were in a hall; and sumptuous meals were provided, the like of which were never seen at Claymont. But I was intent on cracking down on myself, so fasted the ten days. This, I thought, was Work, denying myself available plenty. Initially, I was unaware of topping up on pride. My sense of superiority over non-fasting fellows, and of conquering appetite, grew. Sham sacrifice evolved into perdition.

The challenge during fasting was avoiding thoughts of food. We'd been taught that the best technique was to cultivate the breathing exercise. I meditated on air and how, though we each inhale individually, air remains undivided; how it's the bearer of light, sound, magnetic and electronic forces and is endlessly generous; that we could do without water for hours but only a few minutes without air. Three rounds of Turkish Sufi, Hasan Susud's *zikr-i-daim*, as transmitted by Pierre, and I was recharged; the holding and forced expulsion of carbon dioxide being crucial to harmony. Its enduring appeal lay in simple repeated patterns without force, mantras or directing thoughts.

Bhante led a stretching routine after breakfast. Then we chanted Buddha's blessing before settling into meditation with his slow, barrel-bellied vowels enriching the prayers. Relaxing with closed eyes and allowing the light to dance inside the lids to rouse a blob of green, wasn't challenging for me; I could register other colours, too, with a little coaxing. But sustaining that single colour for more than a few minutes was a challenge.

He was big on water as a healing agent and would study its transparency and weight in the glass as he sipped, drawing attention to its vitality. He recommended bottling it in green glass containers a fortnight before drinking. Green, green, green: we were definitely in the right location and season for this meditation. Other than the fern-gullied foothills of childhood and excursions in the sub-tropics, I'd neither encountered nature this green, nor questioned water quality. Beer-drinking mates would joke that they abstained from water as fish had sex in it. At home I used the recently popularised charcoal filter to reduce additives such as chlorine and fluoride, trusting the maker's claims—it had been devised to purify drinking water from the disease-ridden Thames, early in the nineteenth century. Though inspired while meditating in a Thai jungle, perhaps Bhante's advice grew partly in response to the polluted Ganges flowing near his Benares ashram.

Prior to one session, Bhante recounted a dream to us. 'I am in crowded train as it rushes towards city. When I get to my station the doors open but platform is no there. The doors close and train continue. Again, at next station I try. Again, no platform. The driver talk through intercom saying this train now returning to place of origin. Then I wake up. What you think this mean?' No one ventured an interpretation of the master's subconscious. He chuckled, 'I think it mean, we all mad'. How to understand such a man and his riddles?

Between meditation sessions, he suggested that taking on the suffering of others was man's noblest deed. He'd probably repeated this countlessly during his long teaching career, and I was too engrossed in my own suffering to let it sink in. Gina was edging away, and my thoughts trailed her trajectory. What did the other guy have that I lacked? Was I too controlling? Perhaps my dedication to the course work repulsed her?

Each day we took a walking meditation session outside, practising on maintaining mindfulness. Walking was done alone. I preferred the moving state anyway, no matter how slow, and found the green saturating nature more appealing than that beamed through the lens in the meditation hall. On one occasion, wandering the upper reaches, I found a pasture and lay in the luxuriant grass where I promptly fell asleep. For how long I didn't know. A cow's rasping tongue on my cheek roused me. I sat up startled, surrounded by a small herd of curious bovines quietly observing the miracle of my mindlessness.

Despite Bhante's exhortation that we were in for ten challenging days, the program seemed simple. Just sitting and concentrating on the emerald light would be a relief from Claymont's relentless round of graded attention and sensitivity training as we laboured in field, kitchen, forest or class. Nothing could be further from fact. The more I endeavoured, the more my mind's circus of imagery strayed from its green objective. Peace, happiness, love and compassion weren't bedfellows, and the third eye enlightenment Bhante promised never troubled my brow.

On the final day I approached him, admitting interest in art, asking for advice on colour. The doctor-monk unhesitatingly recommended T.D Jones's *Art of Light and Colour*, a reference that leaned more towards the science of optics than I cared for. There was no inference of Bonnard's intuitive deployment of complementary colours that kept my eyes wedded and enflamed by touch. A fellow student, however, suggested Californian architect, Christopher Alexander's study of 'centres' in his *Pattern Language* that contained a wealth of insights about achieving harmony, including colour. He recounted the intimate process by which we humanised artefacts by permitting light its role. Enthusiasm for Alexander was shared by several students, as were the educational systems of Steiner and Montessori, the latter befriended and endorsed by Bennett.

***

While the Long Creek property delighted me, green light meditation took no hold. Soon after returning we performed the *sema* for Dede who'd arrived from Konya to see how his son was seeding Mevlana's message in the States. Featherweight Dede in his mid-seventies was accompanied by his wife, Ferishte. He presented a radical contrast with Muzzefer who, as we say, seemed to have grazed in a good paddock. 'Cok cok guzel,' 'very beautiful,' he cried, so thrilled he rose from the bleachers, made his way to the octagon floor, and spun rapturously. That moment made all the months of training worthwhile.

Students performing the Warrior Dervish Movement in the Octagon, 1984.

The main impression of these visits was the Brotherhood's connectedness. I'd never encountered such intuitive responses to each other's needs. How different from our striving for individuation, the small school experiment, or footy mateship. As for prayers, there was an insuperable chasm between the lullabies of Sunday School and the physicality and power of Sufi hymns. Our taste of Church was lame compared to their dramatic swaying, bobbing and weeping.

Despite the introduction of different practices at Claymont, there was no directive or insistence that anyone should devote themselves to this or that. Nearing the end of the course, Pierre reviewed our possibilities. What we had experienced were tastes of Work. Some of us, he suggested, might choose a particular line. Take a discipline that benefited you and commit to it for life. Tools had been provided. Some students followed Bhante's Buddhism. Others assumed Arabic names and branches of Sufism. I held to Pierre's advice not to talk about the Work unless practically engaged in some line.

No one at any time demanded anything of me or tried to convert or convince me. The exercises roused me from the passivity Gurdjieff reckoned was the result of modern education. Deep relaxation had for the first time, produced mental stillness in me. Practising awareness and attention to gestures strengthened will. Will was not the same as thought, feeling and sensation, and I came to understand it could overcome distaste, habit, fatigue and other inhibitions or stimulations—not permanently perhaps, but sufficient to keep afloat and productive. I had no interest in gaining a soul nor was I inclined to a faith to enrich the significance of my life, or human life in general. I was not a big-picture man. I needed to feel good about myself and, if art-making was the way forward, to have pride in my product. If cosmic energies were to play a part in this, I would remain ignorant of them and, in Gurdjieff's acerbic phrase, 'die like a dirty dog'.

Gurdjieff's formidable sci-fi allegory remained a challenge despite Bennett's efforts to unravel its neologisms and message in accessible English. What could I tell friends? That I felt more open to experience, more accepting of differing beliefs, and grateful for some practical means of self-discipline? I needed to assert myself with the vigour and enthusiasm I applied to sport. I resolved to give myself five years to establish an art identity through exhibitions. I wouldn't compromise my art to fit perceived fashions. If I couldn't find satisfaction in resolving each painting, what was the point? I had to please myself. But I needed reliable income, too.

***

One of the residents sharing the dormitory was Indigenous American, Richard Rising-Sun. As the course was winding down, I mentioned my sorrow and anger while reading *Bury My Heart at Wounded Knee*. He recommended Ruth Bebe Hill's *Hanta Yo*, whose quasi-anthropological novel was a vivid account of his people's plight.

Before quitting the States, Gina and I joined my Dayton friend in his parents' Kombi and struck across the western plains through Denver and over the Rockies, taking in the Sequoia forests and Grand Canyon. Occasionally, we passed pyramidal stacks of bones fronting farmhouses that our friend said were antlers. I reflected on the government's post-Civil War injunction to weaken Plains Indians' resistance to settlers by slaughtering their prime food source—680,000 deer between 1871 and 1874.

News of Little Feat's brilliant guitarist, Lowell George's death at 34, stunned me as we swept across the Corn Belt. I'd been unaware of his drug-fuelled excesses. The stocky guy we'd seen in Melbourne not long ago had swollen into the 'Orson Wells of Rock', according to a colleague. I'd been untouched by the early deaths of celebrity songsters, Sam Cooke, Tim Buckley, Morrison, Joplin and Hendrix. But we'd witnessed George up close, vital and personal. His passing felt acute.

We alternated driving duties reading *Hanta Yo*, that gave historic and cultural dimensions to the country and recast my image of the old West. However questionable the reconstructed language and conduct of late eighteenth-century Lakota Sioux was, Hill's re-imaging of the silver screen Indian kept me looking for their contemporaries in the streets of mid-western towns. Perhaps I was expecting them to be walking out of Hollywood Westerns so failed to recognise them in civilian duds. Movies romantically falsified Indian lives, rarely venturing cameras on reservation life. And so it was for Australia's First Peoples, in their remote communities.

Not until we were heading back through Arizona did we pick up a Navajo hitchhiker. It was uninhabited flat desert, save some distant buttes. How had he come to be there? What was his name? We couldn't engage him, so assumed he had little or no English. He remained silent throughout our hours, indicating with a faint grunt his wish to alight. There, in a flimsy roadside stall, a young woman held to the shade, a rug spread before her displaying jewellery, woven mats and gee-gaws. There'd been neither a 'hello', 'goodbye' or 'thanks', courtesies I assumed crossed cultural boundaries. Had he no equivalents? Perhaps he was mute? Were we providing an obligatory service in his country?

***

Though I'd not transformed one iota, I emerged with a sense of superiority, having accessed some very select instruction: a member now of an elite club. Belonging, was gratifying and I hoped it wasn't just another mystery club like the Masons. Yet selfless people ignorant of Gurdjieff, were conducting good, compassionate work the world over. How then to expunge this seed of conceit This seed that prevented me from seeing that my self-righteousness and carelessness was like everyone's, and the antithesis of the love alluded to during the course. My script had been inked in terms of possessing the partner who now spurned me. How then to be open to the lives of others?

I headed home through London, Paris, Istanbul and Tehran. Gina would meet her Italian in Greece. Our dance was done. I had been unable to express anger or neediness as my place in her life diminished. Outbursts of negativity, of expressing yearning or criticism, I foolishly believed were not Work-like.

Dulles airport was closed due to fog, so I was diverted to Richmond. Just its name had The Band's defiant lament, *The Night They Drove Old Dixie Down*, ringing between my ears. No surprise then that the Stars and Stripes weren't evident at the terminal. Indeed, behind glass display cabinets were the Confederate flag and grey-uniformed mannequins of the defeated South. Enmities endured, at least here in the former Southern capital.

Having rung Royden from Heathrow I got directions to his abode in Highgate. He'd asked friends, Dr Toby Green and wife, Alison, whom he'd boarded with in Beaminster during deckhand days, if they'd host me for a week. I joined Alison on her daily horse romps through the fields, relieved to quit the city streets now the province of Punks who'd emerged in our absence. Lime-green, orange-and-purple-dyed Mohawks, ripped clothing, razorblades and pins stuck through lips, cheeks, and brows, were a shock to my eyes and physically confronting on the pavement. Royden was tossing up whether Europe was finished for him while urging his young English friend to try out with Peter Brooke's Paris-based theatre group. I was in a hurry to head east, and to leave them in their quandary.

At Gurdjieff's menhir, 1979.

In Paris, I stayed a few days with fellow student Susanna Bloch, in her Paris apartment. She was refining research in breath control and emotion that she would soon develop into the Alba Emoting Technique. Her partner, Yves, whisked me away in his Citroën through fog-filled roads to Fontainebleau.

Here were the forests that inspired nineteenth-century French landscapists of the Barbizon School. Maybe we complemented those images, lounging on a rocky ridge, demolishing bagel, cheese and cabernet Yves had stacked in his wicker hamper. Having quaffed handsomely, we idled through the vast gardens of Fontainebleau. Then we proceeded to the Prieure chateau and Gurdjieff's inauspicious grave amongst the Armenian's family plot in nearby Avon. There was nothing elaborate about this unmarked *menhir* standing amongst some roses between mother and wife. Grey was this day as I acknowledged a chapter's end in my life.

***

I'd written from Claymont and arranged to meet Argentinean folk chanteuse, Leda Valladares, whose voice had sprung from speakers in a Georgetown bookshop. Apart from food rushes on exeats, I spent considerable time to sampling and stockpiling discs that were hard to find and cheaper than at home: *David Ackles, Willie de Ville, Television, Talking Heads*, and *Pierre Bensusan*.

Valladares had spent a lifetime researching and recording songs of her country's remote and endangered Indigenous people. It turned out, replied her manager, we'd be in Paris at the same time. I'd distanced myself from the maudlin, west-coast pop that dominated radio. Dylan's grip, too, had weakened. The rapture and pain of *Blood on the Tracks* was my last referral and I couldn't abide his capitulation to Christianity. Outrage and alienation were the language he'd armed me with, not conceited proselytising. Now foreign languages, instruments and arrangements gave fresh life to themes of love, yearning, separation, anger, and joy for me, even where translation of lyrics disclosed similar banality.

Leda's hotel was an hour by train from Susanna's and directions given by her manager-interpreter made locating it simple. Both women were at the door to answer my knock, smiling and gesturing towards the sofa. The younger woman produced a tray of biscuits and almond cake and went to make coffee. Leda kept beaming from her seat, waiting for her friend to help with conversation. She was so small. What source did this frail elder access to conjure such mellifluous song? Then whipbirds and bellbirds, too, had bodies incommensurate with their strident voice. She was tired from the previous evening's concert, said her friend. Leda motioned to the kitchen bench, and her friend fetched two cassette tapes, copied in anticipation of my visit. They were field recordings, they said, that Leda learned under instruction of the jungle tribes over many years during which trusting friendships developed. I'd written of the thrill of hearing her startling voice in Washington and had hoped to buy a record if one could be sourced. This unexpected generosity was wonderful.

***

Another rainy autumn day across from Notre Dame, I ducked into a subterranean theatre to escape the weather, neglecting to note what was showing. Arriving after introductory credits, I was ten minutes into what appeared to be black and white moving images from Medieval times. It was *Rublev* again—the 1969 biographical historical drama directed by Tarkovsky—in company with the hooded monks trudging stook-filled fields in that grainy dampness, reminiscent of the bleak outdoors left on the pavement. The reconstructed gritty ambience of the era was totally convincing.

Early cinema audiences rushed from their seats when a filmed locomotive seemed destined to run them over. I'd laughed at their less sophisticated sense of 'reality' but had been similarly fooled by Peter Watkins's pseudo-documentary, *Punishment Park*, in 1973, enraged at the injustice witnessed on screen. And for several minutes I'd been fooled once more. When I'd first seen *Rublev* at Melbourne University, I knew nothing of Tarkovsky. His mould-bloomed detritus, mottled flora and deteriorating surfaces of sodden earth were revelations. The sensate world was interlocked with the inner states of the characters, the camera penetrating earth's textures with tactile reality.

Rublev's encounter with adolescent Boriska epitomises Tarkovsky's achievement. A master bell-founder is sought by the Prince's emissaries to replace the bell destroyed during the Tatars sacking of Vladimir in 1228. They learn from Boriska that his bell-making father died during a plague. As they turn to leave, Boriska, sensing opportunity, insists his father has passed the bell-making formula with his dying breaths. It's a lie.

On a rise, from which Vladimir can be seen across a river valley, his father's team starts the dig, Boriska in dubious command, flouting his novel power. Rublev is seen at the rim of the hole, eyeing proceedings. Boriska resents his presence, possibly realising the monk senses the deception. There is a link between artistic vision and nature when the youth, preparing to cast the bell, wrenches a root, which the camera tracks to its tree. The camera rises above Boriska to reveal the pit's Herculean scale. He has succeeded in his task, instinctively locating a spot to dig, grasping the right viscosity of mud, and judging the requisite amount of metal for casting.

Tensions mount as the creaking rope supporting the bell gathers momentum. Its ringing seemingly resounds through the entire world as a celebratory gong. Not for nothing does Tarkovsky locate this act on the spot of an earlier crucifixion fantasy, thereby linking and restoring Christ's sacrifice, with Boriska. The lad demonstrates supreme faith in mastering technology with absolute risk. His life had hung in the balance. Throughout, the camera moves like some innocent eye, slowly uncovering the truth of what it encoun-ters, maturing Rubelov's artistic vision in the process.

Boriska's success inspires the monk to renounce his 16-year vow of silence and abstinence from painting. The camera moves from Rublev nursing the lad, pieta-like, to pausing on the embers of a fire which flickers and flares into colour, morphing into his *Trinity* paintings. Tarkovsky thereby promotes the sense that what we've seen of Rublev's story requires incineration to facilitate the birth of his icons. Once more, I dwelt on the monk lugging his female companion, she a mute and he silent. For me, who'd struggled for words and meekly farewelled Gina, a bell tolled.

At street level it had just gone 6 o'clock, and the last of the business world was making its way home in drizzle. I looked for a bar, curious to try Gurdjieff's preferred blend of Old Calvados before jumping on the night train to Venice. The French can savour their bitter apple distillation, but I would not trouble it again. Having not slept a wink, I searched for accommodation as soon as the train halted at Venice's Santa Lucia terminal, and on arrival, collapsed on the hotel bed.

Next morning, I woke early to scout around the city before the evening train to Trieste. I crossed the pigeon-clad *Piazza San Marco* and glanced at Tintoretto's work in *Scuola di San Marco*. There was too much to see in so short a time. My hasty impertinence was guided by Gurdjieff's scant regard for Western Art. For him it was subjective and regretfully, I accepted his authority without encountering most of the city's treasures. Ouspensky and Gurdjieff's 'objective art' apparently resided mainly east of Istanbul which, with winter approaching, I was in a hurry to reach.

The train rattled across the border through tawny Belgrade to a spectacular Bosporus dawn. Istanbul bathed in amber pollutants as its vendors stirred the sidewalks, its domes the colour of ripe cantaloupes. I felt peculiarly at home all week walking the bazaar and mosques, recognising the skyline from dreams I'd had years before. The train trip had been exhausting and uncertainty of exchange rates allowed Yugoslav border guards to harass and diddle me of my American dollars.

With sporadic sleep and little food since Venice, save some greasy chicken legs and a stale croissant in a Belgrade bar, my throat was raw and my stomach pinched. The Pudding Shop opposite Hagia Sophia was the popular hangout for backpackers in the former capital. On mentioning my woes, the waiter insisted *salep* would help, and indeed the orchid broth soon doctored gut and throat. Just uphill from the Pudding Shop was Hafiz Mustafa's marvellous confectionary where I scoffed shredded cheese *kadayif* with a syrupy coffee chaser.

Kerbside of the shop, a number of Kombi vans advertised fares to Kabul, Tehran, Lahore or New Delhi. No thanks. None looked reliable and the company was questionable. I'd trust the public system. But first to discover the city. The frenetic bazaar dazzled with ceramics, glassware, spice shops and rug sellers. Moustachioed merchants sipped chai from tulip-shaped glasses insisting I join them whenever showing the slightest interest.

By week's end I'd had my fill of pistachios, pear-sized figs, and baklava. In back rooms, I'd been subjected to a crash courses in rug provenance and witnessed wool cleaned, beaten, combed, spun, dyed and woven; and women singing to children patterns their arthritic fingers could no longer translate to carpets. I watched a dealer demonstrate the authenticity of fibres by ruffling a carpet, rolling the gathered threads into a ball and holding a lit match to them. Genuine wool would not ignite. Here, I heard that the yellows derived from larkspur and crimsons from insects living on mulberries. But I was assured, aniline dyes would not run or fade like these natural ones. We'd learned at Art School that their mid nineteenth-century invention heralded the expanded palette of Impressionism's sun-drenched landscapes.

Istanbul, once Europe's most splendid, had been besieged throughout millennia and vestiges of Roman aqueducts and churches, such as the spectacular mosaics of the Chora, remained.

It was a short trot downhill to the Topkapi Palace built under the auspices of Ottoman sultan, Mehmed, soon after conquering the hitherto Byzantine capital in the mid fifteenth century. Though estimates vary, the fifty-day battle cost more than 10,000 lives. What was I beholding? Standing before those fortress walls I imagined their defence, destruction, and those multitudinous corpses? Being insulated from the world's great skirmishes, I'd not seriously questioned the injustice or greed mobilising wars. Neither friends nor I had been directly affected by Vietnam. Here, as I'd first done on those Civil War fields of Antietam, I pondered lost lives.

Our violent impulses assume infinite forms. On the paving outside the Palace's Imperial Gate, a score of bystanders gawked at the grizzly spectacle of a dancing brown bear. The tattered specimen, no larger than its master, was collared to him by two metres of chain. It shuffled left and right in sync with the man's *gadulka* and his son's tambourine, hardly the jaunty melody driving Randy Newman's dancing carnivore. The torment and humiliation in the animal's eyes shocked me. Had this act been cut adrift from some dismantled circus or zoo where in childhood I'd last witnessed bear sufferance? I turned away in horror as the boy inverted his instrument and wended through the spectators in hope of filling it with some paltry lira. Even the bear's halting performance had seemed like pleading.

Adjacent to the Topkapi lay the expansive Gulhane Park. Rooks, parrots and herons occupied treetops while pigeons, wagtails and seagulls squabbled between garden beds of yellow, crimson and white tulips. Nesting boxes had been tacked high on poplars and cypress trunks to keep chicks safe from the ubiquitous cats. Beneath the shade of venerable plane trees were folk wishing for long-awaited babies, better health, or to avoid mishaps. Dozens of handsome hounds of various blonde hues lay about the park. These were descendants of Anatolian sheep dogs, the Kangals, whose unrivalled sense of belonging was accentuated by pedestrian indifference. They shared the paths and lawns with undomesticated tortoiseshell tabbies, all fattened by the doting public.

***

Bennett had been posted to Istanbul for two years after cessation of hostilities in 1918. As well as playing a pivotal role in Middle-Eastern military intelligence he'd made connections with Armenian secret societies, the Turkish royal family, Ouspensky and Gurdjieff. Here, he was introduced to Islam and Sufism.

Strolling the streets, I was drawn uphill towards the most prominent feature on the skyline. The Suleyman Mosque proclaimed the name of the city's longest-reigning Sultan. I wandered in and around the complex then retreated to the nearby Sahaflar Carsisi, a hive of second-hand bookshops and site of Turkey's first printed book. At the back of one the many small, book-crammed retailers I chanced upon Helveti headman, Muzaffer, in busy conference with a fellow ancient. Though Pierre had told us that the sheik was a bookseller I'd forgotten until now. Should I interrupt? Shyness ruled. What would I have to talk about? Anyway, I'd rather not remind him of the impertinence marking our brief Claymont encounter. But another encounter rounded out the week.

Breakfasting on the rooftop of my hotel was fiftyish Tahir, a civil servant from Tunis, visiting the city for the first time in 30 years. He invited me to his table to meet his Moroccan wife. Slightly built with honeyed complexion glowing beneath salt and peppered hair, he had a ready smile revealing a gap between his upper incisors. I was won over by his grey eyes flecked with gold, and mild temperament, in sharp contrast with the brash Turks I'd bantered with in the bazaar. Conversations in trains and shops had joined quickly then dissolved. Here, though, we fell into natural companionship, trading anecdotes and finding shared interests in music, art and literature. He loved Sufi music, Paul Klee and Canetti's, *Voices of Marrakesh*. 'But if you want an insider's angle on the place, you must read Choukri's *For Bread Alone*,' he advised. So besotted with Klee was he that he'd purchased a holiday house on the northwest coast at Ghar el Mein where Klee once stayed.

He offered guidance during our days, apologising the few occasions his recall of streets and locations lapsed. He opened doors for elderly commuters, assisted a woman with her cases to a taxi, stopped traffic to walk a child across an intersection, even spent half a day in backstreets hunting down a wooden trumpet I wanted.

Some streets, crammed with small workshops, were so narrow, materials were transported to and fro by porters. According to Tahir these were Kurds from eastern Anatolia, strapping weird saddles to their backs to accommodate freakish-sized freight. Only displaced Kurds from the bottom of the social order would do such donkey-work. A row of a dozen of these *hams*, chatted and smoked among themselves, propped in their saddles/*semers*, waiting for the summons to haul loads up narrow cobbled alleys, inaccessible to even the tiniest trucks. The loads, frequently topping 100 kilos, caused hernias, ruptured spinal discs and caused arthritic knees; but they had no access to social security or worker's compensation.

Tahir's considerations reminded me of the Halvetis, seeing and helping wherever he could. I'd not even seen these people until he'd interacted with them. He was no different with his wife, Fatima, shining on me the shortcomings of my relationships. Here was a suppression of ego I should emulate. Once more we breakfasted on the rooftop on *pide*, fetta and coffee. Hearing percussion and chanting in the street below, we stood and peered over the balcony, responding with reverie to the rhythms. Grabbing a broomstick leaning by the rooftop cupboard, raising it with both hands to shoulder-height, he closed his eyes and commenced a gentle circular dance. The band stalled. Its vocalist twirled a sword to accompany a chilling solo, causing Tahir to open his eyes. As the beat resumed, he motioned me to join him and we danced until the song ceased. He grinned while telling me that the ruckus celebrated the inauguration of an American Jeans' department.

On our final day together, he wished to impart a technique passed to him by his father, a religious leader in Gafsa, on the rim of Saharan Tunisia. Its promise of balancing stress and re-invigoration found in me a willing candidate, and I offered the benefits of Hasan Susud's zikyr in exchange. Having been talked through the procedure, I lay shirtless on my back while Tahir thrice stemmed my carotid arteries to the point of fainting. Each time he revived me by spraying a mouthful of water on my face and upper body. He massaged my neck, shoulders and legs, followed by the stomach with four clockwise twists. I followed his advice, lying motionless a few minutes, then stood refreshed and utterly relieved. He hoped, *inshallah*, we'd meet next in Paradise, and demonstrated the Muslim custom of wiping both hands over face and chest for protection, adding that the virtue of patience was the reward supporting all other virtues bestowed by Allah.

***

Someone at the Pudding Shop recommended the mail boat as the cheapest means to Izmir. I crossed the quivering Galatea Bridge to the terminal near the Mevlana *tekke*. Here was the place Bennett and Ouspensky most likely witnessed Gurdjieff's ballet, *The Struggle of the Magicians*, in the early 1920s. The pier also seemed to be floating, as I stood mesmerised by scores of jellyfish visible through the oil slick. 'Su am' said a man at my side. Sensing my incomprehension, he edified, 'water cunts'. I nodded knowingly at the anatomical resemblance. Or did misogyny lurk in his snarky grunt.

Having found freshly squeezed pomegranate juice irresistible, I'd imbibed more than was sensible: purgation beset me, so I hastened in search of a quayside toilet. Deplorable though this shithole was, having toilet paper on hand was more than could be said for public toilets in the coming weeks.

The evening boat was about to leave and the sole remaining bunk adjoined the engine room. Having stowed my pack and appraised the cramped quarters, humidity and throbbing engines, I went back on deck as the ship left dock. A portly, turbaned citizen in a dark waistcoat felt obliged to farewell us with a raucous prayer, thrice kneeling then standing and singing aloud his *Allahu Akbar* to the amusement of some and consternation of others.

The engine room was intolerable and sleep, a distant prospect. A lifeboat, one of several strung against the railing, offered an alternative. I slipped beneath its canvas flap hoping to evade detection, and was up and out before dawn, thankful by mid morning to be docking at Izmir and abandoning the sea's incessant roil. From here I intended to travel cross-country through Iran, Afghanistan, possibly India and then enter the more familiar territory of the Malay Archipelago before flying home.

Izmir, formerly Smyrna, was less congested than Istanbul. Kemal Ataturk's soldiers had systematically incinerated the port and city in 1922 when they wrested control from the Greeks who'd governed it as part of the Allied Forces post-war strategies. Greeks and Armenians, predominately Christian, were targeted, and tens of thousands died. Thus, was the carnage as the multi-ethnic Ottoman Empire mutated into a nation state, a scenario repeated elsewhere as nations replaced Empires.

The army still remained omnipresent. Young shaven-headed guys patrolled the streets in similar numbers to their monkish Thai counterparts. But there, the likeness ended. Uniformed Turks brandished an intimidating assortment of handguns, bayonetted assault rifles, and sub-machine guns. And there was little chance of forgetting Ataturk, either. Statues of him, grim and defiant, proliferated in towns and villages, his eyes fixed on hopeful horizons that from my standing were yet to be fulfilled. Here and there a sculptor had caught Kemal wincing as though he'd struck bone in his kebab. If his secular Republic hoped science and reason would reign over superstition and dogma, diligence and merit to dominate ethnicity and religion, it required strong military presence.

Izmir was the closest by boat I could get to Ephesus, as its once legendary harbour had silted up centuries before. Ephesus had been one of the great learning centres of the ancient world; and according to Bennett, both the biblical John and Paul had preached there. I flagged a taxi for the hour's drive to that town. Although I had little interest in Greco-Roman ruins, the driver insisted on showing me them prior to climbing up its mountain to visit the Virgin Mary's house. On arrival there we were immediately diverted from the colonnade and amphitheatre, as a film crew was mid-shoot. The driver told me a famous Turkish actress, her name lost on me, was starring in an advertisement, and I suspect glimpsing her had motivated our detour.

The stroll up Mt Koressos at sunset was pleasurable, to see and feel for myself the alleged place of the Virgin's final years. Leaving the plausibility of virgin birth to one side, who knew the provenance of this humble stone room? Apart from local Christians, no one knew of its existence until the early nineteenth century. Had she died there and was its ascription as the house of the Mother of God riding on earlier associations in the area with fertility goddess, Artemis? A small number of devotees quietly made their way in and out of the chapel, curious and perhaps hoping for contact with 'sacred' influences. No such presence stirred in me. So often I've confused the literal with the symbolic that I defer such speculation to scholars, as I do with the bits of Jesus's body stored in Christian countries or The Prophet's numerous teeth and hairs in Muslim lands.

East of Istanbul the packaging of familiar consumables soon petered out. Coke, Marlboro and Toblerone numbered among the few retaining their grip in roadside stalls. The further I moved, the more the population resembled Ataturk's era. Men in battered fedoras, fezzes, sports coats and pantaloons filled the chai shops, attended by tea boys. Moustaches were fashionable, though only the venerable encouraged beards. Women held to field labour or homes, scarfed and skirted in hectic floral patterns, their blunt, high-cheeked faces tanned by sun.

The less said about accommodation near bus terminals, the better. Holding my breath and squatting over dubious toilet holes, I couldn't avoid their history of turds; I started eating only on alternate days, to limit possible contagion. Then it was freshly made yogurt for breakfast and *pide* with lentil or chickpea *chorba* after the day's travel. That tended to, no matter the size of town or village, I made for the public baths.

From Ephesus I bussed to Antalya and Konya, taking up Dede's invitation, and visiting Rumi's tomb. The drab three-storey Dergah Hotel was on Mevlana Caddesi, and as the address suggested, was close to the saint's tomb. My second-floor room was clean, the bed hard but thankfully bug-free. Though toilet fumes filled the air, I couldn't locate it without interrupting the men sipping tea and smoking before the TV in the lobby. Their chai boy was summoned to show me the top floor where it sat forlornly at the end of a corridor of door-less bedrooms, each overrun by chickens.

I had been given the address of Ahmet, a Dede acolyte, whose carpet shop faced the hotel. He soon corrected my mistaken impression of Konya's peaceful atmosphere explaining that soldiers at the university he attended outnumbered students, two to one and recently, when there's be a protest on campus, several students were pushed from upper levels to their deaths. Students weren't permitted to talk to each other in class, and five was the maximum allowed to assemble on campus. Ahmet feared Turkey had moved too far from Allah, citing its immense financial problems, increased begging, the communism of young teachers, and the impact of TV, as signs of distraction and degeneration.

With Suleyman Dede in his home near Rumi's tomb, 1979.

I sat behind him on his motorbike to visit Dede and Ferishte, craning my neck at another 90cc machine hauling two bulky guys, two sheep and four live chickens strung from the passenger's belt. Just as well Ahmet was driving. Though only 20 minutes from the hotel, I'd have been hard pressed to locate Dede's home through the labyrinth of lanes. Though clearly fatigued, the old couple were pleased to greet and offer us fresh *pide* stuffed with spinach and sheep cheese. Bhari, his Jamaican student, translated Dede's concern about not hearing from his son in Claymont. He reconfirmed that it was fine to practise *sema* by one's self and that a Sufi is one pursuing a spiritual path. Thus, Claymont graduates fitted the bill.

He donned his tombstone hat and black cape, then led me upstairs for Bhari to reel off some photos, and gestured to the walls where hung half-a-dozen other framed photos of him with visitors. Finally, farewelling us at their gate, he again asked if news of Jalaluddin's whereabouts and doings came my way, to get in touch. Before leaving Konya, Ahmet sourced me a pair of the kid leather *meshta* dance slippers I'd seen on Jalaluddin.

From Konya the roads deteriorated, so it was a slow 300 kilometres-slog to Kayseri. The majestic extinct volcano, *Mount Erciyes*, sat 15 kilometres to the south of the city. A stiff breeze blew across its slumbering snow-capped shoulders, rendering me as cold as bronze Kemal astride his mount in the central square. At one edge of this square was the thirteenth-century *Hunad*

Hatun Madresa containing Anatolia's first hospital and *hamam*. Here, I took a bath and was scrubbed and massaged on a marble slab as had innumerable bodies through the centuries.

Cappadocia, so named by its first settlers, the Hittites, for its wealth of beautiful wild horses, was nearby. Its cave dwellings once housed early Christian refugees. The bug-eyed Christ images in their chapels had been defaced by Islamists, perhaps from the same fear of the gaze from beyond the grave that moves us to close the eyes of our dead. In so many places, invading peoples, keen to reduce the humanity of their opposition, had lopped the heads from sculptured bodies, or chiselled out or painted over the fundamental feature of the human personality, the face.

In this town ten years earlier, Pasolini had set much of his retelling of *Medea* with its mesmerising, ritual sacrifice of a handsome youth—was he drawing parallels with the thousands of youths dying in Vietnam as the film was made? Their involuntary deaths suggested little had changed. Accompanied by droning voices and chirping crickets, in his depiction of this ancient tale, the participants dip their hands in the youth's blood, smear it on trees and leaves, and tap each other with twigs, before joining in celebratory dance. It's a fertility-increase ceremony. The visceral power of the scene's documentary detail is unforgettable.

Millenia ago, iron, sulphur and calcium had spewed from *Erciyes*, subsequent weathering leaving the region scattered with weird formations that, though tagged as fairy chimneys, camels or kissing couples, were glaringly phallic. I suspected religious etiquette forbade reference to these erect, circumcised penises that dominated the valley. As seen at the four-storey underground city of *Kaymakli*, hundreds of early Christians had chiselled dwellings, into these rock formations, replete with communal dining areas, cold storage for fruit, vegetables and grain, as well as water and wine hollows not only for baptisms, but I suspected, to endure the dour days of hibernation. They were refuges from sieges, both Romans and later, Muslims.

***

Stoked by Sufi contacts, I headed east, first to Hacibektas where there was the tomb of revered Haji Bektash Veli, a thirteenth-century saint from whom the town had been renamed and who'd given rise to another order. From there I skirted the southern shore of Lake Van and the city of that name, heading northeast for Dogubeyazit. Chatting in limited English in minibuses, it seemed a formality to ask whether I was Christian or Muslim, and my interrogator to study my sturdy Chippewa boots, now conditioned from the year's hard yakka. I exchanged glances at fellow passengers' threadbare sandals and sneakers. Did they have covetous intentions, or were they simply assessing my wealth and place of origin? Even had I claimed spurious Christianity, I would be regarded an infidel. 'When in Rome, do as.' Though far from Rome, chameleon-like I uttered my *salaam alaikum*, right hand covering the heart, Sufi style, and trusted the small emblematic Australian flag glued to the flap of my haversack would provide immunity. Thumbing my *Lonely Planet* for maps, it fell open on cuisine, captioned with a European head stewing in a cauldron. Lonely Planet indeed! I shrunk in embarrassment. And how to apologise to my neighbour about the cross heading the entry on religion? Would a garbled history lesson about Constantine's conversion and Istanbul's earlier name help? I shut the book and tucked it in my pack.

Arriving at Dogubeyazit's bus terminal, I envisaged Gurdjieff as a young boy in the adjoining chai house, in this conflux of Kurds, Azeri, Turks, and Yazidis. Alighting there from the bus's capsuled warmth, I was greeted with icy air, 'as cold as death warmed up' as dad would say. Breathy white skeins of cloud marbled the sky. Gurdjieff would have been one of the eight-year-olds serving interminable tea to the shrewd seniors who sucked smokes while fingering and evaluating wool fibres. Here, he would be schooled in the art of rug making and hustling described in his autobiographical, *Meetings with Remarkable Men*.

Grey haired men fitted with caps of regional and religious significance, fingered their amber *misbaha* beads while silently mouthing Allah's names just as I'd witnessed Jalaluddin doing on his forest jaunts at Claymont.

On the footpath in front of their tables, a man wrestled a sheep to a standstill and, with one arm tucked under its front legs, with the other he drew a knife and, uttering *bismillah*, slit its throat, sweeping left to right. The sheep gave a slight shiver as its blood emptied into the gutter. Three metres downstream a relative, reduced to cubes, was skewered on a kebab stick spitting over a small iron grill of charcoal for us commuters as we heated our chilled cuffs and awaited the bus to the border, Tabriz, and Tehran. Its sad head was simmering on the adjacent hob as the bus arrived.

Given news from fellow travellers that Shah Mohammed Reza Pahlavi had just been exiled from Iran, I should have been prepared at the border for anti-American aggression. Ayatollah Khomeini's Shi'ite revolution promised to purify society of Western corruption, characterised by the CIA-installed

Shah's private hedonism and public repression. Perhaps the century's greatest revolution had commenced. Fundamental Islam's repudiation of Western values bore no resemblance to the openness of the Sufis.

The young American queuing in front of me had his boots seized at gunpoint by the border guard and sent back, in his socks, the 200 kilometres to Erzurum, to re-validate his visa. This blatant abuse unsettled both of us. I proceeded unscathed but felt for the young American, wondering if he'd bother testing his accent at the border again.

American influence hadn't disappeared overnight in Tehran; I joined an all-male audience to watch a Charles Bronson Western and was amused with the unanimous cheering at each appearance of good guys, and equally vehement hissing and tongue-clicking at their foe. But most of the week was spent carpet buying at the bazaar, or at galleries on the soon-to-be retitled, Pahlavi Boulevard. The tree-lined boulevard was one of the few spacious enough for motorbikes not to be tempted onto footpaths and endangering pedestrians.

I thought I could conceal interest in my desired object and realised premium rugs weren't placed on top of the stacks. Grizzled Tariq ran me through the usual provenance routine, weft, knots per square inch, pure wool, silk blends, the merits of organic plant dyes versus synthetics. He claimed he could gauge provenance by smell. Who was I to challenge him? Rug after rug he flipped, allowing light to wander over the ply and exalt the quality of various peach, madder, burgundy and rose hues. 'You don't wash genuine rug or colour will run.'

An ornate samovar was placed at our feet where I squatted on a large carpet, sipping chai, while Tariq tirelessly unpacked the stacks, extolling each rug's virtue and venturing interpretations of my interest. Between entreaties, he ground his jaws, cud-like, with emphasis at odds with his unwavering gaze. I smiled. He seemed to be eating his own words, yet the last laugh was his. My poker face hadn't fooled him. He sensed my attention on a silk-wool piece bordered with dark rose *guls* or flowers, on a superb camel ground with octagonal footprints of ultramarine illuminated with celestial blue spots. He knew he had me and threw in a dense, woollen *Baluch* which I'd shown no interest in, when agreeing to his 'special price'. It would be more attractive still, he added, if I first exchanged money at one of the black marketeers lining the boulevard. The fraught times Iran was entering, with the Shah's dismissal, fed his patter and my compliance.

News broke that a busload of tourists had been held-up on the Afghan-Iran border. A Canadian had been shot, presumably mistaken for a Russian.

Persistent tribal rivalries and the election of a Soviet-backed President in Kabul had given rise to Mujahedeen insurgents. This, I learned in my hotel lobby from Afghan university student, Ghareeb, who interpreted reportage from the flickering TV.

Rumi had been born in Balkh and I'd hoped to see its ancient ruins. Gurdjieff's inference of the enigmatic Sarmoung Brotherhood's presence in that region of Afghanistan was another lure. Whether this was fact or allegory I was as ignorant as I was of the country's history and politics. The Brotherhood, Bennett believed, was a fount of Gurdjieff's music and sacred dances. My wild and naïve aim was to see whatever I could see for myself, albeit lacking Bennett's scholarship and linguistic facilities; wild, in the sense that I'd no more planned or foreseen the ground ahead than on my foray to Lake Tali Karng.

Mum and Dad, 1979.

Exhausted and apprehensive, Dad's aerogram at the poste restante confirming the bus incident was all I needed to fly to Melbourne. Self-preservation prevailed over esoteric titillation. My relieved parents greeted me at their doorstep as I stooped beneath my backpack, a carpet under each arm. Several rugs had been left with Tariq who promised to freight them.

Weeks passed and they hadn't arrived. After several letters I received a reply that there had been issues with export and postage, but not to worry as the carpets are safe, 'even if you have to wait 100 years'. This was no comfort. Dad called the Iranian Embassy in Canberra. That same week, without note or word of explanation, both rugs were left at our door—souvenirs of travels in terrain from which I'd tasted rituals whose origins I had little understanding.

10
Crossroads

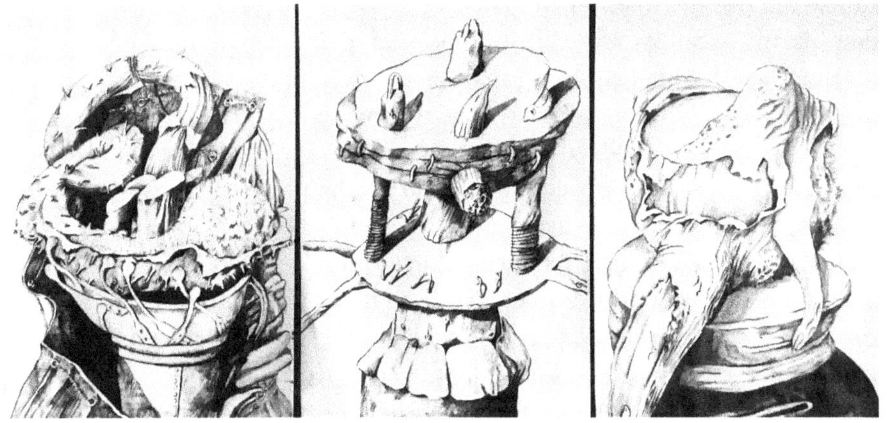

Three Stigmata (After Grunewald), Rod Moss, 1980.

How to find my bearings? I was home, but with little sense of it being home, as the house had never been one of utter comfort. The bush, once my solace, had been savagely compromised. No more Far Away tree. No more black wattles, mushroom rings, or wild orchids. Initially, I stayed a few weeks, setting myself to paint the spouting of the house and dig steps in the rear embankment for easier access to the large, thriving back garden to which my parents were devoting increasing attention.

Chores steadied me. Despite the Work's clues for dealing with negative emotions, I felt abandoned. Images of Gina, of her naked body, recurred cruelly in unbidden flashes I carefully polished. The glint of desire in her eyes, her butterfly fingers as we embraced, our gathering pace as we peaked as one, then lay unwrinkled between sheets. Then the painful realisation that we were apart, and I was alone.

Were those Sufi rituals attempts to mimic the exaltations of coitus; the vigorous bending and swaying, the altered breathing tempo, the flooding of the brain with oxygen? My suffering must have been similar to that I'd inflicted on Jan. By attending to my hands at work, spreading pine-green paint across the spouting, the grain of the shovel handle as I shaped steps from the creamy clays of the backyard cliff, slowly, the hold these images had, weakened.

Domestic dynamics had changed. Dad had retired and, with all their children having 'flown the coop', was devoted to mum's bidding. He'd commandeered bird imagery. 'This house is still your nest,' he insisted one evening. Apart from a few boxes of books and records, I hoped not to have given the impression of settling in. 'Chook,' he turned to mum and for the nth time reminded her that, 'when I fall off the perch our place'll be bulldozed for flats like the rest of the street'. It was one of his games: inviting endorsement of his stoic good health, long-living male bloodline, and the labours he'd devoted to the property. He wouldn't be dying any time soon.

Within three months he'd completed the projects he'd planned would occupy retirement. Now, he followed her around the house waiting instructions on what to pursue, or sat in his armchair by the lounge window, solving magazine crossword puzzles in his bold, inclined lettering. At 4 o'clock, he'd announce it was 'time for our tiddly mother' and head to the glass cabinet in the kitchen corner; his ration of sherry, hers lemonade-diluted. Other than a brief stint of making home-brewed beer, I'd never seen them drink.

Supper done, she'd settle in her armchair in the opposite corner to knit pullovers for Marilyn's three kids and socks for African child refugees, purl and plain in steady discourse as they had been since taking up the needles for Second World War servicemen. Despite rueing the scats spotting the car, dad slipped out the back door after supper to feed scraps to the possums nesting in the garage whose combative squawking punctured my sleep.

Instead of shopping at Coles supermarket at the end of Hastings Avenue, they drove six kilometres to Upper Ferntree Gully where, as dad never tired of saying, he'd completed his upper primary years in the school next to the National Park. They scanned familiar aisles, mum reading from her list, dad trailing with trolley. He was about to join the local Probus Club, while mum maintained friendships with a gentle weekly tennis hit-out. She was also learning Tai Chi and was soon to embark with her class on a Tai Chi tour to China, dad in tow. He planned to tour England and Norway to retrace his mother's forbears in Trondheim, incorporating the spectacle of fiords and the midnight sun.

A fernery housing two fishponds was now established outside the kitchen, where the Larkin brothers once ogled our supper from their perch on the banister. Several mature ferns had been pilfered from gullies in Sherbrooke Forest after dark, transplanted midst hanging baskets of maidenhair. The Hills Hoist that once dominated the space had made way for this verdancy, and a collapsible clothesline bestrode the septic tank on the shaded side of the house.

Mum's sanctuary could be savoured from inside through the windowed walls of the kitchen where on a coffee table, a plant treasury in a terrarium replicated the outdoors in miniature. She drew my attention to things growing and flowering, or the advent of birds that hovered and nested there. Though no scholarly botanist she knew the common names of all local trees, shrubs and flowers, and regularly offered friends and family cuttings from her garden. She had the confidence of her feathered friends and hand-fed a magpie on Saturday mornings, hoping to boost our team's fortunes.

There was a petulant poodle providing animation, an echo of great uncle's manicured beast, with bejewelled collar and ribbons that had begged around our Christmas table. This, too, was a nervous companion readily roused to high-pitched yapping. The carpet and couch reeked of dog, though mum and dad didn't notice. They walked it two kilometres around the block past the bowling green, returning down Boronia Road hill, once a steeper struggle for the Church Bus, but now two-lanes of bisected tarmac roaring with traffic.

How had these two beings, one left motherless at birth, the other fatherless at five, matured? Had they sought surrogate parents in each other by marrying so young? What model did they bring to their partnership? We children had been well fed and clothed, taught table manners, encouraged in sports and enjoyed car outings. Each benefitted from the education they aspired to. What more could we ask? But how much damage did we carry from dad's verbal assaults, and for us boys, his lashings and bashings? How much of mum's submissiveness would influence our own relationships and parenting? Politeness ruled her gentle probing about Gina. I discouraged further talk, saying I was okay and suspected the same for her. Mum glanced wistfully to her right, the matter closed.

I recognised an inner shift, hugging dad on seeing him, something of a first. He was no longer the threatening authority in whose shadow I'd partly stood. He melted into my arms, his eyes at last, momentarily, engaging mine with what I felt was shame, if not apology, for those beatings. Was it this affection that had been missing all these years, why he had not befriended other men, and consigned mum as his sole source of warmth? Men, as I'd seen the Sufis do, could embrace each other and trust a hug, though not apparently the Moss men. Abandoned at birth: the hard wiring.

This unarticulated tussle between father and son. Was he suspicious or resentful of the decision and direction I had taken: sacrificing steady employment, failing to establish a relationship? My path so contradicted his. The circumstances of our arising presented possibilities and skills that nurtured different languages. Content as provider, dad was pleased with his progeny whose achievements he added to his own. But there was no enquiry about what I'd been doing, no reference to Gina, or interest in art or literature. Without his invitation, I felt no need to volunteer information that might draw us closer. Keeping things to myself. What manner of independence was this?

Clocks had assumed residence; a grandfather gonging every fifteen minutes in the hall and a rowdy cuckoo in the kitchen on the half hour. Why this countdown, this noisy reminder of mortality? Would clocks accompany them in their coffins?

And as if to punctuate these observations, the great tree that defined the centre of our avenue was gone. It had defied attempts at removal, a grader and chain in one instance. It was the pivot around which cars turned in our narrow track, home-base for countless games of hide and seek. Coming, ready or not, we'd bellow, our voices partly buried in its puckered bark. Those immense, consoling arms had served shelter and ear to supine George's intoxicated soliloquies many a night. What else had stood so long as testament to all who'd settled in our avenue? With brutal speed our track had transformed into a thoroughfare whose noise caused dad to construct a two-metre-high wooden fence. Just as remarkable, George, grog addicted for forty years and now functioning on one kidney, had sobered up and become a gardener. Their backyard was now a large vegetable patch whose produce he shared, as he'd once done with mincemeat, sausages and racing tips.

***

With changes to my immediate environment and uncertain job prospects, adjusting to Melbourne was more difficult than the challenges of Claymont where decisions each day had been accounted for by the curriculum. The last thing I wanted to do was teach. For several months I went on the dole while determining a forward path. I was determined to be open to whatever came my way, not locked into old routines.

John Scott mentioned an available room adjoining his South Yarra flat, and I jumped at the opportunity. He was lecturing in Media Studies at Swinburne; his grasp of film and television scripting was prodigious, as were his researches in critical theory. His poetry continued, too, charting sexual tensions in relationships. I was surprised he was starting into prose as well, though I suspected novels would reach a wider readership. His partner, Betty, had written a children's book and she asked me to illustrate it. I set to with pencil and gouaches and illustrated its 32 pages. Though she received favourable responses from several publishers, the cost of colour reproduction was a deterrent, and the project was dropped.

When John shifted to larger premises, I accepted an invitation to share house across the Yarra in Richmond with documentary filmmaker, Trevor Graham and partner, Sharon Connolly, a Brinsley Road graduate. The award-winning, *Mabo: Life of an Island Man*, featured among Trevor's achievements. Sharon later headed Film Victoria and Film Australia, as well as writing, editing, scripting and directing documentaries and TV dramas.

Their company in this Greek neighbourhood promised enhanced sociability as other ex-Brinsley Roaders dropped by. Some had become writers, others, filmmakers or painters; the ferment was certainly captured in Brinsley Road alumnus, Richard Lowenstein's, *Dogs in Space*. Trevor and I frequented the Celtic Club in the city, chancing on Irish favourites, The Chieftans, one night in the congested barroom. Otherwise, I sought musical links to the Work with albums by Peter Gabriel, Robert Fripp, Kate Bush, and pianists Elan Sicroff, who'd worked with us on the course, and Keith Jarrett.

At this time, I bought myself strips of Huon Pine, a vice, plane, and circular saw to construct and carve seven and nine-sided tables, inspired by the enneagram and the mosque doors I'd seen in Turkey and Iran. I also incorporated the experience with the students at Argo Street, keeping the carving to the perimeter and constructing a jigsaw of animalia with gouaches on the central panel. However, when Royden returned after five years in England, he was keen to make films.

Australiana Table, Rod Moss, 2010.

He found inspiration in the films of Werner Herzog and after seeing his compelling *Enigma of Kaspar Hauser*, had considered working with him—Herzog's films being exalted in obsessives and alienated eccentrics that Royden identified with.

Peter Brook's theatrical work also enthralled him. Brook had recently repaid his debt to Gurdjieff's teaching by making an unremarkable film of the author's *Meetings with Remarkable Men*. Only the promising *Contest of the Ashoks* prefacing the film, and the Movements performed towards its finale hinted at the life in the book. The expertise of the dancers showed what might be achieved with years of practice. Considering the performances Brook extracted from his brilliant stage work, I was disappointed at the clunky acting. What was he thinking casting Warren Mitchell as Gurdjieff's father? I knew Mitchell as the Cockney, 'Alf', in the popular BBC comedy, *Till Death Do Us Part*. Whenever he appeared in the film all I saw was this bigot rather than the father who helped shape Gurdjieff's formative years. Terence Stamp's portrayal as Prince Lubovedsky was equally disappointing, lacking the allure of his angelic stranger in Pasolini's, *Teorema* a decade earlier.

Though lacking expertise, Royden wanted to make a feature film. Further, would I transpose Frank Herbert's lesser known, *Soul Catcher* from America to Australia? Herbert's hurt and vindictive young Native American kidnaps the young son of a high-ranking politician, intending to sacrifice him in reparation for the wrongs done against his people. It's a dark look into the human mind and the bond that forms between captor and captive. Royden envisioned an Indigenous Australian kidnapping the Prime Minister's son who he takes bush and educates in cultural matters before sacrificing him. Herbert gave the go-ahead but advised us to contact his publisher.

We had a look at Mike Edols rhapsodic, *Lai Lai Dreamtime*, and decided that if the project was to be realised, it would be great to have his superb cinematography on board. Edols had worked in close collaboration with his Indigenous crew whose input had guided production.

When sufficient script was developed, we held a public meeting to drum up financial support and talked with the Film Council, arranging an interview with Indigenous star, David Gulpilil. We filled an Ashburton hall with enthusiasts, courting their support. Royden's persuasive powers seemed to have reignited. The Film Council was less convinced, though. Royden had placed great store on securing Gulpulil's commitment; we were fans, particularly in his pivotal role in Nicolas Roeg's classic, *Walkabout*. Gulpilil had presence in spades, his appearances dominating the screen. However, despite agreements from his manager, the actor evaded meetings, and the project ground to a halt. Was he sending a message?

Over the months, I grew uncomfortable with the script's assumptions. We were ignorant about Indigenous thinking; I was concerned that we would be repeating colonial malpractice. Given their fraught and lowly political position it would be a challenge to develop the relationship between the young black guy and the white youth with Royden's pitch as symbolic separation between 'spirit' and 'soul'. Apart from questioning the existence of this dichotomy I doubted Australian audiences would view an Aboriginal man on screen as a 'spiritual' being and it seemed to me that such designation was patronising anyway. The cinematography would have to be exceptional to avoid literalism. I felt awkward withdrawing from the project, that I was unable to assist Royden in the realisation of his dream, especially as it would inevitably add to his disappointment with Gulpilil.

Fellow lodger, Steve, said there was work set-building for Pegasus Production's, *Last Outlaw*—yet another Kelly saga—starring John Jarratt and Steve Bisley. We headed to Seymour where a shearing shed had been rented to house an array of goods needed on set. For several days we either scrubbed antiques back to their original state or darkened replicas to a 1870s' patina. Then we stripped stringy bark from some trees to thatch the Kelly hut, then spray-painting it grey under day-for-night lights, the urgency due to a dawn shoot. As the sun rose, the tone was deemed too dark so we doused it tawny brown. No sleep. We cut saplings for the post-and-rail fencing of the racetrack's finishing line just out of camera of the hut. Next, we painted the facades of the four towns, all constructed on the same dirt crossroad. The camera simply swung from one to the other as required.

Time constraints, location shifts, the tense hierarchical structure from stars and director down to we lowly set-hands, combined to put egos on edge. This caste system ensured we dined alone in the crowded mess hut. Gossip was rife with rivalries. A third sleepless night on the floor of a room rented next to Seymour's rail siding was enough. Vigils at Claymont, mostly on boiler duty, had never been so demanding. I felt dysfunctional, brain-dead and short-tempered. Proximity to celebrities was no palliative and the prospective weeks didn't suggest relief. By the end of it, I was pleased to have peeked inside the industry but in no hurry to extend the exercise.

***

Despite its excitements, the Richmond share house hadn't quelled my wanderlust. In company with friend, David Pottage, we planned to drive to the far northwest of the continent and stop in on Dave Morgan who'd been invited to work as the printer for Don McLeod's Indigenous mob at Strelley. Maybe I could redress my ignorance of First Peoples that was so painfully apparent with Royden's script.

I'd acquired a 1970 Holden that my brother, Colin, had sourced; a powder-blue utility which we dubbed the, *The Bute*. 'No matter where you are, you'll get parts for this beast,' he reckoned. Our budget only allowed for a set of second-hand tyres to face the epic haul. Dave alerted friends in the Adelaide Hills and Ceduna to feed and shelter us overnight. We headed out on a bleak August day, fantasising about what exotic and warmer Broome might offer. Having built its fame on Indigenous and imported Asian divers, Broome's pearl industry had produced a unique cross-culture that intrigued me.

Flying across the continent, however much the half-day might have dragged, was nothing like driving east to west. It was three full days to Perth, and the Nullarbor stretch from Ceduna to Norseman seemed interminable. My knowledge of Ceduna was limited to the notorious trial of Arrernte man Max Stuart who, having received a death sentence, was eventually exonerated of murdering nine-year-old Mary Hattam in 1958, but not before serving 14 years behind bars—a typical example of how skewed whitefella justice has been towards First Peoples, right up to the present.

Our contact in Ceduna wasn't home when we arrived, so we waited a few hours in the pub for her to return from work. I was sizing up my lemon, lime and bitters when an Indigenous woman sat on the stool beside me, stroked the inside of my leg and invited me join her out the back of the establishment in return for a glass of beer. I was startled by the manner and immediacy of her proposal, the price she put on her bodily favours, not to mention her inebriation. I bought the drink but diverted the conversation to life at Yalata community where she lived, and where we would also be welcomed, she said, should we detour from the highway.

It was after nine when Dave's friend drove up in front of her house, pointed out sleeping quarters and where we could make breakfast before our early start, as she'd be sleeping in.

How pioneers and explorers traversed the Nullarbor in the nineteenth century amazed me. Hard to believe that in the November heat of 1937, dad's boyhood idol, endurance cyclist Hubert Opperman, covered these 1200 kilometres when it was still sand dunes and corrugated dirt. Time constraints would have differed drastically, but the climatic conditions surely were no kinder. And where was the water? We broke our trip at the Mundrabilla Roadhouse where a pair of tiny thornbills fluttered about our outdoor table, pecking the moisture from our lips with fearless intimacy.

We had no intentions in Perth other than topping up fuel and food; the northwest beckoned and we'd come little over halfway. New Norcia Mission's Spanish origins in the mid nineteenth century 130 kilometres north, had attracted my interest some years before. Though its founding charter involved the evangelising of First Peoples, we saw no sign of them as we walked around the imposing grounds and buildings. I flashed to Gethsemane, the Trappist monastery I'd visited in the US which was also founded in 1848. What parallels might have befallen the Cherokee as the Trappists entered their domain? What were the fates of the converted, and what brutalities had transpired? Did they differ from the troubled stories of Indigenous incarceration emanating from Rottnest Island?

Onwards then from New Norcia to Geraldton and Carnarvon. The entire coast differed profoundly from its comparatively lush eastern counterpart. Fierce sea winds had us regularly wrestling the steering wheel. Trees, wherever they managed to grow and whatever rain fell, had adapted to those forces by leaning at weird, inebriated angles. At Port Hedland we alerted Dave of our imminent arrival before landing on his doorstep, an hour on dirt inland from the continent's most western settlement.

Strelley's few primitive dongas and portable houses served the white teaching staff who'd arrived in 1976 at the request of elders, Dooley Bin Bin and Jacob Oberdoo. Lessons were conducted beneath a bark shelter. There were few trees offering such generous protection on the red sand and spinifex. White and Nyangumarta teachers delivered separate boys' and girls' sessions of two-way learning, morning and afternoon. According to Dave, Brinsley Road had in part inspired their project. Communally driven ideology, maybe. But Brinsley Road's moment in the sun lacked Strelley's long and profound ties to language and country. It had also in common, an energetic and inspired young principal, Paul Roberts, who later made a documentary, *How the West Was Lost*, borrowing the title of McLeod's written account of the mob's fight for independence and justice.

The printery where Dave worked was the lone cinderblock building, reflecting the importance the community placed on literacy. Cyclones battered Port Hedland regularly during the season for them, leaving a destructive trail, often featuring nationally in the summer news. Strelley's damage was worse given the pathetic housing, although never reported. So, at least the printery would withstand a battering. While I was still in Melbourne, Dave had suggested I read *Yandy*, a novel based on the struggles of McLeod and the Nyangumarta people, to paint a picture of the people he worked with. Yet I was unprepared for seeing people living in wurlies and old car bodies. At dusk, however, dark bodies, like Giacometti silhouettes, stood or sat around family fires, and, apart from an occasional yapping dog, serenity ruled; a scene of domestic peace I suspected had altered little during the century.

Though Stan Davey had shifted attention to the plight of Indigenous groups in the northwest at Wyndham, strike leaders McLeod, Bin Bin and Oberdoo remained at Strelley. If the straightened circumstances of their quarters might have changed little over the decades, they had the satisfaction of having achieved a modicum of independence.

The heat in early September was already horrendous and we'd neglected to bring hats. Having breakfasted on Weetabix and disturbed the resident frogs in Dave's toilet, I had to hold a book above my head en route to the printery where he'd invited me to work alongside senior woman, Molly Williams, illustrating her pig stories. Apart from kids who picnicked with us the following Saturday at the de Grey River, she was the only local I had the chance to converse with.

There was grave concern within the community about related families at Noonkanbah who were battling the Western Australian Government, bent on promoting oil mining on their sacred sites. Mining was driving the state's economy, nowhere more than the Pilbara. Our entry to Port Hedland had said as much. We'd watched and waited in amazement at the crossing as two kilometres of ore-bearing carriages rolled by on their way to the docks. Many of the Strelley mob had joined the protesting Yungngorn to form a barricade against the convoy of oil rigs, trucks and police sent by the state premier. It was yet another variant of embattled First Peoples.

The following weekend Dave drove us east to Warralong where several Nyangumarta were branding cattle. Cowboys in action, checked shirts, Stetsons and Levis, some booted, most barefooted; a Western, sprung to life. The courage of these lightly built guys taking on one-tonne beasts was impressive. Their deft handling made the work in the ferocious sun look simple. I knew on which side of the fence I belonged. When someone slipped, or beat a hasty retreat, I had neither the nerve nor skill of those perching on the railings, to join their howls of derisive laughter.

Further inland was Marble Bar, infamously holding the world's hottest recorded run of 160 days exceeding 38.7 degrees. The heat was intimidating. Too hot, in fact, to expose our pale bodies for long at the spectacular jasper reef, bridging the Coongan River. And here was the Bar that I'd assumed was some stone-slabbed furniture housed in the town's ironclad hotel.

Nearby, a cricket match was underway on a field of pink and quartz-ridden gravel. It was a whitefella thing, this cricket. The adage, 'Mad dogs and Englishmen' was never more applicable. Both were represented. A hefty swing from the batter landed the severely scuffed ball near our car in which we sat, hostage to airconditioning. I scrutinised the fielder's attire as he retrieved the ball. Most wore something white. All wore Stetsons, and both umpires and fielders sported belts holstered with stubby holders. Drinks' breaks were held every few overs when the chorus of snapping ring-tops rivalled the circling crows and bowling appeals. They played a different game out West.

Dave Morgan, 1984.

Dave reckoned 80 kilometres per hour to be appropriate for the corrugations though it proved no guarantee against trouble. Two punctures and an hour or so on, we regained Strelley as the day expired. A grass fire raged, fronting several kilometres, making for a spectacular crimson sunset. But this wasn't the Dandenongs and Dave, former resident of The Basin, remembering those 1960s conflagrations, read my thoughts. 'It's a controlled burn,' he muttered from my side, a knowing smile parting his whiskers. Having waited until the wind shifted and weakened, women had commenced firestick hunting, simultaneously cleaning and regenerating the country. Crows and hawks already circled the cindered soils. The vitality of fresh goanna, snake, and perhaps marsupial, supplemented the low-nutrition items bought on 80-kilometre round trips to Port Hedland.

Dave's willingness to accept what I deemed considerable privations impressed me mightily. I doubted, given my skill base, that I was equipped in any sense, to take on such a commission as I thought of the isolation, the living quarters, the food and water quality. The quiet manner he negotiated with the community, his patience, pragmatism and eye for detail, fitted him for service.

Broome had been our destination. The highway was in the process of being sealed and the only passing traffic was dedicated to that end. Solitary, tough men sat silently in graders, rollers, and trucks amid the noise and dust. I raised an index finger from the wheel, mirroring the salutes given as we passed. We refuelled at the forlorn pitstop, Sandfire, and enjoyed toasted sandwiches, constantly brushing aside competitive fly hordes, before pushing on.

Sleepy Broome's few streets of bungalows, fly-wired verandas and shuttered windows were unimpressive. We steered the Bute into a vacant patch of grass in the caravan park and made for the modish-looking pub, pivot of Saturday action, to check out work options. It seemed that every other bloke we spoke with was on a bender from the Argyle diamond mine. No paid work was on offer other than on pearling boats, for which neither of us was experienced, nor, given my distaste for the sea, inclined to.

We weren't swimmers either, so the famed Cable Beach held little interest other than it being my first encounter with sea snakes. Wading near the endless jetty, two coral-coloured reptiles wriggled across the wave ahead of me, prompting a rapid exit from the shallows that David, fitting with laughter on safe sands, described as my walking on water. Another phenomenon awaited us. Elegant constellations of sand pellets were scripted in the sand as the tide retreated—deposits of midget crabs that retreated en mass as we approached. So much for exoticism. It was time to move.

Stopping for petrol before we left, I savoured a singularly ironic *Greetings from Broome* postcard of butchers happily hacking through carcasses in the local abattoir. It was a weird footnote purchased from the service station at the edge of town. Wedged on a flimsy carousel between cassettes of cowboy and trucker's songs, it summarised my impressions. The bleary-eyed gents on the postcard appeared to have assembled after a big night on the tiles. The blood-smeared apron of the nearest guy might have resulted as much from his riddled eyes as the meat on the bench as he catches our glance mid mindless blow. You could sense the stench of the room and its blithe invitation to carnivorous pleasures. The moment must have seized the photographer with much the same awe that attracted me. I bought three to post home to friends.

Rather than retracing our tracks we decided to round the continent, hoping work might present itself as we travelled. Several times in these northern parts, we'd caught prospective employers noting our Victorian number plates, or on hearing where we were from, tell us that nothing was available. Perhaps it was some enmity related to the fierce interstate football rivalry. Long ago, dad had referred to the state's failed bid in 1933 to secede from the Federation. Whatever, Western Australians clearly prioritised their own or maybe just had a thing about Victorians.

We were curious to see where Indigenous man, Jandamarra, had armed a small troupe of followers and resisted settlers bent on establishing cattle runs in the 1890s. There'd been a couple of novels based on Jandamarra's guerrilla activity and the local Bunuba people regarded him as a Black Ned Kelly. As with Antietam and Harpers Ferry, I found that momentous events are made more real when I place myself where they occurred.

So, we'd detoured up the Gibb River Road to Tunnel Creek and Windjana Gorge, enthralled by the magnificent baobab trees peculiar to the Kimberleys. Here, at last, we were amongst cliffs, mountains and sizable rocks—Edol's film had served as my introduction to this country's severe glamour, and the reality didn't disappoint. After a dip with freshwater crocs in the Gorge, we meandered to the cave at Tunnel Creek. Bats flittered in and out of our torchlight as we waded through shallow pools into an immense opening where the ceiling had collapsed and butterflies billowed upwards in shafts of sunlight. This feature would have been the key to Jandamarra's mysterious disappearances. There were infinite hiding locations in the jagged limestone to have kept his trackers bamboozled for years.

The car wound through stands of baobabs, a bowling ball navigating an alley of giant ten-pins, rejoining the highway west of Fitzroy Crossing. The widely scattered buildings gave Fitzroy Crossing a sense of incoherence. This arrangement was amplified outside the hotel where scores of Indigenous people clustered in random groups. On verandas and under trees, wherever shade presented, people loitered or lay comatose, waiting for opening hour. What I took to be quartz-encrusted earth was beer-bottle glass and aluminium cans; a solid mat of litter in all directions. It was unutterably sad, and confirmed Dave's remark about the Nyungamurta drifting into Port Hedland and living on 'green bag' at the tip. Before us was, by and large, the fallout of the Noonkanbah crisis. We were glad to head out of town and camp at Geikie Gorge, though tuning my transistor to the grand final broadcast further darkened the day. Richmond, with our nemesis, Bartlett unstoppable, annihilated the Pies.

In Kununurra, a day's pumpkin-picking was enough for us—back-breaking labour in the gathering humidity—we were not cut out for the pumpkin. At day's end, burned and exhausted, we sat in the Bute surveying vast Lake Argyle that mirrored the flat expanses of cerulean above. I had in my lap the folded leaflet about what lay before us. The history of the Ord River project revelled in the many causes of repeated crop failures, as if to say, 'We won't surrender, no matter what seasons, insects and soils are tossed our way'. We counted amongst the defeated.

Just shy of Katherine, we picked up an elderly Indigenous gent standing motionless on the side of the road in the shade of tree. He hadn't waved us down but accepted the lift anyway, squeezing between us without a word, giving the impression he was doing us a favour. As we neared Pine Creek, he murmured that he wanted out. We watched as he drifted off into the bush. The small black ants he'd left as a calling card migrated up inside my pants. Within weeks I discovered they'd colonised the spongy interior of the bench seat, so set to, powdering the infestation with Ant Rid.

We continued to Darwin. David noticed the cinemas were showing the Neil Young biopic, *Rust Never Sleeps*. Devotee that he was, having secured lodgings in Fannie Bay, we headed back to the airconditioned haven of the cinemas. We'd no sooner sat down than I got a tap on the shoulder. Martin King, also a fan of the bleating Young, and student from Maroondah High days, having majored in printmaking at Caulfield, had recently arrived in the northern capital. He'd picked up work as a technical assistant in Darwin University's Art Department. Moreover, he'd been camping at Uluru the night the Chamberlain child had gone missing and had been chatting with the couple around their fire before it was taken. Martin's account was brief, but the story of mother, Lindy's incarceration for the murder of her infant daughter, Azaria, and the retrial revealing the dingo culprit, enflamed public opinion for years.

Our finances were boosted in Darwin when David got an immediate start as a storeman in a Winnellie factory and I was taken on as an emergency teacher in high schools until the academic year expired. As the build-up to the monsoon season gathered momentum, storms appeared over Fannie Bay late each afternoon which provided spectacular light shows, the like of which I'd not witnessed since Bali. The constant 30-degree heat and humidity were torrid, though; the slightest effort and my clothes were drenched in perspiration which chilled on entering airconditioned buildings, making me uncomfortably aware of my body. Cold showers were tepid at best and stinger season kept most swimmers from the shallows of Casuarina Beach, while crocodiles were spotted in nearby Rapid Creek's briny waters.

What were the outpost's redeeming qualities? Certainly, it wasn't the proliferation of dishevelled, tattooed women strutting the streets, or their male counterparts. Had some large bikie gang taken possession of the outpost? There were the 'long-grassers', black and white, who, lounging in the malls and beneath Moreton Bay figs, contrasted spectacularly with camera-toting tourists and trimly attired government employees. Culturally, had much shifted since the times depicted in Xavier Herbert's novels?

Mark Viney, researching the rock art of Koolpin Gorge at southern end of the Arnhem Land escarpment for his Fine Arts thesis invited Martin, David and me on a field trip. The week commenced with Big Bill Neiji touring us the stories of Ubirr Rock. We filed behind him and as I studied his light steps, Nietzsche's aphorism, *Hath not the dancer his ear in his toe*, crossed my mind. The old man's bare feet glided over the gravel, feeling their way to the galaxy of fish, turtle, snake, and bird iconography rendered with steady deliberation that accounted for the undulations of the rock surface, allowing them and its granulations a voice in the ochred expression.

We camped at Death Adder Gorge, where, coiled beneath the painted overhang was not a fearsome Death Adder, but a prettily patterned python of proportion sufficient to suggest lineage to the Rainbow Serpent Creator Being himself. And in the waterway next to where we'd pitched our mosquito nets, I sat for half an hour before supper mesmerised by a file snake as it snatched a barramundi and devoured it with spasmodic thrusts. It was a big night out, what with mosquito bedlam and the queer bellowing that our host informed us in the morning were the mating calls of crocodiles.

Nourlangie, UDP Falls and Koolpin Gorge rounded out the week. Sitting within the majestic Nourlangie cave surrounded by its ancient images, I beheld the bird-filled floodplains. At my back and overhead were ochre-coloured transcriptions of what throbbed before me. Whatever could surpass this, as my last sight on earth?

Martin joined us as we up-anchored and headed south. At Katherine, David and Martin ventured up the Gorge while I lounged riverside. A scrap of magazine wedged in some scrub caught my attention. It was a page of the *Australasian Post* reporting on Nicolas Roeg's movie, *Walkabout*. Not that it carried critical weight. But given our recently acquired interest in Gulpilil, that this single page should survive 10 years, its advent here on the Katherine riverbank was uncanny.

The heat was searing as we turned east at Three-ways towards the distant coast. Camooweal at the Queensland border, renowned as the Territory police's dumping ground for criminals, was a Western stage set. I imagined gunslingers lurking behind the signage of the petrol station's roofing iron. The heinously priced fuel encouraged these impressions. There was Mt Isa, trapped within its slag heaps, Charters Towers, Townsville and the eastern seaboard, where we camped at Noosa to news of John Lennon's murder.

The traffic thickened as we rolled below Brisbane, to Sydney and into Melbourne for Christmas, where fuel was more than a dollar a litre cheaper and our bodies quickly re-acclimatised to the weather's inconstancies. Remarkably, the car had been trouble-free and the second-hand tyres more than worth their weight in, well, rubber.

***

Returning to the Richmond share house I struck up with French woman, Anne, who'd rented the adjacent bedroom and taught English as a Second Language at Waverley High. Propinquity; there were her soft, hazel eyes, her presence beyond the bedroom wall, and significantly, her Claymont experience. She'd done the course the year following mine. Though the structure was similar, the list of guest teachers had differed. The Halveti and Mevlevi were absent. But esteemed Sri Lankan mystic, Bawa Muhaiyaddeen of the Qadiri order, addressed them from his Philadelphia quarters. Pierre regarded the Bawa as an Enlightened One and considered his talks on zikyr and the science of breathing to be the most profound, if challenging, on the subject.

Steve joked that it was Anne's accent that seduced me. True, her voice was thankfully free of anxious Australian upspeak. I rose to her passionately expressed opinions, their temperature and clarity. Her outsider's view of our culture enchanted me. Anne had just procured a set of wooden massage wheels and asked if I'd volunteer my back for a trial run. A few circuits of my ropey spine and I was rattling off things I'd not spoken of since returning to Australia. She deplored and discouraged my high-school French, and her grammatical knowledge of English easily outstripped mine, facts that caused frustration and humour. Her wit and judgment were razor sharp. When Steve told us he was vacating his flat on the other side of the Yarra, we assumed those more spacious quarters on Alexandra Avenue.

I missed the Gurdjieff Dance Movements, less their challenges to attention than aerobic satisfaction. Their value lay in group Work, and the few sessions I trialled with the small Melbourne group lacked Claymont's intensity. But my brother, Colin, coaxed me to one more season of football at distant Lang Lang in the South Gippsland League. Ian also heard the call and we three brothers played together, if unimpressively, for the first time. My career finished late in the season in the dying minutes of a game, caught under the elbow in a heavy tackle. In well over 150 games in my life, it was the only injury ever to keep me from the field. A ruptured shoulder required a sling for a month and stopped table production, which I'd resumed on returning to Melbourne. I needed to find non-combative activity.

Soon after, in the nearby Darling Gardens, I came across Weng Lee, a Malay Chinese, who practised Tai Chi. He agreed to let me join him each morning. So commenced the acquisition of a skill, without the disjunctions of the Movements, that was easily transportable, and didn't require a group. Tai Chi encouraged an emptying and filling of energy from one side of the body to the other, keeping as low as thighs permitted, with the abdomen kept as open as possible to facilitate deep breath.

A couple of months on, he mentioned that he was shifting to the outer suburbs, but insisted we explore alternatives to further my practice. Tibor Tziglani taught Tai Chi Wu close by in a Glenferrie dance studio. He'd start with his back to us prior to turning to adjust errors. Keeping our feet correctly placed was the foundation on which upper body gestures were built. But it was the grace of his hands that became imbedded in my mind and my practice, none more than the elegant 'cloud of hands' sequence. This slowing down and accompanying attention I never tired of with repetition.

Anne wanted me to meet her parents and sister in Brittany, so we flew via Amsterdam, visiting a van Gogh museum, and Rembrandt and Vermeer in Den Haag. Van Gogh's letters had always moved me more than their accompanying reproductions, the only actual work I'd seen in Melbourne being an unimpressive dull ochreous green head of a man. However, its insipid palette bore no resemblance to those in Amsterdam. Colour leapt from the frames, pulsing in thick ribs of oil, each motif ruffled and radiating light as if possessed by supernatural fields of energy.

The works of the older Dutchmen couldn't be more different. Vermeer's serene, domestic scenes invited close attention to colour harmonics and subdued brushing. His images of eternal tranquillity give no hint of his eleven children, the angst and resistance attending Catholic Spain's occupation of Protestant Nederland, or the explosion of the gunpowder store that had flattened much of his city.

The *View of Delft*, *Woman Reading a Letter* and *Girl with Pearl Earring* thrilled me. A print of that girl, hung in Boronia High's corridor, was my first love affair with art. I was twelve and actual girls were yet to arouse me. I would pass her several times a week as we shifted passed the enquiries office to and from the school's academic wing to the Art, Music and Domestic Studies' rooms. Her silent glance caught me each time and, not wanting to share the secret of our intimacy, I would avoid her eye if accompanied by classmates. How inviting were her succulent, parted lips. Unfortunately, this day in Den Haag she was absent. A note in her stead informed of her year in the private gallery of a Texan millionaire.

If Vermeer dealt with impossible unity his older contemporary delved in disturbance. His people's inwardness is at odds with the nervous evidence of

Rembrandt's stressed and timeworn faces. Where his subtle tonal shifts of light are achieved through suppressed mark making, Rembrandt lauds his brushing with swift deposits of the oil and a dazzling array of touching. Most astonishing was the central drama of *Nightwatch* whose darkness threatens to engulf Captain Cocq and his militia. A shaft of light is thrown over the dwarf at his rear. Warwick had drawn attention to the claw of the dead chicken strung from the dwarf's girdle, echoing Cocq's glove. Its presence, he added, symbolised the name of the militia and served as a visual pun on his name.

We took the train to Gare St Lazare, a cavernous structure still recognisable from Monet's painting, then headed west to stay a week with Anne's parents at coastal Dinard. Despite our lack of common language, her father Jacques, and I enjoyed netting fish together when monstrous tides, the like of which I'd not seen since Broome, retreated in the late afternoon. There we stood, he in rubber boots, me in rolled pants with toes shrivelling, as we hauled in a modest catch of silver bass and John Dory. Before supper Jacques knelt before the fireplace where a set of stone shelves harboured his wine collection. He joked that the arrangement allowed him to supplicate in homage to his favourite 'saint'—vinegariest, Louis Roque in Souillac.

The surrounding villages were exquisite, each presenting fresh produce in street markets. Small livestock, chickens and rabbits, were sold there. *Lapin moutarde* on couscous became an absolute favourite of mine. We toured San Michelle, and shopped in San Malo and Rennes, me mostly enslaved to recorded music.

Back to Paris we headed, to wander Notre Dame, the Louvre and Impressionist Galleries. There were also pet shops near the river with caged birds, cats, dogs and rabbits. I couldn't resist the doleful gaze of a Pyrenees Mountain pup. We nudged noses between the bars. I should have left such amours at dogsville, but an extraordinary Flemish rabbit lured me from its nearby hutch. I pressed close to this grey giant. It sniffed. I sniffed. Then it bit a sizeable chunk from the tip of my nose. Weren't they herbivores? Was this the Rabbit World's Revenge? Anne rushed me in search of a pharmacy. Not for the first time in France, I thought how brilliantly she handled the language, forgetting she was French. The chemist and Anne enjoyed a chuckle at my expense. I would like to have some dignified explanation for the bandage plastered to the centre of my face. But the rabbit tale had unique allure and those who looked, then looked away, were left to their own conclusions as we overnighted on the train to Spain.

What an eyeful! The Prado, the Alhambra, Cordoba's Mosque, Matisse's chapel, Gaudi's *Sagrada Familia*, and Picasso museums along the Cote d'Azure. We also caught up with her relatives at Bezier and family doctor, Ropars, outside Nice. This was the man who'd delivered her 34 years previously.

A glass cabinet in his waiting room was stocked with esoteric literature. I noted alchemist, Fulcanelli's *Mysteries of the Cathedrals*, something on Krishnamurti's language, Frater Achad's *Crystal Gazing*, Jean Chevalier's *Dictionary of Symbols*, and books by Eckinkar and Bennett. Bennett's name came up as Ropars greeted Anne. Bennett had written of his esteem for Indian homoeopath, Chandra Sharma, so it wasn't so surprising that Ropars also practised the centuries-old, 'like cures like' medical art. Books also crammed the shelves of his consultation room. The desk was strewn with odd-shaped bottles of medicines, a test tube of coiled red wool, a packet of millet, a green bottle of peanut oil and a pack of wholegrain rice. He was small, probably early seventies, hunched and hardly an advertisement for health, it seemed to me.

When settled in his carpeted kingdom, his face lit up, the many fine wrinkles of his forehead gathered as one between snowy, tufted brows. Hooded eyelids, Arabic nose, rodent dentures—Ropars brought the Flemish rabbit to mind. He read the pendulum of alkaline and acid solutions, held above a rectangular copper plate on which Anne's hand rested. Without explanation, he turned to the blotches flaring below my nostrils, while airing disappointment about her father marrying her mother. I submitted my hand for pendulum diagnosis. He told her she had her father's chromosomes, and then wondered how we were related to Gurdjieff's Work. He'd driven Bennett around France, and had been 'opened' by Javanese guru, Pak Subud's *Latihan* exercise—another of Bennett's enthusiasms.

Had we met Bennett, he wanted to know? He'd not heard of him for 10 years, which was no surprise, since Bennett had passed away in 1974 prior to the first Claymont course. Ropar's contact with the Work had been through Louis Pauwels whom he'd treated for tuberculosis. Though Pauwels believed he'd contracted the disease from Gurdjieff, he was grateful for his teachings in Paris after the War. Ropars regarded Pauwel's theories about tuberculosis and his book, *Morning of the Magicians*, as nonsense.

He must have considered us chronics, measured by the bag of remedies we lugged from his rooms. Microloan, magnesium, chelidonium, hepasane, tubed sulphys, arsenium, and a tube of graphite. I had not the slightest idea what these were or how they corresponded with what swirled through my system.

Anne had been given a needle in the buttocks, disturbing the remainder of her day. I was told to 'stop jogging and eating yoghurt. It poison!' he scoffed, the only words addressed to me in English. I realised I'd not seen a single track-suited jogger. After all it was winter; perhaps the French exercised indoors. If we had further complaints, he added, post him nail clippings or hair for him to swing his pendulum number.

The credibility of the physician is crucial to positive outcomes, and ministry as vital as remedies. As a child, I trusted treatments visited upon me, being at the mercy of adults more knowledgeable than me. As an adult I scrutinised practitioners and felt their humility contingent to healing. Consider Dr Maurice Wong whose hypnotherapy session I'd attended to cure insomnia. It was a gamble with an untried therapy, though I'd witnessed, years ago, that Ian's high jumping improved after some sessions.

Sleep deprivation can promote desperate decisions. After a week at my parents' one Christmas, I noted a hypnotherapist in a nearby street. It hadn't occurred to me that the sloppily attired gent on the pavement grinding a butt beneath his slipper was my man until he followed me through the door. There being no other clients I had an immediate appointment and took a seat.

Everything about his waiting room bespoke improvisation: the steel furniture, the absence of reading material, the vase of dead flowers and equally dead flies crowding the window sill, uncapped *Mortein* can at their side. A dozen survivors circled lazily near the ceiling. Occasionally, one broke from its rotations to test my tolerance. Five minutes passed before he reappeared and ushered me into his consultation room. A Taiwanese registration certificate hung lopsidedly on otherwise bare walls above his chair, a chair of the same tubular steel as the one opposite that he waved me to park my butt on. I felt I was imposing on his precious time, that he was uninterested in my complaint as he hurried through the process of relaxation, glancing now and then at his watch and, as much as possible, avoiding eye contact which I'd deemed crucial to the exercise. Gurdjieff had made quite a business from hypnotherapy and his penetrative gaze was renowned. At no point did I feel I'd 'gone under', but twenty minutes later he assured me I had. I parted with my cash which he carefully counted and stuffed in his wallet, adding that if it didn't 'take' to return next week.

There was a used bookshop nearby and I was browsing its back shelves when he came rushing through the door behind which the owner was propped. Without pause or noticing me he unloaded on the shopkeeper recent troubles with his insurer, oblivious to the man's refusal to be distracted from his computer. This snivelling tirade destroyed my lingering trust. My doctor should, at the least, appear to have mastered himself. Forget next week. Insomnia continued its tricks until I resumed my routines at home.

Setting is important. Not that I expect plush surrounds and piped music, though dingy dentist clinics are less inspiring than ones glistening with chrome, have functioning adjustable chairs, and the sharp clove and formaldehyde air that promise efficiency. Coffee table literature comprising women's issues and sportsmen, I can pass. Prestigious Certificates of Merit may convince or soothe some clients. Crucially, dentists must have reasonable fangs and not exhale rotten breath beneath the spotlit glare of their inquisition.

I dutifully consumed Ropar's pharmaceuticals and, failing to obtain the promised results, tamed the rash with *Dermaid*.

***

I lacked the energy and entrepreneurial front to sell tables in the emerging Australiana stores, and it took three months to do the carpentry, carving, and research the imagery for the painted panel. Having made a third Huon pine table, ex-student, Andrew Otto, suggested using Jelutong–a part of the Oleander family from southeast Asia and very popular with carvers— which he used for pattern making. It lacked pine's honeyed perfume but was easier on wrist and pocket. Despite cutting production time, I still couldn't compete with David Wang's imported camphorwood tables. Australian content remained with stained-glass kookaburras, koalas and rosellas in the 'aunts' Federation homes; sales of my dozen tables barely covered material costs.

John Anderson suggested reproducing them in fibreglass. He'd been using it in his sculpture and his son's surfboards. John was the most accomplished person I knew. Gardening, automobiles, cooking, building, property investment—there was nothing he turned his hand to that he didn't master; or topics friends seeking his advice on, might profit from. John was also master of the sardonic one liner. As he cleared a bench of its tubes of oil paints to make room for the tabletop, he caught me frowning at the neat red and blue pellets scattered amongst them. 'Rats. They have a high-end diet of cobalt and vermillion,' he chuckled, turning over a gnawed tube.

We cast a mother mould from one of the carved tops and John stirred a green onyx brew to fit. Polymer accelerator was used to set it. Immediately, my head throbbed and a rash appeared on my face and ribs. I had to abandon the project and returned to painting, aiming for a second show at Profile Gallery in Glenhuntly, with works featuring native animals trapped in man-made structures.

Like the Andersons, my mate from Mallee years, Graeme Drendel, had a daughter and son to support. Over the years, our friendship never wavered, and we'd shared the ebb and flow of painting, music and football passions, not to mention the mixed fortunes with our sweethearts. Having served his indentured teaching term, he'd turned to music. Country Rock best described his *Riverina Playboys*. They were part of the inner-city circuit but never broke big enough to support a lifestyle. He returned to another small experimental school for disadvantaged kids in Collingwood and started painting. Drawing on his Ouyen experience, Graeme developed whimsical narratives staffed with adults oblivious to their surrounds and each other. His sombre brown-green palette and passive figures reminded me of Quattrocento devotional paintings. When visiting him he'd grab his guitar or plonk at the piano and we'd harmonise *The Band's* haloed numbers, restoring our Ouyen days.

Royden completed a filmmaking course at Swinburne Institute and his graduation film, *Shadows* won the short film section of the 1982 Melbourne Film Festival. He planned to make a film featuring the dance modes of Indian-Malay Chandrabanu and Gulpilil. When plans didn't mature, he sensed more promising directing opportunities in Sydney and relocated there to embrace its open-styled culture and balmier climate. Although we kept in phone contact, I saw much less of him.

To pay my way, I did some hay-bailing in Alexandra, life modelling at Huntingdale Technical College, and reluctantly signed onto the Relief Teaching roster, even though the last significantly depleted energy for art. Melbourne and Richmond High occasionally notified me. But St Kilda Alternative School persisted, coaxing me to a full-time position despite me clarifying my intent to venture to northern Australia. Anne knew that since journeying into Aboriginal Australia, Melbourne had ceased to quicken my pulse. I'd applied for teaching work in the Territory, without response.

In 1982 the St Kilda School seemed devoid of ideology or method, and the bulk of new staff were unaware of its past. Dropouts and street kids dominated. Given my history with the school, Phil the interim principal, asked me to consider his role. I restated my northern aspirations, but ended up staying more than a year, deferring relocation, due to the bond with Anne and interest in seeing the results of the curriculum I helped fashion.

Over the Easter break that year, Claymont was offering an Intensive Movements Course for graduates. I decided to take the opportunity to touch base with the atmosphere of the place. Though Anne was happy for me to attend, she had no interest in pursuing the likely ardour of the trip or the Movements during her holiday. I'd maintained correspondence with fellow graduate, Scott Jones, who picked me up from Dulles Airport and dropped me outside the kitchen, wishing me the best, while adding that his recent Buddhist practice felt more congenial.

None of the 30 graduates were from my year and most of the former residents had moved on. I sought Pierre's approval of Movements I'd created for the St Kilda students, showing him diagrams of choreographies I'd prepared which he liked, encouraging me in developing them further. We worked on the Movements thrice-daily, heightening sensitivity between muscle tension and relaxation. Most Movements were configured in six lines. Occasionally, I caught glimpses of the mathematical patterns underlying the displacements in the rows. The precision of the gestures was paramount. Pierre voiced concerns that the precious knowledge contained in the Movements not be allowed to degenerate. Better not to do them than to lose their significance through inaccuracies.

The heightened feeling of co-ordination that regular practice engendered carried into other activities. Our outside labour was singularly dedicated to painting the entire dormitory and octagon, necessitating a thorough scrubbing of the cinder blocks and masonry and the constructing of scaffolding. Meals were shared with the 30 or more novices partaking of a three-month course and in whose company, we presented as veterans.

Scott kindly delivered me back to the airport, happy to hear of my month but restating his abhorrence of Claymont's regime. Congeniality wasn't on the menu. I'd forgotten how tiring it was and fell asleep before the plane lifted from Dulles runway, waking briefly in Auckland while the 747 refuelled.

Back at the school, I adapted some of Claymont's means of working with sensitivity and mutual respect. We introduced a morning circle, all 60 students sitting on the floor where we entered into diaries at least one thing we intended achieving during the day. This we re-dressed in another circle fifteen minutes before the end of the school day, followed by group reading of a pertinent novel. The simplified Movements still challenged the students' co-ordination and when I led twice weekly sessions, all eagerly participated. I made no attempt, though, to teach Gurdjieff dances; far deeper understanding and practice would be required if I were to transmit them.

We set themes, as per Claymont, encouraging self-reflection and disclosure before the group. To kick-start the process staff agreed on a clutch of key concepts, respect, pushing through, rights and obligations, completing tasks and the like. These would form a common language and their use in speech was encouraged. This wasn't an overnight sensation or uniform assent to confession. It was marvellous to hear students express themselves before their peers. Sitting in a communal circle we shared the sound of someone, hitherto quite incoherent, breaking into clarity. All voices were equally valued. Though not openly applauded, such effort gave confidence to others to do likewise. To hear the boys in particular—whose communicative skills were expressed through games, rough play and slagging—grope for appropriate words, was illuminating. It was a struggle I'd known since childhood.

Despite these successes I felt trapped in a place I really didn't wish to be in, nor could shrug without resigning. From the get-go, I'd regarded Melbourne as an intermission before experiencing more of Aboriginal Australia. Again, I quit the Education Department to concentrate on exhibitions of paintings in Manuka, Canberra, and tables at Distelfink Gallery in Hawthorn.

My old mate and colleague, Alan Tasker, had shifted to another alternative school at Ardoch Village in Prahran. As an interim measure prior to my heading north, he invited me to paint a *trompe l'oeill* mural on one of the school walls. He was so pleased with the result that he asked if I'd help him roof The Lakehouse in Daylesford, a venture in up-market Bed and Breakfast he was embarking on with former maths teacher, now partner, Alla. Both possessed the vision, energy and range of culinary, manual and entrepreneurial skills to ensure success.

Potter, Karl Otto, who'd volunteered his skill at the school while his four children attended, joined our labours on the steep gables of The Lakehouse. All day, I hammered and nailed, noting how best to hold the hammer, ease its oscillations, and to strike it home without slipping from the roof. Karl and I had been friends since his children started at Brinsley Road and I'd kept in contact, enjoying my visits with him and his wife, Rosemary, a lecturer in Education at Latrobe University.

Hearing of my impending move north, Karl showed me his copy of Baldwin Spencer's, *Native Tribes of Central Australia* that reproduced many of the images I'd first seen beneath the museum, explaining that the publication had influenced Freud and set Europeans, Roheim and Eliade, on the trail of the Arrernte. He suggested Lutheran pastor Carl Strehlow, who'd administered the Hermannsburg Mission in Central Australia in the early 1900s, might interest me, too, although he doubted his work had been translated from the German.

We chatted about the pleasure work gave us, less its financial rewards, than work as its own reward; that we need engagement with work to open and connect us to the world. I mentioned that the attention exercises we'd undertaken at Claymont were linked to practical work. He recommended Henri Focillon's essay, *In Praise of Hands*, that he'd returned to over the years for inspiration and reflection.

I could imagine that my beloved lecturer at Caulfield, Warwick Armstrong would have enjoyed incorporating Focillon into his lecture on Rembrandt's touch, his *Bathsheeba*, *Prodigal Son* or *Jewish Bride*. I knew he'd recently returned from a Residency at the Karolyi Foundation in Vence, France and, having retired from Caulfield he was mustering thoughts for a book on Picasso's re-workings of Delecroix, Manet and Velasquez, and been hopeful of interviewing his widow, Jacqueline Roque.

I rang him soon after, only to find the lines were jammed. Mt Macedon was ablaze. A week later, he told me he and his wife had been evacuated to a Gisborne motel. Though their house was untouched, those either side were destroyed. Alton was also spared though many of the nineteenth-century mansions were incinerated. In the rush to get out, he was astonished to find that the things he valued most were not his books but their cats, Hillary and Boris. Even though their house and contents were not burned, the trauma prompted a shift to Queenscliff. Perhaps their brush with mortality explained his renewed interest in Krishnamurti, whose conversations with physicist, David Bohm, promoted as *The Ending of Time*, had just been published. He and his wife began attending discussion evenings in a South Yarra mansion devoted to the guru. Remembering my interest as a student in the guru who professed not to be a teacher during his 70-year lecturing career, Warwick gave me the address. I didn't, however, get the chance to ask him why Krishnamurti remained on his radar. At this time, I preferred the practical exercises I'd picked up at Claymont rather than suggestions that our ills derive from attachment to thought. For better and worse, lucid or muddy, thought was my lot and art, music, literature and dance were its fruits.

***

In addition to Rembrandt, I'd meant to mention to Warwick Goya's 'black' paintings at the Prado in Spain when Anne and I had visited it. First stop at the Prado had been Bosch's *Garden*. Much has been made of its cornucopia of biblical symbols. Scholars even likened its symbolic scope with Gurdjieff's tome. What riveted my eye were the pair of pinned, severed ears in the Hell panel, phallic scissors wedged between, an exposition of Man's bewilderment. Bosch had been lauded by the Surrealists and received further airing when pop culture, notably, *Pearls before the Swine*, adopted his imagery for album covers.

Undoubtedly the hope of expanded consciousness motivated much of my reading. What mental state facilitated Bosch's congestion of morphed and hybrid imagery? Had ergotism (poisoning from eating food affected by ergot), so prevalent from eating the staple black ryebread of his time, induced fervid thoughts? His hybrid creations reminded me of our school game, drawing a head with two projected neck lines, folding the paper and passing it to a mate who'd draw a body and leg lines, fold and pass it back for me to pen in feet. We'd unfold the paper to chuckle over our preposterous images.

Velasquez's *Les Meninas* was privileged with its own room. When lecturing on the Spanish master's extreme exactitude, Warwick had bandied about pure consciousness, the aspirational state I took to be the aim of the *sema*, the *vipassana* and repetitive chanting. How did Velasquez's pure visualisation tally with pure consciousness? His countryman, Ortega y Gasset, regarded Velasquez's paintings as documentaries of unsurpassable verisimo but at the same time as phantasmagoria, an effect Tarkovsky achieved with his camera's immersion in the thingness of things.

The royal ghosts of *Les Meninas* stalked me through acres of Goya's less troubled, Rococo years. Then came the room of gloom that extended Bosh's Hellish theme. No darker suite of paintings have I witnessed. Left of entry was the forlorn dog's head, sniffing pitifully at the creamy sky. For some reason, el Greco's *Cardinal* came to mind. Warwick suggested dogs represented the separation between Man and his world, and their purifying gaze saw him for what he was. How the presence of dogs in paintings mollified Man's sense of despair, intuiting there is something beyond the limits of their own condition. Like us, they feel extreme emotions such as desire and jealousy. Though they know they cannot become men, in their hearts, dogs that associate with men, wish to become men. The sadness we see in their eyes results from this unrealised wish. Goya's mutt, abandoned to its fate before a tsunami of dust, incited memories of dog loyalty, bravery, ferocity, of nuzzling between my knees for solace, sharing warmth and doggie breaths. These speculations I'd, have to be put on hold until Warwick visited Alice Springs.

With the exhibitions done, the call to Indigenous Australia could no longer be ignored. Could I persuade Anne to join me? Perhaps a trip to India could buy some time, given my reluctance about parting from her. Our energies and interests were compatible, and she was attuned to me as I to her. A camel trip through Rajasthan's desert might serve as antidote to grey Melbourne. Was she interested? Though her affection for camels hadn't wavered since her Djibouti childhood as daughter of a Legionnaire officer, she didn't consider a camel camp the respite from teaching that I did. Not that I had the slightest interest in camels. But the allure of dry desert air was strong as was the prospect of budget-level guidance. I booked a ticket to the subcontinent, a zone that till now I'd deferred, in fear of contracting the very ailments, exhaustion and stomach turmoil I'd been suffering.

Boxed Quoll, Rod Moss, 1984.

11
India

Trampoline, Rod Moss, 1976.

It seemed inevitable that I'd visit India. Peter Gabriel's WOMAD label had generated my interest in music from the subcontinent, notably the Sabri Brothers, whose *qawwali* harmonies of longing and desire had sensual appeal. WOMAD's growing popularity reflected the curiosity resulting from the travellers who, like me, had stretched beyond the established routes of Europe and America.

I was infatuated with the symmetrical beauty of Indian faces, and frequented the growing number of restaurants in Melbourne. Previously, I've foolishly described facial traits as if they were common to all Thai women. And so it is with symmetry or proximate symmetry. But these elements, in combination with erect bearing and light, mincing steps are more prevalent among our Asian sisters. And obesity had yet to plague their population.

Tandoori cooking, *pashwari naan*, *malai kofta*—I couldn't get enough of them, nor the polite table service. The abruptness, even hostility, Anne and I experienced from Australian waitresses at this time, was legend. Breakfasting at a roadside cafe near Robe, for instance, we'd passed casual comment to the waitress on the numerous flies surrounding us. She huffed off to the kitchen, returned with spray and liberally dosed us our eggs and toast. Had she served an apprenticeship with Airport Quarantine or graduated from Basil Fawlty's School of Etiquette?

Things Indian, yoga and music, had slowly emerged since the hippy sixties when the Maharishi, unruly long hair and kaftan, struck a note on stage at Monash University. The East beckoned when Royden showed Satyajit Ray's *Apu* trilogy at Tecoma, and I'd fallen for Sharmila Tagore. I'd taken every opportunity to attend concerts of Indian musicians ever since, and thrilled to the interpretation of the *Ramayana* by Chandrabhanu's dancers.

On the *Air India* flight, I was enchanted by a hostess, gracious in her sari, her black hair hoisted in an extravagant bun exposing neck and ear I'd love to nuzzle. While Australian airlines no longer attracted the young, there seemed an endless supply of youthful subcontinental hostesses. Others identically dressed didn't match her faultless proportions. Her sari belonged with her body. I made small requests, more than I ordinarily would, hoping not to tire her, while scanning the sum of her perfection. The delicate nose, dark orbs and lashes, full lips that, on sharing an accommodating smile, parted slightly over immaculate teeth. As much as there was poise, her unhurried awareness of each act respected the physical world without wasted effort. My greedy eyes followed her along the aisles.

Nearing Delhi, I plucked the courage to tell her how beautiful she was. My energies were returning. No bra straps, cleavages or calf muscles on which to speculate. I was content with faces, bared midriffs and graceful fingers. There was beauty in their bearing, depthless black eyes, and the care taken in dressing so colourfully for the world's eyes.

Grey-bearded Bikram Singh, no doubt alert to my attentions, sat at my side by the window beaming beneath his yellow turban. He'd lived in Melbourne this recent decade while his sons completed degrees, one in Law, the other Medicine. He returned to Delhi annually to reunite with family and procure spices for his brother's Richmond restaurant. Having described his business interests he asked what kept me in Melbourne. I mentioned Anne and my exhibitions at Manuka Gallery and Distelfink. Without images to show, words were a poor substitute. He said, though no connoisseur, his few encounters with Australian art revealed deficient critical juice. Though technically competent, he felt it aped art in Northern metropolises; and was mediocre and mostly inconsequential, lacking the intensity of a distinctive visual language.

I suggested he search out John's work on his return to Melbourne: that John's expression of sexual longing and pursuit of material fulfilment depicted in dream language, might touch him as it did me. Singh countered that it was Aboriginal Australia that intrigued overseas visitors rather than colonial art. What was he referring to? Namitjira came to mind but he was long gone and the tepid watercolour landscapes I'd seen replicated on place mats and biscuit tins would hardly register internationally. Best not judge the artist by the kitsch offspring of his work. Original art, especially so delicate a medium as watercolour, was rarely served justice through reproduction.

***

The first and lasting impression of New Delhi was its population. Bangkok and Tehran had nothing on these masses of bodies of varied shapes and colours. The shock of sheer numbers, moving in a great slow tide through the streets from dawn to dusk, displaced self-concern, instantly. What was that in the air? From the hotel balcony Delhi's odour had an unidentifiable herbal richness. Travel brochures made no reference to it. The desk clerk said the low cloud draping trees was fuelled by cow dung. Morning and evening fires stirred sinuses I'd been unaware of and were sufficiently dense to revive claustrophobia I'd experienced in Melbourne fogs. Forget the sandalwood or rose incense of our twee Indian import shops. Here midst the ceaseless hum of traffic floated the essence of place.

I browsed copies of the *Hindustan Times* in the foyer while a rain shower passed. I skipped the bold print's political matters and soon found pages devoted to stabbings and shootings by police and army—violence on a scale that rendered Australian strife trifling. There followed a sizeable section advertising suitable marriage alliances. In the main they declared women's attributes: good Christian, Muslim, Hindu girl, pale skin, academic credentials and, for good measure, astrological signs by an authentic consultant. Higher status was attributed to pale skin. Ideals I'd projected on the country were challenged: injustices and terrors that cried for catalysts of Tagore and Gandhi's calibre.

I wandered a broad boulevard, shaded by plane trees, towards the city centre. There was a park with several cricket pitches occupied by boys vigorously pursuing wickets and runs. A ball was belted and rolled towards the boundary where I'd paused to watch. When I stooped and returned it to the wicket keeper I was hailed as Australian fast bowler, Dennis Lillee, and urged to join. The comparison was flattering but ludicrous. Perhaps 50 overs in local Grade cricket as a spinner, I had produced a handful of wickets. I'd never sprouted a moustache or chested a gold chain. Nevertheless, when I was handed the ball and marked a short run to the crease, the first ball, to my joy, shattered the batsman's stumps. Triumph in India! No matter the victim was an 11-year-old sapling. My over complete, the game halted as a young mum emerged from nearby tenements with a tray of cakes and cordial. I thanked her and quit while ahead.

About a kilometre from the park, the boulevard morphed into a square before reforming on the other side. A throng attended a medicine hawker, plonked on a carpet in the shade of a massive peepal tree, surrounded by a multitude of bottles. These were filled with powders and fluids ranging the full colour spectrum. He praised the place from which each component had been sourced, in particular mountain regions that alone nourished mineral and herbal potencies. Each was touted for its medicinal virtues. He paused between items while his assistant tipped each into a large stainless-steel bowl. When all had received ample benediction and stirred, the apprentice decanted the potion into bottles for sale. It was a brilliant performance, deserving its willing clientele.

Less rowdy were young flower vendors clasping posies, grateful for the few rupees from each sale, seemingly sufficient to the day. So it went: a sale with a smile, hop the wall and fetch another bunch from the riverbank: such minimal fuss separating them from the mendicants strewn elsewhere. Getting and spending, surviving and persisting; this infinite weight of humanity. What dreams were nurtured in each breast? Freed from labours for six weeks, I was here only to spend, and twinged with sadness at the multitudes of children working, their childhood passed in the streets.

Several score of heavily garbed families with glum faces sat propped against a stretch of shop fronts: Tibetan refugees, I was told, who had been re-assembling there each day for years. I knew next to nothing about China's invasion of their country 30 years before, re-populating it at the same time as destroying its unique culture. Or that mountainous Tibet's rich mineral deposits and source of Chinese rivers had made it a target. The exiles didn't appear to be begging or offering items for exchange. I wondered briefly about their fate, what privations and ordeals had provoked emigration, then wandered on, feeling mildly helpless about their plight.

What a challenge for me to exist here, having grown in pampered circumstances and broad spaces with little gratitude or grace: unexamined privileges arising from birth in another quarter of the planet. But for that singular event far from here I, too, might clamber for sustenance with the white-clayed figures slumped in doorways and dim corners of footpaths. Or the tiny mothers clutching infants to breasts as they searched for alms at bus windows.

Just waiting in an infinite queue for my *post restante* challenged patience. An American in front of me reached his limit. Advancing for an hour, and about to face the teller, he was jumped by a small Indian. Grabbing him from behind the man, the bigger man lifted him aside, but the Indian gripped the grill with such tenacity he brought it with him as both men crashed to the floor. This violence was ramified minutes later in the letter the American opened at my side. He dumped its news on me—his girlfriend had been stabbed to death in Georgetown, Washington. I stared at him as if he'd spoken a foreign language, without words. High above, the ceiling fan whirled giddily in our moment of shared silence.

'Like a bull in a tea-shop.' Did the expression arise from India's colonial past? Roan cows meandered unmolested through crowds and lingered in shops. No one turned a head. They competed with the poor, rummaging rubbish gathered in gutters. Among the sea of black heads was a young red-bearded European. Tattered long hair and besmirched, he claimed he'd sold his passport for drugs. I was confused and walked on, bottling pity and revulsion. How had he become so reduced? Street level: the ultimate leveller.

Where had these masses come from? Everyone was on the move in what felt like an evacuation. Australia's entire population seemingly passed by on the hour. Where did they go, each on private missions midst this human jungle? Such luxuriance in nature was throttling. This seething vitality was at huge variance with the tempered society back home. I trusted our laws to protect my freedom of speech and access to reliable medical assistance. There were supermarkets to satisfy my appetite and productive work enabling decent shelter. But what public institutions could grapple and serve this immense populace? I thought, too, of litter and death. Whatever one's position on reincarnation, cremation lessened the pressure on real estate.

Someone's wedding or religious holiday seemed to be celebrated each day with sufficient significance to attract a crowd, moving slightly out of sync with the omnipresent masses. Elephants decorated to the hilt led these parades, their freighted favourites robed in complimentary finery. I wondered how appointments were met when such crowds need be factored into plans.

But it was camels I'd come for and they were in Rajasthan, 460 rail-track kilometres west. Despite leaving the hotel at what I'd assumed was pre-peak hour, the taxi laboured an hour through three kilometres of crowded roads to the equally crowded station, where individuals and families had overnighted on the platforms. There were a variety of carriages, some resembling our obsolete red rattlers, and single carriage freight trains like our redundant Fast Parcels' trains. The traffic conditions we'd just experienced didn't suggest that, unlike Melbourne, India would be switching to road transport any time soon. Station hands still passed a communication bamboo ring to the guard as the train departed, as per my student days.

Boarding the locomotive provided another surprise. As it approached the platform, hordes swarmed across the rails towards the moving carriages, throwing baggage and blankets through its windows, desperate to secure seats. The train to the walled citadel of Bikaner gave relief from the smoke. Then dust took over with similar effect. Mine was a second-class seated compartment shared with Chetal Upadhyaya, who was returning from a meeting in Delhi of regional prison wardens. He had the Bikaner gig and asked, time permitting, if I'd like to visit the prison. My hotel desk clerk would provide directions. Did he enjoy his work?

'No. I am not satisfied,' he rattled defensively as if still at his Delhi meeting. 'A satisfied man is a dead man. However, I like the job.'

On arriving in Bikaner, several young men hovered outside my hotel lobby and invited me to their home. Had they some pecuniary intent? What was I here for if not to partake of local hospitality? They returned 20 minutes later in the smoky dark on bicycles—a spare one for me—and 20 minutes later I was crammed in their lounge, nursing a guitar, strung inversely and with unfamiliar tuning. A dozen people lived under this roof, three generations of family. Bedrooms, kitchen, lounge would fit inside my lounge. All shelf and wall spaces were impeccably kept and choked with pictures, photos and mementos.

The guitar was passed between the men as each in turn played. Several others arrived and took turns. Everyone, no matter how young, had songs and was unabashed about performing. They wished to hear anything I could thrum; I responded as best I could on those tunings with some husky Dylan that earned unwarranted applause. We danced and sang and a few hours later they accompanied me to my lodgings where silent smiles marked our parting. Would such a delightful encounter occur in Australia? Communal singing and repertoires had long been on the decline, more so since the advent of television.

Narput Singh, about my age, met me at the hotel and we taxied to the prison. Singh, apparently of some royal lineage, would assist my sojourn with Rajput cameleers. His humour and decisiveness shone throughout the weeks in the Thar Desert. Chetal greeted me just inside the gates of this men's prison with a tentative handshake as if only dimly recalling our encounter.

Given its monastic peace I asked him what crimes these polite fellows had committed. Over 90 percent were murders. Honour killings, a crime I'd not known about nor was mentioned in the newspaper. How long were their sentences? 'Life. That's 20 years if well behaved.' He toured me through well-groomed rose gardens to the carpet factory where the production of rugs and kilims of notable reputation, helped fund the prison program. Having chosen a lime green kilim, on his urgings, Narput arranged for its delivery to Melbourne.

Already the mélange of human faces in Delhi had been refined. Distinctively dressed Rajputs dominated. Men favoured dhotis, electric orange and yellow turbans and constantly preened long moustaches, admiring the results in small shards of mirror or polished tin. Women and girls decked themselves in vermillion saris and shawls, wore rings through noses and toes, and bracelets on ankles, wrists and biceps.

'Bride wealth', said Narput, when he caught my curious eye. 'Look at the gold fillings in their teeth.'

Half an hour with my camel was sufficient to recognise we were incompatible. I dismounted and walked the remainder of the morning. The camel was lame. 'Flat tyre,' Singh jested before berating its master, sending him back to his village with loss of significant rupees and reputation. Between stints on foot, I joined the two Muslim musicians, Fadu and Babu, on top of the cart bearing food and bedding. Our days concluded with their soaring songs of bravery, romance, treachery and hubris. One morning, while yet to master Hindi diction, I found myself whistling their melodies with novel bird-like trilling. My tongue fluttered against the roof of my mouth as I breathed, enhancing volume and tonal range. The cart cruise was the apogee of the trip and I rarely left their company, learning songs during the day and dancing with them around evening fires.

Babu on dolak and Fadu on wheezy harmonium, Farouk attending, 1984.

As we circled the fire one night a woman sprung from the dark and danced to Fadu's fevered voice. Tiny bells dangled from her wrists and ankles, and her mascaraed eyes gleamed above her veil. Everyone was enthralled by this feminine eruption. I declined her invitation to dance. All eyes were trained on her. Then she removed her veil. It was Babu. This was a hard act to follow though Yado, the head cameleer's son, made a gallant attempt performing the *Talvar Chalana* sword dance, twirling and slashing the air with a fire-lit blade. No sooner done than he repeated the act with a fire torch, scribing brilliant arcs against the starry depths.

Our regular cook stepped aside on evening while a goat was slaughtered for supper by one of the Muslims. The old man read from the Koran before killing it, invoking Allah's name as he swiped his knife across its jugulars, allowing the blood to soak into the sand. I was unaware of religious disharmonies and though the two in command were Sikh and Hindu, Muslims were equally represented on the trip. However, if meat was to be shared by all, a Muslim must do the killing. Not that meat much featured in Rajasthan dishes. Many sects prescribed vegetarianism, and aridity imposed limits on herd-raising and meat consumption.

I joined the men in a boisterous game of *kabaddi*, an exhausting but appropriate desert recreation. Singh said it was an ancient game played throughout the country, but these men had their own version. The word *kabaddi* is repeated by whoever volunteered to cross the centre line of the court, scribed in the sand. The number of contestants determined the scale of the precinct. The protagonist inhaled deeply and slowly expelled that one breath while chanting *kabaddi kabaddi* and attempting to touch as many of the opposing team before successfully regaining his territory. The opposition was not lax. If they could restrain him before he retreated, gasping for air, his efforts were nullified. A man from the other team then advanced and turns alternated until one side was completely vanquished. There were no rules regarding the means of attack or defence, and players employed ingenious gymnastic means of contact. The game abated after half an hour of fierce and honourable contest. I'd done nothing like this since those testosterone tussles of schoolyard Piggyback, Hoppo Bumpo and British Bulldog.

Day six and before we started out for the day's travel, I was asked to contribute rupees for a dietary boost to facilitate a camel coupling. 'Please, a photo for you.' I wasn't prudish but this wasn't an act I'd invited. Nor had I a camera. The cameleer persisted. Molasses was poured over oats and quaffed with relish prior to dutiful humping. Whatever turns you on, I guess, though the encounter seemed joyless for both beasts.

The journey's unfolding rhythms were deeply satisfying. The dry moderate temperatures were an elixir as was the exuberant company. Luxuriously, I didn't erect or dismantle my tent. Nor did I prepare or cook meals. That was left to Lama, a Himalayan Sherpa, who complained the climate was beyond his comfort zone. Everyone retired around 8 o'clock and woke at dawn to the bellowing camels. Only the cameleers needed to face the chill and tend their farting beasts. I remained cocooned in my swag.

Chapatti and chai greeted me at the tent flap. 'You want sugar?' Babu asked. 'No'. 'Milk, perhaps?' 'No,' I replied. 'Perhaps no water,' quipped Narput Singh slouching beside me in the tent while translating songs I'd learned the previous days. There were friendly exchanges regards the sexual mores of Indian and Australian women and the observation that Indian women made good wives but less satisfying lovers. 'The fabric of our women is hard to penetrate,' he said, with a wry grin. Where was this leading? The ideal embodied in the air hostess had not been rivalled and my appetite had slackened with exposure to vast masses that strayed from it.

Narput changed tack, pointing to my freckled arms. He claimed they resulted from eating beef. 'You shouldn't eat your Mother,' he admonished. 'But I rarely eat meat and never touch beef,' I replied. 'Perhaps your parents ate meat, no?' Couldn't deny that. They probably ate more in a week than these locals did annually.

My health continued to improve. Work travails, clinging students, the uncertainty of heated staff meetings—all dropped from mind. Constant novelty demanded attention. This was supposedly India's least populated zone. Weren't deserts deserted? Even here, villages Baru, Satya, Nauk and the rest, were less than an hour apart, each with its well and communal stack of cow dung. Peacocks perched in the occasional bushy scrub, making their peculiar cry as we passed, their shimmering colour resonating with Rajput attire in thrilling contrast to the drab desert. A few sheep and goats, an emaciated cow or two, strands of maize and mustard and the knowledge of how to weave grass into rope or roof expressed the local response to life.

On the second last day, zoned out on desert narcosis, we encountered the windswept fertility temple of Kaladhunga. A red prayer flag flapped in the cold wind. Randomly resting on this rocky outcrop were red votive powders in dishes, stained stones of goat sacrifices and carved baby cradles left by grateful parents who'd conceived after praying here.

Jaisalmer was where we parted company after a fortnight in the desert. My rupees, of course, brought me privileges and rendered me an honoured guest. But love of song—that common language—forged an undeniable bond with the zestful musician-cooks. Babu accompanied me to my hotel room, cresting a peak within the city's crumbly yellow walls. At the hotel he wound a silver thread five times around my left wrist endorsing friendship, then waved goodbye and disappeared down the dark alley to the camels gathered in stubble at the city's edge. I watched from my window until he was lost from sight then noticed a gargling sound. It was toilet water flushing from the room below to the alley where pedestrians were busily balking at the putrescence.

Sleep between clean sheets, on a bed, in a room. What luxury! But before retiring, I was beckoned by hotel staff to the lobby and surprised to see a performance akin to Mevlana whirling. A turbaned young man in a flowing red dress over white pantaloons entertained the small collection of tourists. There was neither allusion to spiritual endeavour, nor Jelaluddin's rapturous intensity. This was after all, touristic enterprise, and the medieval town traded on its ruined looks and such presentations to attract our kind.

I purchased a pair of embroidered leather slippers from a cobbler close to the hotel. All the cameleers wore them, and on them, they looked splendid. Less so on my feet and the rigid leather rubbed both achilles raw within 20 minutes. I removed them to study first my wounds, then the slippers' floral embroidery. Fecundity. That's what I respond to so positively. It drives so much central and Southeast Asian design. Though I suffocate in the intensity of actual crowds, such writhing figuration attracts me to Bosch, Tintoretto, even Bonnard. I'd seen multi-limbed Shivas, Kalis, Vishnus and multi-trunked Ganeshas cavorting on temple walls. Sex, inconspicuous in Christian imagery, was the preoccupation of many Indian gods. Fabrics, carvings, walls and parchments were riddled with human figurations. Were these expressions of India's compressed public and private spaces?

I also wanted a *dolak* like the small wooden drum Babu encouraged me to tap with fingers and the heels of my hands. Given my present lameness, Narput offered to track one down without my arduous bargaining. The station was within hobbling distance. Ankles taped, the next morning I joined the crowds waiting to board the quaint, white train with its guilt-edged trimmings, justly titled the *Palace on Wheels*. Destination, Jodpur, where we'd overnight in the luxurious Umaid Bhawana Palace then take the bus to Jaipur. The masses were less numerous than Delhi or Bikaner but again, I was grateful we arrived early. The seats had been pre-booked though the Delhi experience hadn't inspired confidence.

I turned for a final glimpse of the hilltop town and heard the distant reports of cannons. With raised eyebrows I turned to Narput. 'Artillery,' he said, shaking his head, a 'yes' in these latitudes. And so, this city, constructed millennia ago as fortress against sabre-bearers and archers on elephants, now defended the Pakistan border: my desert reverie halted with awareness of potential violence. Ethnic, class and religious divisions still percolated. Gauging by those guns, titanic tensions between Muslims and Hindus threatened to erupt.

How virulent had been the sectarian strife in Australia between Catholics and Protestants? I'd heard of friction between Irish and English settlers in the nineteenth century, but none like those in Ireland. Much had been made of these differences in retelling the Kelly saga and the rebellion on Ballarat's goldfields. Apparently, the conscription referendum during World War I between Protestant Prime Minister Hughes and Catholic archbishop Mannix exacerbated a quarrel that lingered for decades, dividing the sects. Hughes was adamantly pro-conscription and Mannix objected. Mannix's death in 1963 coincided with a growing educated middle class and the softening of sectarian differences.

Only in adulthood had I learned about atrocities based on race, the appalling violence against First Australians defending their country, the anti-Chinese attitudes arising on the gold fields, and the infamous White Australian Policy that featured in early sessions of the Federal Government and persisted well into the twentieth century. Boronia thrived midst the coastal settlements' white majority. It was easy in cities to remain oblivious to the tensions corroding the fabric of remote Indigenous communities where white discriminatory acts against Aboriginal people—persecution, stolen lands and children—persisted.

Re-entering the scheduled world, I boarded The Palace train, formerly the property of a Rajput prince, and enjoyed sumptuous passage to Jodhpur, famed for the its azure buildings. The fittings and service on the train were like Melbourne's Menzies Hotel on wheels, though no such train ever graced Australian rails. The Jodhpur palace was no less impressive, its squash court and spacious indoor pool, in particular.

I alighted from the bus in Jaipur where the smell of cow dung reasserted itself. And the crowds. How quickly had the desert sojourn erased memory of their pressing numbers. Jaipur was named in honour of its genius mathematician-astronomer, Jai Singh who'd developed the work of Samarkand's equally illustrious Ulugh Beg. The UNESCO World Heritage listed observatory, built in 1738, brought to mind Le Corbusier's elegant, stripped-back lines who'd, incidentally, left his architectural mark to the north, in the gridded city of Chandigarh. Aesthetically, the observatory stood apart from Jaipur's homogenous pink buildings whose opulent alabaster decoration I found wearisome.

From there I took the bus to Agra, detouring to the Bharatpur bird sanctuary. Constructed in the mid eighteenth century by the local Maharaja for his private pleasure, it had recently been designated a national park and made accessible to the public. Its forests and marshes stirred with unfamiliar birdcalls and sightings of cranes, kingfishers, ibis, warblers and spoonbills. The man-made lake had long since been reclaimed by nature. The intense bird cacophony provided a wall of sound I'd only encountered in sub-tropical forests jn Kakadu

The bus depot was close to Agra's famous mausoleum, on the banks of the Jamuna River. I'd heard that the full moon enhanced the Taj Mahal, but that evening, it was a mere cuticle when the bus arrived. Entering the precinct through a high red gate, I paused on a marble bench at the head of a strip of water, interspersed with fountains and cypress avenues. Young couples strolled either side of the waterway motioning to lotus lilies, hushed in awe of an image familiarised by reproduction, now transformed into hyper-reality. Only the trombone pia-ow call of peacock pairs disturbed the tranquillity as they strutted the commons fanning their 50-eyed tails.

Photography failed to convey the geometric interlock of building with its gardens. Its size awed me, the way natural phenomena like the Grand Canyon or Uluru do. What staggering wealth and belief were consecrated here? How much had Lord Curzon's restoration altered its original decoration? Agra was in poor shape in the nineteenth century as was the jewel in its crown. Curzon replaced the flowerbeds, orchards, and rivers of water, milk, honey and wine—said to evoke paradise—with English-styled forecourt lawns. It wasn't the pristine white marble I'd expected from photos, more an austere pale grey. But in congregation with reds, browns, and the cypress greens, it was luminous. The bulbous main dome was flanked by contrasting red, sandstone structures crowned with white marble domes. Inside, intricately patterned floral webbing graced white marble.

Jasmine swamped the evening air. In diminished moonlight the dome's cupolas and four candle-like minarets conversed harmoniously. A slight tweaking of imagination proposed a celestial sister to a fuller moon, linking above with below. Turcoman tents had found their evolutionary end point; the moon's mirror carved from milk.

Across the river from the Taj at the Red Fort, 1984.

Did the Taj fit Gurdjieff's notion of objective art and evoke universal responses? Ouspensky had rattled on about this shrine as he had with Notre Dame, the Sphinx and pyramids. I couldn't discern objective from subjective art. Praiseworthy press had circulated for centuries and travellers, favoured by fortune, bathed in its presence. Mumtaz-i-Mahal's shrine seemed effortlessly made, quieting crowds, a rare harmony in the built world. That it was a tomb was secondary to aesthetic satisfaction. What multitudes of men and elephants had been sacrificed in its accomplishment? Shah Jahan's monumental indifference to suffering in the name of love wouldn't be permitted on contemporary Australian construction sites.

***

It was time to head home, one mostly bereft of domes and none with such poise. Remarkably, I'd not once worried about foodstuffs or drinks. Restaurants and stalls, the meals served as camels bellowed, none had troubled my fragile digestion. Mother India. Not my mother, this land so stressed with prodigious numbers. Begging, a phenomenon I'd encountered occasionally in southeast Asia and not at all in Australia at that time. Here, it was common, and it left me feeling impotent. What institutions or charitable gestures could respond? As with Buddhist Thailand, I wondered if belief in reincarnation condemned people to their social stations. Perhaps behind facades, ashrams and orphanages tended to the needy.

I had little grasp of the culture and only casual interest it. The caste system decried by Gandhi must have persisted everywhere without my understanding. Child brides, the burning of widows, gender inequality in education, hadn't caught my eye. Though fascinated by India's stunning costume, cuisine, music and architecture, I couldn't embrace the beliefs that inspired their expression. I might whine about shortcomings of secular democracy, but travel reminded me of freedoms I wouldn't enjoy elsewhere. I'd barely lifted a finger while beholding its spectacles. It had been tourist cream, this sensorium, taking me out of my country and my deflated self.

***

India only further stimulated interest in Indigenous Australia. Returning to Melbourne, its mercurial weather continued to absorb my vital energy. I'd ride to work with a newspaper stuffed inside my shirt to staunch Antarctic winds howling up Punt Road. My immunity was at an all-time low and I worried about taking another winter in the south under stress. Colds had been more frequent and were taking longer to shrug. A recent bout of fever left me with diarrhoea. Anne recommended her Melbourne homeopath, Dr Joseph von Moger, who operated out of his Kew residency.

There was no need to make an appointment. Despite reservations sparked by the Ropar's experience, I rocked up and stood outside behind several other bods until seats were available in the waiting room. There was little to gain other than pleasing Anne, but also little to lose. At least 20 people sat inside. Passage to the consultation room was rapid. Clients swung in and out of the room every three or so minutes. He looked at me as I entered the room and was scripting medicines even before I sat to state my issues. No checking of pulse or blood pressure, no wielding of stethoscope or thermometer. He passed the script to present at the dispensary at the rear of the house, dismissing me with a suggestion that Melbourne's climate was unsuitable for me. I should shift to a drier, rockier climate. I heard what I wanted to hear, even if the benefits of the tinctures were to prove negligible.

Late in 1984, I was off in Dave Morgan's direction to belatedly accept his invitation, with little idea of the road ahead. The climate and animated fellowship of Rajasthan firmed my decision to quit the south—its vibrancy and openness absent from my Melbourne rounds. Dave never got beyond Darwin. Needing to fatten his wallet for overseas travel, the only water he'd crossed was the Arafura Sea to Millingimbi, a tiny island just of the coast east of Darwin. Eleven years he'd lived there, before the Strelley gig. On each Christmas trip to his mother and siblings, he'd talked up the place and culture that turned his life in unexpected directions. How was it that my friend, attuned to the best of Western literature and art, found enduring sustenance in Indigenous lives? What common ground had he uncovered?

Just prior to heading north, Anne joined me at Monash's Alexander Theatre for Jack Davis's *The Dreamers*. The veteran Indigenous dramaturge's dialogues were sprinkled with *Nyoongah*; in one terrific passage, drunkenly dancing a half-recalled tribal dance to radio music, before collapsing. At another point a man, ceremonially painted, conveyed the contiguity between the real and supernatural, so central in Aboriginal culture. The play ended with the family about to implode, one son imprisoned, the old man dead, and continuing tension and fighting. This lacerating confrontation with Indigenous realities touched me more deeply than the soapbox anger of black radicals.

I made a final call to Great Uncle in a Port Melbourne nursing home. The old man was 99. For three months he'd been bed-bound, regretting his inability to front that year's Anzac Parade. The previous year he'd sat in the open leading car. Now he was weak but comfortable, requiring help to the toilet along the passage. Struggling out of bed revealed his need of diapers. He was resigned to his demise. But then, he'd never disclosed emotions; he'd been a paragon of equanimity.

Had he been different in callow youth, suppressing his feelings after the trenches? Or when returning to France after his Ouyen land inspection, finding his French damsel had married another? What might he tell of that Great War? Over the years I had tried, without success, to prompt him. Like Warwick, he'd served in the Ambulance Corps. Surely, he could speak about the gassing, 'Nothing you'd want to hear now,' he said, recomposing beneath the quilt.

'What's your father up to? Hammer and nails, I suppose.' He managed a grin through watery eyes, the prominent blackhead buried at the flank of his right nostril still unattended after all these years.

As I rose to go, he'd pulled from his bedside drawer Frank Hardy's, *The Unlucky Australians*. 'You might want to know about this, where you're going,' he smiled. Well I wasn't heading to the Gurindji country depicted in Hardy's classic, or following activist, Stan Davey. But it was north, and despite the courageous work of my predecessors, little significant advantage had transpired for First Peoples.

With reluctance I left Anne. She was pragmatic about my decision. 'You love me and care for me,' she said. 'But you do not need me.' No way did she wish to dwell so far from the sea; she who had regularly driven to St. Kilda's pier to inhale the salty air. 'It's visceral,' she had declared, 'not some nostalgic thing'. Though our interests so often aligned the sea's hold was not among them. The warmth and respectful space we gave each other would be sorely missed. I'd fed off her excitement, her critical eye, even her disgust with Australian complacence. Moving to the frontier would sacrifice our intimacy.

My few belongings were stuffed into a haversack. We said our goodbyes and I flew to Darwin where Dave waited.

After Strelley, he'd shifted back to the Territory to print for Batchelor Teachers College, a hundred clicks south of Darwin. It was time to see what he'd been talking about—the warmth, the space, the belonging, I aspired to. I joined him in the printery, applying for work with the College and an Arts position in fledgling Alice Springs Community College. Before the end of the year I was in Alice, lecturing, with Warwick's notes as my guide. Anchored in the centre of the continent, I found a setting that fully engaged me. It was as far as imaginable from the Top End island where I'd figured on finding employment as an art advisor or teacher. Nor did the job promise contact with

First Peoples. I'd have to re-invent myself as a purveyor of art knowledge to adults, another role I was keen to try.

As the plane descended over the MacDonnell Ranges, I saw what Sidney Nolan had seen decades before: clumps of vegetation dotting vistas of varied reds, pale pinks, and glistening quartz sweeping to the ranges. The snaking line of the flinty ridges brought Goya's savage San Isidro landscape to mind. It was November—hot, dry, and clear. Coming from the wet season build-up, it was a total release.

The hours passed differently for Indigenous and settler cultures. Nowhere, certainly not at Batchelor, was there such distinction: two streams of people busying themselves, with indifference to each other. Apart from humbugging around bottleshops and supermarkets, First Peoples kept their affairs to themselves.

It was nearly a year before I met Arrernte man, Xavier Neal. Like most of my encounters, this was serendipitous. Though I'd availed the opportunity by shifting to the Territory, Xavier's approach was the catalyst for what I, belatedly, regard as my calling. He might only have been asking for a match to light his friend's cigarette, but it soon ignited much more. I'd encountered a local Indigenous man about whose life and his associates I was hungry to know. He'd resourced a whitefella from whom he could expect consistent loyalty.

Rock Musiques, Rod Moss, 1984.

Accounts of Europeans' first contact with Indigenous people date from seafaring explorers who were often accompanied by missionaries and scientists. Artists and writers followed, famously R L Stevenson and Gauguin. My encounter was more akin to Ishmael and Queequeg's, in *Moby Dick* in that neither man had departed from what he regarded as home. Well, I'd left my parent's home, but not my country.

I unhesitatingly responded to Xavier's elementary requests, hoping he'd favour me with perceptions of his country. It was soon apparent he was not similarly searching for some lost or hidden part of himself. Despite his home being overrun by settler culture, suffering the deaths of both parents, brothers and numerous relatives, despite alcoholism, he was at ease with himself, purposeful and not a man to cringe, or self-pityingly, feel in debt to me.

Through long association, I came to realise that his confidence benefitted from subtle interrelationships nurtured in all Arrernte. Rich family and kinship systems tied people together which fostered responsibilities for particular others. Distinct from settler culture, grandchildren were obliged to care for grandparents. Such responsibilities were made clear from infancy, through language and handling, and were inextricably connected to the country in ways that rendered my affection for it superficial. TV weather reports lacked the sensitive environmental readings Arrernte made of shifts in temperature, wind direction, and the seasons' unfolding life patterns.

Not long after I asked Xavier if I could photograph him just as he was with his bare-chested display of mourning cicatrices. He'd arrived for a lift into town with shirt bunched in hand. It was a mugshot in the mode of Baldwin Spencer's *fin-de-siecle* ethnological photos, more journalistic than art. I reproduced it life-size in graphite and allowed the body to be its own expression, standing against some grid structure, present in other work of that time. The structure featured *frottage* of stone paving at the Telegraph Station where part-Arrernte had once been incarcerated. As events quickened and our familiarity thickened, narrative work ensued.

Our rapport vaulted me into the Eastern Arrernte families at Whitegate fringe camp where elder, Arranye Edward Johnson took me under wing, travelling throughout his country and telling its stories. This was direct material, unavailable in most of Australia, though as the old man's semi-nomadic life story admitted, it was being quickly undermined by settler culture. Among First Australians, human qualities still count far more than they do with we settlers whose institutions continue to work by momentum even where human qualities are questionable or lacking. The workings of the plethora of institutions serving the town campers remained opaque to his generation.

Arranye's threadbare existence and vigilance were adapted to hazard, a broad calendar and abiding history alien to me. Participation in the summer ceremonial camps when boys are transformed into men was of special moment. These formal occasions had the ring of deep seriousness and an intensity I'd only experienced in the Sufis' ritual dancing where stamping feet and chanted proclamations of belonging to earth and air were enacted. There was much more; the cohesiveness of extended family, the spontaneity and warmth, their understanding of the country and identification with it. I was at the beginning of a learning curve that kept me in thrall to Central Australia.

The light and colour of the place unleashed the palette I'd harboured since encountering Bonnard. Topography exposed a language of rock, tree and scrub as nowhere else, demanding description in panoramic scale with textures mimicking its prickly surfaces. The venerable Lloyd Rees had mooted that metaphysical art in Australia was linked to loving its soil. I was far removed from the art of First Peoples who claimed such attachment. Guplil's dance, Gurrumul's haunting voice, or the canvases of famous female painter, Nyurapayia Nampitjinpa Bennett, declared their belonging to country, of being earthed. But I could sympathise with injustices they felt. Stolen land, stolen children, deaths in custody, denial of basic life necessities, control of income and where to live—what adversities cried as loud. I would place the people front and centre.

A few years after re-locating to Queenscliff, Warwick visited me with his wife, Margo. She warned that he was suffering signs of dementia, but that he was keen to see the Centre. Though his conversational powers and curiosity remained, he manifested signs of that dreadful illness on the trip: going missing at the Adelaide rail terminal when Margo's back was turned, being passive and confused about simple decisions regarding when and what to eat, and anxious when she moved from his sight.

We made short trips east of town where he asked to stop to make a meagre line drawing in his pad, following the wobbly crest of the MacDonnell Range's caterpillar creation story. There'd always been a youthful openness about Warwick, but the innocence induced by the onset of dementia brought to mind his description of the little boy 'drawing a line around his think'.

He was reading Bachelard's *Poetics of Space*, and reckoned the Frenchman's evocation of a rustic abode complemented Heidegger's paean to the peasant hut in the Black Forest, both sharing a reverie for maternal, womblike, and sheltering homes. Bachelard's phenomenology of internal and external spaces, examined through the lens of poetry, had inspired painters and architects, not least Christopher Alexander, whose notes on creating 'inner light' I'd resorted to in class. Given Alice Spring's miniscule settlement pitched midst the might of surrounding desert, Bachelard's thoughts on the miniature and immensity had particular pertinence.

Our exchanges lacked the vigour of earlier years. Still, I was unprepared for John Anderson's alarmed call later that year. Warwick's decline had been rapid, and his wife had placed him in respite care in Queenscliff where they'd relocated after the Macedon fires. During Christmas, John and I drove to Portsea and crossed the Heads on the ferry. We were ushered into the ironically named, activities room. It took us a minute or two to recognise this, our teacher, amongst the dozen rugged and drugged bodies in wheelchairs, staring vacantly at a TV bracketed high on the wall. We rolled him outdoors and tried unsuccessfully to engage him in things he'd left undone, his notes on Picasso, and the painting in his studio he'd sat and pondered for months. This dribbling homunculus, was this our cherished mentor, the most sophisticated mind on cultural matters we'd encountered? Where had he gone? We rolled him back into dull humidity and returned in mute despair. He died a few months later.

12

Where gods once walked

Rumjungle Drawing, Rod Moss, 1985.

Three decades have elapsed since those jaunts overseas. The central deserts and Indigenous inhabitants were so absorbing I barely lifted my head from local circumstances. The memoirs mentioned in the foreword account for them. Endemic poverty, poor health, inadequately funded schools, the ignominy of overcrowded housing, institutional injustice, racial oppression, lack of prison reform and rehabilitation—these are the realities of Arrernte lives as is retributive violence and soaring domestic injury. Participating in this reality has, ineluctably, adjusted the lens through which I see things.

At first, I'd been confounded. I'd encountered poverty overseas but had arrived with romantic notions of Indigenous people enjoying intimate relationship with their country. It was, afterall, the heartland of the much-documented Arrernte. They did, but it was overridden by other images. Government initiatives in the 1970s, intended to enhance prospects for First Peoples. Yet the setting up of legal, health and town camp services, seemed to have had little impact in lifting esteem and connecting to the quality of life middle-class Australians assumed as their entitlement.

What esteem and quality of life amounted to for Alice Spring's original inhabitants, I could only imagine, from visits to the National Museum of Victoria in Swanston Street, housing the photograph and artefact collections of its first director, Baldwin Spencer. Dispossession and government control were yet to dominate lives as they do now. While sullen apprehension is captured in some of Spencer's photos, there's no indignity. It would take time to form trusting relationships for that anticipated intimacy with Nature to be revealed.

What I enjoy as my privilege was at the cost of Arrernte dispossession. They'd been ripped apart by colonisation and the creation of Alice Springs. Families were forcibly removed from their ancestral lands. The town was a prohibited area for them from 1928 to 1964. I witness the attempted destruction of their language, the imposition of ill-fitting political, economic, and justice systems, and the blame they endure for failing to enthuse or thrive on Western aspirations.

Adding to the perpetual crisis in the lives of Indigenous Australians, the federal government discontinued services to remote communities and outstations to concentrate on hub centres. How was autonomy to be nurtured in these circumstances? The hubs required extra administration with new positions usually filled by non-Indigenous Australians. Restructured community work programs contributed to unemployment and income loss. Many people moved to Alice Springs, leaving massive estates unprotected from fire and feral animals.

Tourism is vital to Alice Spring's economy. The region's phenomenal geography and potential interactions with the world's oldest living continuous culture are its drawcards. First Australians, whatever their enthusiasm about museum status, seized on the word to identify traditional ways and claim respect to hold against the tide of sickness, crime, and early deaths, resulting from the battle to adapt to the lifestyle and economy of their colonisers.

Many people place Indigenous culture at the high end of performance arts, painting, song, dance, and theatre; and embrace the supreme skills of Indigenous athletes. With a world art market welcoming desert dot painting in the 1980s, ironically, non-Indigenous Australians followed suit. Aboriginal galleries in the Alice Springs mall do brisk tourist business. Airlines adorn their craft with dotted imagery. Car manufacturer, BMW, in an advertising ploy, did likewise. Michael Jagamara Nelson was commissioned to do a mural for the Parliament House courtyard.

I could live in populous coastal cities and be unaware and untroubled by the failure to recognise the full humanity of First Australians. With minimal toil or sacrifice, I benefit from crimes committed by my forebears. So far as I know my forefathers had no hand in violating First Australians. Yet they, too, lived with the belief of their superiority, enabling subjugation and dispossession.

***

My partner, Lareena, did the sums and rented out our house to cover overseas accommodation in hostels and hotels. Her practical aplomb and foresight in these matters far exceeded mine. Having completed high school, our eldest daughter, Ronja, was a teacher's assistant at the local Ross Park Primary prior to pursuing studies in Film and Television at RMIT in Melbourne. Raffi had entered an apprenticeship as a flat-board plasterer in Canberra. He'd shot up in six months and now towered above me.

What could be more removed from my situation than a small Mediterranean island? Sicily would fit comfortably inside a few cattle stations surrounding Alice Springs. Lareena and our seven-year old daughter, Anjou, had gone ahead, searching for relatives of her deceased mother who'd left the village of Licodea Ubea as a child. I was booked for a double hernia operation that would keep me in Melbourne a fortnight recouping, staying between my parents and the Andersons. Meanwhile, Lareena had placed Anjou in school, hoping she'd pick up rudimentary Sicilian.

I'd read Lampedusa's *Leopard*, Robb's, *Midnight in Sicily,* and scanned the violent images in Battaglia's staggering portfolio, *Passion, Justice, Freedom,* all of which made me wary of Palermo's Mafia society. Each articulated the social without reference to the island's spectacular topography. It would surely contrast with my arid, predominately flat home country, with its extreme summers and winters, where seas were too distant to influence weather; whereas Sicily was obedient to its injunctions, its infidelities of sunshine and rain. And, of course, there'd be different light. Northern zones are softer than the desert's laser beams where all is revealed in crystal definition and the eye runs to the horizon with few humans troubling the intervening space.

I dropped though Catania's chilled air to meet Lareena and her relatives, Salvatore and his son-in-law, who'd driven the hour from their hilltop village. We motored steadily across the larval plains, thin elms and poplars bordering the road which opened onto fields of maize and wheat. The two men up front talked incessantly, the driver's hands disconcertingly leaving the wheel for emphasis. I didn't speak their language nor they mine. Knowing only Melbourne Sicilians with English fluency, I'd neglected the possibility of a language barrier. My impasse with foreign languages persisted. We slowed through a town or two. Cloud omelettes coagulated above the 600-metre rocky eminence rising from the fields on which perched Licodea-Ubea population of 3000, predominately farmers, though few owned the land they worked. Lareena's relatives worked the land and had a spare house we could rent.

Looking east over Licodea-Ubea, 2008.

A ruined castle graced the eminence's eastern peak. Like much of the island it had succumbed to earthquakes or volcanoes: in this instance the quake of 1693. Cliffs and valleys isolating the community were sprinkled with wild artichoke and prickly pear. The pear's pink flesh was distilled into a delicious liqueur, served after supper with a dainty cup of coffee. A mountain of spaghetti was ladled onto my plate and topped with vegetables picked that day. Salvatore, Rosetta, their two sons and daughter and offspring surrounded us, wide-eyed and enthusiastic. Lareena was the lone family member to have ever sought ancestral roots. They had eaten hours before and watched our progress, gauging my response to their generosity. I was warm, sated, but exhausted from 40 hours of sleepless travel. We embraced. Everyone could retire. Lareena led Anjou and me to our abode in the next lane, and up three flights of stairs to the bitingly cold room and welcoming bed.

Though the village head-count approximated that of the Arrernte of Alice Springs, the spaces the two communities occupied could not be more different. Nor could the buildings: a cluster of ancient grey-brick, terracotta-tiled dwellings in Licodea-Ubea compared to the hurriedly improvised tin shelters and overcrowded cinderblock buildings on Alice Springs' margins. I was a head taller than the locals, accentuating self-consciousness as I strolled the Fiat-ridden, narrow streets. They owned a ruffled vitality, were casual and gregarious with each other, though cautious before my conspicuous paleness and uncalloused hands. Teaching hadn't toughened the outer layers.

How introspective were these villages? Vizzini, 10 kilometres distant had many words at variance with Licodea-Ubea. Hilltop vantage points had been chosen to protect them from each other when more strained and violent circumstances played upon the plains. Tiny tractors descended and ascended to and from roll-a-door stables to the fields each day, following former horse and donkey tracks. In contrast to Alice Springs' sizeable numbers of Sudanese, Vietnamese, and Indian inhabitants, both villages were composed solely of Sicilians.

Some mornings I sat and sang in the stairwell of the small apartment, melancholic warblings that rose to the floors above and were bottled in the third-floor bedroom. They were songs of hope tinged with the regret of failed intimacies. My limited vocals stretched over Dylan, The Band and Jesse Winchester tunes, as well as self-penned material. Sufi chants learned at Claymont had led me to *mugham* exponents, whose vocal acrobatics I attempted. The few windows were small and set high. The low and narrow passage to our bedroom, built Sicilian scale, necessitated stooping. At each step, pain stabbed my groin as the hernia stitching registered its complaints and amplified my mournful balladry.

Caricatures of Old People, Rod Moss, 2008.

I sketched the curved tiles gracing rooftops from the balcony. The view alone was a novelty as no buildings in Alice Springs rose above two floors. Their rippling passage terminated half a kilometre west at the base of a wooded range. Broad scabs of lime-green lichen decorated the tiles, the odd cat lurking there with predatory intents. In the stairwell alcoves unblinking pigeons prospered over belching babes.

I created caricatures of the marvellously worn faces encountered on the streets. These were not flattering images, but I was attracted to wrinkled faces, extraneous hair, drooped eyelids, and the fiercely knotted buns of old women with their bulbous noses. Was it the infirmities and sufferings of age that attracted me: that beauty is found elsewhere than in youth? On what criteria had I set my standards of beauty and ugliness? I, who am neither one nor the other but inhabit the great middle ground.

My catalogue of the grotesque includes Bosch, Bacon, Breughel, Goya and Grunewald, who'd committed the horror of physical degradation and violence to paint. Global awareness of twentieth-century ruins, exploitation and chaos has enlarged the charter of artistic distortion and fragmentation. Salgado, Koudelka or Polidori's photography, for instance, have aestheticised ruin and tragedy. More often, the compassion in older art has surrendered to ugliness.

Beyond the stairwell, April sped by. The Mistral's vagabond fingers reached inside my coat as I explored streets and hills. The wood stove required daily searching for firewood. We huddled around the small oven door while beans simmered, dicing tomatoes and potatoes. The early dark and cold encouraged us to our blankets soon after sunset where I'd lie and read an hour before sleep and remain likewise after dawn.

Sleep rattled with roofing irons, Venetian blinds, cat squalls and protesting birds. The century-old building felt flimsy beneath their percussive assault. I rose when the wind dropped, and followed the yeasty perfumes permeating the alleys to the bakery, avoiding dogs whose dreamy indolence disregarded traffic. Peg-littered lanes echoed the hill's contours. Scraps of clothing, swept and crumpled against walls, would need a second wash.

Pigeons puffed and preened on balconies, reciting from meagre songbooks. Together with those other-world citizens—starlings and sparrows—they dominated the streets, great in number but poor by comparison to the 30 species frequenting our garden. No rummaging babblers, no melodious butcherbirds, scraping bowerbirds, or chattering galahs stirred Licodea. Maybe it was too early for bird-attracting blossoms, lerps, or insect multitudes.

Spinach and ricotta pastries were my favourites. I strolled to the walled western crest and scanned the plains below where poppies suppurated through fields of durum. Butterfly symbols were engraved upon windows, stencilled on doors and walls of most houses. As winter weakened, real butterflies fluttered above the flowering fields.

Meals were simple and fresh. As in India, most foodstuffs were locally grown. Citrus fruits and tomatoes had a mineral richness unparalleled in Australian organics. Community vitality thrived without supermarkets and health food shops promoting mineral and vitamin supplements. Indeed, the absence of billboard advertising freed my eyes to luxuriate on so much else.

I wandered to the cemetery at the edge of the town, ringed by a three-metre brick wall. Locals made lavish memorials to their dead during the recent century. Prior to that, the poor were dispatched over the cliff. Were not the funds for these grand edifices better deployed on the living? Photo portraits of the gazing dead, presumably enjoying the promises of their Saviour, featured on more expensive headstones. There were low-relief carvings of the flagellated Bartholomew and Michelangelo's *Pieta*; the one all wounds, the other in ecstasy.

Though Lutherans had established a mission at Hermannsburg, 100 kilometres west of town in 1877, church business and burials for my Arrernte friends began with Catholic missionaries in the 1930s. I'd attended their numerous funerals and was familiar with this impulse to guard the dead, and prevent their rotting unprotected in the earth. But nothing in Alice Springs shared this Sicilian bent for monumental tombs, far grander and more permanent than their homes. The most prestigious housed the wealthy, and so on down the pecking order, reflecting post-war wealth and the rise of individuality yet to touch the Arrernte.

The sole occasions on which Arrernte church numbers rivalled Licodea's weekly congregations were funerals. Depending on the significance of the deceased, families travelled 1000 kilometres from Darwin to the north and Port Augusta, due south. Given the struggle in siphoning pension monies, it was often weeks after a death until families had funds to cover costs. That death rapped so frequently at their doors compounded the dilemma.

What the villagers shared with the Arrernte was ancestral connection to particular places. I couldn't, as they did, speak of my country soaked in struggle, or the cries of its austere lessons, of my family's blood in the soil. My presence, as Arrernte said, was 'only yesterday'. My wellbeing didn't depend on the power of specific locations demanding my presence. Sure, give me the dry hard light of the Centre rather than Melbourne's damp greyness or Darwin's humidity. But that this tree or that rock had particular significance, required knowledge and belief I lacked.

Near the gates of the cemetery, a florist did a brisk trade with visitors who preferred her bouquets to the oleanders, absinthes, geraniums, and marigolds flourishing between the tombs. She had flower arrangements for specific relationships to the deceased. I wasn't a flower man myself but recognised that her lilies, carnations and chrysanthemums weren't growing round the graves, and likely had symbolic import eluding me. Pragmatists that they are, the Arrernte favoured the price and durability of the plastic product from the two-dollar store.

Dad's atheism had ensured religion had had minimal influence during my childhood. A compassionate, merciful god had lost credibility during the Great Depression as had the slaughter of the Wars. Like his Sunday School teaching grandfather, he'd imagined a Big Man, a major Being, ruling the world from His Heavenly Throne from whom justice, goodness, truth and beauty emanated. How could the church's truths be the province of any one religion? If lasting peace was religion's objective, all had failed. How could a loving God abide the scale of such horrors? What kind of creator placed man before injustice, suffering and evil: to tolerate tsunamis, cyclones, disease, or earthquakes? Nature behaving naturally was surely just nature. Had prayer ever spared people from these tribulations? Whose mercy sorted the saved from the perished?

No prayer or grace bookended our meals. Dad ridiculed the millions obedient to Holy Rome's representative on Earth and the ceremonial garb of figures conducting church ceremonies. He scoffed at the feathers and tiger heads of suited heads of state in post-colonial Africa. The Freemasons, too, were eventually rejected, their rituals recognised as variants of the church.

Ian and I had happily ceased Sunday School, having been caught accidentally landing a rock on the roof of the church bus as it climbed Boronia Road to the tall house on the hill. For several Sundays, dressed in Sunday attire, we'd played truant, opting to volley rocks at absconding brothers on the opposing cliffs of the cutting leading to the church. Our game was up. To save further embarrassment, we quit. Mum's religious ambitions for us submitted to dad's atheism.

'There's the church and there's the steeple,' she'd once instructed, pressing her hands as if in prayer then pressing index fingers together forming a spire. 'Then turn it upside down,' this done with interlaced fingers, 'and there's the people'. The Church of Christ had just lost two small fingers. Our church had lacked festive fervour, too. The significance of Christ at Easter was lost amid chocolates, hot cross buns and roast chicken.

So, the Easter parades coinciding with my arrival in the village were a charged spectacle. The entire population wove in steady file from the lower eastern-most church to the most elevated, ancient and sacred—the western-most, on Mount Calvario. A dozen young men carried mock Christs and Marys, whose ghoulish likeness I'd only seen in art. One sad Mary was pinned with the *Seven Swords of Sorrow*. A sword was plucked from her side. Several doves eased themselves from her shroud and fluttered into the darkening sky amidst cannon smoke. Jesus, on his chariot, rocked and rolled in joyous Resurrection. Crackers exploded in riotous clamour.

The procession halted outside the Mount Calvario church. Light rain fell as Christ was lifted from his coffin and Mary, draped in black, was divested of her halo and sword. One man sang a lament, chorused by six acolytes in a magnificent slow dirge. As if on cue, a shaft of sunlight beamed from the east as ominous clouds gathered. A herd of long-muzzled brown goats joined the assembly on the damp cobbles, their pungent odour seizing hold of my nostrils. The effigy-bearers led the villagers inside, clasping drenched umbrellas to their thighs.

***

How had these parades changed during the centuries? What recollection remained of the seasons when leaves sprouted, and pagan gods fertilised the earth with sperm as winter descended? Had people been happier with multiple gods to fit their moods? Here, ritual spoke of heroic suffering leading to resurrection. Yet suffering might also lead to retaliation, to letting go, to insights, even love. Sicily had chosen sorrow and the victimhood of a nailed corpse who'd died and was resurrected for them.

The call to prayer resounded each Sunday with a clarion rendition of 'Ave Maria'. The faithful clogged the pathways outside the four churches. The convivial gatherings in the piazzas after Mass bore witness to social glue reminiscent of Arrernte 'loitering', the pejorative directed by whitefellas at Arrernte chatting with kinsfolk while busying themselves with nine to five routines.

In the cafes, coffee, cake and ice cream orders kept the waiters on their feet. At home, smokers were shamed in restaurants and public buildings. Here, it remained a passionate pursuit. I mingled in their warmth, envious of the security offered by religious zeal. Dignity and self-respect were not trifling traits. The weekly hour seemed small change to smarten up for. Did their devotions contribute to social services and alleviate stress? How did the sermons travel through their days?

I wondered about this longing for guaranteed outcomes we carry into our activities. We admire the daring of lives exposed to dangers, tightropes, downhill bike-racing, rock climbing and the like. We know risk-taking brings us into a fuller condition of life; that it's the essence and song of life. Even the unpredictability derived from travelling outside one's familiar zone heightens the senses. Not that I felt particularly vulnerable or in need of confiding in an infallible Creator. Perhaps experience, both present and historical, had villagers seeking assurance that human mismanagement and natural disasters would be averted or eventually be corrected.

When asking who might respond to my questions, I was directed along a lane to the staircase and home of Lucia, The Faithful. She had the history of the town and its families in her head. Diminutive Lucia squeezed into the space just off the diner to brew coffee. Sink and porta-stove only, an altar to caffeine. She poured it into a delicate china cup and placed a tray of sweet biscuits beside it. Over bitter coffee and biscuits in the wizened woman's cramped quarters, we bantered beneath votive images of Mary that adorned tablecloths and tea towels. Even the gauzy curtains bore her sorry face.

No one mentioned that Lucia lacked English. She answered my queries about the village rituals by leading me around the room, placing my fingers on implements, lifting a doily to my cheek, pressing information into my body. Would a common language have enriched our experience? Would it have helped me understand her belief in the young man on the cross, his miraculous birth, death, and resurrection?

I was impressed by her displays of affection, kissing the photographed faces of her deceased husband and their progeny. Pride of place was their wedding snap. Released momentarily from oppression and toil, they obey the photographer, posing grimly in their formal wear. Lacking common language, my impertinence soon wearied. Coffee done I stood to leave. She was as pleased with my going as my coming, wrapping the remaining foodstuffs in tissue and squeezing them into my hand at the door.

Within a fortnight, novelty had frayed. Elsewhere, had become Somewhere. The town's four streets ran in parallel along the east-west axis. The lower bore its three-dozen shops. The upper skirted the cliff where the wealthy had privileged views of the plains. I remained a passive onlooker assessing routines, estimating when the tiny man with a limp would smile and wave to me as he ambled to morning coffee with cronies; when the florist waiting on the warming sun would proffer pots of flowers on her pavement stand; which children stormed the steep lanes to and from school; and when the bakery van would honk in the lane above our dwelling. The silent clockwork of other lives was the same one ticking in me, and never more tellingly than when we perched at that cafe to indulge scrumptious *Cioccolata calda*, whose creaminess outbid caffeine cravings.

Long Journey: Easter on Akelurre Apwerte, Rod Moss, 2017.

On clear days Mt Etna could be seen dominating the eastern skyline. It was a colossus accounting for coastal contours from Messina in the northeast to Catania in the south. Pasolini gave this eminence a role in several films, including the dramatic scenes of Christ's temptations. His Christ's strident assertions were a world away from the limp, lamp-holding guy in the old maid's home in Boronia. Inspired by Pasolini and Caravaggio, I made a drawing deploying Arrernte friends in Stations of the Cross; hopefully the meaning of this mural-sized piece would reach people beyond denominational allegiances.

Etna was magnetic. You couldn't live so close to it and not visit. We set off by car, noting the black cobs and twists of lava circling its base through Bronte, famous for once being part of Lord Nelson's estate, a gift from the King of Naples for victory in the Napoleonic Wars. Thousands of British troops occupied Naples during the last vestiges of feudalism. I'd sourced this from the lone English text in Licodea's library, Pratt's *Nelson's Duchy*. Anjou cracked us up with her observation that Etna reminded her of Ear's Rock, her mishearing of Australia's most cherished monolith, Ayers Rock, now recognised by its Pitjantjatjara name, Uluru.

Etna's fertile soils in part accounted for Sicily's frequent invasions; the Greeks introduced corn, vines and olives; the Romans used it as a granary to feed its empire; the Arabs brought sugarcane, cotton, date palms and citrus fruits. These products still accounted for half the island's income. But by the time we passed Nicolisi such lushness had submitted to Etna's monochrome bleakness and brutality, evidenced in burnt-out buildings and houses solidified in lava and ash.

The mountain's peak was doused in dark emulsion. Cars wended with caterpillar caution towards the car park, an hour's walk below the summit. A legion of minute lemon butterflies drifted over the melting snow as we made our slow ascent. Anjou's persistence was impressive, fuelled by her first sighting of the fluffy stuff. At 3,320 metres, the air was cool and the ground lava-warm. I'd been geared for volcanic fireworks and advised to wear work boots to quell the heat. It smelled like a chemistry lab. When I tripped on a rock its underside revealed earthy blacks, yellows, reds and greens. One circuit around the charred lips of the largest crater was sufficient. Hefty winds challenged us as we stared into the snorting orifice. Sulphur fumes stirred intestinal juices and clawed at the back of my throat.

The newly formed soil filled me with wonder. At home, I assume the earth's antiquity and stability. Alice Springs is well-fitted with elegant rocks. I marvelled at the abundant hummocky hills of gneiss and granite. Their placement, scale, shape and proportion, I mused, was the handiwork of a gigantic Zen gardener. Indigenous friends didn't regard its crystal solids as dead mass moved by gravity and thermal force. They invested its geological scars with ancestor status, humanising its indifference to draw it near. The big shifts happened millions of years before humans walked the earth, and its low-grade soils were the consequence of gradual weathering.

On scrubby land a kilometre from my door, was Whitegate or *Irrkerlantye*, occupied by Arrernte families aeons before European settlement. My understanding of what they called 'country' derived from our 35-year association. Kite hawks circled and stooped above it whenever thermals advantaged them. They were *irrkerlantye* sharing their name with the low ridge bordering camp. Sites of particular significance to the families dotted the hills and plains, water places, rocks, trees, their descriptions and interdependence recorded in ceremonial song and dance. Their big-picture mapping was filled with song. No such poetry resonated in the settler mind. Our maps lacked music.

Etna, too, bore myths of the monster, Typhon, trapped within by sky god Zeus, whose thunderbolts were forged by three-eyed giants. These were the portholes venting eruptive fluids. Typhon's restless stirrings, expressed through fiery lava flows, grumbled throughout millennia. How did the Greek gods stack up against the one the locals revered each Sunday? Had they all been accommodated, just as the Arrernte had incorporated Catholicism into their creation stories?

We hastened our descent, avoiding the switchbacks by sliding on our butts over the snow. Among the mountain's myths was its role in the evolution of gelatos since the late eighteenth century. A shepherd had conserved some snow in straw for summer refreshment. His success escalated into commerce and by the early 1800s flavoured ice was fashionable in Paris. Sicily was infatuated with iced confectionary. No matter how small the town, no matter the temperature, Sicilians had access to their adored confection. In the southern coastal city of Agrigento, I was stunned to see a guy order a great wad of ice cream wedged in a hamburger bun. This was after we'd dared the *stradas*, joining our hired car to the island's Fiat fleet, and toured the provinces.

The end of April marked the end of school term and Anjou's most joyous day. Her class took the bus to Catania to visit the butterfly house. We'd not expected the school to make concessions to a foreign student arriving unannounced. With only one English speaker on deck, the weeks were an endurance test more than academic success for staff and her.

Having greater motivation, Lareena made steady progress with her mother's language, aided by dictionary and lessons with Francisco, a lawyer returned home after having worked for years in Chicago. She'd study during the day while I read Goldsworthy's, *Three Dog Night*, a fictional account of a man touched by Indigenous law in Central Australia in ways echoing my own experience. After supper, we sat around the oven fire and read aloud Sally Morgan's painful but gratifying, *My Place*, where in middle age, she slowly uncovers her Indigenous identity.

Lareena booked a car in Catania and we took the 7 a.m. bus to fetch it. Miss it and we'd have to wait until midday for the next one. The day prior to take-off, Salvatore showed us the vineyard and orchard on which he and eldest son, Roberto, laboured. At breakfast, dark clouds had grumbled riotously without divesting a drop. The moment passed, and a cloudless sky encouraged us to wash our dirty clothes in the bath and drape them on the rails of the third-floor balcony. Salvatore drove us the eight kilometres to the hillside plot and pulled up midfield by the tool shed beneath the shade of some olive trees.

Roberto interrupted his pruning to stroll us along the rows while his father busied himself with provisions from the trunk of the car. When we returned to the shed, he'd erected a trestle table and laid upon it plates of olives, breads, cheeses, tomatoes, pasta and a flagon of fruity home-made red wine. I was surprised and delighted—Lareena had told him this was my birthday and, as he raised his glass of grappa in my honour, an unannounced burst from above drenched us. We packed hastily and headed home to wring and stuff our sodden clothes into plastic garbage bags for drying in a Catania Laundromat.

An international licence presumed competencies that didn't clarify regional road habits. Seatbelts were optional, infants sat on papa's lap behind the wheel, bike helmets were a rarity, and parking courtesies resembled dodgem-car circuits. Cars were left double and triple-parked in narrow village thoroughfares while their drivers chatted over coffee and cigarettes in cafes—characteristics amplified in Catania and Palermo. Battaglia and Robb had nurtured apprehensions about the latter. Traffic was thick but the crowded footpaths were no more threatening than those of Licodea-Ubea. Yet we'd not witnessed poverty in the village.

Confronting us as we came and went from Hotel Olympia was a beggar torso and head only, propped in his suitcase on the pavement, money bowl at his belt, a pitiful sight beyond those catalogued by Velasquez and Herzog. Incapacitated and immobile, he seemed helpless. And yet, surprise, surprise, a few days later and many mountain ranges to the southeast he was in Catania's busiest piazza, none the worse for wear. What agency manipulated him, I had no idea.

Begging perplexes travellers. For one thing, in Australia, though I was in the lowest income bracket, superannuation savings financed my trip. Unlike the Arrernte poor, whose context and particular needs I knew when put upon, or 'humbugged' in local parlance, I could respond accordingly. Here, I did not know the circumstance and extent of suffering. Lareena was less troubled, and I admired her instinctive generosity. Rather than drop coins in cups she'd trot off and return with a meal. Her compassion for animals was equally impressive. Where chance presented itself, she'd buy apples to feed famished horses and donkeys.

The most striking of Palermo's buildings was set on the so-called Royal Mountain overlooking the city and its seaport. Monreale Palace, built in the twelfth century was where Normans and subsequent rulers situated themselves. The Norman structure was less impressive than the chapel's interior, a hypnotic fusion of eastern and western conventions. Restraint was not the order of the day. A Pantocrater (depiction of Christ) overlooked the assembly from His customary position high in the apse. Constantinopolitan craftsmen had decorated the nave walls with lively mosaics narrating biblical tales, their figuration soon to inspire mainland fresco masters, Cimabue, Duccio and Giotto. An amazing variety of Arabic geometric patterning filled all other surfaces. It didn't require a trained eye to detect the conjunction of distinct styles. It left me wondering where in our post-colonial era, such hybridity might be tolerated.

***

From Palermo we took the route through foothills housing sheep that flocked against the Fiat's flanks, a sea of dirty wool, clanging bells, and dogs barely distinguishable from their charges. The world's first car rally undertaken by rich enthusiasts in the infant years of the twentieth century, coursed through the donkey trails of the Madonie Ranges. We followed that trail, now tarred, as it snaked through sheer sides of limestone and lava valleys.

An abandoned power station, overgrown and straddling a stream, drew our attention. The odour of bat shit predominated over congealed oils pooled on the floor. Within its concrete confines, amidst the debris of glass and dismantled generators, lay a 1960s newspaper whose front page featured a photo of the Maharishi and The Beatles, relics of other powers riding the currents during the station's years of decline. I flashed to the crowded Great Hall at Monash University, 1966, amongst whom I'd squeezed with Tadpole and The Devil to soak up the guru's teaching. Good enough for The Beatles. But Transcendental Meditation and its promise of expanded consciousness steered past me and kept on going.

We walked half an hour up the valley, sprinkled with long-abandoned walnut, peach and cherry trees, disturbing a family of black boars who broke from their hide, and unsettling a kaleidoscope of butterflies. The path occasionally devolved into scrub and concluded at an empty reservoir perched at the head of the valley, and possibly explaining the station's demise. We admired the valley then stood and stumbled back by what seemed to be a shorter route but proved not so. Brush that appeared benign at a distance hid man-sized boulders entangled in briar thickets which presented greater challenges than the crumbly ascent. Frustrated and fatigued, we welcomed the sight of the main track.

The car slouching in shade also gratified us, as did Corleone several kilometres up the road; a town coterminous with the Mafia. A body of local professionals, I heard, was currently lobbying for a name change because of its

Mafia associations. Lampedusa had asserted Sicilians were trapped between extremes of immobilising torpor and shattering violence, their compulsions rooted in profound anxieties and disposed to darkness. Centuries of peasant revolts transpired before Garibaldi and his thousand followers overthrew the occupying Bourbons and nationalised Italy in the 1860s. Lampedusa's narrative was set during the moment of land reform accompanying the diminished powers of the titled aristocracy.

Subsequent reforms did little to eliminate peasant disadvantage, and the compost of rebellious centuries created an outlaw response—the *sistema* dubbed 'Mafia' which dealt justice through the ancient code of '*Lu sangu lava lu sanga*', or 'blood washes blood'. This mode of settling disputes and delivering justice reminded me of the retributive violence in Indigenous communities still confounding the Alice Springs court.

We wandered through the town's Mafia museum with its unabashed display of news clippings and photos of bushy-browed bosses disturbed during conference. Some of Battaglia's gruesome images of street assassinations counted amongst them; blood pooling on footpaths made starker in black-and-white. Our guide assured us that the gun-toting days related to the 1970s. The Mob's hierarchy had moved into white-collar business, chiefly banking and real estate. He added that the poorly lit village streets were safe after dark. Good. The sun was buried behind the hills and we were famished.

When we arrived, the trattoria was already crowded. We were led to a table, and starched napkins were draped in our laps. Five men, some with ties and all in business shirts, occupied the next table. White-collared businessmen perhaps? I worried about the vast quantity of pasta they were wading through and it was only their entre. I decided to skip the preamble, preferring direct access to a volcano of pesto gnocchi.

The region had spawned centuries of bandits resisting the constabulary of various absentee overlords. Sicily was prized by Greeks, Phoenicians, Romans, Byzantines, Saracens, Normans, Angevins, Aragonese and Bourbons who'd all had a turn of ruling the island and had left their chromosomal imprint. Resentment of these tax masters was recorded in ballads reaching back to the fourteenth-century Normans.

The isolation of Madonie villages—Polizzi Generosi and Piano Battaglia— gave them a sense of contented self-sufficiency. Sun-enriched faces, young and old of both genders, promenaded arm in arm, clutching the inevitable gelato. They were rich unto the day. I partook of pleasantries in Polizzi Generosi's pastry shop, sipping chocolate. In a gelato bar I was warmed by the simple courtesies of those who must endlessly repeat such services: images so distinct from those sombre Mafioso.

Old men sitting silently smoking and sipping coffee dominated the village piazzas. The anti-smoking lobby hadn't found its way here, either. Copper-skinned runts, be-shawled and cane wielding, clustered on benches, bent in rictus as if still shovelling their pastures. I thought of the isolation of my octogenarian parent's long hours, sitting in the lounge awaiting their soapies and the news. Where they scanned the western horizon for Melbourne's faint outlines hoping for a blaze of sunset to redeem the day. Corellas and cockies now dominated the maples, elms and poplars. Where, in clear weather and on a closer ridge, they identified the residence of brother Ian, and his family on Wheelers Hill.

The canopy of gums no longer impeded their view. These were eradicated when the dirt track was bitumenised and the great tree felled. The daffodil fields had gone the way of subdivision with streets named after Chandler progeny. A few rows of pines survived. An errant bulb sometimes sprouted in a backyard. The property of the two old maids at their rear was stacked with brick veneers. Childhood experiences pertaining to these places were demolished with each development. Nowadays dad scanned obituaries in *The Sun News Pictorial* for familiar names, reading to mum who, nodding, muttered acknowledgment.

***

As the weather warmed, sparrows, spruce and agile in contrast to its inhabitants, flitted through Licodea's milky sky. It wasn't a bad place for an old guy to run out the years, as Sam Risotto was doing. He paused at our door whenever he saw me squatting on the doorstep. Beneath a Gatsby-styled golf cap he sported tortoise-shell specs and steadied himself on a silver-toed stick. His cardigan was buttoned beneath his sports coat and his tie was tightened at the throat. He reeked of shaving lotion. I welcomed his English fluency. He was the first of several locals I met who had left, only to return permanently or visit regularly.

Retired schoolteacher, Joe, for instance, born in Melbourne and now fifty, had returned with wife and kids to be with aged parents. Francisco, sent to relatives in Chicago after high school to study law, felt more meaningfully employed in the village where his children would benefit from nurturing grandparents. And Pasquale and wife, also from Melbourne, where he'd established a hosiery factory in the 1960s, came each year. It turned out they lived in Coburg behind my musical painter mate, Graeme Drendel.

Sam had been part of Sicily's post-Second World War emigration wave that washed up on Australian shores. Poverty had confronted Sicilians for centuries, and survival if not prosperity beckoned in the United States and Australia. For Sam and others of his generation who'd returned, the roots to country and familial history outbid the comforts of Melbourne's northern 'burbs, despite the fraternity of its Licodea-Eubea Club in Brunswick. Immigrants like Lareena's grandparents introduced fresh energy to Australia's predominantly Anglo-Celtic population at the time. The construction industry, restaurants, market gardens and groceries greatly benefited. The discrimination and 'wog' slur confronting Sicilians would later embrace Vietnamese, Afghans, Iraqis, Lebanese, Sudanese and Syrians, many fleeing horrific circumstances unimaginable to Australians.

Sam was pleased with his lot; a house in Syracuse, another in Licodea-Ubea, pensions and relatives in both countries. He dipped his hat again on parting, saying that his air-pilot son was due to visit him Syracuse that afternoon. Up the hill, he tottered to his charcoal Rover, which he rolled down the cobbles. From my cliff-side watch I saw the vehicle darting through the durum fields.

His generation was outside the economic concerns of working folk. Would they continue to struggle with the Euro underpinning unified Europe? Disparities between rich northern Italy and its poor south remained. Locals bemoaned their devalued labour and the longer hours required to satisfy basic needs. But I heard of no one about to emigrate. If anything, movement was in the opposite direction. 'Boat people' fleeing Africa and the Middle East were arriving in numbers that made a mockery of the fraction of asylum seekers my government objected to on our northern shores. The millennia's greatest migrant movement was underway.

I had seen how impoverished economies and repressive regimes forced workers to seek employment beyond their countries, accepting work where wages and conditions promised more than mere survival. Even in the 1970s I was surprised with the numbers of Kurds, Romanians and Bulgarians adding to Istanbul's influx of unemployed rural peasantry. Australians, far removed and buffeted by wealth, had little or no response to the refugees' plight.

Sam reckoned Erice was worth a look, so off we motored. The tiny Norman village towered 750 metres above the western seaport of Trapani, a cluster of houses and stone alleyways capping its cliffs. Its twelfth-century appearance hid earlier occupation. Castles had been built over ruins. Most significant had been the temple of fertility goddess Astarte, whom the Romans subsequently dubbed, Venus. I marvelled at buildings perched on blunt outcrops, seemingly driven into the earth, their construction baffling me. I wondered how dire the need of defence was for men to risk their lives on such precarious pinnacles. Those who'd first trod these cobbles had long departed with their gods.

The veracity and durability of the stone-walled structures bore evidence of the hands that had hefted, stacked, trowelled and capped them. Rarely did enamelled metals, plastics and reflective glass, so resistant to deterioration, enrapture me. The old had an inherent aura. Boronia's 'old' dated to 1920, with the opening of the station. Only a small arc of originals, including the anomalously named Progress Hall, remained. A McDonalds franchise occupied my school ground. Shopping malls dominated as small businesses struggled. Coles and Kmart, a mandatory hot bread shop, tacky Two-dollar stores crammed with shonky Chinese produce, and coffee shops comprised a 'burb now contiguous with Melbourne's eastern suburbs.

Alice Springs, too, was snared in developmental claws that lacked interlock with its environment. By subscribing to America's retail philosophy, with lookalike franchise stores, both towns had sacrificed distinctiveness. Ironically, those small towns like The Basin that by geographic quirk had not caught the eye of developers were now reaping tourist dollars from their involuntary resistance to growth.

The ache of the wrecking ball angered at least some Sicilians. When asked by a bunch of Americans what purpose the gargoyles studding the façade of a small church served, their local guide snapped, 'Bad spirits, then. Today, developers.' There was a snigger from this knowing crowd who'd not come to drool over post-war suburbs. Like me, they were citizens of pre-fabricated places, and familiar with impoverished post-war architecture. Worse still, unlike war-ravaged Europe, we witnessed the planned destruction of our few repositories of memory, beauty and love.

Given its fortressed vantage point and impregnability, Erice had once been strategically significant. Nothing of its kind ever existed in my homelands. Our pioneers needed no forts to overtake the land's prior occupants. Guns against spears. Negotiations were few and the languages of weaponry and Bible forged crude dominion. Where were the grand edifices expressing Indigenous beliefs and governance? The conquerors saw no evidence that the First Peoples revered nature's power sources or performed obligatory service to them.

I made small talk with a young woman working behind the counter of the Osteria di Venerea Café, eager to place her foreign looks. Yasmine would return home to Tunisia as soon as savings permitted. Though an Arts graduate of Sfax University, she couldn't find work there, in Sousse or Tunis. Her older brother, Mohammed, with a Master of Engineering, was on the island, fruit picking. Only one graduate from her year had found employment—in his father's architectural firm—doing work unrelated to his degree. Her own father had loved teaching, but the profession was poorly rewarded in Tunisia, so when starting his family, he'd no choice on such a pathetic salary but to join the family carpet business. Tough times in Northern Africa, and Sicily, so close, was hardly a thriving alternative.

North of Erice where mountains steepled into the sea, were stunning quarries of pale, striated marble, the source of the old buildings' longevity whose stone bodies contrasted with the concrete ghettos skirting most towns' original hubs. Steel rods projected through the slab-roofs of first-floor dwellings, suggesting future, though improbable, construction. Thus, were legalities, inspections and costs left in abeyance, with all parties aware of the building code's loophole. Your Mafia at work.

My hair now needed trimming, so when I spotted a pair of spiralling blood-red and white-wreathed poles supporting a veranda, while shopping for ceramic plates in Caltagirone, I slipped inside for a clip. With no other customers, I was immediately ushered to a chair, the toreador barber waving his cape at bullish me. Most things were reassuringly familiar: the white jacket, the chair, mirror and cabinet of utensils. Giuseppe had spent years in Melbourne and was soon spieling about the recent decline of his Richmond football club's fortunes. Confessing my allegiance invited his retelling of Bartlett's role in eclipsing Collingwood in the 1980 Grand Final. Did I imagine the clippers ratchetting up a gear? Not only did barbers across the hemispheres seem of similar vintage, there must be some universal school of cutting and conversational male-speak. Perhaps he learnt these arts in Melbourne. It took some persuading to deter the inevitable short back and sides, and settle on the trim.

Catching my reflection as the clippers climbed the back of my neck, I was shocked. For years I'd tended my styling so didn't recognise the skin I now owned: this reptilian epidermis of senior years. Was that my tonsured pate? Covertly, my hair had joined the flight pattern of my lower incisors. Giuseppe tended tufts sprouting from my ears, nostrils and eyebrows. No clients intruded as he told of recent heart surgery he'd undergone. He proceeded to remove his jacket and shirt to reveal the massive scar careering across his chest. He moved to the door to check on passing traffic. There was none. Back beside his chair, he unzipped to show the skin graft from his right buttock. Done and dusted I rose, paid for the clip and sideshow, happy to face the wide and vacant piazza.

The barber pole's reference to times when barbers doubled as dental surgeons had taken a personal twist.

***

Taormina's Piazza, 2008.

Sam had also insisted we visit Taormina, spectacularly poised 200 metres above twin bays, sporting a shopping drag the equal of any in elegant Florence. In the late eighteenth century, Goethe had described it as 'a patch of paradise'. Its third-century-BC Greek amphitheatre, set above the Gulf of Naxos's watery vista, still staged concerts. Dylan played here in 2001 with erupting Etna providing backdrop pyrotechnics. Having frequently referenced Italy in songs and interviews, he surely was aware of ancient audiences baying for gladiator blood on the stage whereon he, and now we, stood.

The town was prime postcard material, featuring a handsome piazza for newlyweds' photography, as well as the clanging quartets and solo musicians courting the tourist dollar. Tarkovsky had been similarly charmed, snapping Polaroids back in 1980 while in self-imposed exile, working on *Nostalgia*.

It was also where Lawrence penned *Women in Love* and the snake poem we'd studied at school. Author and friend, Barry Hill, told me of Lawrence and Frieda's three-year stay at the Villa Fontana Vecchia. Thirty years later it was home to Truman Capote. Barry had dedicated a poem to Lawrence's love of the place. Complex and elegant, it evoked the sexual energy in Lawrence's writing and the travel lust that would lead him to Australia. The ban on Lawrence's final novel was rumoured to have germinated from the frolicking of a naked Taorminian with a farmer. The ban on *Lady Chatterley* had not long been lifted when we'd studied *Sons and Lovers* at school, the latter mirroring my family dynamic in some respects and gifting me the voice of Paul Morel.

Visitors crammed boutiques in the main drag. So thick was the crowd that we lost Anjou for 20 anxious minutes before she arrived escorted by police, pursued by a journalist who wanted to report her plight in the *Taormina Times*. Anjou would have none of it. Nor were we eager to expose incompetence. Most tourists were mainland Italians from whom Sicilians maintained proud distinction. Couples of all ages were captivated by the location, upmarket shops and revellers so distinct from the streets of Licodean peasantry.

Close to a church was a shop selling devotional stuff—rosaries, plastic and tin Madonnas, and crucified Christs. My eye caught a plaster-of-Paris cast of Leonardo's *Last Supper*. That the painting had been reduced in scale and rendered sculpturally was amusing; figures un-housed from the master's carefully calculated architectural space. I fixed on its central figure. Paint and lacquer had failed to conceal the cancerous air-bubble nibbling The Lord's beak, giving a fresh explanation to the disciples' dramatic reactions.

At the da Concettina Bed and Breakfast, I shared the kitchen table with Brazilian architect, Nestor Cenal who was on weekend leave from a conference on liturgical architecture, in Rome. Christianity was always at hand in Italy. He decried the disharmony of modern churches that didn't acknowledge liturgical space and were the outcome of what he called, 'ego-tecture'. Well-groomed liturgical space factored in natural light and candlepower. Electricity had ushered in convenient freedoms at the expense of the 'sacred', he explained, the dark nave representing the body of Christ and that, moving eastwards along it to the altar, one moved towards the light and an elevated state. None of the dour churches I'd entered had moved me the way Rheims, Chartres or Notre Dame had. With an unstable earth to consider, Sicily's fortress mode seemed sensible.

'Do the great Gothic works express this space?' 'Yes, especially Our Lady,' he replied. And Hagia Sophia, whose massive dome I'd seen floating as if by miracle on a ring of tiny windows, did it possess liturgical space? Though he recognised its significance as Christian architecture, he'd not seen it. I recalled the sudden shock when confronted by that huge Pantocrater. Even minus a good many tesserae, the Christ's icy gaze insisted, 'don't mess with me'.

Nor had Nestor heard of Keith Critchlow's Puttaparthi Hospital. Surely Critchlow, graduate of Summerhill School, consultant for Krishnamurti's Brockwood Park Centre and student of sacred geometry, would interest him, just as he'd influenced my table designs.

The course at St Peter's in Rome sought to redress this dearth of liturgical space and reinstate its significance in shaping rituals. 'These should be places where we experience silence and clarity,' he insisted, adding, 'You must see my favourite *chiesa* (church), San Bernardino in Umberto, just north of Rome.'

We spoke of European art, and he urged me to see Rembrandt's *Prodigal Son* in the Hermitage. 'I underwent analysis years ago in Buenos Aires,' he added. 'I was told to meditate. It led me through issues to do with my father, and then I discovered the Rembrandt. Standing before it resolved things for me. I've seen it once and hope to again.'

It was a painting Warwick had tellingly sequenced slides to zoom in on the father's hands, isolating the artist's supreme sense of touch. Tarkovsky also references it towards the end of *Solaris*, where the psychologist returns from his space mission and is reunited and reconciled with his father. The image of forgiveness imputes the resolution of guilt the psychologist faced over his wife's suicide. *Solaris's* perplexing final shot perhaps asks if it's better to love an illusion than not to love at all.

***

Other artists were on my itinerary. Not far north was Messina, departure point for the Aeolian Islands. But first there was its regional museum after a sleep-deprived night, losing my battle with a mosquito; the mighty once more humbled by the miniscule. I knew Caravaggio stayed here between 1608 and 1609 and I wanted to see what he achieved. At this point of his precarious 38 years, Caravaggio was on the run, sleeping with a knife beneath his pillow, wanted for murder in Rome. Critics, even of his day, yoked his temper and sword duels to his art. Some said he'd quit Messina, again on the run, and succumbed to complications from facial wounds exacted by his pursuers. Others mooted that he perished on a beach after drinking contaminated water.

There was a delicate, small crucifixion by local master, Antonello Messina. No weeping or gnashing of mourners beneath Christ as fellow insurrectionists writhe in elegant ecstasy, their weight conforming to the contours of the dead trees on which they're strung. Christ hangs rigidly on his cross, carving the painting in two, calm as the countryside and sky.

There were two paintings by the criminal artist, *Adoration of the Shepherds* and *The Raising of Lazarus*, deploying large areas of black to highlight the pathos of the gestures. The charged emotions were the antithesis of Messina's serenity. Scholars suggested that Lazarus might be a self-portrait, possibly conveying his hope of clemency, if not redemption. The works had suffered from cleaning which may have accounted for the dreamy thinness of the paint-body and pervasive enervation. Perhaps this wispy brushing expressed the state of death returning to life with its Christ gesture reminiscent of Michelangelo's, *Adam*. Neither work had the juicy corporeality I'd expected from reproductions.

If Caravaggio's imagery moved me, it was for its life-like conviction and tender handiwork. The eroticism of its tactile immediacy was unnerving. He was the first Italian painter to identify with the powerless poor and thus an affiliate of my affections. Italian realist cinema would echo this portrayal of the disenfranchised. Like Caravaggio, Pasolini recruited untutored street-poor to perform as themselves. Caravaggio's figures shelter in anonymous dark spaces, bodies tense with imminent neglect. Just as Pasolini's, *Gospel*, had re-invigorated a biblical tale with recognisable individuals, Caravaggio's edgy confrontation with affliction disturbed and inspired me as they had the audience of his day.

***

The ferry soon filled, then proceeded to chug through the Tyrrhenian Sea's cobalt depths to Lipari, Stromboli and neighbouring islands. Stromboli seemed more volatile than Etna, belching fumes so weighted with sulphur they hugged its slopes in transit to the sea. It was a serious sight, a persistent threat to life. Small wonder its brave inhabitants had shrunk to a few hundred. San Bartolo's few narrow lanes were a-putter with scooters and the tiniest cars imaginable. Behind them, greater engines churned: lava lungs continually cooking.

Lastly, we shipped south from Trapani to Pantelleria. Iberians, Carthaginians, Romans, Arabs and the French had been there centuries, if not millenia before us; archaeological digs had unearthed stuff dating from 35,000 years. The elliptically shaped island, 25 by nine kilometres, was barren and encrusted with the rare magma, pantellerite. There were no buses and few taxis. We hired a car and circumnavigated its rocky coastline within the hour, then wound up the narrow bitumen strip to the summit of the immodestly titled, Montagna Grande, a mere 830 metres high, from which the shimmering Tunisian coast could be seen.

We skirted Pantelleria's airfield constructed by Mussolini in the 1930s as a military defence and subsequently seized by the Allied Army in its conquest of Axis powers. The island, no less than Sicily, had forever been a strategic hotspot. Near the airfield lay the spring-fed Lake Venus where the goddess had bathed and preened herself in its mirror, preparing for Bacchus. We dipped in her tepid 'milk' waters, sloshing ourselves with its reputed healing muds. There were no trees, so we retreated to a bird hide to shade from the sun's hostilities bouncing off the lake's blonde beaches.

Smaller springs sprinkled the coastline where we waded in thongs to avoid cuts from serrated submarine rocks. Most intriguing was Santaria, a cave housing a warm spring, legendary love nest of Ulysses and Calypso. Circe allegedly cavorted here, too, and charmed the wanderer.

Such mythical gods and heroes weren't a feature of Australian cartography after white settlement. When it came to naming early coastal settlements, our maps cited dignitaries and explorers—the English who conquered and the French who nearly did. As settlers moved inland, Indigenous names like, Ouyen, Mildura and Patchewollock were adapted from local languages, acknowledging occupation of the country prior to settlement. Nearly 200 years elapsed before our High Court accepted this as fact by revoking the fiction of Terra Nullius.

Interestingly, Art has assisted Australia's settler culture recognise Indigenous connection with land. In Alice Springs two modes evoking Central Desert experience enjoy market appeal. Namatjira's style, popularised during his lifetime—1902 to 1959—persists. Back then the prevailing patronising attitude regarded him as an example of successful assimilation since he'd adopted European understandings of illusionistic space, light, form and colour.

Emerging in the 1970s, the dot style achieved worldwide acclaim. This style transferred ancient iconographies, scribed for millennia upon the earth with ochres, into bolder-coloured acrylics on canvas. As their narrative significance added credibility and gained acceptance, similar virtues were sought in Namitjira's work.

Neither mode attends to the desert's vastness, throbbing heat and inherent dangers in ways that challenge me, which bespeaks the ease and intimacy the artists enjoy with the place. The recessional space of the landscape style unfolds in delicate veils that allows trees, rocks and ranges to float permanently in meditative peace. On the other hand, freed from such spatial duties, the decoratively dotted canvases deploy a fuller spectrum, with patterned metaphors of the country inspiring them. For me these maps of journeys and food resources haven't the utilitarian value they do for Indigenous audiences versed in their symbols. But the vigour and deft touch of the more subtle patterns in the dot paintings is undeniable.

It was difficult to credit local hopes for Pantelleria as a potential tourist destination. The physical attractions were limited, and their generating myths obscured by time. Water scarcity was also an issue. Rain was harvested from the white domed *dammusi*, the unique dwellings that had drawn us to the island. Was it the inference of celestial bodies, or invocation of egg or breast? Perhaps the ancients had similar thoughts. There were several igloo-like, basalt burial chambers or *sesi*, perhaps the proto-types for the *dammusi*. Ten radial tunnels led to the chambers of these stepped rotund structures. Speculation dated these as contemporaneous with Egypt's pyramids. Once more my limited archaeological knowledge was tested, found wanting and failed to excite further curiosity.

Promises of an Afterlife reach way back. Cosmologies were premised on an everlasting soul, the acquisition of which drove notions of transformation and self-perfection, states that elude me despite my midlife strivings. I say 'yes' to the 'spirited' company of friends, or the 'spirit of the game'. With deep seriousness, Arrernte friends regularly relate conversations with spirit entities. 'You seen that *inke* there, Rod,' they insist as we sit by an evening fire. 'Little people there might be come to look after us.' But I neither see nor feel any presence. Nor do I see auras around people. And I know it was dad's coat pegged on the kitchen doorknob at night that prompted nightmares, just as other dreams playfully re-order my daily doings. 'Soul' music's roots in African American culture strikes accord. While Jungian psychologist James Hillman's work revels in these terms, in the main I find they are so profaned I avoid them.

Though the black and twisted rock of barren Pantellaria embodied the grotesque, I very much doubted I'd return. Mainland Sicily was another matter. Encounters had been uniformly pleasant without requiring involvement with the strivings and desires of Sicilians Indeed, I was inoffensiveness incarnate in all exchanges, yet felt tenderness for its buckled terrain and people.

✳✳✳

We had two more months of travel. Georgia had been on my agenda for years, particularly its capital, Tbilisi. I also wanted to visit Baku. *Trip Advisor* reckoned an Azerbaijan visa was best obtained at their Istanbul embassy, giving me an excuse to return to the city I retained fond memories of. I was keen to see what changes had taken place during the intervening decades.

When we arrived, Istanbul was celebrating Rumi's eight-hundredth birthday with an exhibition in Hagia Sophia, the magnificent massively domed structure, dominating the city, that was originally a Greek Orthodox cathedral, later re-fashioned into an imperial mosque, now a museum. Rumi's whirling dervishes were on deck for tourists in a way inconceivable in 1980 when Sufi practices remained underground subsequent to Attaturk dissolving the various Orders in 1925. Now, Rumi's poetry and Sufi studies proliferated in bookshops. I was startled, too, to note the muezzin's prayer-calling was now recorded. Touristic culture was milking the buck. Snow-globed Blue Mosques and whirling dervishes were probably not far away.

Unsurprisingly the decrepit nineteenth-century wooden buildings around Hagia Sophia hadn't survived. The new blocks of high-rise apartments replacing them had retained the scale of their predecessors, as the historic cultural sector was crucial for tourism. Those exclamations of modernism, the glistening steel and glass towers of high finance, had grown on the Asian side of the Bosporus.

But I was startled that the bazaar, once a crowded sensual feast, had succumbed to a more sanitised persuasion. It had hummed differently when artisans had been present, tinkering and weaving. Produce that seemed barely separated from its place of origin was now behind glass-fronted, airconditioned shops. Floors shone. Retiled in jasper or marble they reflected myriad fluorescent fittings. Abundant spices and fruits were stacked in cone-shaped piles, spruikers standing aside, tempting passers-by with titbits. Yet the spectacle was compromised and with it the happiness I'd once found in that discordant den of commerce.

Even the Pudding Shop had followed suit. No longer a bedraggled hippy hangout, it had gone upmarket. Waiters wore trim uniforms. Stuffed capsicums, bean dishes and kebabs, were at prices that would keep hippies on the street. And what message were the mural-sized photos on its walls sending? In faded sepia, images of the place it once was, a record of how far the establishment had progressed and a nostalgic memory trip for those of my vintage.

No longer did Kombi drivers on its kerbing, canvas for company to Kabul, Karachi or KL. Absent so long from tourist hotspots like Istanbul, I'd been unaware of what travellers these days found fashionable. For one thing, veteran vanity no longer donned the kaftan, sarong or gold jewellery in its bid to disguise vanishing youth. The ear stud and tattoo prevailed. Tattoos, a legacy of eighteenth-century European marines consorting with Pacific Islanders, were flourishing in parlours as never before. The aesthetic coherence derived from ritual, communal significance had succumbed to individual whim, resulting in a malignancy of confused imagery.

Beads and headbands had been forsaken for the man-bun, ponytail, dreadlocks and shaved heads. Both sexes glamourised the body with piercings and tattoos of dubious artistic merit, rarely flattering pale flesh. Disruptions and disfigurations to the body that Picasso's art enacted prior to the Great War were now vogue. Baggy denims worn low on the butt to advertise underwear had succeeded their floral-patched forebears. And an aerial Silk Road had opened to Istanbul. Chinese out-numbered all comers five to one, and thronged between Hagia Sophia and the Blue Mosque, posing for group photographs before the Muslim masterpieces.

Close to the Pudding Shop, was Yerebatan, a large subterranean cistern once servicing the Topkapi Palace across the road, built in 532AD and filled by the Valens Aqueduct from a forest to the north. Sixty cisterns had operated during the Byzantine era: vital resources when besieged. I wandered over its wooden platforms in the damp gloominess to the rear of the enclosure where two Medusa heads of unknown rock were set at the base of columns, one upside down. As columns were appropriated from earlier sites, speculation arose that this inversion was commentary by Christian workers about Roman paganism. As I peered into the dark waters, sturgeon swept past, entrancing a quartet of cats and me until roused by the muezzin's midday call.

Curious to witness the Mevlana Dervish ceremony, I ambled down an alley one evening to a mosque that'd been converted into the Hodjapasha Cultural Centre. A packed crowd sat three-deep in a semicircle before a low stage. Two vocalists stepped slowly across the stage and stood behind stands holding copies of the Koran from which they'd recite. Four musicians filed in and sat on the opposite flank. Red sheepskin rugs were ceremoniously placed on the floor by two of the dancers who then retreated from view. The eerie notes of the *ney*, the Turkish reed flute, introduced all five dancers, evoking for me the melancholy call of the curlew, though I overheard the fellow beside me mutter to his companion that it sounded like someone stepping on a cat's tail. The dancers knelt then bowed, thrice kissing the floor before rising in succession to commence dancing, their arms folded across chests, lowered by their thighs then unfolding like emerging butterflies about to fly.

A year's tutelage under Jalaluddin's watchful eye didn't qualify me as an expert in Mevlana matters. Yet my sense of the *sema*'s meaning being corrupted by the presence of we gawking tourists was unavoidable. As with Licodea's Easter Parade this was a solemn affair. What was at odds lay in the nature of spectacle. If the atmosphere of 'sacred energy' meant anything, then its absence was as clear as it had been with the whirling Rajput in Jalsimer. The thirst for the exotic was at play. That the performance's neat one-hour time slot was abbreviated to fit market-place expectations said a lot. Watching and doing the whirling were distinctly different. Some may have felt blessed or graced. I didn't. 'I don't sell my Dreaming,' my friend, Xavier Neal's reply rang in my ears when I'd asked him, years before, if he, like so many desert people, had joined the legion of painter artists peddling their work in Alice Spring's main tourist drag.

Architecturally, I am a friend of curved space and indifferent to the straight line. The pleasure of the dome with its incontestable completeness is my favourite. Does it stir primal experience of the womb or breast? It presents in the igloo, the yurt and the geodesic, and is found in the convexities of the fruited world, pumpkins, gourds, avocados, and figs. How comforting to roll a loquat or lychee pip against the domed roof of my mouth! Or ponder the silk innards of a honeyeater's nest. And with the same pleasure I'd once fondled the gold radials of my boy cub's cap, in a Pantelleria bedroom I'd commenced sketching the construction lines of its multi-cupped ceiling. I continued taking notes of alternate structures and now in Istanbul, in the walled gardens of Gulhane Park I chanced upon the dome's supreme expression.

It was laminated maple from Japan according to Armand, an engineer graduate working onsite who'd noticed my admiring eye. The dome was intended to attract visitors to the soon-to-be-opened Museum of Islamic Science and Technology, housed above the former stables in the nearby wall. He guided me through the display of immaculate miniature waterwheels, optical, medical, chemical, astronomical devices, and weaponry; inventions predating their European equivalents by several centuries. The Muslim intellectual centres of Bokhara and Baghdad, he claimed, were the antecedents of discoveries attributed to the European Renaissance. He neglected to mention that many Muslim achievements had relied on Greek texts.

I followed him up narrow stairs to the ramparts from which he advised I'd best view the interlocking arches. We stood high above the dome on the very edge of the roof. Immediately a sequence of images crowded my mind, perhaps induced by the elevation. A pinprick beneath billowing silk blooms into manhood as a parachute nears touchdown. Once grounded the parachutist lies in a foetal pose. The parachute expires in a crumpled heap. I was replaying the *Rubelov* prologue, another extraordinary Tarkovsky passage. We see people preparing a primitive balloon for flight as others on horseback approach, threatening to stop their endeavour. As we follow the aerialist upstairs of a church, a black horse trots through a doorway away from the pursuers. We gaze from the church window to witness the equestrians reach the balloon, and see the man holding the rope at ground level have his eyes plucked out. The aerialist feels he's escaped his pursuers and we hear breathing as air escapes the balloon. He is fulfilling man's wish to be freed from gravity, to see the unity of things; the earth and water in the landscape blended together. Someone said of this masterpiece that it's feels as if the entire world itself was trying to force its way through the screen. It's *the* great movie about the significance of the artist questioning the meaning of existence.

Armand disturbed my reverie. I clicked off a few photos, thanked him, and returned to our hotel to pack for our overnight bus to the Georgian border.

I was thrilled when Pierre Elliott entered my dreams that night. His recent death and our advent in the lands of his Sufi Brothers coalesced. He was summoning me to Claymont where, on arrival, a resident told me that despite apparent vigour, Pierre had only four days to live and had invited me to sit them through. At his bedside a young Tibetan monk was reciting *The Tibetan Book of the Dead*. Pierre told me he intended fasting to death and asked if the monk and I would assist his passage by joining his fast. The Work, he confided, wasn't about raising efficiency in life, developing higher powers, increasing concentration, or better health. God, truth, exalted states, whatever, were simply concepts. We must strip our illusions to allow Life itself to be our Teacher. Then he turned to Lareena who'd just arrived with Anjou. What he communicated I wasn't privy to but could tell from her expression that it had been of some moment. Then, having bent in conversation with Anjou, he turned and let me know she was an exceptional child.

✳✳✳

Historically, Georgia had been poised between Persian and Russian powers, though Tartars, too, had once controlled it—each a bloody conquest. Soviet Russia's dissolution in 1991 paved the familiar forlorn path of peripheral territories in declining empires. The subsequent power vacuum was contested by smaller, local ethnicities. Yet Georgia's unique written and spoken language had survived. From Pasolini's film, *Medea*, I knew part of the Golden Fleece legend was set in Georgia, originally called Colchis. And, as if to literalise the legend, mountain villagers in Svaneti had recently been observed using sheepskins to trap the fine gold particles in rivers flowing from the Caucasus Mountains.

The bus station at the border town Sarpi, was incredibly shaded by a majestic red gum, reminder of home. I'd forgotten how its durability, resistance to predation, quick growth and evergreen status made it an attractive export. Gauging by the tree's girth it may well have predated World War I. Its gnarled bark with scrotum-like bole festering at its base reflected ancestry from our stringent climate. It brought to mind Hans Heysen whose legacy endured in the works of hobbyists embracing the eucalypt as the standard bearer of the landscape genre. Like most Germans, Australian citizenship couldn't save him from the barbs of patriots during the Great War. Germans were interred and German nomenclatures, such as his village of Hahndorf, were extinguished. Had he shared the irony that his sturdy gum tree paintings became icons of Digger stoicism and heroism in the trenches?

Other than the occasional dream, I'd long ceased contact with Claymont though some interest in Gurdjieff lingered. The revolutionary turbulence of 1917 had forced him and his students from Moscow, through Essentuki and Tbilisi to Istanbul, before establishing a more permanent school near Fontainebleau. He'd lectured on his system and publicly performed the dances for the first time in Tbilisi's Opera Theatre, still standing in restored form in downtown Rustavelli Street. It turned out that Tarkovsky, like so many artists, was intrigued with Castaneda and Gurdjieff. I wondered if some of *Rubelov* had been filmed in Georgia.

To the northwest was the Ukraine from whence schoolmate, Nic Ouchtomsky's parents had fled. It was the scene of the Crimean War in 1854 where England's charging fusiliers, I'd first observed above old Niven and Thomas's organ, were defeated by Russian artillery. What I knew of the conflict amounted to what I'd seen in their reproduction. Likewise, my knowledge of the port city, Odessa, the site of the precursor to Russia's Revolution, known to me only through Eisenstein's film of the protesting sailors on the *Potemkin* in 1905. With access to all-weather ports on the Black Sea, and as a superb grain producer, Ukraine remained a contested zone.

Georgia had been under various Russian regimes during recent centuries. Having gained independent sovereignty in 1991, it confronted internal instability. While the 2002 Rose Revolution secured reasonable peace and suppressed its Mafia, a palpable fatigue hung over Tiblisi; Istanbul's hustle and bustle was worlds away. Georgia's sovereignty was still threatened by Russian incursions into the provinces of Abkhazia and South Ossetia as the Bear sought control of its former states.

Mid-afternoon we secured lodging on the fourth floor of a dilapidated, overcrowded boarding house, a few kilometres from the city centre. Irine Japaridze was the proprietor, a formidable chain-smoking Jewish woman about my age. A family of Israeli tourists we'd shared lodgings with earlier, recommended her. She was on the third floor, lounging on her divan before a small computer screen, scrolling through 'hits' on her Facebook site. I noted other Israeli hits praising her hospitality. Humidity and smoke clouded the confined space, despite her fanning flushed cheeks with a tourist brochure. The bold floral print of the divan matched her kaftan. Both were similarly stained and shared the fur of the fat, marbled cat squatting on her shoulder. Disdainful and visibly tired, she waved us upstairs, saying to square with her in the morning.

We dropped our packs and I accompanied Anjou downstairs to the rear courtyard where I chatted with a couple of Australian lads tending their motorbikes. They were the first voices from home we'd heard in months. I was mightily impressed with the scale of their enterprise from Durban to Europe across to China, trailing the Malay Archipelago, boating to Darwin from Timor, and then heading home to their Barrow Island mining camp. Two months to go. They'd accomplished a Moscow to Vladivostok trek this time last year, said Tristan, replacing tools in the pannier, having fitted a new tyre to the rear rim and adjusted the brakes. Displays of simple mechanical skills still filled me with awe.

The young colts in their mid-twenties were mechanics on Barrow Island, a hundred kilometres off the Pilbara coast at the American giant Chevron's oil and gas plant.

'That's the place environmentalist, Harry Butler raved about on his TV show in the 1970s,' I said. 'I thought it was protected wilderness.'

'He's still there, mate,' said Liam. 'Inducting new workers about the island's unique wildlife.'

He noticed me looking at the other spare tyres strapped to their panniers.

'If you reckon roads in Georgia aren't up to scratch, you ought to see them in Central Asia. They make the Tanami Road look like a super highway. Even a camel would struggle,' he huffed. 'But you want to see Khiva, Bukhara and Samarkand. They more than make up for it. Brilliant cities, mate. Masterpieces.'

There would be sections, he added pointing to a jerrycan, where fuel would be scarce and its octane level uncertain.

'You fill up and you're a few clicks down the track when your motor starts coughing.'

Liam rolled up his trouser leg to show a nasty burn on his left calf muscle from the exhaust pipe. 'Just a taster, mate.' He grinned. 'Nothing like the dogs that mauled us in Siberia.'

With dog references still in the air, Anjou wandered over to join a young girl playing with her large scruffy mutt on the far side of the yard. It broke from its leash and greeted Anjou with a nip on her knee. She ran to my arms as much in shock as pain. While the graze didn't look serious, it sent us into a spin, searching for antiseptic in nearby shops. We weren't aware of the presence of rabies but knew she hadn't had a tetanus shot. Failing to find a pharmacy, Lareena resorted to the antiseptic in our medical kit, by which time Anjou had almost forgotten the incident.

But I was on the far side of health that night with an immobilising fever; floppy of body, scorching ears, and incinerating heat on the roof of my mouth. It couldn't be the weather's mild 20s; I was far exceeding that. Hot. Cold. Then back again. My ears boiled and blood broth filled my skull. I rose slowly but sensed my consciousness lagging on the pillow. The heat and pain contracted to my throat. Maybe some fresh air on the narrow balcony would help. A string hammock was suspended there which I flopped into.

Frater Albertus, Salt Lake alchemist and founder of the *Paracelsus Research Centre* appeared in my delirium, arm around his wife's shoulders strolling along Myers Creek Road, Healesville, heading towards Mt Slide on their evening constitutional after the day's lectures.

In 1976 a colleague at the Argo Street School encouraged me to Frater's alchemical prima. Her husband had devoted three years to the guru's courses and mentioned that Albertus had succeeded in transmuting minerals into the legendary philosophic stone. As Art students we'd read in Koestler's *Sleepwalkers* of Renaissance scientist-astronomers who were alchemists attentive to astrology. It'd been pretty much abandoned during The Enlightenment with the likes of Boyle, Lavoisier and Davy's penetrating chemical analyses. Curious and gullible, however, I enrolled.

Swiss physician, Paracelsus, contemporary of Luther and Erasmus, influenced Albertus. Alchemists preferred three 'philosophic' principles to the Greeks' four elements of Earth, Air, Fire, and Water. Mercury, Sulphur and Salt were likened to smoke, fire and ash respectively. Mercury gave lustre and hardness to a substance, Sulphur gave colour and combustibility and Salt conferred solidity and resistance to fire. There were correlations between planets and bodily organs. The language regarding plant and minerals was imbued with unusual reverence, the shape and structure of each grain and particle perceived as fingerprints of God.

Albertus especially admired alchemist Fulcanelli's, *Le Mystere des Cathedrales*, a book I'd noticed on Dr Ropar's shelves. Fulcanelli, it was claimed, had produced stones, and even high-end, alchemical gold. His reading of the icons decorating Notre Dame and Amiens cathedrals differed substantially from Male's, *Gothic Image*, another of our college texts. According to the alchemist, they contained the recipe for the philosophic stone of gold. Some adherents claimed he warned of the imminent dangers of atomic fusion decades before Hiroshima.

During the week, we studied links between the Kabbalah, astrology and practical laboratory work; a three-fold exploration of the cosmos and one's place within it. We were invited to meditate on the symbolic Tree of Life whose hidden roots were the Root of all Roots, and sap of the hidden God. Its 10 Sepiroth were sacred emanations flowing from sky and plant. Again, I struggled with metaphor.

I borrowed mortar, pestle, flasks and beakers from my brother Ian's laboratory for grinding, boiling and macerating freshly sourced rosemary, the novice's introductory experiment. Start from the vegetable kingdom and progress to the mineral and animal. On Albertus's advice, I harvested some sprigs when dew still clung to it at the appropriate phase of the moon. A concentrate, or purified stone reduced from the chosen substance, allegedly had healing properties capable of attracting universal energies and potentially altering the atomic structure of what it was placed in contact with.

Astrology was another language floating above my radar. It'd been a 1960s conversational byword to enquire of one's star sign and its ascendant: a given for understanding potential relationships. I was sceptical about the veracity of these claims though aware auspicious couplings, even war plans, for centuries, had relied on astrological consultations. Indian astrologers, for instance, were adamant the carnage during the Partition could have been avoided had Mountbatten chosen a more propitious date. No less a dignitary than Nancy Reagan, wife of the late US President, consulted an astrologer in regard to propitious dates for him to act.

Albertus explained how our weekdays came to be named. I'd not noted our setting aside Sunday for religious observance derived from pagan 'sun' worshipers. Nor that 'moon' day followed, being next in importance for early astrologers. Mars, Mercury, Jupiter, Venus and Saturn completed the sequence and Albertus spoke of their alignment with various metals and plants. Certain times for harvesting were more propitious than others, he claimed.

Tucked between sheets, and sheltered beneath a roof, I rarely scanned the night canopy and was inconsiderate of stellar settings. I did not navigate according to their dictates, nor plant vegetables by lunar reckonings any more than I consulted the *I Ching* as a basis for decisions.

After relocating to Central Australia, it's dry weather under vast, lucid skies invited camping. I'd thrown my swag down beside Arrernte friends and listened to their sky stories. Rather than joining the dots to find animal counterparts in the sky, Arrernte often accounted for images in the spaces between stars. Some coincided with European counterparts. Many did not. Their days had no need of naming, nor were their years numbered. I regarded the stories as the work of men and women with creative imaginations requiring more analysis than I was prepared to undertake. They remained as spurious unities.

In the scheme of distant planets and receding galaxies, surely our doings on a small planet were inconsequential. What trust could I place in the chance scattering of star clouds? I didn't discount myths. They were fascinating, and every culture I'd grazed on had its spin. Talk of spinning, the annual shifting of our planet on its axis meant that the zodiacal sign toward which the sun was pointing at the time of our births is no longer the one we thought it was. This doesn't stop me applauding the mathematicians who figured the harmonies underpinning nature. If studying the motion of celestial bodies has inspired buildings, artefacts, music, and perhaps the whirling, so much the better.

Frater gave us to understand that real personal transformation, even the promise of eternal life, would accompany successful laboratory work. The leaves were pummelled and boiled in a beaker, but the hours required for the cook exhausted my patience. I polished my motto, 'doubt springs eternal', and dropped Alchemy. My inner scientist would remain content with the crystal gardens of childhood where I'd suspended a thread of wool in supersaturated salt and watched as burstings and buddings of plant-like growths sprung into being.

Wrapping up these reflections, I returned to the pillow and slipped into sleep. In my dream it was raining, and the sea lapped at an empty beach. Albertus appeared standing statuesquely at water's edge. He morphed into an albatross swooping low then returning to his nest prodding a large, glass egg. A crack appeared and a puff of sulphurous gas plumed. The fissure widened and from it trickled sawdust. The bird scratched the sawdust looking in vain for something. Above, the sky hoisted its dark skirt around its neck and rained the painted dead. Pale bodies littered the beach with crimson script tattooed on their thighs.

A small blue aperture broke through the grey, and from it a stream of cirrus spilled, forming my name. The albatross flew above, its shadow a bruise wandering the beach. I followed the shadow to the nest where the bird had resettled and asked why the dead were scattered here. It grinned and I noticed blood in the corners of its beak. My wrists were wet. Had I dipped them in the sea? I looked closer and saw they were bleeding. I shook myself awake.

I'd slept prostrate for two hours with hands beneath me blotched with pins and needles. The sheets were wet but the fever had receded. Other bodies in the dormitory still slumbered. I moved slowly between the compress of beds back to the cool of the balcony air.

Before me stretched the silhouette of Tbilisi's western suburbs through which we'd arrived by bus. Bisecting the panorama was the silver thread of the Mt'k'vari River, the Trialeti Range at its rear, hemming the suburbs. Across the river, spires sprouted in sharp contrast with the feminised feel of Istanbul's domed sprawl.

Tbilisi's redeeming feature resided in the medieval charms of the central complex's wonky wooden houses, latticed balconies and rustic caravanserais. Istanbul had looked like this in the late 1970s. Weather and age had harmonised the pastel pink, blue and green planks with a delicate patina. *Rublev*-like icons beckoned from several shop windows, affirming Christianity's enduring presence. Other than a young mum with babe tugging at her breast and hand outstretched on the steps of a church, poverty seemed confined to the suburbs. A busker stood near her whipping the air with his fiddle in hope of tourist coins.

Civilian wars in the 1990s had reduced Georgia to poverty. There was little or no construction or reconstruction. In rural areas lush cornfields surrounded communal buildings with windows smashed and walls decked with graffiti. Cows roamed the roadsides undeterred by fences or traffic. Cancered concrete balconies crumbled underfoot. A ganglion of power lines dangled dangerously at head level.

The car inventory amused and saddened me. Most would have been sprouting grass in Australian junkyards. Here it was common to see 1970s' models with bonnets prised, women bent beneath, or pushing, with a man at the wheel, to petrol stations. Few petrol stations functioned. Only in impoverished Aboriginal communities had I seen such things; the siphoning of fuel from jerrycans, the abandoned vehicle upturned for access to spare parts. Here, taxi drivers routinely switched off the engine when cruising downhill to conserve fuel. Endemic lassitude was rife. Time stalled in perpetual twilight. War widows and elderly women begged at street corners of inner-city suburbs. Several times students approached with no intention other than to practise their English. Georgian was their first language. But they were bent on breaking ties with older generations who kept Russian as their second tongue.

Such were my thoughts as I stared into the dark 'burbs. At this hour, with no sign of humanity other than those dozen heaving respirators bedded in the dorm at my back, I found the skyline soothing. Perhaps my tipsiness was viral. Suddenly the skyline and the valley before me were transformed. The same buildings and trees that were silhouetted became illuminated. Did this viridian, turquoise, cadmium, and lilac spectacle derive from contagion? Was it sitting before my eyes or projected from behind them? What chemical was irrigating my brain? It faded with the rising sun an hour on. Surely this chromal ecstasy was an illusion. Perhaps thinking of those crystal gardens had evoked the event. What lightness of being, this viral reverie.

***

The streets seemed peopled by Tarkovsky 'extras', an illusion enhanced by the crumbling Narikala fortress, cresting the hill above the hot baths that gave Tbilisi its name. It might have been the set for the tartars sacking of Vladimir. The unremitting desolation and suffering in *Rublev* were replicated in Tiblisi's pensive rhythms.

I trundled downhill from the fortress to the baths, another place Gurdjieff frequented. Sentiment aside, I partook of public baths wherever opportunities presented. Two middle-aged women were washing clothes in the overflow from the baths. One passed me a towel and I followed her to a bare stone chamber where jets of sulphur-smelling water poured into great basins in the floor.

After 20-minutes' immersion she returned with a chamois in which she folded a cake of soap and produced a rich lather. She washed and scraped, then dowsed me repeatedly with bowls of hot water. A man of similar size and age appeared and led me to the massage slab. Prone, I was pummelled and stretched in unaccustomed directions, held by the hands and arched backwards, then dropped to the slab, resulting in some relief and the sense of feeling several inches taller, leaner and exhausted.

Narikala Fortress viewed from the Baths, 2008.

It remains for some idler to compare and contrast the world's massage methods. Perhaps it's already the subject of a thesis elucidating how cultural temperaments are expressed. Though I know of no Roman Baths in Australia, most forms are available. There's Swedish sweatbox, Samoan ritual huffing and thumping, Andean Shamanic style with hot river stones, Japanese acupressure, Bowen technique, Turkish bone-shaking with skin grate like I'd just undergone, or Thai. Australia boasts the dressing rooms of its footy clubs. I opt for Thai. It alone has a range of touch attuned to the body's call, alternating between affectionate foreplay and vigorous assault, and falling just shy of congress. If Thai massage is integral to temple teachings, long may Buddhism flourish.

We took a bus from Tbilisi, a few hours east to Azerbaijan, the bathing session having set my cold on a sprint. Though the city provided that epiphany, I doubt I'd be hurrying back to Georgia engulfed as it was in a cloud of numbed grief. The delights of local folk ensembles might have added to my pleasure. No one could help point us in the direction of regional music. We were left with raucous Russian Punk, blaring from taxi radios and cassettes, so offensive as to make Sid Vicious sound like a choirboy.

Baku, capital of Azerbaijan beckoned, the home of mugham folk music, and my passion these 10 years. Its master, Alim Qasimov, drew me. He was the national hero, the one with an international profile. Without disrespecting either man, I explained to friends he was like Roy Orbison yodelling on caffeine. Mugham was central to national self-consciousness and identification. The term had circulated for centuries before UNESCO nominated it a world heritage masterpiece in 2003. Though sung in neighbouring countries, Azerbaijan had especial claims on it.

But first there was the border. Given the Embassy's warning, we anticipated delays. Formalities however were minimal and a student on vacation from the State Economic University in Baku taxied us to the Zaqatala terminal. A five-kilometre colonnade of poplars formed entry to the town, suggesting improved fortunes. A few metres back from this colonnade stood concrete walls painted black and white, imitating mortar and stone.

The Tala River formed a natural border to the east of Zaqatala where mulberries and hazelnut groves completed the town's picturesque setting. The terminal had three small bedrooms at the rear of a tearoom serving dried biscuits, cheese and roasted sunflower seeds. We booked overnight rooms, intent on moving in the morning.

It was an uphill walk to the town centre where we passed two-storey dwellings in red-brick, limestone and river-rock. The streets were immaculate and litter free. Backgammon players occupied the town square. Beyond the modest shopping complex was a sliver of park dominated by two primeval plane trees, their girths fitted with steel benches on which townsfolk of all ages idled. Zaqatala, like most of the region had passed through Russian and Georgian powers before Azerbaijan became a constituent Soviet State in 1922.

Just as crowded was the rambling cypress park of Heydar Aliyer on the hill above, sporting half a dozen weary fairground rides. Faded streetlight flickered through the trees, lancing the paths winding round fountains. The hill housed a statue of a *Potemkin* mutineer who'd participated in the 1905 rebellion, one of the final vestiges of the Russo-Japanese war. Abutting the park were the ruins of a Russian fortress that served as a prison for the mutineers.

My knowledge of the mutineers' tragedy derived from Eisenstein's movie, famous for its montage of the violent suppression of their supporters by Tsarist troops. There was the slaughter on the Odessa steps, the nurse's smashed spectacles and scream, conflated decades later in Bacon's version of Velasquez's *Pope Innocent X*. Bacon's assault on papal authority, in part, embraced the tragedy of the insurrection. Bacon, how resonant the name with his obsession with damaged flesh on meat rack or Cross. He'd joined the formidable lineage of Grunewald, Titian, Caravaggio, Rembrandt, Rubens, Courbet and Soutine who'd maximised the possibilities of pliable oils to evoke human flesh, piteously so in his case.

Revolution seemed far removed from the children clasping parent hands and ice creams. We savoured Anjou's kid joy with the frolickers for a half hour and searched for supper. She'd been wonderful throughout our trip. Though the Sicilian schooling wasn't a success and she'd battled Lareena's maths tuition, she rarely complained, and kept us buoyant. Her large dark eyes and blonde locks coaxed conversation and occasional small gifts from fellow passengers, diners and hoteliers. Vital, curious and natural comic, she had ready appeal.

The only eatery open at 11.30 p.m. was a Turkish restaurant where we welcomed pea and lentil *chorba* with warm *pide* before rambling downhill to the terminal. A wild cortege of wedding vehicles circuited the terminal car park at breakneck speed, tooting and yelling. The racket continued after midnight during which time I realised the temperature in the bedroom was rising. Was the fever returning? In the morning, the woman at the front desk pointed to the malfunctioning water system, indicating the empty water tank and dysfunctional communal shower. The kitchen-hand drew water from the well, boiling then tempering a bucket for our ablutions.

We overnighted in several mountain villages before heading to intriguing Xinaliq. It was situated high in the eastern Caucasus and was accessible only in summer. Quba was as far as regular buses ventured. Having booked into the cavernously stark soviet-era, Shahdag hotel, we crossed the footbridge over the Kudyal River and wandered the streets of Quba's all-Jewish smaller sister, Krasnaya Sloboda. This shtetl of mountain Jews had endured pogroms by Persian warlords, repression under communism and the rise of post-Soviet nationalism. Viewed from the hotel, the order of its red-roofed buildings promised satisfying cuisine. Though immaculately kept it was completely shut. No sign of cat, dog or its five thousand people lurked about. Perhaps religious customs were being observed. Then two yamulke-wearing young guys appeared from a side street and hailed us. Lacking a common tongue, we gave to understand our hunger, and within seconds they phoned a taxi. All aboard, we headed back across the river to a ramshackle restaurant where they ordered food, paid for both taxi and meals, wished us well and departed back across the river. How impressive was that!

In the morning we taxied to Quba's marketplace seeking a driver destined for Xinaliq. None were inclined to the mountains which frustrated us, until a weedy guy in denims and army jacket jabbed towards his ancient army jeep and yelled, Xinaliq. Seated silently in the backbench was a young woman in an ankle-length floral skirt with acrylic vest fitted over an emerald cardigan. Anjou sat next to her. What seemed to be the last passenger, Afaddin, made seating up the back tight. We tried to negotiate fares, even at one point ejecting him. He argued for a few minutes with the driver and squeezed between Anjou and the young woman. Though we wealthy Westerners would bolster the driver's pocket the trip might take place without us but not him.

The vehicle bulged with bodies by the time the engine fired up. At the last moment an old woman haggled for passage and lugged her mattress onto the rear bench. The driver protested feebly, shrugged, and the journey commenced; two hours of four-wheel driving through prodigious passes, and twice halted by teams clearing avalanches. The Rutosh River roared through sheer clefts of pewter-coloured rock. Their foreboding volatility contrasted sharply with the inviting, earth-hugging red rocks of home. Here and there savage slabs of rock had dropped to the cinnamon waters bisecting the canyon.

Mountain pass to Xinaliq.

Xinaliq's dwellings, housing its population of two thousand, were built of deep-grey slate from where they nestled on the narrow shoulder and gentlest gradient of the lowest mountain. Its name stood for the henna rusting the surrounding slopes. Their thick walls were stacked tight with rock and reinforced with timbers from a source somewhere lost to sight, forests being a thing of the remote past. This means of construction was the ingenious response to tremors in all mountain villages.

As with most remote villages, tourist facilities were non-existent and we needed to find lodgings, or thought we did. The road curled past a substantial two-storey school where a crew were busy finishing construction. The driver stopped about halfway up the slope. The young woman, silent throughout our trip, alighted with us. So too did Afaddin. We followed them down the path leading to their house and then climbed stairs to a narrow balcony where Afaddin smiled faintly and grasped my proffered hand. Some silent collusion had transpired. Perhaps everyone was related, the shrew, the driver, Afaddin and as we now realised, his daughter.

Xinaliq, 2008.

No one spoke English, Turkish, Russian, or possibly Azeri in this isolated region. The melting snow was piped directly from Mount Shahdagh, the giant amongst neighbouring peaks and yet another fabled resting place of Noah's ark. Locals referred to themselves as his children. Vast sheep pastures climbed the ranges until massive black rocks forbade access. Women flounced their laundry in troughs dispersed along the pipe, and domestic needs were drawn from it as it rushed to the river, bisecting the wide valley.

Moustachioed Afaddin chain-smoked, his fawn fedora pressing his ears forward. His eyes, dark as currants, quizzed us. We did our best without a common tongue. His wife remained out of sight as he introduced the silent daughter and two others. They were possibly a year or so apart, sturdy, dark-haired, all in floral skirts and scarfs, with notable gold fillings, glimpsed through courteous smiles. The youngest had consulted a doctor in Quba and retired to the couch. The others led us to the room below where two cows munched hay. One daughter stayed to milk them. The other showed us the drop toilet perched just below the road leading to houses on the upper terraces. A lynx-like spotted cat slept by the slatted door.

Horns were tooting. Winding up the dirt road 50 metres below were two overcrowded cars, red ribbons flying from windows and aerials. Beneath the bonnet of the front vehicle rose a cloud of smoke. Passengers were remonstrating with the driver who belatedly stopped. Villagers with water-buckets ran to dowse the flames, accompanied by several hysterical dogs. Within minutes the procession resumed.

Afaddin, who'd watched bemusedly, stood and motioned us through the door. We followed to the level above where the cars had stopped, scattering ducks and chickens, daubed with blue paint, presumably a sign of provenance. It was another wedding in this summer of weddings. The groom and his buddies, in suits and ties, clamoured from the cars and single-filed up the narrow path to the bride's house.

A quartet had assembled amid the villagers. Clarinet, drum and accordion beat a cordial cacophony above chatter and laughter. A vocalist strained to be heard. Everyone, ourselves included, dipped their 'pinkie' in a dessert bowl of liquid cow manure to formally conclude the welcome. A sheep bedecked with red ribbon, was prodded past our legs to its fate on the spit. Red seemed to be a theme as many of the women, young and old, had hennaed hair. Afaddin urged our introduction to the bride's father and, though given to understand that our chance presence conferred a blessing, we felt intrusive and opted to retreat.

We joined the shy daughters in the narrow dining room. Mrs Afaddin appeared from the outside stairs with a plate of fresh chapattis. She'd been buried in the small hut on the lower terrace, a room sufficient for a stove and from which a column of smoke climbed through a tin pipe. The breads were ladled onto a plate next to another with slabs of cheese. A bowl of honey appeared, and black tea. This was supper. Afaddin sat opposite in his battered tweed coat, elbows propped on the table, not eating, but scrutinising, waiting some indication that provisions had sufficed.

There was no network reception but the girls, ranging between 18 and 23, had DVDs and posters of Charles Bronson and Steve McQueen adorning walls. Having cleared the table, they slipped a disc into the set and sprawled mute before it on the floor. I commented on their knitted slippers that they indicated were made this summer. The long winter hibernation was devoted to rug making, a ready money maker in good times.

The movie was something to do with Spartacus. Computer graphics simulated towering precipices overlooking troops advancing across a plain. The valley presenting through their window required no such computerised enhancement. Mountains filled the view from the window. A narrow band of pale sky rode their rim. I imagined invading Russian troops swarming the slopes. How strange, encountering this retold epic here where television news of the day was not received, and distant Baku rarely, if ever, visited; and provisions were sourced from Quba every six to eight months.

We, men, remained at the table. Affadin propped on his arms, deep creases between his brows, pinched and ready to detonate. It was time for money talk. I had no idea of the going rate and based my offer on what we'd paid at hotels that wouldn't register on any star system. There was no dispute over my 30 marats per night. For all I knew it was a month's pay. He held my eyes as he had since our introduction, weighing me up, then raked the notes with a croupier's dispassion across the table with his forearm, pocketed them, rose briskly and absented himself on some business. His wife returned to her kitchen.

Affadin had indicated we would take the master bedroom. Husband and wife would sleep on the dining room couch. I was troubled by this deference, but our host insisted. Sheepskins formed a mattress of sorts. Cushions stuffed with wool served as pillows. It was a low-ceilinged cavern with earthen floor, rear wall banked against the damp earth and separated from the dining room by a heavy woollen blanket pinned above the doorway. We retired into the dark recess. There was no light but one of the daughters handed me a candlestick and box of matches. It was warm, even stuffy, despite the altitude. The enclosure prompted unwanted thoughts.

It was 1973 and I'd driven to Royden's abode in Sherbrook Forest. He'd demonstrated a casting technique during high school, and I'd been using it in my classes at Maroondah High. I had the idea of casting my body in the manner of Caravaggio's, *Entombment of Christ*, head thrown back, arm dangling from a bedroom closet; a funereal, white, fibre-glass sculpture emerging from sheets. Echoes of Michelangelo's *Pieta*, and David's *Death of Marat*, also played in this pre-figuring of my demise.

It was a warm afternoon, perfect for curing plaster-of-Paris. I cut an aperture in a piece of card through which I'd poked my face to the depth of my ears and made myself comfortable on an outside bench while Royden placed the card over my head and fitted straws into my nostrils. He mixed the plaster and squeezed drops of lemon in for a smoother finish, carefully applying it around nostrils, eyes and lips before piling the remaining surfaces. It was cold and especially heavy on my eyelids.

Twenty minutes passed and the plaster got colder and heavier. Thirty minutes and exhalations were condensing in the straws and retreating up my nostrils. Royden held my hand and said to squeeze if I was uncomfortable. Forty minutes and we realised the plaster had gone off. I squeezed his hand. My breathing staggered and I sat up, allowing gravity to wrench the plaster from my face. We'd forgotten to grease my hair. The Vaseline was still in my kit. Though freed of plaster, now mostly on my lap, great clods were locked to my scalp. Royden rang the Poisons Board. There was no solvent for partially set plaster. He produced hammer, chisel and scissors. An hour later with loss of hair and vanity I was liberated. We repeated the process the following weekend, redressing our oversight. The sculpture was fabricated in fibreglass from further body casts. Thinking I'd expunged my fear of dying, I buried it unceremoniously in the backyard.

Fear of suffocation could still disturb my sleep in airless rooms. The television grumbled from the other room as I drifted off. Two hours later all noise had ceased, and I awoke in a panic. In which room was I: that of the previous night, of my Alice Springs bedroom, or indeed, that of my childhood?

Silence clotted the deaf dark. Once more I confronted my exit into death's Great Nothingness. I needed to pee but couldn't find matches or candle. I groped around the wall for the opening. I was about to call out and reluctantly disturb the household when I fell through the blanket. I fumbled down the stairs and peed beneath the icy stare of the moon, cooled and calmed, the dank bedroom no longer a threat. Voluminous pissing. Fleshy me seemed made of water! I wished for sleep's restorative powers to plunge into its depths and snuff these galloping thoughts.

***

Breakfast was a repeat of supper, though this time Afaddin planted a generous spoon of strawberry jam in my tea and, aware I'd not done so, doused my cheese with salt. Again, he sat while I ate, not partaking until I'd finished. The sky was lightly clouded, and the mountains glistened metallically. On mentioning the fire temple Ateshgah, he lit up, summoning a daughter with paper and pen on which he scrawled a rudimentary map. Trip Advisor had alerted us to the existence of Azerbaijan Fire Temples including Xinaliq's. Was I sharing one of his enthusiasms? No two-dimensional rendering suggested the vertiginous climb confronting us.

The first hour on a gravel track followed the raucous cataract upstream. It was shallow and lucid. Intermittent reefs reaped clusters of white froth. They broke in curds that hugged the banks. Strawberry plants bearing small, delicate fruits, spotted the banks, the likely source of the morning's tea-sweetener. A great carpet of sheep grazed on the grassy, lower slopes. From this emerged two huge surly dogs whose wolf heritage was clearly evident. They charged downhill towards us. A shepherd, alerted by their barking, appeared from behind a hefty boulder, halted their advance and waved us on.

We consulted Afaddin's map. The path to our right seemed likely though it petered out within half an hour. As we descended, I noticed a more defined track on the adjacent shoulder. We clambered down then up through grey scree that kept slipping beneath each step, till we gained the track. Up and up until my thighs burned. I could see Anjou wilting without complaint. Cliffs of stupendous verticality dropped to the stream so distant its roar was lost and its motion frozen as in a photo. Chickens scratching their village patch looked like white confetti.

Salan with Equestrians, 2008.

On the cusp of surrender, another shepherd, a young man on horseback, appeared round a bend and beckoned us a further kilometre to the permanent flame of *Ateshgah*. Anjou had had enough. She and Lareena clambered up behind the horseman and headed uphill. I was exhausted. The surprising rescue and sight of Anjou on her first mount caused my snort of hysterical laughter as they departed. Despite the chilly air the strain had me peeling off my jacket while pausing to muster energy for the final leg. As if attracted to the banksia motifs on my green shirt, a black bee landed, joined by a massive yellow fly, then three butterflies of differing colours. They clung on as I rose to follow the others before abandoning me for whatever else flowered at this barren altitude.

Ateshgah's eternal flame, 2008.

The equestrians had dismounted some metres below the track around an unprepossessing hearth. What an odd phenomenon just below the summer snowline, the middle of a nowhere for me, but a crucial somewhere for locals! Those dogs had done their doggie thing protecting their turf. It would be impossible to huddle sheep on these unfenced pastures without them. Now, horseman Salan, in like fashion, was rounding up us stragglers. We squatted by the flame over which lay a large flat rock for cooking chapatti and boiling tea.

It was still and bright. A bib of glacier sat above on the naked mountain. But high overhead, big winds were heaving and seemingly wrenching cloud carcasses from the snow-capped ridges. Their gauzy bodies were in hectic disarray, teased to the limits of visibility, whereupon they morphed into monstrous vertebrae.

There was no indication this was a Zoroastrian Fire Temple, remnant of the ancient religion once occupying Persian minds. No ruin with hints of a ritual past. Such edifices remained in the south of the country though I was unaware if the religion remained in vogue. The flames from these oil founts had given rise to Zoroastrian monotheism that praised their purity as a sign of god's light and wisdom. In turn, the religion inspired Greek and Judeo-Christian thinking.

I'd taken this from Bennett's *Dramatic Universe* which spoke of a great moment in the evolution of human consciousness. Apparently, cultural innovations and advances emerged synchronously across Eurasia in the period of Classical Greece, early Rome, the Prophets of Israel, the Upanishads and Buddhism in India, and Confucius in China. For Bennett, this period introduced the culture of mind and love, and was the great leap towards recognisable ancestral roots. These fellows, according to him, were preaching the right of every person to find their own salvation and, like Zoroaster, conveyed the notion of the sacredness of the individual, an attitude unfamiliar prior to 600 BC. Bennett's imaginative gifts were the equal of the best historic novelists. In such matters, basically, I was once more befriending my ignorance.

Elsewhere I'd gleaned that Zoroaster had been born laughing in 600 BC and murdered in Balkh. He'd incorporated older Aryan and Mithraism fire worship, reckoned God descended to earth via a miraculous birth, and was resurrected after death. He allegedly nominated Sunday as the Sabbath on December 25th. Sounded familiar. Coincidentally, the three magi journeying from the east were claimed as Zoroastrians.

Nowadays, oil empowered aeronautic and automobile narratives have taken purchase on minds as zealous as any religion. Car ownership, the private chariot, became the aspiration of the multitudes. And flight, the dream of centuries—though nightmare for those subjected to aerial bombing—was available to people of even my modest means. Clearly, however, the disparity between my pension and whatever Salan, squatting at my side, subsisted on remained incommensurable. Superannuation wouldn't even be a dream. Though my privilege must have glared at him, he politely declined my offer to compensate his kindness.

This small flame had supposedly ignited god-filled myths to explain Nature's powers. Had it ever been more than an improvised kitchen? Breathing the air in rare altitudes and beholding so grand a panorama was enough for me. There were no sheep here. Was Salan simply the site's custodian? Simple reduction? What was I thinking? How marvellous is this fundamental element flaring interminably through this fissure. Fire raised the energies of raw foodstuffs and forged our metals. How often I'd squatted around Arrernte campfires mesmerised by their flickering choreography as damper and tea simmered. And here was a flame that might have flickered before humans thought to rub two sticks together. As a passing presence, I was poorly placed to presume local experience.

Our conversation was limited to exchanging names, and half an hour later, we started descending. My thighs were weak from the ascent and I involuntarily cantered downhill behind Salan who was soon lost to sight far below. He reappeared by the cataract, now at a gallop, heading for Xinaliq. Had his invaluable presence been fortuitous? Given the village network it was entirely possible that Afaddin had sent him in advance. The resourcefulness and self-sufficiency so evident in Xinaliq's foodstuffs, clothing and shelter depended on close collaboration.

***

Tomorrow, bargaining passage to Baku and hopefully a taste of *mugham*. What had attuned me to it? In the sway of Sufism after Claymont, I'd made my way from Istanbul to Konya, participating in *Mevlani* and *Qadiri* rituals, and taking Dede's advice to visit Shams Tabrizi's nearby mosque, exchanging a few coins with the caretaker for a sachet of symbolic salt. I'd been slapped and pummelled in Kayseri's Turkish baths and toured Cappadocia's bullet-shaped geology.

I'd bussed east and visited the ruins of the tenth-century Armenian Church of the Holy Cross on Aghtamar Isle, a few kilometres from Lake Van's shoreline. I hurried through Van, encountered *Naqshbandi* Sufis, and overnighted at Dogubayazit before bumping past iced-capped Mount Ararat, north of the highway. Noah's disembarking brood wouldn't have been enamoured of their prospects in such conditions. But here was my highlight.

From the Iranian-Turkish border to Tehran, the young Kurdish bus attendant, distinguished by his rust-coloured hair and green eyes, polished the windscreen at each depot and provided soft drink and cologne-scented tissues to passengers. I'd encouraged him as he leaned against the dashboard, facing the aisle, ready to serve. Between duties he sang songs of his homeland, cupping his right hand to his cheek and singing Kurdish *guranis* in a tremulous falsetto. While some melodies maybe yearned for love others surely expressed Kurdistan's long struggle for independence from Ankara, Baghdad and Tehran governance. Voicing his language was sufficiently rebellious to raise tension between its austere beauty and the hissing from seats up the back. But he stirred feelings in me as deep as any I'd ever experienced. And I'd found those soaring laments in *mugham*.

***

The built environment of Baku's central grid was typical late nineteenth century, a time marking the development of its oil industry and the internal combustion engine. Fortunes were made, notably by Swedish magnate and inventor of dynamite, Alfred Nobel. An estimated 20 percent of the money used to grant annual international prizes came from the extraction of Azerbaijani oil. The Nobel family had supplied military equipment to Russia as far back as the Crimean War. Prior to oil extraction in 1879 the Nobels had been sourcing Azeri walnut trees for rifle stocks.

None of this oil wealth was immediately evident now, however. Baku's historic elements had been either erased or camouflaged save a few acres of immaculate touristy old city.

The grid abutted the Caspian Sea, and the President and his cavalcade rounded it each day at 1 o'clock, stopping traffic and waving to his mute minions, forced into detention on the streets; a remarkable show of imperial power. I watched this from the footpath, standing beside a tall Sudanese who told me he was here playing professional football. Ahmed was not enthralled by the autocrat speeding by but admitted Baku provided a sporting career denied him in his war-torn country. Still, football didn't pay all the bills which explained the brilliant candy-blue suit he was wearing as concierge outside the Sapphire Inn Hotel. He was aiming to attend Baku State University despite the dubious status of its degrees, telling me that students with cashed connections could purchase degrees even if they failed exams. 'Bribery,' he shrugged. 'If you're clever, no worries. But money helps very much when you are not a genius.'

Ahmed was the first African I'd seen since Palermo's street corners and median strips where, at the change of traffic lights, small contingents of Africans left their plastic ground sheets of transistors, watches, sunglasses and sundry smallgoods on the pavement, and swooped on stationary cars, offering to wipe windscreens. On the wide scrubby medians of Palermo's peripheries, mini-skirted Sudanese prostitutes plied their trade, sponsored I was told, by the Mafia. My source added, that they helped Africans get an economic footing. Ahmed had seen nothing like that in Baku but admitted corruption was rife and that 'money from trafficking people is much more than from drugs'.

The struggle for money had a peculiar cast in Central Australia. Clearly there was poverty, limited employment opportunities and welfare dependence. Government strategies operated beneath a circus of bureaucratic acronyms that hadn't significantly reduced suffering. Well-intentioned plans frequently failed due to poor negotiation. Schemes were re-invented, overseen by short-term administrators lacking the history of previous endeavours or trusting relationships developed with those they served. Millions of taxpayer dollars were absorbed in administrative costs. Much of the money targeting First Peoples didn't reach them. Welfare colonialism controlled their lives, robbing self- esteem, stifling enterprises and initiatives and destroying hope.

Summer was stifling and the bitumen buckled accordingly. There was nothing romantic about Baku's public buildings or sense of a glorious past. No slumbering mosques or palaces softened the skylines as in most Muslim cities; big-bosomed domes cornered by minarets. No muezzin caterwauling from towers summoned the faithful. Nor were there burqas or flowing caftans. After the conservative attire in rural villages the sight of glamorous women in fashionable western garb was surprising.

Substantial four to six-storey buildings fronted the Caspian. Ice-cream vendors traded on a shady seaside promenade. Brisk onshore winds pleated the water with white-capped corrugations. Some fairground rides laboured under their enthusiastic freight, heedless of the accompanying gaudy music. A tiny zoo sat centre-point, but the grim animal imagery painted on its fascia board and miserable, caged monkey at the entrance, proved disincentives for us.

At the south-eastern corner of the grid sat the old walled city. The much-lauded twelfth century Maiden's Tower, *Giz Galsi*, appearing on currency, was near the entrance. It was a challenge to link the Rapunzel-like tale inspiring its name with this stumpy watchtower. Few tourists wandered the streets. Within an hour we'd seen the main features. I'd hoped, in vain, to encounter cupolas of eggshell, campanula, sapphire and peacock-blue tesserae, that distinguished the Silk Road cities of Samarkand, Bukhara, and Khiva. They were famed learning hubs long before Greece took precedence as the foundation of western culture. It had been the Gurdjieff literature that first alerted me to them. If old Baku felt manicured and sanitised, 10 minutes beyond the main grid, footpaths and roads lapsed into randomly paved disrepair. As with post-war Sicily, prefabricated brutalism held sway.

Art follows money as the treasures of Florence, Paris, Madrid, Amsterdam and New York attest. Baku's boom certainly wasn't reflected in its art galleries. Maybe the best art and big money crossed the borders. More likely, creative energies were directed towards music and wool. Close to the old quarters was a three-storey museum celebrating Azerbaijani carpets. Anjou accompanied me while Lareena rested in the hotel. The displays were arranged in regional zones, providing a travelogue of the country. The fields of dominant colour, patterns and borders were stunning, but the symbolic intent of animal, geometric and botanical designs escaped me, as did their ribbons of Kufic script. Nevertheless, the blood-reds and indigo skies riding through the knotted piles spoke the universal language of harmony.

I gravitated to rugs from Quba and Baku, represented by geometric images featuring dark backgrounds on which flowers were saved from slipping into a Prussian blue abyss by lighter blues. Alice Spring's desert art also featured natural motifs with braille-like, acrylic dots mustering the great wild into rectangular canvases. Geometry within the rectangle; nature made small. But it's not nature-inspired imagery alone that they have in common with these rugs. And like esteemed twentieth-century painters, Klee and Bonnard, they understand how subdued colours factor to brilliance.

It was wonderful to have a choice of restaurants again. Lebanese, French, Italian, Indian, Chinese, and Turkish fare fed the streets; I was a captive client after the limited diet in Caucasian villages. A hoarding embellished with portraits of Tutankhamen and Nefertiti, advertised Egyptian food. It was subterranean, a test for apprehensions about enclosure. Engineering and electrical fittings east of Istanbul were often improvised, and here, a dull bulb flickered ominously in the stairwell. But the temptations of hummus, falafel, kushari (rice, lentil and macaroni dish), fava beans and grilled sturgeon overcame our hesitation. We wandered down and were ushered towards the rear of a long room where three couples sat at wooden benches. I ordered while scrutinising the hieroglyphs and profiled images on the walls, glancing at the fabulous food fronting our neighbours. The perfume of fresh *aish* (Egyptian bread) and *baba ghanoush* fizzed with herb-enriched lamb *kofta*.

I chuckled as hummus and beetroot dips arrived: buckwheat bread appeared unappetisingly advertised as 'bug wheat'. Someone might consider having a translator of translations bewildering or beguiling the traveller. Then, of course, we'd be deprived of such whoppers as *Grilled Aborigine* instead of *Grilled Aubergine*—yes, I have actually seen that on a menu; a genuine mistake, not intentional, thankfully.

Suddenly, we were plunged into darkness and my smile died. No one spoke, though the eclipse didn't disturb others. Severed from signifiers, I panicked until rustling hands found mobile phones whose pathetic light allowed us to resume eating. Entombment thwarted pleasure. I like to see what I'm eating. Though the couple at the next table invited us over and candles came from the kitchen, I couldn't share their nonchalance.

Hurrying the meal, I thanked them, covered expenses, and groped along the passage. Emerging on the street in the only rain of the week, we hailed a taxi and gave the name of our hotel. I was wary of the service as many unlicensed drivers, doing a second or third job, simply placed a light on their cabin roof and had no meter or sense of direction. Once more the tell-tale cracked windscreen and dysfunctional needles on dashboard dials. Not for the first time in Azerbaijan we felt we were taken further from our destination than necessary. After a second circuit of the hotel we insisted on alighting and stood beneath its veranda until power was restored.

Alim Qasimov in full flight, 2008.

Fantasia Haman tearoom, 2008.

There were many exponents of *mugham* as I discovered in CD shops and on a dedicated TV channel in our hotel lobby. Most were middle-aged like Qasimov. His agile tenor possessed, or as he claimed, 'channelled' that oceanic cry of elation that keens into our depths and vivifies the sensual world. His intimate coloratura technique was heightened by an ability to soften his tone at will and float a delicate falsetto. In Shaki, Ismailli, Mestia, and Quba I'd asked after him and was told on arriving at the village of Lerik that he'd visited an old friend there only days before. Whilst he was known throughout the country, none of my informants knew of his whereabouts.

We visited the Mugham Club housed in the caravanserai of the old city. The food and service were solid up-market fare but the jazz-imbued version was less impressive. Symphonic mugham also failed. Only a chance encounter in the Fantasia Hamam saved my utter disappointment; and here it was an unaccompanied voice. Having bathed, I entered the chai room en-towelled and ordered *chai*, sitting to one side of the churning fountain. Beyond it at another table sat three men. The oldest placed sugar cubes between his teeth and sucked tea through them, as is customary here. Between sips he entreated his fellows with recitations, some hummed, some intoned in sweet tenor scales. The domed ceiling swirled his notes across the fountain. He occasionally followed them to check my response. When I rose to leave, I advanced on their table where the maestro was explaining something of his text, to thank him. I asked if there were public performances of *mugham* and that Alim Qasimov enraptured me. He gasped.

'Ah, Alim. We two, together, this 10 years,' he reaffirmed by aligning both index fingers in a manner I'd only seen Arrernte men use when referring to initiated friends, or *alyeye*. 'My name, Qulu Esgerov.'

Later, I sourced one of his CDs in the main drag, Nazimi Street, named in honour of the nation's beloved poet. Did any Australian thoroughfare honour a poet?

Alim, however, proved elusive and I contented myself on Azeri Air with the in-flight *mugham* channel apposite for high altitude transportation. Above peregrine-curved clouds the music rose. Was that the legendary 1930s' master, Bulbul, *The Nightingale*, at one point, dive-bombing on swarms of stringed instruments? At thirty thousand feet this was the closest thing to whatever heaven might propose.

✳✳✳

Threshold, John Anderson, 2008.

To this point, for me contemporary art had been uninspiring, well-mannered replays of Western Modernism. I'd poked my head through gallery doors in Palermo, Istanbul, Tbilisi, and Baku but found more interest in rugs, ceramic bowls, bridges and medieval buildings on precipices. I enjoyed the museum of the streets, its garb, gestures, and varied physiognomy more than the stuff of galleries. Few painters challenged street life with the verve of my mate, John Anderson, however.

317

He connected with the figurative tradition established by Italians and Spaniards during the height of the Baroque. Mastery of the messy oil medium was taught through the laborious studio system until the advent of schools like the one we'd attended. Apprenticeship in the old masters' studios guaranteed that even mediocre practitioners had skills superior to contemporary artists. By the 1960s, with synthetic polymers all the rage, lecturers with oil painting expertise were scarce. John's technical prowess had been an arduous slog, an eye on his canvas, another on the old guys in European galleries, as he honed his astonishing imagery. He intuited that their dark spaces were the appropriate vehicle to float discontinuous dream narratives of the kind we see in filmmakers, Tarkovsky, Sukurov, and Lynch.

Reproduction serves him poorly, tightening images that are brushed to the brink of irresolution. Sprawling figures, buildings, trees, swimming pools, and domestic animals cavorted in juxtaposed spaces. These chimerical presences disrupt space and time in surprising folds inviting us to ponder the nature of ambiguity. The restlessness of breeze-driven leaves, the squirt of breaking waves, activates our gaze. Eros romps through this kingdom of lurching males, provocative femme fatales, raunchy Chevrolets and buxom Holdens: allegories of hormonal release conveyed through the tug and sway of brush and rag.

With *Threshold*, a crimson floatie is the fiat between a dark male domain and a luminous pool, where a girl stretches invitingly; a Freudian riff that survives through the largesse of his colour vocabulary. The moody beiges and blues circulating in the dark are electrified by the unexpected shot of a cobalt fender, twirled by the donut, and stabilised by a column of phallic drapery. As arousals of lust his lexicon is unsurpassed.

Having flown from Baku we took the train to Venice intent on visiting Tintoretto's works in the Scuola grand di San Rocco, while Lareena and Anjou took a boat to the famous glassworks on the island of Murano. In 1979 I hadn't been aware of San Rocco's existence where Tintotetto had laboured for 20 years. The room housing his *Crucifixion* took my breath away.

I perched half an hour on the viewing bench, dumbstruck before exiting to sense the world outside, then returning for a second session. How had he brought me to tears? Everywhere, pockets of interest were subordinate to the whole; the challenge of unifying numerous elements at considerable scale produced this living thing. I sensed how easily they might topple into darkness, that death was contained in life. This wariness of brinksmanship made for the sadness I feel underpins great art.

Eighteen elegant horses bear witness to the surrounding tumult; busy backs dragging, swaying, swerving, supporting, tugging, weeping, conferring, pleading, wondering, and writhing. Here, the barren crest of Golgotha supports an athletic Christ, arms fanning like wings preparing for Ascension. We float with Him above the verb-riddled canvas. At five by twelve metres, the figures are near life-size. Pinned to wood, beyond pain, He surveys the grieving apostles, soldiers, executioners, and equestrians in finery. Some turbaned easterners gaze dispassionately at Him. One thief waits to be nailed in place, sitting up, watching. The other is being pulled from the front and pushed from behind. Christ's pale torso contrasts with the warm-blooded shirts, capes, pantaloons and turbans thronging below. His gaze is masked in shadow; His halo operating as both natural light and revelation, illuminate this magnificent disturbance, this quiver of humanity, blessed by His forgiving arms.

***

So much for Tintoretto's anguished canvas. More intimate news was testing. Lareena was intent on separating and shifting to greener, east coast pastures. Another failed relationship and, as with its predecessor, intensified by separation from children. We'd successfully shared Anjou's parenting but our disconnection had become increasingly apparent. Lareena wanted to catch up with an acquaintance in Switzerland, so having come to terms with separation, I departed with Anjou for Melbourne. But not before sighting Caravaggio's savage light at Santa Maria del Popolo in Rome.

No more saints and virgins posing eloquently in wealthy garb for thuggish Caravaggio. These were the artist's buddies in ragged street gear. Chiaroscuro had ripened. These paired paintings showed him at the top of his game. If Tintoretto initiated dream space while re-casting the bible, Caravaggio was the progenitor of dark danger. Eye-popping presence. That hindquarter of horse, or St Peter's vein-wrinkled brow, here now, made fresh and pertinent as if he inhabited the figures in his narratives. His realism transcends the centuries expressing a humanity I hadn't detected in contemporary galleries. What enabled their profundity? Technique alone didn't explain how he kept the wonder of life before us.

***

An exhibition of my work was due to open in Melbourne and our flights were scheduled accordingly. I was anxious about separation and also about the prospect of showing in Anna Pappas's gallery for the first time. A

319

simultaneous solo show was being staged at the City Library in Flinders Lane. It was a challenge to savour these events.

I perused the newsagency at Rome's airport. Alice Munro's, *Dear Life,* was one of the few books in English guaranteed to appeal to me. There was email access here, so I proofed the booklet Anna had posted in preparation for the show. Ronja had emailed. Her Film and Television course included Francois Truffaut's *400 Blows.* She'd heard me mention his name. Had I seen the film and reflected on the experience? No, I replied. I'd seen only *Day for Night* and read his interviews with Hitchcock. Anjou and I searched the food court for sushi, and I opened the Munro, munching rice, tuna, and avocado rolled in seaweed. On page nine of the first story was a reference to *400 Blows.* In none of Munro's books had I read of film citations. I could hardly believe my eyes. At the very least such synchronicities arouse a sense of order beyond my reckoning.

I had no illusions of being a mainline event, so it was encouraging to find a director game to take on controversial work. It was one thing to acquire dot paintings as a sign of interest in First Peoples, albeit at a distance from affairs in the desert. As decorative pieces they brightened walls. For some the content invited deeper contemplation of terrain rarely, if ever, visited. My work redescribed actual lives, bearing the hard truths of colonisation.

Anna's attractive booklet, *Even as We Speak,* would help promote the show and she'd arranged radio interviews. Two friends, artist John Wolseley, and senior curator of anthropology at the Melbourne Museum, Philip Batty, would share the introductory remarks. Who else might attend? Most city dwellers fail to see the depth of meaning in the lives of Aboriginal Australia or the suffering colonisation has wrought. Would Anna bring fresh eyes to my descriptions of life on the fringes of White Australia? Who was interested in First Australians given the fear of Others promoted by politicians and the paralysing nonchalance of the suburbs?

13

Postscript:
On the road again

Origins of the New Poetics, Rod Moss, 2015.

Seven years have elapsed since Lareena and Anjou settled on New South Wale's mid north coast. Christmas looms and I'm driving south. We've survived separation well enough. Anjou has flown from her mum's to meet me for Christmas. Having two such contrasting settings inspires her. She's halfway through high school and excelling, though not enjoying learning as much as she had in Alice. I've met her at the Alice Springs terminal and we're on the long trek to Melbourne family and friends. Tall. Goodness. Like her brother she's way taller than older sister Ronja's trim 155 centimetres. She's recently returned from three months with Lareena in Jordan, so there's plenty to catch up on and her jocularity is welcome company over the hot bitumen expanses. I have Sean Penn's reading of Dylan's *Chronicles* to fill lapses in conversation.

As usual we start well before sun-up and its chorus of cooing pigeons. Each pitstop bears a memory of my car woes through the decades. A hole in the petrol tank at Kulgera, a rollover at The Marriott near the South Australian border, a burnt-out clutch plate, leaking gearbox, stuffed solenoid, flat tyres, a collision with a bull's corpse straddled on a jump-up shy of Marla, the loss of the crank's harmonic balance and the two-hour tow back to Coober Pedy. The ledger is full and damning, a recitation risking Anjou's confidence in me, my cars, or both. No car had been less than 15 years old on purchase. But I'm still here to testify and her furtive glances my way bear no censorship.

North of Coober Pedy we enter the flat desolate wastes of the state's northern plains. The opal-mining town's cones of limestone tailings prove eccentric surprise, though the town has never offered more than brief respite, as indeed have the few roadhouses either side of it. The afternoon sun blares piteously over the hallucinatory void, vast and shimmering. When had moisture ever visited to sprout the sparse flora supporting hoppers, lizards and mice? South of Glendambo there are sheep, black of face, some owning that colour on their flanks. They are as inert as the saltbush and boulders. In the gathering dusk, were it not for those patches, they'd be indistinguishable from their dun surrounds. What manner of gut-juice had this herd to cope with gravel? They add variety to the kangaroo carnage that increases as we descend the plateau below Pimba.

I stop to haul them from the highway, less from respect for the dead than from increasing the eagle toll. With stupendous wingspans the wedgetails are reluctant to quit nibbling and hit the high thermals. They rise slowly as I advance, black rags auguring round the savage sun. This last 'roo, a large buck, wore a gaping aperture at his breast fringed with a coagulation of dark blood, ants and flies. Between ribs, its ruby flesh seethed with maggots. I need both hands to grip its tail and drag its warm corpse to the verge. The five birds caress the sky at great elevation. It's not the height of indifference. They're intent on me and the meat I've shifted. One cruises back to the verge before we've driven 100 metres.

We have exhausted Anjou's reportage for now. She'd helped her mum sort clothes for Syrian and Iraqi refugees in Amman. She'd visited the place where John the Baptist had waded, and waded herself, in the Dead Sea. This she tells, coincidentally, as we cruise past Lake Gairdner, a salt vista of such magnitude the biblical sea would disappear within it. It houses an island floating apparitionally on its white crust. What did the local Kokatha people call it?

Anjou has thankfully resorted to her headphones. Much as I enjoy Adelle, constant repetition lessens the charm of her plaintive repertoire.

There's a grove of Myall an hour out of Port Augusta, unkindly called the 'gutter' though its waters do reek of sulphuric refuse. I wish not to overnight in those airs. So, we pull into the grove and unfurl our swags. Had some prodigal topiarist trimmed them? Their spindly leaves, silver tipped with seasonal growth, sit incongruously at spacious intervals in neat clumps on craggy limbs.

Too spent to light a cooking fire, I spread Nuttella on Ryvita for Anjou and tahini on mine. Crumbs cause a detachment of small black ants to cut from their solemn column between tree and nest and rush the morsel with impressive tenacity. The snarl of flies that had clung to us since leaving the car, disappears suddenly with the sun. No bird or bat calls from the trees and I'm left with a current of crickets, and tyre-hissing tinnitus as the highway's white lines run across my eyelids. My vertebrae re-align as I unwind on the swag. No need to crawl beneath the canvas until the chilled early hours.

In the far west is a low, silhouetted range, carving a table from the sky. Arrernte friend, David Kwemen Johnson, once confided the discovery of his countrymen's bones as he'd traced the ancestral *achilpe*/native cat's songlines in his youth; calcified evidence of a family's tragic misadventure he attributed to whitefella bullets. Kwemen, too, has passed on now though his tale, like *achilpe's*, persists.

A cool moon rides through the stencilled limbs. I watch it intermittently as it wheels west, stars winking as they have forever, in the abyss, occasionally abetted by satellites. We cheer ourselves over this cheerless array, naming promontories and declivities on planets so removed from our orb, scribing geometrical patterns, measuring space and time, and possible adventure. Doomsday speculations have been based on the imminent appearance of comets and millennial destruction, predicated on Christian and Aztec calendars.

At dawn, roused by the distant roar of road trains on tar, I grope for the sandals at my head to find them gone. I rise and follow tracks of my stealthy visitor. The dingo, finding them unappetising, has discarded them 15 metres distant. The wind that startled me in the small hours has delivered cloud, now bunching over the bevelled range and its liver-coloured cliff. It's perversely chilly. Perhaps it does rain after all. Anjou, slow to sociability first thing, stalls with her salted avocado and dried apricots.

We're soon on the road, swinging east through Port Augusta before its traffic stirs, and head via touristic Burra where I top up on caffeine at a cafe run by an older guy and his young Balinese, artist partner. Anjou settles for hot chocolate which compares poorly with its Sicilian namesake. Next, are the Riverina towns with their acres of olive, citrus and pistachios bordering the road. As we close on the first of these at Morgan, a herd of goats wanders unannounced across the highway. The 30 metres between them and us cause an adrenalin rush and increased vigilance on this final stretch of unfenced scrub. Please, let there be no additional chapter of car grief. Though the day is dwindling, I remain hopeful of showing Anjou the place of my initial posting in Ouyen.

It's more than 40 years since I first drove to the town, and the Calder Highway now signposts the possibility of Mallee fowls crossing. Sure enough, I spot a pair just 10 kilometres from town. They're in no hurry and would have been skittled had I not beamed them in the falling dark and hit the anchors. Ouyen's streets are bereft of bodies, much as they were in the 1970s. The town is shrinking, its population halved, and the traffic is mostly southbound. It's a rural story repeated throughout Australia where industrialisation and market forces have combined to eliminate labourers from the land. One index is the contraction of the town's footy teams into an affiliated squad in a distant league. My club no longer exists.

I met Graeme Drendel back then. He was the outstanding student artist. We'd both played footy with Tiega and he'd drop by after school to absorb The Band and Dylan on my turntable. Listening to The Band's music, he reckoned, was like going to church, referring to the reverence we shared for the rocking rural ambience conjured in their early discs.

We left town simultaneously, him to pursue art teacher training and dwell in the city's northern suburbs. Both he with his wife Wendy, like the Andersons, have enjoyed long and fruitful relationships in which I love to bask. He has a third child now with Wendy. Graeme has enjoyed sufficient critical and commercial success to shelve teaching duties. Andersons' offspring have careers and children of their own in the city.

John and Leonie have purchased 10 acres on Cape Schanck with a nineteenth-century cottage they've restored and extended. John's studio is shared with his other love, an early 1960s Cadillac, which receives his doting renovations, and makes periodic appearances on canvas. Both couples have shared struggles, pleasures and disappointments as trust and friendship matured.

The tiny rural town's tug is regularly revived by Graeme's humorous accounts of visits to family and the foibles of friends remaining there. He's played in rock bands, taught art, continued to make paintings and play the art game. He's surely the only important artist to have emerged from the town.

The pitstops on the Calder are busier than the shops in Ouyen's main drag, Oke Street. Many are boarded up. There's more action at the Senior Citizens Club than the pre-school. Would I recognise formerly fleet-footed footballers crowding the bingo tables? As I cruise past the Roxy I recall the ennui of Bogdonavich's, *Last Picture Show*. Locked in a post-war time capsule it portrays so many places existing far from urban excitements. The only architectural registers of economic success, marking the days of hope here are the Victoria Hotel and Commonwealth Bank.

Fuelling up at the main crossroads, I sense in the distanced gazes of the mechanic and the farmer on the other side of the pump, the troubled consequences of their diminishing returns. They'd been 14 when last encountered—bright, charming, and enterprising. Who were these drawn and withered men of middle years? It hurts me to look into their fear.

Graeme must feel this acutely on his native soil when he returns here, no longer able to call it home. His paintings darken and moisten the Mallee's implacable aridity. The long aisles of golden stubble and eucalypt boundaries are there. So too its distant horizons and big skies. A signature silo occasionally appears. But the tyrannical heat and insects are drained off. Also absent is the suggestion of throbbing birdlife that animate trees and freckle the fields.

The Outsiders: Beyond Agriculture,

The Bathers, Graeme Drendel, 2012.

Despite occupying the middle ground his folks' gazes rarely lock with ours or invite intimacy. Immobile and immune to meteorological gloom, they daydream in silent, self-absorbed lassitude. The patient brushing and tonal shifts remind me of Vermeer, as do the subjects' uniform age and inwardness. Unlike the people staffing the Dutchman's rooms Graeme's are unhoused and engaged in meaningless tasks. In part the paintings gently reproach rural futility. They are not bucolics but displaced urban sophisticates, clothes and skins unruffled, innocents breathing despair, groomed hounds leashed at their sides. There is no evidence of the generations, no nurturing oldies, no energetic kids.

As much as Indigenous art affirms belonging, Graeme's exist in a limbo of non-belonging without a built environment to impute claims to place. Might this be the supreme significance and power of his images: this profound psychic disconnect with the country, that seems the lot of our settler culture? They speak of the divorce between coast and country and their separately coded languages with misaligned aspirations. It's as palpable as that between Indigenous and settler cultures whose suspicions and enmities are projected upon the Other: fear and distrust as constant companions.

While Graeme shifted south, I moved further north to the centre of the continent where he's never ventured. Its lure had been with me since those days of Cowboys and Indians in the bush next door. Bush, rather than the city, enlivens me. As a young teacher thrust unwillingly into remote and arid Ouyen, I'd lived the protagonist's trials in the menacing film, *Wake in Fright*. A more eloquent cinematic account of Australia's relationship to its interior has yet to appear. We know little about the novice teacher's background other than he hails from Sydney to teach in the outback. We see him departing at year's end to the city on a station set on featureless plains. A city girlfriend beckons to break his tedium. But at the mining town hub, he misses his flight and is lured to a game of two-up. Losing all his money, he descends into chaos and joins the drunken nihilism of the locals. His toxic derangement concludes hitching hopefully to Sydney, but a wrong turn finds him delivered to the same forlorn platform facing another year at the remote school.

City-educated colt encounters rural masculinity. Like him, my encounter with local Aboriginals was minimal. Educational credentials don't confer the superiority he feels entitled to. There was the excessive drinking and surreal behaviour of denizens snared in small-town claustrophobia. Even the appalling kangaroo hunt replicates my experience. Yet I'd surmounted those extremes. Maybe he hadn't done the larrikin boozing, played footy, been nurtured in bush like Boronia's, or served summers on a farm flushed with a farmer's perennial wry humour.

We lodge in a motel opposite the footy ground. All rooms but one are booked by a construction crew. Mining for zircon, rutile and ilmenite is happening in sands northwest of town. At dawn, I run a devotional few laps before breakfast, after which we head east towards Swan Hill, crossing the Murray and continuing to Deniliquin. Dry country all of this, with untidy Mallee gums hugging the highway bearing their name. Nearing Swan Hill, river gums announce the Murray's presence, their agonised limbs scripting arabesques. I like this dry heat. My body sings. I'm less encumbered. And this I realised in Ouyen.

***

As I close these pages, I'm heading north up the Stuart Highway towards my Alice Springs home. Anjou and I stayed a week with my brother Colin, in Deniliquin. It's a farming community dependent on irrigation, so talk of water levels in the Edwards River was the salient issue. The government, responding to CSIRO's research on the health of the Murray River system, is buying water lots back from the farmers. Many have little choice but to opt out of sowing. The rice mill is retrenching workers. Colin's woodcutting has also been throttled by the state government's decision to ban culling from state forests. The government envisages the forests as tourist parks. It means he'll have to negotiate with farmers to clear dead wood from their blocks. Leaving state forests untended increases fire hazard as well as throwing 80 or so woodsmen into redundancy.

Christmas dinner at my sister's was superb. Her daughter laid in vegetarian fare, favoured by my girls, and Marilyn pulled out all stops on a Pavlova, and gratified Ian, with an abundance of rum balls. He'd added the spoils of his recent diving trip off Wilson's Promontory—a three-kilogram crayfish— knowing the crustacean is a winner with mum and Marilyn.

After many relocations, Marilyn and Andre have circled back to Mornington Peninsula. They seem incapable of staying in one residence more than a few years. From the park opposite, gulls pleaded to partake. Their home abounded with the generations and, judging from their smiles, the struggle to get my parents to and from the car as well as the hour's drive, repaid the effort. 'You know how much it means to your mother to have you all together,' dad reminded me when settled in an armchair. This he followed with his usual claim, 'Seventy years and not a cross word, hey mother,' rhetorically tuned and thrown with his customary sideways glance in the hope of agreement.

Raffi flew from Canberra with news of the rendering business he's started since topping his apprenticeship year. His flair must harken to an earlier generation. I'm amazed at his eye for finish. His recall of issues on building sites and the various characters of his work crew had us in fits. His rapier wit comes from mum. Dad's never been a joker or laugher, facts that have kept him at a distance from us kids. Ronja was her effervescent self, and on the final leg of her media course, intent on icing her media qualifications with a Master of Education, specialising, in Indigenous Studies. Anjou and she sparked off each other's musical passions and piano skills.

The Andersons and Drendels were well, too, despite lamenting the state of the secondary art market since the Global Financial Crisis. The paucity and quality of art reportage in the popular press was likely linked to this general decline. Figuration had capitulated to illustration and dependence on computer-generated photography, making it indistinguishable from advertising. Though having published a string of acclaimed novels, Scott wasn't reaching the wide readership he deserves.

How wonderful it was to hear that fire still burns in the breasts of old schoolmates. Nick, the 'Russian Honeybear', has custody of his father's enthralling family saga: journeying from the Crimea via Harbin—city of White Russian émigrés in Manchuria—to Shanghai, the Philippines, and finally to settle in a more welcoming Australia than we currently present. As the leather-bound journals have been typed in Russian, Nick's immediate task is to translate them. The 'Tassie Devil' is also busy with ancestor business. His partner's grandfather, Ted Ryko, undertook an epic bike journey from Adelaide to Darwin before World War I, and made superb ethnographic images of his experience both there and in the Arnhem Land escarpment. A documentary with reconstructed action beckons; it's been scripted and awaits funding. Dave 'Anteater' Morgan is engaged in bilingual education archival projects, and the promotion of a major Milingimbi Museum art collection. Jack O'Dowd, in addition to crafting cigar-box guitars, has been constructing jelutong blanks for me to carve and paint tables. Tony, 'Loupas' Linterman's recent poetry collection, *Weather Walks In*, resounds with poignant, often darkly humorous reflections of family and place. Shane 'Tadpole' Bourne is a decorated actor on both large and small screens. And post-war Boronia's ferment was crucial to our flourishing.

***

I dropped Anjou at Tullamarine for her flight to Coffs Harbour. Three-dozen ex-students from Brinsley Road were reuniting at the former site on Australia Day, or Invasion Day as some Arrernte say. Peggy Cole attended, so too the Goldman and Otto sisters, and James Dean with photos from those halcyon days. We talked also about those absent, the promises fulfilled, and the early deaths. Weird—these children with children of their own, and careers well advanced. The ten or so years that separated us in the 1970s seemed to have shrunk this second half of our lives. The trees remained but the building was long gone. It's a park, as is Argo Street's half acre. The Fitzroy Street Methodist church hall was reduced to cinders decades ago. High-rise offices dwarf the old bluestone church next door, now heritage-listed and webbed with ivy.

We Meet Here to Talk About Water, Rod Moss, 2015.

By dusk, I'd headed to overnight with Rose Bygrave and Barry Hill in Queenscliff. A book-lined passage ran the length of their house. Rose was putting finishing touches on a collaboration with long-time friend, Marce Howard. *Pearl* soared with love of family and country, a sisterhood of sound. Barry had researched, *Peacemongers*, charting Tagore's visits to Japan between the wars, appraising and praying for peace. I'm selling short his exploration of Indian and Japanese scholarship. His empathy for fellow travellers glows through its language. He recounts Hiroshima's devastation from survivors. War crimes are put under the lamp as are Tagore's warnings about unfettered bombing.

He was a torrent of talk, projects running concurrently and those to follow, when Tagore was done. He bundled me off to bed with a clutch of articles and sections of books he knew would arouse interest. I bounced between thoughts of my kids, Hiroshima's destruction, memories of Sokurov's stunning biopic of Hirohito, and the plight of *Irrkerlantye*. The precarious tenure of the families in camp has been exacerbated by lack of water. Their town supply was cut while nearby road works were underway, and the Minister of Community Services has refused to redress the situation. They read this as one more effort to push Native Title holders from this slip of land into town, a prospect none of them willingly accede to. Without water where would any of us be? To date our protests have failed to move government and I've been carting water from home for people, dogs and Jenny, the goat.

Such thoughts were unlikely aids for slumber. Knowing too well what lay ahead, I skipped Barry's promised breakfast and hit the road at 3.30 a.m. heading north through Adelaide and Port Augusta.

It's almost 30 years to the day when I first drove the Stuart Highway, though it was mostly dirt then and demanded modest speeds. Somewhere around Pimba where bitumen gave way to horrendously rough dirt, the Bute was towed ignominiously from a washout by a Safeway road train, the signage on its rear doors mocking me through 100 metres of door-depth muddy water.

✳✳✳

My parents have reluctantly trialled a nursing facility less than a kilometre from their home, during which time I've house-sat Hastings Avenue. It'd been a challenge, mostly conducted by Marilyn and Andre, to get them out of the house. Though dad insisted on keeping his promise to mum that she'd be carried in a box from the street she'd lived her 89 years, the fortnight made them realise the necessity of full-time care. Colin retrieved their pampered poodle, which, though well-fed, was riddled with fleas.

Had fear of loneliness kept them bonded and secure from the world's terrors in airconditioned comfort? The local radio burbled information from the 10-kilometre radius of their door. At 4.30 p.m., *The Bold and the Beautiful* summoned them to the lounge, followed by a succession of TV news stories, varying little on each channel. Horrendous war clips were juxtaposed with pet yarns, the trivial jostling with the profound, masquerading as news; snippets that did little to encourage conversation.

Dad acknowledged he'd lost the strength to twist the cap off their soymilk and fully close taps. He encouraged me to take any tools from the garage I might use. And though Ian comes each Saturday to attend chores, their cherished garden was reverting to nature. Mum says to take anything I like from the shelves. Her nick-knacks have no sentimental value for me, though. Cooking consists of meals on wheels, re-heated in the microwave. I ask for her stoneware mixing bowl and wooden rolling pin, those implements I'd helped her bake with in the 1950s.

I carry them into my days. They are not heavy. Nor do their voices pester or plead. That's never been their style. Their interdependency oscillates between respect and resentment of their failing selves. They rest with brave decorum, gripped by the terror of death and the loneliness one of them will incur. The liquid ambers and maples planted 70 years ago have predeceased them. The birdbath outside the lounge window no longer quenches the thirst of blackbirds or thrush. Parrots and cockatoos squabble for water rights.

At 94, dad's beyond caring for her and struggling with himself. Great Uncle's 99 years tugs at his mind. There'll be no Christian burial in womb-like coffin, epitaph, or headstone for him. He'll not feed worm-rich cemetery soil. He's written his eulogy and wishes to have his ashes tossed at Rickett's Point in the Bay, the waters of his childhood. He's convinced mum to do the same, though she prefers to be scattered in Sherbrooke Forest and says I know which hollowed tree. I watched his frail shuffle around the house as, refusing the walking frame, he searched the wall for support with one hand. With the other he held pants that would, otherwise, slip from his withered hips. I lapsed into thinking he was only acting being old. He moved along the passage to the bedroom from which sexless light classics serenaded them from the bedside radio. These cautious steps, this cashewed body, skewered to one side: when would he straighten himself and stride forcefully again into the business of his day? Had his ears enlarged or refused to shrink with the rest of him? Can this be the man whose bursts of anger and strength intimidated us?

Mum and Dad, 2014.

How well do I understand him? He crept about the house as if in hiding, storing some secret, veiled even from himself; dimly aware perhaps that something has passed him by, that he has little connection with his world, with people, with family. He was careful not to clatter cutlery when washing up, or shut doors too firmly and disturb his pact with silence. Their silence: the house and him collaborating in some dark and private truth. I recognise this secrecy, the one I keep for painting and writing, though exhibition and publications force me from my hide.

Mum's knitting needles rested on the quilt draped across her lap. She napped briefly, respite from insomnia and distraction from arthritic joints. Even reposed her face retains its sweetness. Elsewhere, failing muscles have acceded to fat, inhibiting her walk, her bluish toes lost in puffy feet, her crooked fingers dimpled and translucent. Spittle crawled from one corner of her mouth. She complained of cracked lips and ulcerated gums which explained why her dentures lay by the needles. I bent over her and moistened her lips with a kiss, thinking of her wretched dental visit as a teenager to have all teeth removed in a single sitting, in the city. How the school dentist's fillings caused their blackening. Of how the city guy had yanked them out and whacked a plastic set over those bleeding gums. Then the long train trip home with grandma, in a haze of chloroform, vomiting blood.

Both were lucid but had little to say to each other than noting medical and optician appointments, and the timing of their respective pharmaceuticals.

Father's recent incontinence had him whisked into hospital for prostate surgery. The doctor reported on his success. 'No more colostomy bag, Beryl. You'll have your boy back in three days.' But from decrepitude there is no such return. He'd accepted that his driver's licence should not be renewed this April. The car, vestige of pride and independence, has returned with Colin to see out its days.

***

I've camped on the gibber plains south of Coober Pedy and it's the darkest hour. Good to get the remaining 700 kilometres completed before the afternoon furnace. Venus rides the eastern rim, so radiant, it sucks all light from surrounding sisters squatting in patient isolation. Kangaroos form a silent guard of honour beside the bitumen strip, pale and still, flashing in and out of the high beam. Other than momentary glances, they resume their verge-side meals. A joey sits on the white line without inclination to move. I slow to a stop and it continues, unnerved, to gaze into the door, indifferent to it or me as I lean through the window and wonder at its fearlessness. It's still there, motionless in the weak taillights.

There's another dull glow out east. I speculate that some mining town must have sprouted since I last drove here. Controversial fracking has been going on for decades in these mineral-rich soils. But it's the sun making gradual passage to dominance. It never wearies. As it rises, the gibber glows. In the brief half-light, infinite quartz pebbles mirror the sky. Chevron clouds shunt slowly south, shot with crimson. An emu stalks toward the road, also indifferent to my passage. Eagles and crows crowd the carcasses. Apart from rare fuel depots, no human inhabits these endless plains that remain the domain of our emblematic fauna.

Will summer's hammer have beaten the seedlings into submission, or its winds whipped limbs from the eucalypts? Perhaps the house has been broken into. My mind races ahead of the car. It's easy to forget the speed I'm doing. Lacking significant ranges and saltpans to mark passage, the highway stretches long and straight.

To still thoughts of home I slip on Dylan's *Basement Tapes* and unwind the window, giving encapsulated air its freedom. Protean Bob, word warrior of sexual desire's torments, a veteran with the croaky old man voice he'd feigned in youth to gain folk credibility. His recent work speaks to my aging self with as much relevance as it had in adolescence. A sense of mortality pervades the songs. But this is the weird folksy stuff he made with The Band in retreat from the 1966 World Tour, the songs that started my rapport with Scott, in the school staffroom. Warm air whips at my ear as Dylan's words are drowned in road noise, and for a few minutes my thoughts are too. Onwards, ever onwards, the bitumen highway more resolute than my shifting self.

A large limb has crashed through the colour-bond fence in the backyard. A honeyeater is plucking the *aperaltye*/lerp flakes dandruffing its leaves and feeding its chicks whose beaks nudge their nest in the nearby whitewood. Both fishponds are brimming. Erratic breezes ruffle the bulrushes. Irises peek between their shifting cover. Leaves fidget across the surrounding sand. Finch-sized shards of sky flit between the citrus. They are grasshoppers whose glossy wings disappear on landing.

An unprecedented week of misty rain coats the grasses, silencing the quaking crickets, keeping them beneath the rocks. The lisping rain unleashes a delicious perfume from the starved soils and rocks. Dust particles have been earthed and the resulting lucidity is startling. A fainter fragrance is carried by masses of yellow and violet flowers peppering the red earth. If old Arranye Edward Johnson were still with us, he would have sung the *merne*/plant-food-increase song over a poached-egg daisy. There are mushrooms, fungus and the momentary triumph of mould.

Arranye Edward Johnson, 1998.